UNDERSTANDING MODERN WARFARE

A major new study of the theory and practice of warfare in the twentieth and twenty-first centuries. Using relevant examples from recent history, this book provides a complete introduction to the issues, ideas, concepts, context and vocabulary of modern warfare. The expert team of authors explores the conduct of war across land, sea, air and space, in addition to addressing key issues relating to contemporary strategy, weapons of mass destruction and irregular warfare, including insurgency, terrorism and civil war. They provide an incisive and structured grounding in military theory and argue for the importance of understanding warfare within the joint (interservice) context and as an evolutionary rather than a revolutionary phenomenon. By providing the tools required to truly understand contemporary military doctrine this accessible survey will be an invaluable resource for any student of military history or international relations, as well as for military professionals.

David Jordan Defence Studies Department, King's College, London, based at the Joint Services Command and Staff College, Shrivenham. His previous publications include *Battle of the Bulge* (2003) and *The Fall of Hitler's Reich: Germany's Defeat in Europe, 1943–45* (2004).

James D. Kiras School of Advanced Air and Space Studies, Air University, United States Air Force. He is the author of *Special Operations and Strategy: From World War II to the War on Terrorism* (2006) and was awarded the Air Education Training Command civilian 'Educator of the Year' award for 2006–7.

David J. Lonsdale Department of Politics and International Studies, University of Hull. His publications include *The Nature of War in the Information Age: Clausewitzian Future* (2004) and *Alexander the Great: Lessons in Strategy* (2007).

Ian Speller Department of History, National University of Ireland, Maynooth. He also lectures in defence studies at the Irish Defence Forces Military College and in maritime strategy at the UK Defence Academy and at the National Maritime College of Ireland. He is the author of *The Role of Amphibious Warfare in British Defence Policy, 1945–56* (2001) and the editor of *The Royal Navy and Maritime Power in the Twentieth Century* (2005).

Christopher Tuck Defence Studies Department, King's College, London, based at the Joint Services Command and Staff College, Shrivenham. He co-authored, with Ian Speller, *Amphibious Warfare: The Theory and Practice of Amphibious Warfare in the Twentieth Century* (2001).

C. Dale Walton Department of Politics and International Relations, University of Reading. Among his publications are *The Myth of Inevitable US Defeat in Vietnam* (2002) and *Geopolitics and the Great Powers in the Twenty-First Century* (2007).

UNDERSTANDING
MODERN WARFARE

DAVID JORDAN, JAMES D. KIRAS,
DAVID J. LONSDALE, IAN SPELLER,
CHRISTOPHER TUCK AND
C. DALE WALTON

CAMBRIDGE
UNIVERSITY PRESS

CAMBRIDGE
UNIVERSITY PRESS

University Printing House, Cambridge CB2 8BS, United Kingdom

Cambridge University Press is part of the University of Cambridge.

It furthers the University's mission by disseminating knowledge in the pursuit of education, learning and research at the highest international levels of excellence.

www.cambridge.org
Information on this title: www.cambridge.org/9780521700382

First published 2008
8th printing 2014

Printed by CPI Group (UK) Ltd, Croydon CR0 4YY

A catalogue record for this publication is available from the British Library

ISBN   978-0-521-87698-8   Hardback
ISBN   978-0-521-70038-2   Paperback

CONTENTS

ILLUSTRATIONS

BOXES AND TABLES

Box

Table

PREFACE

This is a book about warfare. It focuses on the conduct of war in the twentieth and twenty-first centuries. It is designed to be read by anyone with an interest in the subject, and the reader requires no specialist prior knowledge. Indeed, the book has its origins in an unsuccessful search by the authors to find a source that could provide an authoritative yet accessible introduction to the theory and practice of modern warfare. There are numerous good books devoted to an examination of aspects of modern warfare, and even more that address its history over the centuries. Despite this, we found none that offered the reader, in a single volume of manageable proportions, a thorough grounding in the critical issues, ideas, concepts and vocabulary necessary to develop and articulate an understanding of the conduct of war in its various forms and in its different operating environments. *Understanding Modern Warfare* is intended to fill this gap and has been written accordingly. In addition to providing a general introduction to the subject, however, it also addresses concepts and issues that are important to those seeking to develop a sophisticated understanding of the complexities of modern warfare. Therefore, as well as the general reader, the book is intended to be of value to students of war studies, military history and related subjects, and also to military professionals. The latter may include enlisted personnel and officer cadets embarking on their careers through to more senior personnel undertaking staff courses and their equivalent at a later stage. Whichever category the reader falls into, we hope that this book will do what it claims on the front cover and help them to develop and refine their understanding of modern warfare. Tragically, one need only tune into the evening news on any major television or radio station to recognise that such an understanding is likely to remain as important today and in the future as it was in the past.

The contributors to this book have all benefited from experience in teaching students at civilian universities and military establishments. We owe these students, uniformed or otherwise, a debt of gratitude for the stimulus and challenge that they have provided over the years. Exposure to their different ideas and innumerable questions has forced each of us individually to explain and defend our views and opinions many times over. This book is therefore partly a result of such debates and, hopefully, will provoke and inform many more in the future. An additional debt is owed to our colleagues in the various departments and institutions in which we work. They are too numerous to mention individually but, without their assistance and, sometimes, their forbearance, works such as this would not be possible. Particular mention must be made of Professor Dennis M. Drew, Dr John Sheldon, Dr Jon Robb-Webb, Dr Niall Barr, Dr Deborah Sanders and Dr Aoife Bhreatnach for their comments and assistance. Michael Watson and the editorial staff of Cambridge University Press provided the perfect balance between enthusiasm and encouragement on the one hand and firm guidance on the other. We would also like to thank the anonymous reviewers of the manuscript who provided a number of keen insights that improved the quality of the work. Finally, it should be noted that the views expressed in this book are those of the authors alone and do not represent the views of the US Department of Defense, the US Air Force, the UK Ministry of Defence, the UK Defence Academy or any other organisation. Any mistakes are, of course, our own.

HOW TO USE

This text includes a variety of learning tools that will help you to navigate your way easily through it and that will strengthen your knowledge and understanding of modern warfare. This section provides a guide to those tools, showing you how to get the most out of your textbook.

Detailed contents lists at the start of each chapter provide you with an immediate and accessible guide to the content of each chapter.

THIS BOOK

KEY THEMES

- War does not have an indeper
  However, the relationship bet
- Strategy requires serious stud
  intellectual fashions.
- Strategy has a constant nature
  be respected.
- Strategy is complex and does
- Strategic theory can help the
  guarantees.
- There are various ways in whi
  Military force is a flexible, if b

Key themes listed at the beginning
of each chapter summarise the key
arguments and give you an immediate guide to the principal themes and
issues discussed.

Box 1.2 Gray's dimensio

- People
- Society
- Culture
- Politics
- Ethics
- Economics and logistics
- Organisation
- Military administration
- Information and intelligen

Text boxes on key concepts are
provided throughout the text.
Examining critical issues in greater
depth, the boxes broaden your
understanding of the main chapter
text. Listed at the beginning of the
book and highlighted in the text,
the boxes can be easily referred to.

Further reading guides at the end of each chapter direct you to sources for further study. Short summaries of each text provide an accessible guide to other resources for key issues raised in each chapter.

FURTHER READING

Black, Jeremy, *Rethinking Military Hi*
A bold critique of much contemporary
the subject from 1500 to the present.

Gat, Azar, *War in Human Civilization*
In this thought-provoking book, Gat c
people engage in war.

Gray, Colin S., *Another Bloody Centur*
A challenging look at the future of wa
studies.

An extensive **Glossary** at the end of the book enables you to find definitions of key military and technical terms quickly.

Air superiority	The ability to use air power at a g a given place without prohibitive from the enemy.
Air supremacy	Air superiority in which the ene of effective interference.
Aircraft carrier	A warship designed to carry and numerous fixed-wing aircraft at
Amphibious operation	The landing of military forces fr hostile or potentially hostile sho
Attrition	The reduction of the effectivenes formation caused by the loss of e and/or personnel.
Battalion	A military unit usually consistin troops divided into 4 to 6 *compan* battalions may be grouped into or more may constitute a *regimen*
Battlefleet	A fleet, usually composed of the warships, designed to contest *con* in combat with the enemy.
Battlegroup	A flexible *combined-arms* force us around the nucleus of a *battalio* infantry or armoured unit and other arms.
Battleship	A large, heavily armoured warshi primarily with large-calibre guns. mid-twentieth century these wer most powerful warships.
Battlespace dominance	A US concept that encompasses dominate the three-dimensional

Illustrations and diagrams are included throughout the book.

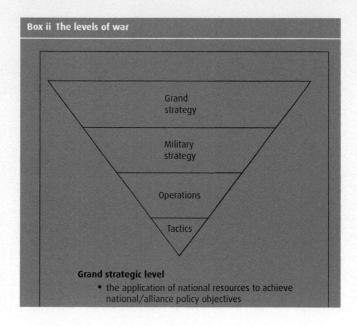

Box ii The levels of war

Grand
strategy

Military
strategy

Operations

Tactics

Grand strategic level
- the application of national resources to achieve
  national/alliance policy objectives

INTRODUCTION

IAN SPELLER AND CHRISTOPHER TUCK

You may not be interested in war, but war is very interested in you.[1]

The purpose of this book is to provide an authoritative yet accessible introduction to the practice of modern warfare: hence we chose the title 'Understanding Modern Warfare'. Of course, adopting this rather ambitious title inevitably leads to two questions: what, in relation to the scope of this book, do we mean by 'warfare' and what on earth might the realm of 'modern' warfare encompass?

According to the *Oxford English Dictionary*, war is a 'hostile contention by means of armed forces, carried on between nations, states, or rulers, or between parties in the same nation or state'.[2] More succinctly, Hedley Bull, the renowned scholar of international relations, described war as 'organised violence carried on by political units against each other'.[3] Other definitions distinguish between armed conflict and war. They tend to focus on the scale and degree of violence employed, suggesting that 'wars' are characterised by large numbers of combatants, heavy casualties and/or high-intensity fighting. In the words of contemporary British military doctrine:

Armed conflict is a situation in which violence or military force is threatened or used. War is the most extreme manifestation of armed conflict and is characterised by intense, extensive and sustained combat, usually between states.[4]

A recent guide to the key concepts in international relations suggests that, according to conventional wisdom, for a conflict to be classified as a war, it should result in at least 1,000 battle deaths. This is a far from satisfactory approach. Does it mean that a conflict that results in 998 fatal casualties is not a war unless two more people are killed? Does a conflict suddenly become a war when the magical casualty figure is reached? Definitions that focus simply on a body count are simplistic to the point of absurdity, ignoring the political and legal implications of defining war, in addition to saying nothing about the actual conduct of military operations. Other definitions focus on legal issues, identifying 'war' as a state of law that regulates armed conflict between groups, usually states. Such definitions reflect the conventional understanding of war, as reflected in international law and treaties, as organised rule-bounded violence conducted between the uniformed armed forces of states. They tend to exclude the activities of sub-state groups whose use of violence is not given the credibility or legitimacy of the title 'war'. Given that, thus far into the twenty-first century, most armed conflict has occurred either between sub-state groups or between such groups and conventional militaries, such definitions, while logically coherent, may be too restrictive. For the purposes of this book, Bull's more expansive definition seems more satisfactory.

Contemporary Western definitions of war are profoundly influenced by the work of Carl von Clausewitz, whose posthumous *magnum opus On War,* published in 1832, stated that war is 'an act of force to compel our enemy to do our will . . . a clash of major interests, which is resolved by bloodshed'. Famously, Clausewitz emphasised the political nature of war, stressing that 'war is not merely an act of policy but a true political instrument, a continuation of political intercourse, carried on with other means', a statement that is as widely known as it is frequently misquoted. Far from advocating war as an alternative to politics he intended to show that war was driven by politics and could only be understood in that context. In consequence, the means of waging war can never be considered in isolation from the political aim that it is designed to support. As Clausewitz put it, '[w]ar may have its own grammar, but not its own logic. The logic is determined by the political aim.'[5] Of course, the political aim might be to achieve an economic goal or to meet some cultural imperative, such as a requirement to fight for status or honour, and the term 'political' must be viewed here in its broadest context.

The study of war therefore implies an investigation that is not limited to the battlefield but that caters for the intrusion of political factors. Indeed, such enquiry, commonly described by university departments and military academies alike as war studies or, displaying a degree of reticence as to the real subject matter, peace studies or defence studies, is necessarily a broad discipline. A sophisticated understanding of war requires one to take account of the impact of social, cultural, political, economic and technological factors (see figure i). The eminent military historian Michael Howard has recalled that, when given responsibility for establishing the War Studies Department at King's College London in the 1950s, he sought to recruit as widely as possible from other disciplines in the knowledge that the understanding of war required their input. To put it succinctly, 'the study of war was too important to be left to military historians'.[6] Any attempt to examine and explain war, in its broadest sense, is therefore a huge undertaking. As Azar Gat points out, '[w]ith war being connected to everything else and everything else being connected to war, explaining war and tracing its development in relation to human development in general almost amounts to a theory and a history of everything'.[7] This book does not attempt to do this. There are many excellent works covering the

Figure i A US Army soldier attached to 3rd Armored Cavalry Regiment hands out informational flyers in Mosul, Iraq, January 2008. The current conflict in Iraq provides ample illustration of the need to understand social, cultural, political and other factors in addition to more traditional military matters if one is to understand war.

broader aspects of war. Instead, we have focused the efforts of this book on the conduct of warfare.

The study of warfare is a sub-set within the study of war. Warfare is about the conduct of war and is defined by the *Oxford English Dictionary* as 'the action of carrying on, or engaging in, war'. Warfare is thus primarily about the employment of organised violence. It is about fighting. The degree of violence, and how it is applied, varies according to circumstance. Indeed, some might argue that there is currently an identifiable 'Western way in warfare' that emphasises the requirement both to take and inflict minimum casualties. In some respect such approaches are reminiscent of much older non-Western attitudes, such as those espoused by Sun Tzu, writing in China in the fourth century BC.[8] Nevertheless, at its heart, warfare is about the preparation for, and conduct of, organised violence, something that is well reflected in Sun Tzu's work. The study of warfare implies a particular focus on armies, campaigns, battles and engagements, the basic hard currency of war. This does not mean that political, social, cultural, economic and technological factors are not relevant. Nothing could be further from the truth. These factors set the conditions within which warfare is conducted, and all play a part in determining how different societies or organisations approach the conduct of war. The same can be said of legal and ethical constraints, which are themselves a reflection of the social, cultural and political environment in which they originate.

The impact of societal factors on war is often neglected in the vast and continuous outpouring of popular literature with which the field of military history is blessed or cursed, depending on one's perspective. However, the impact of war on society has, for a number of decades, represented a significant, perhaps even a dominant, approach to the study of war within the academic world. The 'war and society' or 'new military history' approach involves an examination of such issues as the impact of war on literature or on attitudes to class, race and gender, all very worthy areas of study. By moving the focus of enquiry away from the actual conduct of war to its broader impact, this approach has allowed liberal-minded academics and institutions to avoid the opprobrium that some believe is, or should be, attached to the study of war. As Jeremy Black has noted, in some respects this approach demilitarises military history by moving it away from war and battle, a process that Michael Howard has characterised as a 'flight to the suburbs' of military history.[9] Such studies may say something about society, but they tend to shed little light on military capability or performance. They do not usually develop our understanding of warfare. At the heart of such an understanding is, to quote Howard, 'the study of the central activity of armed forces, that is, fighting'.[10] In his influential book *The Face of Battle*, John Keegan made a strong case for the primary importance of 'battle history' within military history, arguing that:

it is not through what armies *are* but what they *do* that the lives of nations and of individuals are changed. In either case, the engine of change is the same: the infliction of human suffering through violence. And the right to inflict suffering must always be purchased by, or at the risk of, combat – ultimately of combat *corps à corps*.[11]

Not everyone is happy to focus on such issues. Stephen Morillo has noted that military history is not the most respected branch of historical enquiry, and the root of this disapproval lies in its subject: war.[12] By extension the same thing is true of war studies. Of course, despite what some may think, study does not necessarily imply approval. One need not believe that war in general is, or individual wars in particular are, justified or necessary in order to think that the phenomenon of war is worthy of study, any more than one needs to believe that communicable diseases are a good thing in order to study the history of the bubonic plague in fourteenth-century Europe. The same also applies to the study of warfare. However, in the latter case, the particular focus on the actual conduct of war is often linked to recommendations on how to wage war more effectively, potentially influencing the actual behaviour of armed forces in future conflicts and, conceivably, contributing to the notion that armed conflict can be functional. The line between study and approval may indeed be blurred. There may not even be a strong dividing line between commentator and practitioner, particularly in a discipline where many authors are serving or ex-military personnel and where many academic commentators are employed, directly or indirectly, by armed forces. The obvious justification for books such as this one is that, to paraphrase Sun Tzu, the conduct of war is of such importance, quite literally the province of life and death, that it is vital it be studied carefully. It should never be forgotten that wars always result in death, destruction, waste and human suffering, all too frequently on a truly staggering scale. However, ignoring the phenomenon is unlikely to make it go away. Indeed, one might suggest that in a democracy in the twenty-first century it is particularly important that as wide a range of people as possible should understand the nature of modern warfare in order that they are equipped to make intelligent judgements about the way in which their own governments seek to employ military force. The requirement for military personnel to understand warfare should be too obvious to require further elaboration, particularly given the historical correlation between ignorance and military incompetence.

The title of this book suggests a focus on 'modern' warfare. This begs many questions as to what one means by 'modern'. Dictionary definitions suggest that it means 'of or belonging to the present day or a comparatively recent period of history' and 'being of the kind now extant'. This does not provide much of a clue as to what period should be considered 'comparatively recent' when studying warfare, still less what 'of the kind now extant' should include or exclude. In terms of what 'comparatively recent' might mean, it is worth noting that different authors have chosen different timeframes in their own studies of 'modern war'. The starting-point of Theodore Ropp's 1959 study *War in the Modern World* was 1415.[13] Some authors begin with the sixteenth century, the age of Marlborough and Frederick the Great in the eighteenth century, the French Revolution of 1789 or the defeat of Napoleon in 1815. Others focus on the period from the outbreak of the American Civil War in 1861 or from the start of the twentieth century. It is not clear whether the 'comparatively recent' past should include years, decades or centuries.

Similarly, it is no easier to decide what 'the kind now extant' should mean in the context of warfare. Charles Townshend has argued that modern war is the product of administrative, technical and ideological developments that took place in Europe between the sixteenth and eighteenth centuries, transforming the nature of war and, by extension, the way in which it was conducted.[14] Other commentators have focused more squarely on technological factors. One website, popular with unwary students, suggests that 'modern warfare involves the widespread use of highly advanced technology'.[15] Such definitions are not necessarily wrong, but they do rule out many, perhaps even most, contemporary conflicts as

Figure ii US Naval personnel monitor radar and missile-firing consoles aboard the aircraft carrier USS *John F. Kennedy* during operations in support of Operation Iraqi Freedom in the Arabian Gulf, September 2004. Such systems, and the skills required to create and operate them, reflect the technological nature of much modern warfare.

non-modern, because these are often fought with unsophisticated small arms, light support weapons and improvised explosive devices (see figures ii and iii). There is a danger, in any case, of focusing too heavily on weapons technology. Technology is not an independent variable, and the manner in which it is developed and employed reflects a broad range of inputs that are not technological in origin.

In his introduction to *The Cambridge History of Warfare*, Geoffrey Parker identifies technology as just one of five key foundations for what he describes as the 'Western way of war', arguing that armed forces in the West have traditionally placed a heavy reliance on superior technology, often to compensate for inferior numbers.[16] However, technology alone is not enough. He also cites discipline, an aggressive military tradition, the ability to respond and adapt to successive change, and an ability to finance such change as the other foundation stones. Parker is unapologetic in identifying the 'Western way' as a superior way of waging war. Of course, while Western-type approaches to warfare have dominated conventional combat and generally, but not exclusively, defeated their 'non-Western'-type opponents since at least the eighteenth century, this does not mean to say that the 'Western way' is suitable to all circumstances. Indeed, an increasing body of opinion now suggests that future conflict will be characterised by

Figure iii Operation Enduring Freedom has also highlighted the importance of traditional infantry skills and the continued dangers posed by relatively low-technology threats. Here Iraqi soldiers practise urban warfare tactics at an advanced training course led by US soldiers in Mosul, 2006.

low-intensity and asymmetric warfare and that 'conventional' military operations by armies represent a form of warfare that is of decreasing relevance. According to this view, warfare in the twenty-first century will be radically different from war in the past, and it is far from clear that approaches grounded in the Western tradition are the most likely to prove successful. On the basis of such ideas, it is sometimes suggested that the study of 'modern' warfare requires a much shorter timeframe than is usually employed and that too broad a frame of reference is liable to lead one to focus on the wrong issues. Thus, not only is there dispute over what one means by the 'comparatively recent past', there is a similar lack of consensus over what 'of the kind now extant' actually implies.

These issues are addressed throughout this book. It is not intended to provide a history of modern warfare. Rather, it examines the critical issues, ideas, concepts and vocabulary necessary to develop and articulate an understanding of the conduct of war in its various forms and in its different operating environments. The focus is on the kind of warfare that is 'of the kind now extant'. In order to examine this in a satisfactory fashion, an examination of military concepts, organisations and activities in the 'comparatively recent past' is also required. We have tried to avoid being overly prescriptive about what this might actually mean. The degree to which one needs to look back in order to understand the present varies depending on the subject. To understand modern strategy requires one to deal with concepts and theories that were first articulated centuries ago, while an understanding of air warfare implies a primary focus on the period since the Wright brothers' pioneering flight in 1903. Therefore, while the book focuses primarily on warfare in the twentieth and twenty-first centuries, it also draws on issues, events and concepts that pre-date this timescale. When addressing issues that relate to conventional war fighting, there is an inevitable tendency to focus on concepts that do reflect a Western approach. This is determined by the pervasive, global impact of such concepts rather than by any bias on the part of the authors. In any case, our approach is informed by an understanding of the complexity of the subject and the diversity that characterises different groups' and organisations' approaches to warfare and by the dangers of paradigm/diffusion models. The book focuses on both conventional and more unconventional warfare. The latter category includes low-intensity conflict, terrorism, guerrilla warfare and other forms of what is frequently described as 'asymmetric warfare'; it also includes the use, or potential use, of weapons of mass destruction (WMDs). Western approaches are not necessarily dominant in either case.

While much of the subject matter contains a presentation of principles and concepts, we have tried to avoid presenting such matter as wisdom in itself. The conduct of warfare has generated a plethora of doctrine, templates, ideas and rules on the methods through which warfare can be conducted successfully. This is reflected by the way in which many militaries have developed formal 'principles of war' to guide the effective application of military power (see box i). As this book makes clear, however, warfare is not a science. Knowledge of these things is less important than an understanding of the challenges of applying them in any given context. A century ago, Julian Corbett emphasised this point, writing that 'nothing is so dangerous in the study of war as to permit maxims to become the substitute for judgement'.[17] Knowledge of principles and concepts is not a substitute for judgement or understanding, merely a means of fertilising both. We hope, therefore, that in addition to informing the reader, this book will act as a stimulus for thought and reflection on the subject matter.

In this spirit, the first chapter addresses the subject of strategy and its fundamental importance to the conduct of warfare. The particular challenges and opportunities of warfare in particular environments are also subject to the general influences of the nature of strategy. Such factors as the adversarial nature of war (the fact that it is always fought against another, thinking foe) make warfare an unrelentingly complex and difficult activity. The three subsequent chapters examine the land, maritime and air environ-

Box i Illustrative principles of war		
Soviet Union	**United Kingdom**	**United States**
Offensive action	Selection and	Objective
Manoeuvre and initiative	maintenance of aim	Offence
Concentration of force	Concentration of force	Mass
Economy of force	Economy of effort	Economy of force
Surprise and deception	Maintenance of morale	Manoeuvre
Momentum	Offensive action	Unity of command
Annihilation	Flexibility	Security
Reserves	Co-operation	Surprise
Co-operation	Security	Simplicity
	Surprise	
	Administration	

ments respectively. These environments have their own particular concepts and principles that derive from the differing nature of the environments and the attributes of forces designed to fight in them. Increasingly, however, modern warfare has also been defined by commonalities, particularly as joint operations – warfare involving co-operation between the different services – has become a recurrent theme in the conduct of war. The final two chapters of this book consider a form of warfare, irregular warfare, and a set of technologies, WMDs, that have exerted progressively more influence on the theory and practice of warfare in modern times. Events that have taken place since 2000 have given these two subjects even more significance. The debates on 'super-terrorism' and the potential for a coming 'age of asymmetry' also give unconventional operations and WMDs a prominent place in debates on the future of warfare.

Although the various chapters in this book deal with many different issues, they also reflect certain common themes. One is that modern warfare is more of an evolutionary phenomenon than it is revolutionary. Many of the important features of warfare in the twenty-first century have their origins in the gradual development of concepts and structures from earlier periods. A second common feature is the importance of interservice co-operation (joint operations). We have not included a separate chapter on joint operations because their importance is reflected throughout this book and particularly in the three chapters examining the environmental elements that comprise joint operations (land, air and naval operations). A third theme is the importance of thinking about warfare in terms of different, but interrelated, levels (see box ii). While chapter 1 demonstrates that grand strategy is always important, the subsequent chapters illustrate that different environments and forms of warfare have seen continuity and change that manifest themselves in different ways at different levels of war. For example, as

Box ii The levels of war

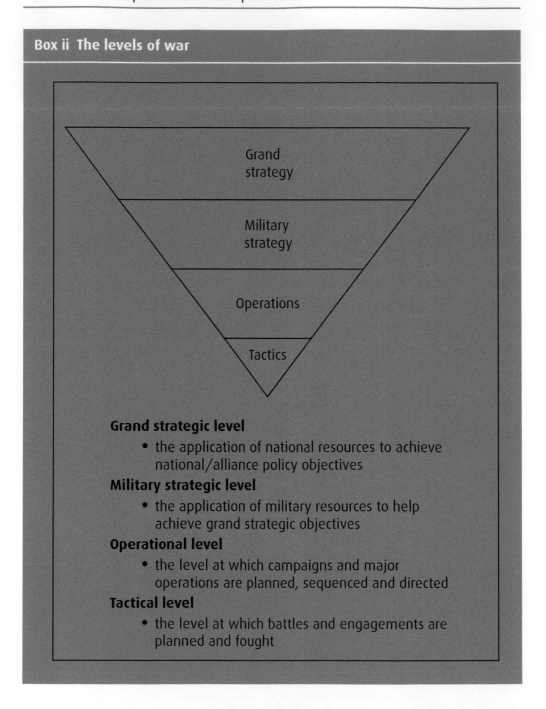

Grand strategic level
- the application of national resources to achieve national/alliance policy objectives

Military strategic level
- the application of military resources to help achieve grand strategic objectives

Operational level
- the level at which campaigns and major operations are planned, sequenced and directed

Tactical level
- the level at which battles and engagements are planned and fought

chapter 3 on naval warfare explains, changes at the tactical level of war do not necessarily invalidate established principles at the operational and strategic levels. Another recurrent theme is that it is evidently rarely easy to distinguish between continuity and change. Consequently, militaries have often found it difficult to predict accurately the future of warfare.

This last theme, in particular, is an important one. Adapting successfully to the future depends in part upon having a grasp of the past and the present. The future is not fixed, nor is it easily predicted. As the eighteenth-century philosopher David Hume noted, 'nothing that we imagine is absolutely impossible'.[18] While *knowledge* of the past and present of warfare may provide part of the foundation for coping with the future, more important is developing an *understanding*. We hope that this book is a useful contribution to that process.

NOTES

1 Attributed to Leon Trotsky (1879–1940).
2 http://dictionary.oed.com.
3 Colin S. Gray, *Strategy and History: Essays on Theory and Practice* (London: Routledge, 2006), p. 185.
4 *Joint Warfare Publication 0–01. British Defence Doctrine* (1996), p. 2.2.
5 See Carl von Clausewitz, *On War*, ed. and trans. by Michael Howard and Peter Paret (Princeton, NJ: Princeton University Press, 1976 [first publ. 1832]).
6 Michael Howard, 'Military History and the History of War', in Williamson Murray and Richard Hart Sinnreich, *The Past as Prologue: The Importance of History to the Military Profession* (Cambridge: Cambridge University Press, 2006), pp. 12–13.
7 Azar Gat, *War in Human Civilization* (Oxford: Oxford University Press, 2006), p. ix.
8 Sun Tzu, *The Art of War*, trans. by Samuel B. Griffith (Oxford: Oxford University Press, 1963).
9 Jeremy Black, *Rethinking Military History* (Abingdon: Routledge, 2004), pp. 49–54. Howard, 'Military History and the History of War', p. 20.
10 *Ibid.*
11 John Keegan, *The Face of Battle* (London: Jonathan Cape, 1976), p. 30.
12 Stephen Morillo with Michael F. Pavkovic, *What is Military History?* (Cambridge: Polity, 2006), p. 1.
13 Theodore Ropp, *War in the Modern World* (Durham, NC: Duke University Press, 1959).
14 Charles Townshend, ed., *The Oxford History of Modern War* (Oxford: Oxford University Press, 2005), pp. 3–19.
15 http://en.wikipedia.org/wiki/Modern_warfare.
16 Geoffrey Parker, ed., *The Cambridge History of Warfare* (Cambridge: Cambridge University Press, 2005), pp. 1–11.
17 Julian Corbett, *Some Principles of Maritime Strategy* (London: Conway Maritime Press, 1972 [first publ. 1911]), p. 169.

18 Quoted in Antulio J. Echevarria II, *Imagining Future War: The West's Technological Revolution and Visions of Wars to Come, 1880–1914* (Westport, CT: Praeger, 2007), p. xiii.

FURTHER READING

Black, Jeremy, *Rethinking Military History* (Abingdon: Routledge, 2004).
A bold critique of much contemporary military history that includes a survey of key themes within the subject from 1500 to the present.

Gat, Azar, *War in Human Civilization* (Oxford: Oxford University Press, 2006).
In this thought-provoking book, Gat combines many disciplines in an attempt to examine why people engage in war.

Gray, Colin S., *Another Bloody Century: Future Warfare* (London: Weidenfeld & Nicolson, 2005).
A challenging look at the future of warfare from one of the world's leading experts in strategic studies.

Keegan, John, *The Face of Battle* (London: Jonathan Cape, 1976).
A classic defence of 'battle-focused' history including case studies of Agincourt, Waterloo and the Somme. Has given its name to a genre of similar works.

Hughes, Matthew and Philpott, William, eds., *Modern Military History* (Basingstoke: Palgrave, 2006).
Provides a brief introduction to key areas and themes of military history and warfare since 1500.

Morillo, Stephen with Pavkovic, Michael F., *What is Military History?* (Cambridge: Polity, 2006).
A short but very accomplished book that goes a long way towards answering the question contained in the title.

Murray, Willamson and Sinnreich, Richard, eds., *The Past as Prologue: The Importance of History to the Military Profession* (Cambridge: Cambridge University Press, 2006).
A collection of essays that seeks to examine the value of military history to military professionals.

Parker, Geoffrey, ed., *The Cambridge History of Warfare* (Cambridge: Cambridge University Press, 2005).
A collection of essays that examines the history of warfare since ancient times, with particular emphasis on the Western way of war.

Stevens, Alan and Baker, Nicola, *Making Sense of War: Strategy for the 21st Century* (Cambridge: Cambridge University Press, 2006).
Provides an introduction to the importance of strategy and identifies strategic choices and the constraints and opportunities facing contemporary commanders.

Townshend, Charles, *The Oxford History of Modern War*, 2nd edn (Oxford: Oxford University Press, 2005).
Written by some of the leading experts in the field, this book examines various aspects of war and warfare from the seventeenth century to the present day.

STRATEGY

CONTENTS

KEY THEMES

- War does not have an independent rationale; it must act in the service of policy. However, the relationship between the two is complex and difficult.
- Strategy requires serious study removed from moral, political, operational and intellectual fashions.
- Strategy has a constant nature, which is violent and competitive, and which should be respected.
- Strategy is complex and does not tolerate simple formulas or principles for success.
- Strategic theory can help the practitioner in dealing with complexity but offers no guarantees.
- There are various ways in which force can be utilised in the service of policy. Military force is a flexible, if blunt, tool of policy.

War is practised in many different environments and contexts. While this has always been the case, the modern period has witnessed a growing complexity to warfare. In the twentieth century the air, space and cyberspace environments took their place as theatres of war alongside the traditional environments of land and sea. With each new environment of warfare come distinct features, challenges and opportunities for the commander to deal with. In addition to these new arenas, the invention of nuclear weapons presented a severe challenge for those involved in using military force in the service of policy objectives. However, the twentieth century was not just about the 'new'. Older forms of warfare also underwent substantial developments. Irregular warfare witnessed a degree of theoretical and practical maturation through the works and careers of such men as Mao Tse-Tung (Mao Zedong) and Robert Thompson. At the same time, regular forms of warfare have had to adapt to new technology and an increasingly joint approach. Finally, political and social developments have added to the challenges faced by strategists. In an age of 24/7 media, legal and moral restrictions on the use of force are more readily applied and upheld.

The following chapters in this book will explore the significance of the above changes to the character of war. Yet, despite the seeming novelty of warfare in the modern period, the very essence of war has remained the same. Across time and place, although the character of war has altered, its nature has remained constant. At the heart of that nature is strategy. Regardless of the specific context, each war has a guiding rationale. Each particular form of warfare, whether acting in isolation or operating in concert with others, must be guided by strategy. This chapter will outline and analyse strategy: that which gives war meaning and purpose. Only with such an understanding can the reader then appreciate the true place of each particular form of warfare in the bigger picture.

This opening chapter begins by identifying the need for an academic approach to strategy. From here, and having initially defined strategy and its various levels, the work will analyse the various characteristics of strategy that make it difficult. In particular, the chapter will explore: disharmony among the levels of strategy; strategy's multidimensional nature; interaction with an intelligent foe; the nature of war; the Clausewitzian concept of friction; and war's polymorphous character. Although the range of these complexities poses a significant challenge for the strategist, he can find some help in works of strategic theory. In this respect, the chapter provides a summary of the two great works of universal theory, Carl von Clausewitz's *On War* and Sun Tzu's *The Art of War*. Brief mention will also be made of Baron Antoine Henri de Jomini's *The Art of War*. With the notion that Strategic Studies is a practical subject very much in our thoughts, it is essential that the chapter include an explanation of the various ways in which military force can be utilised in the pursuit of policy. This will entail an analysis of defence, deterrence, compellence, posturing, offence and the miscellaneous uses of force. It is hoped that by the end of this chapter the reader will have a better understanding of the challenges involved in strategy, and how these can be dealt with so that the use of military force can best serve policy objectives. Finally, the work presents a cursory assessment of strategy today, looking at the current state of the art.

The study of strategy

The study of strategy is currently enjoying something of a renaissance. In the aftermath of the attacks of 11 September 2001 (9/11) interest in the subject has understandably grown. This is reflected in the university sector in the proliferation of related degree programmes and the growth in student numbers to fill them. However, it has not always been thus. Since its inception during the Cold War, Strategic Studies has enjoyed mixed fortunes. During periods of perceived heightened threat (for example, from terrorism or nuclear weapons) interest in strategy has flourished. However, changes in the international security environment, evident failures in strategy or moral repugnance towards war have undermined the perceived validity, desire and/or requirement for Strategic Studies. As Strategic Studies seeks to be a practical subject, of use to the practitioner, the seeming failure of limited-war theory in Indochina forced many to question its continuing utility. Similarly, the difficulties faced in Iraq may well sour contemporary perceptions of strategy.

However, it would be a catastrophic mistake once again to neglect the serious study of war merely on the basis of current dissatisfaction with the subject. Richard Betts is convincing when he states that university 'faculties should decide what to cover on the basis of long-term evidence of what mattered in world politics rather than recent events, intellectual fads, or moral hopes'.[1] The study of strategy is essential to give military activity meaning beyond the battlespace.[2] Without an understanding of strategy we cannot construct a meaningful theory of victory. In this sense, victory cannot be defined merely in military terms. Rather, a strategic theory of victory is concerned with the achievement of policy objectives. Strategic Studies enables us conceptually to make this jump from the battlespace and appreciate the true value of military actions. Thus, in the first instance this chapter seeks to outline the need for the continued development of Strategic Studies as an academic discipline, acting in the service of those who practise strategy in the real world.

The need for Strategic Studies is perhaps at its most intense in response to the complexity of strategy. This complexity, and the challenges it produces, is amply demonstrated in the counter-insurgency campaign in Iraq. Indeed, we can conclude that the complexity of strategy is such that achieving a satisfactory end state at reasonable cost, and within a reasonable timeframe, is often more elusive than ill-informed comment would suggest. As a result, we must have realistic expectations of what is possible from both the theorist and the practitioner. As David Jablonsky notes, 'a true scientific product is not possible from the study of strategy'.[3] Strategy does not tolerate formulas for success; rather, it calls for an approach more suited to art than science. Every strategic context is unique and therefore requires its own unique mixture and application of strategic assets. To appreciate fully the complexity of strategy, this chapter endeavours to dissect the art. This will be achieved by providing a common set of definitions and concepts, as well as analysing those elements that present the most formidable challenges. While undertaking this latter task, the chapter will also provide an answer to the question, 'Why is strategy so difficult?'

In many respects, the development of modern Strategic Studies can be attributed to one man and one invention. The man is Bernard Brodie; the invention is the nuclear weapon (see figure 1.1). The unique characteristics of nuclear weapons, and the absence of a history of use, opened the door for civilian strategists to lead debates about strategy during the Cold War. The rise of the civilian strategic analyst is illustrated by Alain Enthoven, who made the following comment during a discussion on strategic plans: 'General, I have fought just as many nuclear wars as you have.'[4] Brodie's contribution was to call for a more systematic, academic approach to the subject. Ironically, Brodie's call somewhat backfired. In outlining a need for a more scientific approach to strategy, he inadvertently instigated an

Figure 1.1 The invention of nuclear weapons, used first at Hiroshima (depicted here) and Nagasaki in August 1945, played a key part in the development of the academic discipline of strategic studies.

approach (systems analysis) that attempted to reduce the complexity of strategy to quantifiable mathematical phenomena. In response, Brodie later called for the reintegration of politics and history into the subject.

Since strategy sits uncomfortably between two worlds occupied by politics and the military, it has historically suffered from the absence of an intellectual tradition of its own. Political theory has of course a long tradition, whereas, although strategic theory has been blessed with such outstanding works as the aforementioned Clausewitz's *On War* and Sun Tzu's *The Art of War*, the development of theory relating to military matters has tended to be limited to a focus on tactical and operational issues. Indeed,

Brodie bemoans the lack of any real successors to the two great theorists. Since 1949, a number of commendable theorists have emerged, Brodie among them; yet his comments regarding the anti-intellectual bias of the military still ring true: 'Soldiers usually are close students of tactics, but only rarely are they students of strategy and practically never of war!'[5] This seemingly odd statement can be explained by the following comment from Colin S. Gray, citing historian Peter Browning: 'War is a relationship between belligerents; it is the whole context for warfare. Warfare is defined as "the act of making war".'[6] Understanding these two related, but distinct, concepts requires very different approaches. Worryingly, Brodie's lament that military staff colleges focus primarily, and intensively, on training at the expense of true analytical reflection could easily be an observation of the current situation. In modern military colleges, strategic theory often receives significantly less attention than such subjects as defence management and procurement. The result of such an approach is that the military tend towards an overreliance on simplistic principles concerned with tactical and operational issues, such as the principles of war. It also misunderstands the role of theory. As Gray notes, 'strategic theory is about education, not training or doctrine'.[7] As Brodie again notes, within the cultural confines of the military there is simply neither the inclination nor the time to engage in detailed analysis of strategic issues.[8] One might say that because there is no inclination, sufficient time is not created.

This should not necessarily be taken as an outright condemnation of the military profession's attitude to study. Nor should it be regarded as a call for abstract theoretical methodology. In many respects, it is understandable that a profession so rightly focused on practical considerations and results should neglect deep analytical ruminations. Also, since strategy is so bound up with intangible forces (such as morale and will), judgement, rather than endless analysis, is often the key to success. However, these two considerations, while somewhat understandable, do not excuse the neglect of academic analysis. Clausewitz, both a soldier and a scholar, was aware of the value of strategic theory: 'Theory exists so that one need not start afresh each time sorting out the material and ploughing through it, but will find it ready to hand and in good order. It is meant to educate the mind of the future commander, or, more accurately, to guide him in his self-education, not accompany him to the battlefield.'[9] In this sense, theory helps us to understand what matters in strategy and gives us insight into how the many dimensions of strategy interact.

While extolling the virtues of theory in strategy, we should never forget that there are limits to the utility of theory for the practitioner. Indeed, the relationship between theory and practical strategy is a complex one. An overly enthusiastic fixation on the practical can lead to analytical stagnation and an obsession purely with today's problems. A theory constructed and developed beyond immediate policy concerns may therefore have more lasting value and be able to illustrate a range of tomorrow's policy issues. However, at the same time, theory devoid of policy relevance will not further the goal of better strategy, which must be an objective for Strategic Studies; bad strategy kills. It is therefore understandable that, as Raymond Aron observes, strategic theory often reflects the strategic issues of the day.[10] Again, Betts summarises the relationship well: 'Neither theory nor policy can be optimised apart from each other. Central theoretical insights often flow from grappling with concrete questions rather than a priori constructs.'[11] Or, as Gray puts it: 'Most practitioners need to be educated to recognise the relevance of theory to their search for workable solutions to today's problems, whereas theorists must never forget that their labours ultimately only have meaning and value for the world of strategic behaviour.'[12] Ultimately, the strategist has to act usually, if not always, without a complete understanding of the situation. At such times, judgement and moral courage come to the fore. Nevertheless, the further development of strategic theory can only help us to improve our understanding of the complex relationships among the many dimensions within strategy.

In the absence of an intellectual strategic tradition within the military, Strategic Studies has had to develop its own identity within the civilian sector, both within universities and various think-tanks and research institutes. Initially centred in the latter, which resulted in a focus on current policy demands, the subject failed to establish a scholarly framework, as Lawrence Freedman notes. Again, akin to its relationship with the military, academic analysis finds little empathy in the world of policy-makers. Policy-makers want solutions, not further elucidation of the problems and complexities facing them. As Freedman notes, 'Policy-makers became impatient with those qualities that academics believe to be the most valuable: long-term thinking, stretching the bounds of the possible, and taking complexity as a challenge rather than an excuse for not going into too much detail.'[13] Thus, alongside the need for a more academic approach in staff colleges, the maintenance of Strategic Studies in universities is equally critical for the development of a genuine analytical framework and tradition. Within such an environment, the strategic analyst is afforded the freedom and time to develop the interdisciplinary, analytical approach required to enhance understanding of strategy.

Again, the above comments are not designed to denigrate the more practical aspects of military education and training, such as doctrine. However, while accepting the need for doctrine, all those concerned with the development of strategy should also truly embrace a theoretical approach in the Clausewitzian tradition, rather than a slightly more sophisticated version of Jomini's work (based as it is on principles and operational-level issues). Too often, the significance of Clausewitz's work is acknowledged, but only through the citation of an overused maxim. Clausewitz's real value exists in the intellectual development one experiences when dealing with the whole complexity of his theory. Despite the many instances when this chapter will extol the virtues of Clausewitz's work, it should not be taken as an advertising campaign for *On War*. We must heed Brodie's advice and go beyond Clausewitz. Strategic Studies, and thereby our understanding of strategy, cannot develop if all we do is reiterate Clausewitz's ideas. Clausewitz is an excellent starting-point, but we must develop the theory further. This can only be achieved by theorising in an intellectually permissive environment.

In light of the above discussion, a fair question to pose is: do we need civilian strategists? Could not the military and policy-makers construct an effective understanding of strategy between themselves? Richard Betts thinks not: 'If civilian strategists are not to decide along with the professional military, either ignorant civilians will do it, disjoining political and military logic, or the military will do it alone.'[14]

Since strategy is the meeting-point of two different worlds, its complexity cannot be overestimated. Thus, we must resist the temptation to sideline Strategic Studies in response to military failures or moral objections to the study of war as an instrument of policy. The real challenge for Strategic Studies is how to remain useful in the service of policy in a timely fashion, without forgoing the detailed analysis necessary to understand the complexities of the subject.

Strategy defined

Now that we have identified the need to develop our analytical approach to the subject, we must begin our exploration with some key definitions of strategy and its various levels. Extant strategic literature contains various definitions of strategy. For Clausewitz, it can be understood as 'the use of engagements for the object of the war'. Similarly, Gray defines strategy as 'the use that is made of force and the threat of force for the ends of policy'.[15] André Beaufre, however, highlights the dynamic interaction between belligerents: 'the art of the dialectic of two opposing wills using force to resolve their dispute'.[16] An alternative definition that builds upon those of Clausewitz, Gray and Beaufre may describe strategy as *the art of using military force against an intelligent foe(s) towards the attainment of policy objectives* (see box 1.1).

At the heart of strategy is the relationship between military force and policy objective. This relationship can be described and understood in various ways. Gray describes it as a bridge that links the military and political worlds.[17] Similarly, also reflecting the notion of a process that brings the two together, Eliot Cohen described this relationship as an 'unequal dialogue'.[18] In this sense, we can regard strategy as a process by which military force creates political effect. Although the supremacy of policy is well established and understood, and thereby military force must serve policy,

Box 1.1 Strategy defined

The art of using military force against an intelligent foe(s) towards the attainment of policy objectives.

the relationship is not that simple or one-way. Indeed, Clausewitz reminds us that although policy must remain the supreme consideration in the conduct of war, '[t]hat, however, does not imply that the political aim is a tyrant. It must adapt itself to its chosen means.' Thus, the military and political leaderships must engage in discussions concerning what policy requires and, just as importantly, what the military instrument can deliver. Hence, the significance of dialogue becomes clear in the quest for positive strategic effect. However, the dialogue lacks equity because the military instrument must ultimately serve the policy goals (see figure 1.2).

A constructive dialogue may avert an obvious danger in such a relationship – namely, that policy-makers may not understand the instrument at their disposal. As Gray notes, this danger can manifest itself in two ways: 'There is always a danger either that out of ignorance or incompetence policy will ask more of its military instrument than that instrument should be expected to deliver, or that policy will ask less of its "sword" than could, and perhaps should, be secured.'[19] To mitigate the potential for such failures, some modicum of education in Strategic Studies for policy-makers would be welcome but still would not guarantee success. Policy-makers may conduct poor strategy, even in the face of good strategic theory, for a host of different reasons. For example, domestic political considerations may limit the choices available to policy-makers. Note, for example, the House and Senate votes against President George W. Bush's decision to increase troop numbers in Iraq in early 2007. Aside from bolstering enemy morale and will, such a move creates an atmosphere that is not conducive to freedom of strategic choice.

The relationship between policy and the military is seemingly at its most complex in a modern democratic state. In such an environment, the political and military leaderships often have little experience or understanding of their opposite number. For example, in his excellent study of Field Marshal Sir Douglas Haig, John Terraine notes that within Haig's generation there was a substantial amount of mistrust and misunderstanding between the military and civil establishments. In addition, Terraine correctly concludes that Haig's 'absolute lack of interest in politics . . . cannot be considered as other than a serious defect'.[20]

The problems that emanate from the political–military relationship are not restricted to modern democratic states. Although on the surface this relationship seems much simpler for the likes of Alexander the Great or Napoleon, problems still existed. In these instances, the unification of the

Figure 1.2 The US Joint Chiefs of Staff meet to discuss policy with President George W. Bush in the White House, 29 January 2008. Strategy serves political goals and acts as the bridge between the military and political worlds.

roles of both the political and military leaderships creates its own problems. In particular, the absence of an external dialogue beyond the strategic decision-maker can result in a corresponding absence of quality control on his decisions. For Alexander, this became a growing problem over time as he became increasingly confident and paranoid. Towards the end of his campaigns, especially in India, Alexander had lost strategic focus, and his methods became increasingly brutal and one-dimensional. The result of this deterioration in his strategic performance was a long, bloody campaign that eventually provoked a mutiny in the army. Thus, the complexities of the political–military relationship seem to be less a problem of command organisation (although this can exacerbate the difficulties), as both modern democracies and imperial dictators struggle to bring together these two worlds. The problem is more conceptual: it is about means and ends, which at times can be very different in their nature and may sometimes even appear contradictory.

The levels of strategy

A large part of the challenge in strategy is understanding how military force can contribute towards the attainment of a policy objective and then making this a workable reality in the crucible of war. In order to achieve this, the strategist must perform competently across all levels of strategy. It will be instructive at this point to define the levels of strategy and comment on how they interact. At the top of the taxonomy of strategy is *policy*: the overall objective that is sought. The range of policy objectives are essentially infinite, as Clausewitz so ably describes: 'Policy, of course, is nothing in itself; it is simply the trustee for all these interests against other states . . . we can only treat policy as representative of all interests of the community.'

Policy objectives should have a fundamental influence on actions within the other levels of strategy; indeed, more specifically, they should determine the methods used in the campaigns. However, this is easier said than done. Clausewitz's comment that the policy objective should guide the military instrument often creates problems when the relationship between the political and military objectives is not clear and/or direct. For example, the current counter-insurgency (COIN) campaign in Iraq is one such case. How does one use a relatively blunt military instrument to achieve subtle policy objectives, such as economic and social reconstruction? As is often the case, Clausewitz provides us with the answer. He notes that when the policy and military aims are not the same, a military aim should be chosen that leads to the fulfilment of the policy objective indirectly. For example, you should endeavour to give yourself a strong military position from which to negotiate a peace. We should remember that politics, and therefore war, is about power. Perhaps at times we are guilty of over-thinking Clausewitz and have tried to establish too close a relationship between policy and war. War cannot always itself lead directly to a policy objective, but it can alter the power relationships through which policy can be pursued against the enemy. When Clausewitz writes about disarming the enemy, and making him do our will, he is talking about power. A disarmed enemy is easier to influence. Of course, perceptions of power do not come just from physical assets, or the lack of them: the enemy has to perceive differences in the power relationship.

A slight reinterpretation of Clausewitz would note that, while strategy is about the use of military force to achieve policy objectives, this relationship is not always straightforward or direct. In the first instance, strategy is about the acquisition and use of power. Once gained, an imbalance in power can be used to achieve policy objectives. Thus, the attainment of power represents the hidden step in Clausewitz's concept of strategy. Although Clausewitz does not explicitly outline this step in terms of power acquisition, it is evident in his work when he notes that 'war is thus an act of force to compel our enemy to do our will'. This statement by Clausewitz represents a definition of power that is remarkably similar to that offered by Raymond Aron, the theorist of international relations: 'the capacity of a political unit to impose its will upon other units'.[21]

With sufficient power, one can engage in the many subtle activities that achievement of the policy objective calls for: nation-building, civic works, reconstruction and providing security, to name just four. If, however, the enemy still retains sufficient power himself, he can influence events, for example by coercing the population. In this sense, he may be able to challenge one's influence and authority in the contested locale. The relationship between military force and power is central to Admiral J. C. Wylie's often overlooked work, *Military Strategy: A General Theory of Power Control*. Wylie's basic assumption is that 'the aim of war is some measure of control over the enemy'.[22] This is achieved by controlling the pattern of the war, which in turn is achieved by manipulating the enemy's centres of gravity. The means by which this occurs is the physical presence of armed men: 'The ultimate determinant in war is the man on the scene with the gun. This man is the final power in war. He is control.' Control is not an absolute condition. Rather, Wylie notes, it can be 'direct, indirect, subtle, passive, partial or complete'. Interestingly, for the purposes of understanding the role of military force in the acquisition of power, when describing the more indirect examples of control Wylie is happy to use the term 'influence' instead. Thus, when thinking about strategy, we should remember that although the relationship between war and policy objectives is not always direct or obvious, the former relates to the latter through the medium of power.

In order to pursue a policy objective an actor has at his disposal a number of instruments, which generally speaking fall into one of the following categories: diplomatic; intelligence assets; military; and economic. Taken together, these represent the instruments of *grand strategy*. Basil H. Liddell Hart succinctly outlines the function of grand strategy: 'to coordinate and direct all the resources of a nation, or band of nations, towards the attainment of the political object of the war – the goal defined by fundamental policy'.[23] For any particular policy objective sought, the key grand strategic decision is choosing the right instrument, or the right combination of instruments. This decision should be arrived at after taking into account a number of factors, including: the policy itself; the available resources; the nature of potential enemies; the strategic culture; and the geopolitical environment, to name just five.

The aspect of grand strategy of primary interest to us here is military strategy. Once it has been established how military force will be used to serve the ends of policy, the strategy must be put into practice. This is achieved through actions at the *tactical* and *operational* levels. The former is concerned with actions in the battlespace in the face of the enemy. So, for example, under tactics would come the deployment of forces, engagement with the enemy and the interactions among various units. In essence, tactics is concerned with the details of combat. Each contact with the enemy represents a distinct tactical event. At first, one could be forgiven for thinking that success at the military strategic level stems from a victorious outcome in every tactical action. However, successful military strategy requires a more developed understanding of the significance of tactical events. Thus, it is possible that tactical 'failure' can make an effective contribution to the attainment of a military strategic end state. A striking example of the latter is the Tet offensive launched by the Viet Cong in 1968. After initial, but short-lived, success, Tet was characterised by a series of tactical failures. However, the fact that the Viet Cong were able to launch such a range of tactical actions across South Vietnam seriously undermined morale within the United States. In this respect, it is the interactions among the different tactical actions (in the case of Tet, their cumulative effect on public and political perception in the United States) and their relationship with the military strategic level that matter most. It is at this point that the *operational* level performs its role. It is through the operational level that tactical actions serve the requirements of the overall military strategy. Edward Luttwak succinctly describes this function: 'this operational level governs the consequences of what is done and not done tactically'.[24] Put simply, in and of themselves tactical actions may have little significance. Victory or defeat at this lowest level are insignificant without reference to their military-strategic implications.

The operational level has both conceptual and material elements. Conceptually, the operational level provides an analytical framework within which tactical actions can be linked together so that they serve military strategy. So, for example, a series of tactical aerial bombing missions needs to be considered as a whole, so that it produces a decisive coercive effect on the enemy. Materially, the operational level can be perceived in relation to a geographic area of operations. Within this theatre of operations the operational-level commander must manoeuvre his forces while taking account of a number of key factors and features. These include logistics and lines of communication, the position and movement of enemy forces, and such decisive points as cities, bridges and other key terrain features. The above description of the levels of strategy presents a rather linear vision of how they relate to one another. However, while this description is valid to some degree, it does little to reflect the complexity and non-linear nature of strategy. Thus, this chapter will now analyse those features of strategy that make it so difficult.

The complexity of strategy is the product of a number of different factors that, taken together, produce substantial challenges for the practitioner. The aforementioned awkward relationship between policy and military force is but one such factor. There are many other considerations that must be dealt with by the practitioner in his quest for strategic success.

Disharmony among the levels

The strategic practitioner has to achieve a degree of competence in each of the levels of strategy, as described above. However, he must also harmonise his actions among those levels. Actions at the tactical level must be in accord with those at the higher levels of strategy. When considering the feasibility of this, one is reminded of the following sobering comment by Clausewitz: 'Everything in strategy is very simple, but that does not mean that everything is very easy.' Indeed, Edward Luttwak notes that the normal state of affairs is measured disharmony. In his work *Strategy: The Logic of War and Peace*, Luttwak paints a disturbing picture for the strategist, one in which the challenges of achieving harmony are substantial. To illustrate this, Luttwak cites the Japanese attack on Pearl Harbor. Although at the tactical and operational levels the attack on Pearl Harbor was relatively successful, from the grand strategic perspective this success proved problematic. The scale of the attack compelled the United States to pursue a policy towards Japan of unconditional surrender. When considered alongside the uncompromising nature of the Japanese government and the power of the United States, this situation was almost certain to lead to costly defeat for Japan. Thus, harmonisation of the levels of strategy is not necessarily concerned with achieving success within all of the said levels. Rather, it is about ensuring that actions within each level support, rather than undermine, efforts in the other levels of strategy. More limited Japanese action at the tactical and operational levels, although almost certainly aggravating the United States, might have provoked a more limited response, which in turn might not have ended in total defeat for the empire.

Harmony also demands that both policy and grand strategy create a conducive and permissive environment for military strategy to play its part. The dangers inherent in getting this wrong are evident in the case of Germany in the Second World War. Germany's overly ambitious policy objectives and flawed grand strategy ensured that tactical and operational prowess could not be fully exploited. Germany simply acquired too many powerful enemies, who, as a result of the nature of the Third Reich and its objectives, were beyond negotiation. Much like in the case of Japan, the enemies of Germany were set on a course of unconditional surrender. Despite substantial battlefield success for Germany, its enemies were constantly able, and willing, to put fresh forces into the field.

To illustrate this further, we can also look to the Second Punic War (218–201 BC), fought between Carthage and the Roman republic. The Carthaginian commander, Hannibal, was astute at the tactical and operational levels. Thus, he was able to inflict a series of stunning battlefield defeats on Rome during his invasion of Italy. The most notable of these were the battles of Cannae and Lake Trasimene. At the former, Hannibal destroyed two Roman armies, killing 60,000 men in a single day. However, he failed to translate these successes into a favourable policy outcome. In a curious decision, Hannibal chose not to attack Rome itself and thereby failed to put sufficient pressure on the decision-making centre of the Roman republic. Thus, the republic survived and was able continually to exploit its vast manpower resources. Taking into account the nature of his enemy, Hannibal's outstanding successes on the battle-field were out of kilter with the situation at the strategic and grand strategic levels. With the resources at his disposal, Hannibal could not hope physically to destroy a sufficient amount of the Roman military capability. Rather, victory would be most likely to have come from destroying the will of his enemy. Therefore, Hannibal's tactical actions did not coalesce with the overall policy objective, mainly because his military strategy was inappropriate for the situation in hand. The effects of this disharmony were magnified by Rome's strategy, masterminded by Fabius Maximus, of avoiding battle under anything but the most favourable circumstances. This Fabian strategy gave Rome the time it required to mobilise its considerable manpower resources, and thereby over time Hannibal's tactical and operational performance produced diminishing returns. In essence, his military strategy began to fail. The Second Punic War illustrates well Luttwak's point that the challenge of harmonising the levels of strategy is intensified by the actions of the enemy, who ensures that a complex series of interactions is taking place within and among the levels of strategy.

Multidimensional

The notion of 'dimensions' helps us to understand the many different factors that impinge upon or play a part in strategy. Depending upon which theorist you choose to read, the number of dimensions in strategy varies. Clausewitz identified five dimensions of strategy: moral; physical; mathematical; geographical; and statistical. In the modern era, Michael Howard, in his 1979 article 'The Forgotten Dimensions of Strategy', identified four dimensions. In Howard's taxonomy these are: technological; operational; social; and logistic. The relative prominence of each dimension is dependent upon circumstance.[25] More recently, in *Modern Strategy* Gray has produced a considerably more developed theory of the dimensions and by doing so has dissected the art of strategy considerably further than either Clausewitz or Howard. In total, Gray identifies seventeen dimensions (see box 1.2), which he organises into three categories: 'People and Politics'; 'Preparation for War'; and 'War Proper'. Within these categories the dimensions include society, culture, economics and logistics, strategic theory and doctrine, command and time, to name just six. Is seventeen the final and correct number of dimensions? As Gray himself notes, 'the precise number

Box 1.2 Gray's dimensions of strategy

- People
- Society
- Culture
- Politics
- Ethics
- Economics and logistics
- Organisation
- Military administration
- Information and intelligence

- Strategic theory and doctrine
- Technology
- Military operations
- Command
- Geography
- Friction
- Adversary
- Time

[of dimensions] does not matter so long as everything of importance is properly corralled'.[26]

The significance of identifying the dimensions of strategy, and Gray's analysis in particular, is that it highlights the substantial range of factors that must be considered and dealt with. The strategic waters are muddied further by the fact that complex interactions occur among the dimensions. For example, from the perspective of the US intelligence community, before 9/11 the time, information and organisation dimensions interacted in an unfavourable manner. There was not sufficient time or adequate organisational arrangements among the intelligence agencies to make sense of the scare information available on future al-Qaeda operations. Further to this, as Gray discusses, the challenge of achieving competence among the dimensions may be intensified by the fact that in one or more of the dimensions an enemy may hold a significant advantage. Thus, depending upon the context, this advantage may have to be negated in some way, if at all possible. For example, the English Channel gives Britain a substantial advantage in the geographical dimension over continental foes. However, it should be noted that achieving and maintaining an advantage in a dimension is a dynamic process: it is down to the practitioners themselves to exploit them to their advantage. Thus, the English Channel did not prove an insuperable obstacle to the Roman or Norman invading forces. However, once the inhabitants of the British Isles had developed competent naval forces, the significance of the geographical dimension was substantially magnified.

Interaction with an intelligent foe

As Clausewitz identified when he described war as a duel on a larger scale, strategy is fundamentally characterised by the fact that it is conducted against a thinking enemy. Although this is a rather obvious statement, the corresponding reality should not be overlooked or underestimated. Luttwak tied this factor to his concept of the 'paradoxical logic': 'Although each separate element in the conduct of warfare can be very simple . . . the totality of these simple things can become enormously difficult when there is a live enemy opposite, who reacts to undo everything being attempted, with his own moves and his own strength.'[27] Although Luttwak overplays the significance of the paradoxical logic, as an idea it is still worthy of our attention. This pervasive feature operates in many different ways and can perhaps best be explained through a number of examples, which illustrate that the expected does not always occur, strength leads to weakness and advantage does not always flow from a linear progression of events. For example, the paradoxical logic is at play when a manoeuvre that takes the more difficult, less logical route provides success by surprising the enemy. Alternatively, the paradoxical logic suggests that a successful military operation may begin to produce diminishing returns over time. This may occur as the enemy adapts and counters one's own successful operations, or indeed as the advancing forces may have to curtail their campaign because their logistics become increasingly stretched.

The current war in Iraq offers a prime example of the challenges invoked by interaction with a thinking foe. In the 1991 Gulf War, US-led forces easily overcame their Iraqi counterparts. However, in 2003 the defeat of the Iraqi regular forces merely represented the first stage in an on-going struggle. Those wishing to challenge the presence of US-led forces sought to offset the conventional superiority of their enemies and opted for irregular warfare, blending together elements of insurgency and terrorism. In this sense, the paradoxical logic began to operate at different levels for the US-led Coalition. At the tactical and operational levels, roadside bombs could inflict casualties on US forces and their allies while not allowing their conventional superiority to be brought to bear. In addition, the insurgents could avoid contact with the Coalition forces entirely by targeting civilians with car and truck bombs. Such tactics, and the associated casualties and destruction, have created pressure at the higher levels of strategy within the Coalition. Understanding that they could not militarily defeat the Coalition, the insurgents are attempting to break the will of political communities in the Coalition, thus forcing a withdrawal.

The salience of this aspect of strategy is perfectly described by the Confederate General George Pickett who, when asked why the South lost at Gettysburg, replied, 'I think the Union Army had something to do with it.'[28] Put simply, the existence of an intelligent foe affects and complicates every dimension of strategy. It defines and complicates the task of harmonising actions among the levels of strategy. And, as we shall see, it plays a significant part in defining the nature of war, contributes to friction (see p. 35) and gives added prescience to the fact that war has a polymorphous character.

The nature of war

Those seeking to achieve policy objectives through the use of military force also have to contend with the nature of war. In any historical, social or political context, the nature of war poses substantial challenges to the strategist. However, modern Western attitudes to war have further complicated this endeavour. Since war is a political act, it cannot be conducted in a military vacuum. Thus, the strategist must take into account prevailing norms and values regarding the use of force. Although the modern laws of war have existed since the late nineteenth century, more recent social attitudes have increased expectations regarding behaviour in war. This trend has been intensified by 24/7 media and the increasing penetration of the legal profession (often pursuing civil actions) into the military sphere. The challenge posed by this state of affairs emanates from the requirement to balance the above responsibilities with the demands placed by the nature of war.

Like strategy, the nature of war is complex. In a general sense, the nature of war is composed of elements that are ever-present. However, within each particular war the relationships among these elements fluctuate. Thus, each particular war has its own unique, albeit similar, nature. There are a number of conceptual means by which to describe the nature of war and its various elements. In Clausewitzian terms, the 'fascinating trinity' describes the nature of war being composed of rational and non-rational forces (policy, emotion, chance). As the relative strength of each of these components differs with context, the nature of any particular war will be found floating somewhere between them. Thus, using the trinity as a conceptual vehicle, Christopher Bassford concludes that the nature of any particular war results from the dynamics that occur within, and among, the trinities of the various actors involved in a conflict.[29] Clearly, this process, as just described, suggests why the nature of war is so complex.

To muddy the waters further, Alan Beyerchen notes that these complex interactions make war an activity characterised by non-linear dynamics. In such an environment, small fluctuations can have significant consequences.[30] For example, the outcome of the battle of Waterloo was partially influenced by the interaction between such factors as Napoleon's illness and consequent absence during the battle, and the heavy rain the night before the battle. The latter of course had untold consequences for all of the forces present on that day but was particularly significant for the French artillery. Round shot required firm ground to help maximise efficacy. Thus, Napoleon delayed the initial offensive in order to allow the ground to dry out. This delay became significant because, as the battle lasted longer, it gave von Blücher's Prussian forces the required time to make an appearance later in the day. The Prussians' late arrival was so significant because by that time the French forces were severely weakened, in part owing to mistakes made in Napoleon's absence. These limited interactions are but a small taste of the many factors that interacted on, and beyond, the battlefield of Waterloo. In addition, one could also factor in the morale and physical condition of the forces and political pressures, as well as the influence of past experiences on the men and their commanders. Clearly, it is beyond the ability of any human fully to understand and predict how these factors in the nature of war interact and what the consequences will be. This is further exacerbated by the fact that many of these factors, such as illness or weather, occur as chance events. As Clausewitz notes, 'No other human activity is so continuously or universally bound up with chance.'

The complexity and non-linearity of the nature of war are intensified by uncertainty, which Clausewitz regards as a constant state of affairs in war. Indeed, the interplay of uncertainty and non-linearity creates a vicious-circle effect: non-linearity creates uncertainty, just as the latter produces the former. Indeed, interaction among belligerents creates non-linear outcomes that are difficult to predict or quantify. For Clausewitz, the omnipotence of uncertainty is a result of many factors. However, of particular importance is the fact that, in war, information is often unreliable and incomplete. Human involvement also has a role to play here. The inclusion of human actors infuses war with powerful moral forces, again unquantifiable in nature. In addition, information ultimately has to be processed by human actors, who may misinterpret said information owing to error or bias. One can add to these factors the geography of the battlespace and the nature of certain actors (e.g. irregular forces). Thus, we can appreciate how war is often irregular and unpredictable in its nature. All of the above creates a metaphorical 'fog of war', which can be mitigated by technology and good procedures but never lifted entirely. Consequently, the strategist finds himself in a situation where he must endeavour to achieve his goals within an environment of complexity infused by uncertainty.

This is not the end of the matter for the nature of war, however. The practice of strategy is further complicated by another central ingredient of the nature of war: violence, or what Clausewitz refers to as the 'dominance of the destructive principle'. Clausewitz is persuasive when he notes that violence is intrinsic to the nature of war: 'War is a clash between major interests, which is resolved by bloodshed – that is the only way in which it differs from other conflicts.' Although the levels of violence vary in war, it is always present or waiting in the wings. As Clausewitz notes, 'it is inherent in the very concept of war that everything that occurs *must originally derive from combat*' [emphasis in the original]. Although there are those who promote less violent forms of war, its presence and influence can never be eradicated. This is primarily because war has a dialectic nature. As Clausewitz recognised, the competitive aspect of war creates an escalatory dynamic as each belligerent attempts to seek an advantage. Thus, even if one belligerent in a conflict extols a less bloody method, the enemy may introduce higher levels of violence to gain the upper hand. The intensification of the destructive principle may seek to debilitate the enemy's capabilities and/or break his will through the application of violence.

Violence creates problems for the strategist because it has an attritional effect on his forces and capabilities at a physical level but may also have a debilitating affect on the morale of those forces, their political masters and the society from which they are drawn. At its heart, war is a human activity: 'in war and strategy people matter most'.[31] Thus, as Clausewitz reminds us, war is infused with human emotions and concerns: 'The art of war deals with living and with moral forces.' Within the stress and exertion of war the human actor, whether a general or a foot soldier, may be negatively affected in relation to the ability to think and act effectively. This complicates the task of the strategist by restricting his options and freedom of action. In addition, as Gray notes, 'war is usually so traumatic an experience that generally it follows a course and has consequences quite unintended by the belligerents. To go to war is to roll the iron dice.'[32]

Despite this, the strategist must still maintain sufficient will and capabilities to pursue his objectives through to completion in the face of such destruction and human suffering. However, although the violent nature of war adds further pressure on the strategist, he has to utilise it for the purposes of policy. Indeed, policy itself may require significant levels of violence and destruction. For example, there are times when enemy forces may have to be physically destroyed, rather than just coerced or outmanoeuvred. In order to pursue the policy of unconditional surrender against Nazi Germany, as well as to leave post-war Germany militarily impotent, the Combined Chiefs of Staff issued the following directive to the commander, Eisenhower: 'You will enter the continent of Europe and, in conjunction with the other Allied Nations, undertake operations aimed at the heart of Germany and the destruction of her armed forces.' Eisenhower goes on to note, 'This purpose of destroying enemy forces was always our guiding principle.'[33]

The significance of the violent, uncertain and competitive nature of war must not be underestimated. Those who submit to this error run the risk of being at a disadvantage. As Clausewitz warns us, 'kind-hearted people might of course think there was some ingenious way to disarm or defeat an enemy without too much bloodshed'. He continues: 'If one side uses force without compunction, undeterred by the bloodshed it involves, while the other side refrains, the first will gain the upper hand.' In a similar vein, Clausewitz warned: 'The fact that slaughter is a horrifying spectacle must make us take war more seriously, but not provide an excuse for gradually blunting our swords in the name of humanity. Sooner or later someone will come along with a sharp sword and hack off our arms.'

While this advice cannot be ignored without serious consequence, in the same instance war cannot be waged without reference to the social norms of the day. In a modern setting, certain actions in war are simply not possible from an ethical standpoint. In a similar vein, Gray correctly argues that '[war] should be waged militarily in such a manner as not to sabotage its political goals'.[34] A particularly brutal form of war may cause such a backlash that the policy objectives could be lost among the condemnation. As with so much in strategy, there is simply no straightforward solution to this dilemma. Instead, the strategist must rely upon his judgement to create the required balance. Again, Clausewitz is instructive:

> We can thus only say that the aims a belligerent adopts, and the resources he employs, must be governed by the particular characteristics of his own position; but they will also conform to the spirit of the age and to its general character. Finally, they must always be governed by the general conclusions to be drawn from the nature of war itself.

Friction

Much of the discussion thus far concerning the difficulties of strategy can be understood and expressed through the Clausewitzian concept of friction, which can be understood as 'Countless minor incidents – the kind you can never really foresee – [that] combine to lower the general level of performance, so that one always falls short of the intended goal.' For Clausewitz, friction is an essential ingredient in the reality of war: 'Friction is the only concept that more or less corresponds to the factors that distinguish real war from war on paper.' The scope of friction can be appreciated through Clausewitz's 'unified concept of general friction', as identified by Barry D. Watts. In his excellent study on future war, Watts identifies the following taxonomy for the unified concept of general friction: danger; physical exertion; uncertainties and imperfections in information; friction in the narrow sense of the resistance within one's own forces; chance events; physical and political limits on the use of military force; unpredictability stemming from interaction with the enemy; disconnects between ends and means in war.[35]

To complicate matters further, friction can occur as a result of, and be exacerbated by, the paradoxical logic. Paradoxical courses of action, for example to surprise an enemy, may forgo the normal, complete and logical procedures. As Luttwak states, these actions 'will further increase friction and therefore the risk of organisational failure'.[36] Naturally, certain elements of friction are also enhanced by the effects of interaction with the enemy. Losses of men and equipment in battle deplete the capabilities of a force, which in turn can hinder future operations. In addition, the enemy may actively seek to complicate one's actions. For example, the pace of an advance may be severely curtailed by the enemy blowing up a bridge.

Despite the potency of friction and its potential to wreck military operations, its effects can be mitigated to some degree. Having identified this troublesome force in war, Clausewitz notes that certain characteristics, such as determination, can help to reduce its debilitating effects. Gray develops this argument and suggests that a number of practical steps can be taken to limit the consequences of friction. These include: good and ample equipment; high morale; rigorous training; imaginative planning; historical education; combat experience; and sensitivity to potential problems.[37] Nonetheless, friction can never fully be eradicated. Therefore, those conducting strategy should anticipate its presence and endeavour to limit its influence but ultimately prepare to live with its consequences.

The polymorphous character of war

War does not take one, regular form for which the strategist can plan with certainty. Indeed, the reverse is actually true. In this sense, war can be said to have a polymorphous character. Historically, war has always taken a number of different forms. However, from an operational perspective the modern era has undoubtedly produced a more complex environment. Technological developments in the twentieth century facilitated the exploitation of the air, space and cyberspace environments. In addition, the century also witnessed further developments in the theory and practice of insurgency and terrorism. Finally, perhaps the greatest challenge for strategy has been the arrival of nuclear weapons. The extreme destructive nature of these weapons makes them difficult tools of policy. Each of these various areas of strategy will be discussed in detail in the following chapters. For now we must recognise that many of them overlap, creating new opportunities and challenges in the different environments. For example, maritime strategy has had to develop to incorporate both air power and nuclear weapons. Thus, commanders in each geographical environment, as well those running an entire campaign, have to deal with a more complex battlespace.

The pace of technological developments in the modern era has sparked important debates regarding the significance of technology in war. For some commentators and practitioners, the 1991 Gulf War heralded a so-called Revolution in Military Affairs (RMA), or in current parlance a Military Transformation. When an RMA occurs, the advantage is said to go to those who fully exploit and operationalise the latest technological developments. Since the RMA debate remains of such import, both within academic and military circles, it is worth exploring the validity of this concept. In addition, by doing so we can also assess the relative value of technology in deciding the outcomes of war.

The development of blitzkrieg during the twentieth century offers a prime example of a candidate RMA and thus represents an important test case for the RMA hypothesis. In the early twentieth century, a range of new technologies appeared that could be utilised in the art of warfare. The internal combustion engine made possible the development of the tank and related logistics and infantry vehicles. Taken together, these vehicles enabled more rapid manoeuvres in the theatre of operations. The command and control of these manoeuvres was facilitated by the advent of wireless radio. All told, this produced forces that could move rapidly in a co-ordinated manner and thereby achieve a higher tempo of operations.

However, merely having advanced technological capability is not enough. An adequate doctrine is required to exploit fully the potential of new technologies. The significance of this latter point is evidenced by the fact that the various European powers utilised these new forces differently in the early stages of the Second World War. The French, with their defensive and conservative outlook, dispersed their armoured forces throughout their existing infantry formations, essentially treating them as mobile artillery. This was hardly a revolutionary step forward. In contrast, Nazi Germany developed the operational concept of blitzkrieg. Within this new doctrine, concentrated armoured forces acted as the spearhead of rapid offensive formations. The immediate origins of blitzkrieg can be found towards the end of the First World War, when both sides created self-contained formations that could conduct deep and rapid advances along a narrow axis of attack. These concepts were brought to maturity by such men as Heinz Guderian.

Although tanks are powerful and rapid moving instruments, when operating on their own they are vulnerable to infantry-based anti-tank weapons. To guard against this, the Germans developed the panzer division. This new formation contained tanks, infantry, artillery and support troops. This range of capabilities gave the panzer division a degree of self-sustainability and ensured that the different elements could offer each other mutual support and protection.

As evidenced in its invasions of Poland (1939), France (1940) and the Soviet Union (1941), blitzkrieg initially proved remarkably successful for Germany. However, as the war wore on the Germans began to reap diminishing returns from blitzkrieg. This can be attributed to a number of factors. The weather and geographic depth of the Soviet Union neutralised many of the advantages conferred by blitzkrieg. In addition, due to the substantial resources of their enemies Germany was unable to translate its tactical and operational successes into a war-winning outcome. Finally, Germany's enemies adapted to blitzkrieg, either imitating it themselves or discovering ways to offset its advantages. Thus, the case of blitzkrieg demonstrates that the advantages conferred by operational innovation, great though they may be, can be offset. The complexities faced by the strategist do not often permit such straightforward, operational answers to complex strategic questions.

It is all too easy to overestimate the significance of technological developments and their associated operational implications. The noted military historian J.F.C. Fuller is guilty of such a mistake: 'Tools or weapons, if only the right ones can be discovered, form ninety-nine per cent of victory.'[38] However, a closer look at history reveals that many seemingly new operational developments, such as joint operations, manoeuvre warfare or effects-based operations, have historical precedent. There is little, if anything, genuinely new in strategy. For example, Alexander the Great's military method is very reminiscent of the characteristics of blitzkrieg, albeit at a tactical rather than operational level. Chapter 2 below describes how the key to German operational performance in the Second World War was not new technology per se, but the integration of units into an effective, combined-arms force. The resulting force was thus able to manoeuvre more rapidly, deliver shock, penetrate the enemy's lines on a narrow front and finally exploit the gap to strike deep into the rear of the enemy's forces. We see a similar approach taken by Alexander in his three great battles against the Persian main army. Indeed, Alexander was an extremely astute exponent of combined-arms warfare. His rapid tactical manoeuvres were led by a spearhead of heavy cavalry, which punched through the enemy's lines along a narrow axis. This lead unit, the companion cavalry, was supported by an evolved combined-arms formation, which included various types of infantry and troops with ranged weapons. Such an approach was devastating against the more limited tactical formations of Greek hoplite warfare. It also proved to be decisive against the more evolved forces of the Persian empire. Like Alexander, the Persians put into the field a mixed army comprised of cavalry, infantry and missile troops. However, very like the Germans in the Second World War, much of Alexander's advantage came from superior doctrine and training.

Thus, when reading the following chapters, which will discuss the different forms of warfare and how they have evolved, it is important to remember that the fundamentals of strategy never change, regardless of time or place.

What the remainder of this book will reveal is the range and complexity of forms that war can take. In this sense, the character of any particular war can include weapons of mass destruction (WMDs), regular conflict between uniformed and similarly organised foes and/or various forms of irregular warfare, including terrorism and insurgency. The challenge posed by such a variety of forms concerns both the preparation and conduct of war. Each particular form of warfare requires a somewhat distinct set of capabilities, which in turn may require varied types of forces, equipment, doctrine and/or training. Charles Callwell, the Victorian theorist of irregular warfare, notes how 'The art of war, as generally understood [for regular forms of warfare] must be modified to suit the circumstances of each particular case. The conduct of small wars is in fact in certain respects an art in itself.'[39] Almost one hundred years after Callwell, Gray cautions against complacency in the face of the polymorphous character of war: 'Small wars can detract from the readiness of regular forces to take the field against other regular forces.'[40] Thus, the strategist must create and maintain capabilities with a degree of competence in each of the different forms of warfare, so that he can deal with any strategic challenges posed. However, he must also avoid being too specialised in any part of the spectrum of warfare, otherwise he may not be able to adapt to another form of warfare.

The task of the strategist is further complicated by the fact that particular wars often display a complex mix of different forms. Thus, the following counsel from Clausewitz is valid but not always easy to achieve: 'The first, the supreme, the most far-reaching act of judgement that the statesman and commander has to make is to establish by that test the kind of war on which they are embarking.' Such wars as the US war in Vietnam and the American War of Independence contain elements common to both regular and irregular warfare. However, despite the fact that each particular form of warfare presents its own unique challenges, they are all still forms of war. This being so, they take place within the same complex nature discussed above. In particular, they are still violent, competitive conflicts acting in the service of policy. Thus, the battle of the wills is often paramount, and a theory of victory must exist. It is all too easy to give exaggerated significance to the challenges of a particular form of warfare and thereby underestimate these basic truths. This is nowhere more evident than in counter-insurgency.

Modern COIN practice, at least partially based upon such seminal works as Robert Thompson's *Defeating Communist Insurgency*, tends to be regarded less as a form of war and more as a security challenge, with popularity and legitimacy being the key means to achieving the desirable end state.[41] While there is certainly value in the hearts-and-minds aspects of COIN doctrine, we must never lose sight of the fact that COIN is still a form of war. In fact, an essential ingredient of COIN is inflicting serious military setback on the insurgents. This not only restricts their ability to undermine security in the contested territory, it also promotes a sense of authority for the local government and their allies. On this point, Callwell is clear: 'Prestige is everything in such warfare.' Similarly, Julian Paget, in the classic work *Counter-Insurgency Campaigning*, concludes that in order to win the support of the local population 'the Government must demonstrate its determination and its ability to defeat the insurgents'.[42] Finally, Steven Metz notes: 'it is less an assessment of a preferred future that drives insurgents or insurgent supporters than an assessment of who will prevail – the insurgents or the regime'.[43]

The successful British COIN campaign in Malaya provides a telling example. The campaign took twelve years and included some fairly draconian

Box 1.3 Why is strategy difficult?

- The relationship between war and policy is difficult and awkward.
- Strategy is multidimensional (including such dimensions as society, culture, economics and logistics, strategic theory and doctrine, command and time), and success requires a level of competence to be achieved in them all.
- Success requires harmony of actions among the levels of strategy.
- Strategy is conducted against an intelligent foe. The enemy will attempt to offset one's advantages. What worked today may not work tomorrow.
- The nature of war is violent, competitive, complex and constant. This must be respected but puts pressure on the commander and his forces, especially in relation to modern norms and social values.
- Friction prevents war from achieving its maximum operational efficiency.
- War is a human activity imbued with non-rational, emotional forces.
- War has a polymorphous character. It can take many forms, each of which requires a subtly different approach. Often, a particular war will exhibit a mixture of different forms operating simultaneously.

methods. The latter included curfews, the mass forced relocation of 400,000 people, detention without trial and execution for possession of firearms or explosives. In addition, the insurgents were subjected to a protracted war of attrition, during which their numbers were slowly eroded, at the cost of 500 British deaths. In summary, rather than being a competition in popularity, COIN is rather a competition in authority. That authority is heavily dependent on military success.

Efforts to understand the complexities of strategy have been aided by a number of key theorists. Although each particular form of warfare has its own dominant works of theory, there are universal theorists who grapple with the nature of war and the broader aspects of strategy. For the practitioner, these works help to identify and understand the various elements of strategy. In addition, they provide some, if limited, advice on how to cope with the challenges of strategy. Interestingly, the more prescriptive a work, the less universal it tends to be. This is particularly the case with Jomini's work, which suffers in comparison with Clausewitz's as a result.

Although these universal works provide enlightenment on strategy, the limits of theory must be kept in mind. As a general proposition, Wylie's assertion that no general theory can guarantee success should be treated as the first and most important thought on this issue. In this vein, Clausewitz recognises that theory could only ever be second best to what military genius does: 'What genius does is the best rule, and theory can do no better than show how and why this should be the case.' Nonetheless, he does go on to identify the value of theory: 'Theory exists so that one need not start afresh each time sorting out the material and ploughing through it, but will find it ready to hand and in good order.' Indeed, theory has often performed a very practical function within strategy. One of the most striking examples of this is the relationship between the theory and practice of strategic bombing. The influence of theory was particularly evident during the interwar years, when the central theoretical tenets of both precision and area/morale bombing were formulated in the works of Douhet, Trenchard and Mitchell. Williamson Murray notes how pervasive the influence of theory can be, reaching into such areas as doctrine and force composition: 'The theories of Douhet and other early airpower advocates . . . have exercised a great influence on the development of air forces since that time.'[44] In a similar manner, the theorists of nuclear strategy during the Cold War were said to have 'wielded enormous influence, not only over the way an entire generation's thoughts about military issues were shaped but also over the formulation of defence policy in the nuclear-weapon states'.[45]

In order to be useful to the practitioner, theory must coincide with reality. To this end, Murray and Grimsley's declaration that 'strategy is the art of the possible' is an important warning to those who would construct naively optimistic theories.[46] Again, Clausewitz is persuasive when he warns: '[Theory's] purpose is to demonstrate what war is in practice, not what its ideal nature ought to be.' In a similar vein, the Cold War theorist Brodie argues that 'Above all, strategic theory is a theory for action.' Echoing Brodie's wise counsel, Daniel Moran stipulates that 'The goal of theory in any field is to improve our understanding of reality, and our ability to act effectively.'[47] Finally, Clausewitz summarises both the value and limits of theory: '[Theory] is meant to educate the mind of the future commander, or, more accurately, to guide him in his self-education, not to accompany him to the battlefield.' Later on in the work, he elaborates on these thoughts:

Theory cannot equip the mind with formulas for solving problems, nor can it mark the narrow path on which the sole solution is supposed to lie by planting a hedge of principles on either side. But it can give the mind insight into the great mass of phenomena and of their relationships, then leave it free to rise into the higher realms of action.

Clausewitz

Of the universal theorists, perhaps the first among equals is the aforementioned Carl von Clausewitz. He served in the Prussian Army against Napoleon's forces, and his major work, *On War*, was published posthumously in 1832. *On War* is arguably the most influential work of strategic theory to date. Brodie is unequivocal about the value of Clausewitz's work, which he describes as 'not simply the greatest but the only truly great book on war'. Similarly, Gray, one of the most respected of modern strategic thinkers, describes Clausewitz as his constant companion. The practitioners of strategy are no less impressed by the Prussian's credentials. For example, the US Marine Corps' doctrinal publication *Warfighting* stipulates that Clausewitz's *On War* is 'the definitive treatment of the nature and theory of war'.[48]

Despite its prominence in modern strategic affairs, Clausewitz's work is often misunderstood and criticised. Much of this is due to the unfinished nature of the work, and the fact that Clausewitz chose a philosophical framework that, although popular in his day, is now rarely utilised. *On War* was published as a single volume after Clausewitz's widow gathered together elements of the unfinished manuscript. Indeed, in a book of 123 chapters, Clausewitz considered only the first to be fully complete. In addition, Clausewitz's use of the dialectical approach has led to some confusion. Rather than merely present one perspective, this philosophical method arrives at a synthesis after discussing the thesis and antithesis. Specifically, Clausewitz first presents a vision of war that is absolute, escalatory and unrestricted. He spends much of the rest of the book reining in this idea with the various means by which war is limited. So, for example, absolute war is never achieved because it is limited by policy concerns and the play of friction, to name just two. On this basis, Clausewitz distinguishes between absolute war and real war. Unfortunately, some commentators have failed to grasp his approach and have thus criticised Clausewitz for advocating unrestricted forms of war in the early sections of the book.

Clausewitz has come under fire from some of the most prominent writers in modern Strategic Studies. Martin van Creveld, perhaps in an attempt to bolster his view that war is becoming increasingly irregular in character, regards Clausewitz's work as being stuck in a state-centric view of the world and therefore narrow in its utility.[49] The military historian John Keegan likewise regards Clausewitz's view of war as being too narrow. Keegan argues that rather than being merely an instrument of policy, war is in fact a cultural phenomenon.[50] These narrow interpretations of *On War* do a disservice to Clausewitz, whose work is far more universal. Clausewitz's focus on policy as the guiding force in war is anything but restrictive. It is certainly not limited to state-based war fought for purely rational and secular motives. The following statement from Clausewitz illustrates this point perfectly: 'Policy, of course, is nothing in itself; it is simply the trustee for all these interests against other states . . . we can only treat policy as representative of all interests of the community.' The emphasis here is on the broad interpretation of the concept of policy and the use of the term 'community'. Thus, policy may refer to *any* objective for which war is waged. This can include religious issues, territorial disputes, resources or indeed important cultural events.

Clausewitz's vision of war is deliberately complex and dense. Although it is not possible fully to express his ideas in just one chapter of a book, the main concepts can be summarised. However, it is worth noting that there is simply no substitute for spending time analysing *On War* itself. Among strategic thinkers Clausewitz comes closest to defining the nature of war. For Clausewitz, war is a complex phenomenon, which is composed of rational and non-rational forces. Most famously, Clausewitz identified war's rational element as emanating from its relationship with policy. As a tool of policy, war has to be controlled to serve its political masters. However, this rational element is tempered by non-rational forces that make war uncertain, chaotic and non-linear. For Clausewitz, war is infused with chance, emotions and significant levels of friction that prevent war from reaching the higher levels of operational efficiency.

Although Clausewitz spends much of his time in *On War* discussing the various complexities of strategy, he does offer a number of means through which to deal with the associated problems. In a work that places so much emphasis on the human element, it is not surprising that the primary factor that can mitigate the complexities of strategy is to be found in man. Winston Churchill, a man who had to wrestle with strategy at the highest levels, is of the same mind: '[war's] highest solution must be evolved from the eye and brain and soul of a single man . . . Nothing but genius, the demon in man, can answer the riddles of war.'[51] Indeed, Clausewitz's theory of war cannot be fully understood without reference to the role of the commander.

Although Clausewitz fought against Napoleon, it is clear that his notion of the 'military genius' was largely based upon the Corsican. Although the term 'genius' tends to suggest that Clausewitz was referring to a few gifted individuals, we can utilise his concept to discuss the attributes of good command more generally. Thus, good command requires certain cognitive skills, certain moral qualities and an understanding of the human condition. More specifically, Clausewitz highlights a number of characteristics that a commander should possess. These include: physical and moral courage; incisiveness; presence of mind; strength of will and character; and an ambitious nature. Perhaps first among equals, though, is a general's intuitive ability, his *coup d'oeil*, and a determined character to remain faithful to his original plan in the face of doubt and trepidation. Clausewitz was also conscious of the significance of leadership within the chaotic and stressful environment of war. Finally, and rather obviously, a Clausewitzian general must understand the process of strategy by which war is used for political effect.

Important though the commander is, command as a whole cannot be reduced simply to the attributes of the individual. As Gray postulates, an astute commander may be unavailable when the next war occurs. Thus, a process of command must be designed to compensate for the potential lack of genius: 'War cabinets, general staffs, and chiefs of staff committees were invented to function as a surrogate for individual strategic genius.'[52] There are a number of examples of command systems that are able to produce consistently good results. One prominent example, often cited, is the Prussian General Staff. Indeed, T.N. Dupuy argues that the success of the Prussian/German General Staff can be attributed to the fact that 'it enabled men who individually lacked the qualities of a genius to perform institutionally in a manner that would provide results ordinarily achievable only by genius'.[53] Thus, we can conclude that the complexity of strategy can be somewhat unravelled by a judicious combination of the commander's qualities, the command structure and an appropriate command ethos.

In many respects, the main utility of Clausewitz's work for the practitioner may simply be the fact that he identifies the complexities of strategy. To be able to deal with a problem, one must first acknowledge and understand it. However, *On War* goes further. Aside from an important, if not always practical, focus on the military genius, Clausewitz provided a few conceptual aides. Most noteworthy in this respect is the 'centre of gravity'. This concept dominates much of modern military doctrine. Centres of gravity are defined by Clausewitz as: 'particular factors [that] can often be decisive . . . One must keep the dominant characteristics of both belligerents in mind. Out of these characteristics a certain centre of gravity develops, the hub of all power and movement, on which everything depends. That is the point against which all our energies should be directed.' Wylie incorporates the centre of gravity into his own theory regarding the search for strategic success:

The basic problem facing the strategist throughout all these situations, through any war, any time, any place, is this: Where shall be the center of gravity of the war? . . . Control of the strategic weights or centers of gravity in any war, large or small, limited or unlimited, is a basic advantage that should be sought by any strategist. It is the fundamental key to the conduct of warfare.

The above comment by Wylie correctly presupposes that there may be more than one centre of gravity for each belligerent in a conflict and therefore a number of routes to victory. Indeed, it is possible to identify centres of gravity at all levels of strategy. At the tactical and operational levels, candidate centres of gravity may include certain military formations, airfields and fortifications, to name just three. At the same time, an individual leader or the public may be the centre of gravity at the grand strategic level. Generally speaking, Clausewitz concurs with the notion of numerous and various centres of gravity. However, he does conclude that it is preferable to 'trace them back to a single one'. In addition, while Clausewitz's various centres of gravity may include such things as cities, alliance cohesion and leadership, he does finally conclude that 'the defeat and destruction of his fighting force remains the best way to begin, and in every case will be a very significant feature of the campaign'.

In this respect, Clausewitz's work is also noteworthy for the emphasis it places on battle. While this may seem rather obvious in a work about war, it is a refreshing counterpoint to the modern tendency to undervalue engagement with the enemy. Clausewitz was certainly aware of the limits of force, but he also stressed the dominance of the destructive principle and the value of defeating the enemy's forces. The latter is obviously not an end in itself but, as noted earlier, is usually an important step on the road to achieving policy objectives.

This is wise counsel in an age when we may be guilty of over-thinking strategy in our search for overly complex and subtle answers to strategic dilemmas. Indeed, simplicity, one of the modern principles of war, is often overlooked. Yet Clausewitz regarded it as an essential ingredient of his theory of war: 'It seems to us that this is proof enough of the superiority of the simple and direct over the complex . . . rather than try to outbid the enemy with complicated schemes, one should, on the contrary, try to outdo him in simplicity.' And for those who regard a direct, battle-orientated approach as intellectually immature, Clausewitz comments: 'The maximum use of force is in no way incompatible with the simultaneous use of the intellect.'

Regardless of what constitutes the centre(s) of gravity in any particular war, the concept does act as a very useful analytical and planning tool. Nonetheless, as with all theory it does not offer a guaranteed route to victory. Therefore, in order fully to appreciate the relative value of centres of gravity, we must ask a number of questions in each circumstance. Does the enemy actually have a centre of gravity? Can the enemy's centre of gravity be identified? The intelligence and analytical challenge posed by this last question should not be underestimated. For example, a debate still rages over what constituted the centre of gravity within the German war economy during the Second World War. This is not surprising when one considers the size of the task involved in trying to undertake an accurate, macro-level analysis of the German economy at that time. Robert A. Pape acknowledges that the required information was simply not available.[54] Even with the benefits of historical research and hindsight, historians still disagree over which component of the German economy, at which period in the war, represented its key vulnerability. Understanding the functioning of the German economy at the time must have been even more of a challenge. These difficulties are compounded by the fact that the intelligence acquired is often based on a peacetime analysis of the enemy, rather than when they have mobilised their economy for war.

Even if a centre of gravity has been correctly identified, is it always possible to put it under sufficient pressure? As Beaufre argues, 'the enemy's vulnerable points must be set against our own capabilities'. For example, if the Wehrmacht represented one of Nazi Germany's centres of gravity, it was beyond the reach of certain countries at certain times. Until the D-Day landings in June 1944 the Wehrmacht could not be sufficiently engaged by British and American military power. Furthermore, in 1939, although German forces were in contact with the Poles, the latter lacked the required capabilities to put the former under significant pressure. With such a mismatch in capabilities and opportunities, it matters little that you have identified the enemy's key attribute; your defeat will still occur. Finally, the Soviet Union, although able eventually to defeat the Wehrmacht, could only do so at great cost. Other countries may not have been able to sustain such losses and deprivations.

Jomini

Before moving on to the work of Sun Tzu, the other great universal theorist, it is important to mention the work of Baron Antoine Henri de Jomini. Although now somewhat out of favour, during the nineteenth and much of the twentieth centuries Jomini was the strategic theorist of choice. Indeed, so influential was he that John Shy goes as far as to comment: 'Jomini, more than Clausewitz, deserves the dubious title of founder of modern strategy.'[55] As a contemporary of Clausewitz's, who also participated in the Napoleonic Wars, Jomini offers a vision of war that, although it displays similarities to the Prussian's, is still significantly different. As a son of the Enlightenment, Jomini, more than Clausewitz, sought to discover the scientific principles underlying war. In contrast to Clausewitz's emphasis on military genius overcoming the complexities of a chaotic world, Jomini provides the reader with a number of principles, which, all things being equal, if followed should lead to victory. Indeed, rather than describing war as a non-linear activity in which intangible forces dominate, Jomini's approach to war is rather geometric. In particular, Jomini stresses the advantages of interior lines of communication. The significance of these interior lines comes from the fact that they most readily permit the commander to mass his forces against the enemy's weaknesses at the decisive point. This offensive massing of forces against the enemy is the core principle underpinning Jomini's theory of war. Jomini's experience with Napoleon's general staff may have been instrumental in shaping his planning-based approach to the subject of war. This may help to explain his greater emphasis on such concepts as lines of operation.

It is interesting to note that two strategic thinkers from the same period, and sharing some of the same experiences, can produce such different theories. In broad philosophical terms, both Jomini and Clausewitz display a tendency for the Enlightenment's propensity towards rational analysis. Jomini in particular apes Newton in his quest to discover the fundamental principles underpinning the activity of war. However, whereas Jomini is criticised for failing to escape the rationalism of the eighteenth century, Clausewitz managed to create a synthesis of the Enlightenment's rationality and the non-rational approach of German Romanticism with its greater emphasis on the psychological, emotional, metaphysical and intuitive.

However, despite the evident differences between the two theories, Jomini's does share some similarities with the more developed areas of Clausewitz's work. In particular, Jomini does acknowledge that war is an impassioned drama, full of emotion and intangible forces. Therefore, in such an environment morale plays an important role, and ultimately victory is at least partially due to the military genius and his *coup d'oeil*. In the final analysis, Jomini, not wishing to leave his core principles behind, declares that victory is born from a combination of good tactics (based upon Jomini's identified principles), genius, luck, courage and morale: 'war, far from being an exact science, is a terrible and impassioned drama, regulated, it is true, by three or four general principles, but also dependent for its results upon a number of moral and physical complications'.[56]

In some respects, Jomini actually covers areas of strategy that Clausewitz neglects. Although he fails to provide substantial details, Jomini does discuss irregular forms of war and warfare in complex terrain. In this sense, he recognises that his principles of war may need to be adapted to different circumstances. Indeed, for irregular forms of war Jomini concludes that the decisive use of force is not always appropriate, and that appropriate treatment of the local population may contribute significantly to achieving one's objectives. Nonetheless, despite these positive developments in his work, the repeated message in Jomini's theory is too prescriptive and gives too much credence to set principles. Thus, over time the limitations of the prescriptive nature of Jomini's work have become evident, and relative to Clausewitz he fails to provide a more universal theory of strategy.

Sun Tzu

The second great universal theorist pre-dates the Napoleonic period by over 2,000 years. The Chinese strategist Sun Tzu offers yet another, different vision of war. Sun Tzu's work is influenced by the Taoist tradition, with its emphasis on non-material force-multipliers. Thomas Cleary explains that Taoism can be understood as 'the ancient tradition of knowledge'.[57] In this sense, we may conclude that for Sun Tzu, war in its ideal form becomes an intellectual and metaphysical exercise rather than a physical one. For Sun Tzu, war is a necessary evil that represents a departure from cosmic harmony.

In contrast to Clausewitz's emphasis on violent clashes of arms, Sun Tzu seeks the attainment of policy objectives preferably without the application of violence. For Sun Tzu 'to win one hundred victories in one hundred battles is not the acme of skill. To subdue the enemy without fighting is the acme of skill.'[58] In order to achieve this, or indeed to gain victory at minimal cost should fighting occur, Sun Tzu puts great emphasis on the role of information and knowledge. Indeed, much of Sun Tzu's work is built around the need to acquire and use intelligence about such factors as the enemy, the environment and oneself. With intelligence at the heart of his theory, Sun Tzu understandably highlights the significance of deception. His statement 'All warfare is based upon deception' is revealing, since in order to deceive the enemy effectively, one must exert control over information.

Whereas Clausewitz regards a more direct, battle-orientated approach as the most profitable, Sun Tzu is famed for the indirect approach. Indeed, rather than highlighting the gains to made from destroying the enemy, Sun Tzu extols the virtues of absorbing the enemy's resources into one's own: 'Your aim must be to take All-under-Heaven intact. Thus your troops are not worn out and your gains will be complete.' From the above it is understandable why the ancient Chinese strategist has become popular in the modern period. In many respects his approach is ideally suited to a Western, information-age approach to strategy that seeks minimal costs and champions the manoeuvrist approach to warfare.

Whereas Clausewitz's work may be criticised for being too dense and sometimes confusing, Sun Tzu suffers from the opposite problem. Although there is little to argue with his ideas concerning the value of acquiring information, overall his work gives the impression that war is a controllable and predictable activity. Lawrence Freedman goes as far as to suggest, 'Sun Tzu believed that perfect knowledge could be obtained.'[59] In the chapter 'Energy', Sun Tzu provides a picture of combat that appears chaotic, but in fact 'there is no disorder'. Organisation and good communications are the means by which order is produced from seeming disorder. Rather than Clausewitz's gritty 'real war', Sun Tzu provides something of an ideal vision of how strategy can be conducted. Taking Sun Tzu too seriously could leave the practitioner naively optimistic of what is possible in strategy.

While Sun Tzu and Clausewitz offer very different approaches to strategy, their ideas can be effectively combined. This has been most obviously and successfully done in Maoist strategic thinking. Mao's three-stage theory of revolutionary war utilises the indirect approach in the early stages, switches to Clausewitzian battle in the final stage, and throughout is infused by a clear adherence to the idea that war is very much a political instrument. Indeed, Mao was extremely conscious of the fact that his forces were political actors as well as being military units.

Taken together, the works of Clausewitz and Sun Tzu should provide the practitioner with a solid theoretical basis for his future undertakings. However, Gray is right in his assertion that we need more than just *On War*. The greatest – and only true great – book on war, to paraphrase Brodie, should be supplemented. At the level of general theory, three works suggest

Box 1.4 Strategic theory

Clausewitz
- War is a continuation of political intercourse.
- The nature of war is composed of rational and non-rational forces.
- Wars may differ in their character but are all things of the same nature.
- Friction, which distinguishes war on paper from war in reality, impedes efficacy.
- War is violent, uncertain and competitive.
- There are many potential centres of gravity, but defeating the enemy's forces is usually the best place to start.

Sun Tzu
- The acquisition of knowledge is the key to success in strategy.
- Deception has a central role in war.
- More is gained through victory without battle/violence.
- Victory may be achieved through either a direct or indirect approach.
- Know when to fight and when not to fight.

themselves. These are: Luttwak's *Strategy: The Logic of War and Peace*, primarily for its identification of the paradoxical logic of strategy, although its discussion on the harmony of the levels of strategy is also a worthwhile and beneficial read; Wylie's *Military Strategy: A General Theory of Power Control*, which is distinguished by its universally useful concept of control and the related ideas concerning the man on the scene with the gun; and Gray's *Modern Strategy*, which is chosen for its identification of the many dimensions of strategy, its broad scope covering the whole spectrum of strategic matters and its concept that strategy represents a unified, practical undertaking.

Strategy may be complex and difficult. However, perhaps with the aid of theory, experience and, ideally, military genius, the strategist can, indeed must, utilise the military instrument in the service of policy. This can be done in a number of ways. Military force is a far more flexible instrument than many assume. Modern literature on the role of war in international politics tends to underestimate this flexibility. For analytical purposes, the various uses of force can be divided into six categories: defence; deterrence; compellence; posturing; offence; and miscellaneous.

Often, discussion is limited to the first four categories. This exclusion of the fifth and sixth categories may reflect a philosophical and/or ethical shift away from regarding military force as a decisive, flexible or legitimate instrument. However, with the invasions of Iraq and Afghanistan in recent years, this is clearly a naive philosophical approach. Regardless of what the on-going counter-insurgency campaigns in these two countries reveal about the efficacy of force, it is undeniable that the offensive use of military force removed the Baathist and Taliban regimes. It should of course be noted that the actual use of force often simultaneously covers a number of the following categories. It is important to remember that the categorisation of anything in theory rarely reflects the complexities of reality in an absolute sense.

Defence

Understandably, defending the state/community is the primary function of military force. The defensive use of force can have two functions: to repel an attack or to limit the damage caused should an attack occur. What actually constitutes an act of self-defence has become something of a debate since the terrorist attacks of 9/11 and the Bush Administration's response to it. Traditionally, an act of self-defence is only considered to be such in the face of an armed attack, or if such an attack is imminent. However, the Bush Administration's National Security Strategy declares, in response to more insidious threats, that both pre-emptive attacks and preventative war must be considered forms of the defensive use of force. Of course, the problem with this position is that an overlap begins to develop between the defensive and offensive use of force. However, this may only be a problem for international lawyers and academics. If a preventative war achieves its motivating policy objectives, it may matter little how it is categorised. Facts on the ground are more compelling than theoretical or legal arguments.

Deterrence

The defensive use of force is a physical act. In contrast, deterrence, compellence and indeed posturing, although founded upon physical force, are dependent upon the psychological effects of military force. Deterrence 'has the negative object of persuading an adversary not to take an action he might otherwise have done'.[60] This can be achieved through the threat of punishment and/or denial. Punishment seeks to deter an actor by threatening to respond in such a way as to make the costs of the enemy's actions outweigh the potential benefits. Deterrence by denial seeks to persuade an actor that his goals cannot be achieved.

Deterrence will be discussed in detail in C. Dale Walton's chapter on nuclear strategy (see chapter 6). In the context of the present chapter it is worth noting that deterrence as strategy has its own challenges. Increasingly, the reliability of deterrence is being questioned. By default, the efficacy of deterrence is difficult to prove, in that one cannot prove a negative. To have a chance of being successful, a strategy of deterrence must fulfil three criteria: capability, commitment and communication. To deter, an actor must posses the capability and commitment to fulfil the threatened punishment or denial. Just as importantly, these must be communicated to the enemy, otherwise the basis for the deterrent effect remains hidden. Clearly, when nuclear weapons are involved the commitment criterion is problematic. During the Cold War, one of the main challenges for the United States' deterrence strategy was how to persuade the Soviet Union credibly that it was willing to commit suicide in order to defend Western Europe from Soviet attack. This form of deterrence is commonly referred to as 'extended deterrence'.

In the complex world of strategy, fulfilling the three above criteria is not sufficient to guarantee success. As Lawrence Freedman notes, 'deterrence works best when the targets are able to act rationally, and when the deterrer and the deterred are working within a sufficiently shared normative framework'.[61] Cultural differences regarding rational choices may cause a mismatch in the deterrence relationship. It is also plausible that some actors are beyond deterrence. Upon initial analysis, such organisations as al-Qaeda would appear to be immune to the effects of deterrence. However, well-protected targets are often bypassed by terrorist organisations. In addition, as Gray notes, the foot soldiers of these organisations may be dissuaded from participating in the fight should the cause be seen to be losing momentum.[62] In both of these examples the deterrent effect emanates from a perceived inability to achieve the objectives of the organisation: deterrence by denial.

In the final analysis, despite the challenges of deterrence, it has always been, and will remain, an important instrument of strategy. Problems arise when too much is expected of it. Like all forms of strategy, deterrence has its limitations. Thus, deterrence should merely be considered as one possible instrument of grand strategy: 'deterrence does not offer a self-contained strategic relationship but is part of a wider set of relationships'.[63] In the final analysis, it must be recognised that the success or failure of deterrence will be decided by the actor to be deterred.

Compellence

Along the same lines as deterrence, compellence aims 'to be able either to stop an adversary from doing something that he has already undertaken or to get him to do something that he has not yet undertaken'.[64] Like deterrence, compellence relies upon the psychological effects of force. In this sense, because the targeted actor is not completely denuded of his military capabilities, he is left with a choice: 'The adversary must still have the capacity for organised violence but choose not to exercise it.'[65] Thomas

Schelling, one of the most influential writers on the subject, describes this difference: 'There is a difference between taking what you want and making someone give it to you.'[66] The mere threat, rather than the actual use of force, may compel. Violence held in reserve can be a powerful instrument of persuasion. However, although such circumstances are often described as the 'non-use' of force, it is important to stress that the effect is still based upon perceptions of what would occur if that force were used. Compellence can be useful in many circumstances but is particularly appropriate for those pursuing limited objectives, when the degree of violence should be correspondingly curtailed. A more limited use of force may also be appropriate if the attacker wishes to engage in some form of positive, post-conflict relationship with the target actor. Compellence may also prove useful for those with limited resources or without the will to sustain a long and costly attritional struggle. In this sense, a carefully targeted application of force against valued assets of the enemy may bring success at a reasonable cost.

A strategy of compellence rests on one's ability to understand what the enemy values, and the amount of pain that will compel him to alter his behaviour. Sun Tzu's advice to know your enemy is no more useful than in such circumstances. Estimating the enemy's pain threshold is notoriously difficult. For example, during the 1999 Kosovo conflict elements within the US leadership predicted that a mere three days of bombing would bring Milosevic's Jugoslavia back to the negotiating table. In the end, the campaign lasted seventy-eight days. And although the coercive air campaign did have an effect on the Milosevic regime's decision-making process, other factors were also significant. Particularly worthy of mention are the withdrawal of Russian support from its traditional ally, and increasing discussion and preparations for a NATO ground offensive.

Like deterrence, compellence clearly has its limitations. However, it is a vital form of strategy. In fact, few wars end with the absolute overthrow of the enemy. Thus, most conflicts cease when one side has been coerced. In this sense, the compellent use of force is central to strategic effect. However, curiously the ability to inflict pain for strategic effect is often overlooked. Schelling bemoans this oversight: 'It is extraordinary how many treatises on war and strategy have declined to recognise that the power to hurt has been, throughout history, a fundamental character of military force and fundamental to the diplomacy based on it.' This problem, which Schelling noted in the 1960s, has only intensified in more recent times. It seems plausible that 'the power to hurt' has been increasingly undermined by social, ethical and legal concerns. Inflicting pain to achieve policy objectives does not sit well with prevailing liberal values. Nonetheless, unpalatable though it may be (much like the nature of war), the power to hurt must remain an ingredient in strategy.

Posturing

Indirectly supportive of deterrence and compellence is 'posturing'. This use, or more specifically this 'display', of military capabilities often has general rather than specific objectives in mind. Although the display of military force may be aimed at a particular target, it is designed simply to enhance the reputation and/or profile of the actor in question. Examples of posturing include military parades, the purchase of advanced capabilities, military exercises and port visits, to name just four. Since nuclear weapons are still regarded as one of the technical highpoints of military capabilities, one of the rationales for developing them can be to raise the prestige of the developing state in strategic terms. The 'nuclear club' is still relatively small and exclusive.

Offence

As with the power to hurt, the offensive use of force is often overlooked in literature, doctrine and international law as a legitimate exercise in military power. This is regrettable, because it adds substantially to the flexibility of military force as an instrument of policy. Again, we can look to Schelling's work for a discussion of the many uses to which the offensive use of force can be put: 'penetrate and occupy, seize, exterminate, disarm and disable, confine, deny access . . .'.[67] These uses indicate that military force can act as an effective instrument of 'control' and thereby have more direct and physical effects than either deterrence or compellence. More specifically, in its offensive guise military force can be utilised to: seize resources; force regime change; displace populations; or eradicate an enemy's capabilities and resources. The latter may indeed be used to disarm an opponent forcibly, perhaps of his WMDs.

Miscellaneous

Finally, there are other, less headline-grabbing uses of military force. Falling within the miscellaneous category is a vast range of activities, including, but not restricted to: policing; humanitarian aid; disaster relief; ceremonial; counter-smuggling operations; and garrison duties. Some of these activities are often corralled under the heading of Military Assistance to Civil Authorities (MACA). The latter can include providing a stand-by fire-fighting force in the event of industrial action, or helping local civil authorities and water companies during floods. A larger MACA commitment can be witnessed in the use of the British Army in support of police operations in Northern Ireland. Hopefully, the above discussion dispels the myth that military force is a rather blunt and limited instrument. Rather, it represents a very flexible tool of policy, albeit one that ultimately relies upon

Box 1.5 The many uses of force

- *Defence*: To repel an attack or limit the damage, should one occur.
- *Deterrence*: To dissuade an adversary from taking certain actions through the threat of punishment or denial.
- *Compellence*: To persuade an adversary to act in a certain way through the threat of, or actual, infliction of pain.
- *Posturing*: To enhance the strategic reputation of an actor through a display of military power.
- *Offence*: Has many uses, including: occupation; seizure; extermination; disarmament; and confinement.
- *Miscellaneous*: Includes policing; humanitarian aid; disaster relief; ceremonial; counter-smuggling operations; and garrison duties.

violence to exert its influence and power. While the latter point is generally true, this is of course not the case in some MACA activities, which are instead based upon the military's range of capabilities and skills.

As the Cold War came to an end, a certain optimism arose in the defence communities of the West. The Revolution in Military Affairs/Military Transformation appeared to promise a leap forward in the efficiency of warfare. With increasing levels of information available to commanders, the fulfilment of concepts discussed in chapter 2, such as dominant battlespace awareness and full-spectrum dominance, seemed possible (see p. 110). Linked to precision-guided munitions (PGMs), assured kills could become a distinct reality. It was thought that under such conditions a networked, RMA force would be dominant, to the point at which the acquisition of information itself could decide the outcome of a conflict. The possible futures that emanate from such visions promised to revolutionise the very act of war. Attritional forms of warfare would become anachronistic, to be replaced by effects-based operations. The cohesion of the enemy could theoretically be broken by a few well-placed attacks, severely reducing casualties and levels of destruction. In its most extreme form, the future promised 'humane warfare', perhaps without any significant levels of violence to speak of (see figure 1.3).

Much of the optimism upon which the RMA hypothesis was founded emanated from the experience of the 1991 Gulf War. In response to the 1990 Iraqi invasion of Kuwait, an American-led Coalition defeated the world's fourth largest army at a cost of fewer than 500 Coalition fatalities. Further validation came with the Kosovo conflict in 1999. Despite some

Figure 1.3 An MQ-9 Reaper unmanned aerial attack vehicle descends into an airfield in Afghanistan after a mission, November 2007. The Reaper is able to carry both precision-guided bombs and missiles and represents the kind of technology often associated with theories of an RMA.

significant problems of target identification and destruction, NATO forces did finally coerce the Milosevic regime to halt its campaign of ethnic cleansing and withdraw its forces from the province. Most remarkably, this was achieved without any NATO combat fatalities. The promise of low-cost, tightly regulated, humane warfare seemed to be within reach. However, the theorists and commentators of the RMA had largely restricted their discussions to the tactical and operational levels. They committed the error of regarding victory purely in military terms. As already mentioned, a theory of victory must be constructed with reference to the policy objective. Although military success often acts as the basis for policy attainment, in the complex world of strategy it is rarely sufficient on its own.

The RMA debate also suffered from the fact that it tended to focus on regular warfare; 9/11 was a stark reminder of the polymorphous character of war. The al-Qaeda attacks on New York and Washington brought back into sharp focus a form of war that had received little attention among the euphoria of the RMA debate. This is not to suggest that there had not been warnings of the growing threat from irregular forms of war. A section of the Strategic Studies community had been debating for some time the rise of asymmetric forms of war and in particular the potential for super-terrorism. Indeed, a growing body of literature had warned that the very success of the RMA would force enemies of the West to opt for asymmetrical strategies. Stephen Metz defines asymmetric warfare as 'acting, organizing and thinking differently from opponents to maximize relative strengths, exploit opponents' weaknesses or gain greater freedom of action. It can be political-strategic, military-strategic, operational or a combination, and entail different methods, technologies, values, organi-zations or time perspectives.'[68]

In the wake of 9/11 Western defence communities adopted a vision of the future dominated by the Global War on Terror. However, they did not completely abandon Military Transformation. Indeed, they tried to adapt the concept to the new threat, with disastrous results in Iraq. Under the guidance of Donald Rumsfeld as Secretary of Defense, the invasion and occupation of Iraq in 2003 was undertaken with a relatively small force, on the premise that Military Transformation allowed you to do more with less. However, occupation and counter-insurgency have traditionally been manpower-intensive activities, relying less on high-tech weaponry and more on 'the man on the scene with the gun'. Just as limited-war theory was found wanting in Vietnam, so too Military Transformation looked inadequate in the face of the polymorphous, complex character of war as revealed in Iraq.

Just as worrying as the attempt to shoehorn Military Transformation into areas where it does not belong is the debate surrounding the future of large-scale war. The War on Terror has brought into focus such concepts as Fourth-Generation Warfare (4GW) and the dubious claim that large-scale warfare has become a thing of the past. Understandably, defence commu-nities tend to focus on the immediate problem to be faced, sometimes at the expense of preparation for an alternative, complex future. This can have serious and debilitating effects on future performance. For example, at the close of the First World War the British Army was unprepared to return to its duties of imperial policing. The obvious, though challenging, answer to this dilemma is not to assume that the future will be dominated by one particular form of war. From a practical perspective, this means that despite the temptation to focus all of one's attentions on the immediate strategic challenge, an eye must be kept on the future polymorphous char-acter of war. Alternative capabilities must be kept active.

It is prudent to work on the basis that the future, like the past, will be characterised by a mixture of styles of warfare. It is only in our minds that one period of history is dominated by any one form of war. Unfortunately, such an approach can become manifest in the world of war preparation. For example, prior to Vietnam the US Air Force had a doctrinal focus on the delivery of nuclear payloads in preparation for a war with the Soviet Union. Clearly, this left the service initially unprepared for its role in Vietnam.

Our picture of the future is further complicated by the proliferation of WMDs. Although issues of proliferation are quite prominent in relation to such countries as Iran and North Korea, WMD strategy has received little attention since the end of the Cold War. Yet it is essential to keep the strate-gic flame alive on this most challenging of aspects of the art. University undergraduate and postgraduate programmes are currently dominated by students pursuing studies on terrorism and insurgency. It is rare to find one interested in nuclear strategy. This neglect of the subject is also evident in the policy world. One such case is the British Government's policy on Trident replacement. Although the decision to retain an independent nuclear capability was prudent, the Government's policy is worryingly light on discussion of nuclear strategy. One is left with the impression that Britain is a reluctant nuclear power, still clinging to the notion that nuclear weapons have utility only as instruments of deterrence. In contrast, we need an energised debate on nuclear strategy, so that we can construct a meaningful place for these instruments in the modern strategic environment. Undoubtedly, nuclear weapons represent a significance challenge for the strategic thinker and practitioner. However, as was noted earlier, their appearance was responsible for the great classic works of theory in the Cold War. Modern Strategic Studies, in both its military and civilian spheres, must devote more attention to WMD strategy. If it does not, we shall have to rely upon an ad hoc approach when the real challenges appear.

As the following chapters in this book will illustrate, war is a varied activity characterised by constant evolution. In order to be successful, the practitioner must achieve tactical and operational proficiency in each of the environments in which war occurs. This represents a constant challenge, because the technological and doctrinal landscape is ever-changing. However, proficiency at the lower levels is simply not enough. Every use of the military instrument must be guided by strategy: the first-order consideration. Strategy, that process by which military force serves policy objectives, must be the dominant thought in the mind of the commander. What an admiral does with his fleet, or what an insurgent does with his AK-47, must be guided by the policy objective.

The above advice is straightforward. However, those who must participate in strategy at the highest levels have an unenviable task. Not only is strategy an inherently complex activity, infused by intangible moral forces, it is quite literally the province of life and death. Poor performance in strategy almost certainly leads to multiple deaths, but it can also signal the fall of entire nations and civilisations. Thus, Sun Tzu's advice that it be properly studied is difficult to ignore. Despite this, the cause of good strategy has long suffered from an anti-intellectual bias within military and policy circles. As an academic discipline Strategic Studies has thankfully rectified this situation somewhat. The increasing prominence of the subject in universities, and to some degree within the public's consciousness, is to be welcomed. However, much of the progress made could be lost if, due to a changing moral or political environment, Strategic Studies is once again sidelined. Hopefully, volumes such as this one can help to keep the strategic flame alive. At the same time, it is important to remember that Strategic Studies must continue to regard itself as an academic discipline with clear practical application. There must exist a close relationship between theory and practice, while at the same time enabling a permissive environment for academic reflection.

The necessity for the study of strategy is clear when one considers the complexity of strategy in action. This complexity emanates from: its multidimensional nature; the nature of war; the polymorphous character of war; the involvement of humans; the existence of an intelligent enemy; the play of friction; and the fact that it is the meeting-point between the two different worlds of politics and the military. While there is certainly no substitute for experience and military genius when dealing with said complexity, strategic theory enables us to begin to make sense of the multitude of dimensions and interactions at play in strategy. There is undoubtedly much to be gained from studying the work of such theorists as Sun Tzu, Gray, Luttwak and Wylie. Indeed, the present volume may hopefully be able to make a contribution to the various debates and topics with which it deals. However, there is simply no better way to seek understanding of strategy than through the study of Clausewitz's *On War*. No other work comes as close as *On War* to defining the nature of war and strategy. Clausewitz, though, offers few solutions to the many problems faced by the strategist. Perhaps his greatest contribution is, through analysis of his work, to educate the reader's mind to think in a manner conducive to strategic success.

Even with a good education in strategic theory as his aide, the strategist must ultimately rely upon his own judgement to ensure that his use of force works towards the desired policy objectives. In this sense, the strategist must translate theory into practice in a vast range of different, indeed unique, contexts. To this end, he can use force in a variety of ways and for a variety of purposes. Sometimes, military force may be used in a direct manner in a defensive or offensive way. In addition, military force is often used in a more limited and indirect fashion, whereby the effects are felt more at the psychological level in the realms of deterrence, compellence and posturing. Finally, the flexibility of military force endows it with a host of other, miscellaneous uses, from disaster relief to counter-narcotics operations. Regardless of how it is used, it must always be remembered that military force is ultimately premised on the ability to deliver violence. Military culture and our social attitudes regarding force must be faithful to that notion.

NOTES

1 Richard K. Betts, 'Should Strategic Studies Survive?', *World Politics* 50 (October 1997): 41.

2 The term 'battlespace' refers to the environment in which warfare occurs. The term is used in place of the more traditional 'battlefield' to indicate the increasingly complex, and joint, operational environment. Hence, battlespace includes the traditional environments of land, sea and air. It also includes space, cyberspace and the electromagnetic spectrum more generally.

3 David Jablonsky, 'Why is Strategy Difficult?', in Joseph R. Cerami and James F. Holcomb, Jr, eds., *US Army War College Guide to Strategy* (February 2001), http://permanent.access.gpo.gov/lps11754/00354.pdf.

4 Quoted in Fred Kaplan, *The Wizards of Armageddon* (New York: Simon and Schuster, 1983), p. 254.

5 Bernard Brodie, *War and Politics* (London: Cassell, 1973), p. 11.

6 Colin S. Gray, 'From Principles of Warfare to Principles of War: A Clausewitzian Solution', in Colin S. Gray, *Strategy and History: Essays on Theory and Practice* (London: Routledge, 2006), p. 82.

7 Colin S. Gray, 'Introduction', in *ibid.*, p. 2.

8 Bernard Brodie, 'Strategy as a Science', *World Politics* 1: 4 (July 1949): 486–7.

9 Carl von Clausewitz, *On War*, trans. by Michael Howard and Peter Paret (London: David Campbell Publishers, 1993), p. 141.

10 Raymond Aron, *Peace and War: A Theory of International Relations*, trans. by Richard Howard and Annette Baker Fox (New York: Anchor Press/Doubleday, 1973).

11 Betts, 'Should Strategic Studies Survive?', 37.

12 Gray, 'Introduction', p. 5.

13 Lawrence Freedman, 'The Future of Strategic Studies', in John Baylis, James Wirtz, Colin S. Gray and Eliot Cohen, eds., *Strategy – the Contemporary World: An Introduction to Strategic Studies*, 2nd edn (Oxford: Oxford University Press, 2007), p. 360.

14 Betts, 'Should Strategic Studies Survive?', 3.

15 Colin S. Gray, *Modern Strategy* (Oxford: Oxford University Press, 1999), p. 17.

16 André Beaufre, *An Introduction to Strategy: With Particular Reference to the Problems of Defence, Politics, Economics, and Diplomacy in the Nuclear Age* (London: Faber and Faber, 1965), p. 22.

17 Colin S. Gray, *War, Peace, and Victory: Strategy and Statecraft for the Next Century* (New York: Simon and Schuster, 1990).

18 Eliot A. Cohen, *Supreme Command: Soldiers, Statesmen, and Leadership in Wartime* (New York: The Free Press, 2002), p. 208.

19 Colin S. Gray, 'New Directions for Strategic Studies? How Can Theory Help Practice?', in Gray, *Strategy and History*, p. 43.

20 John Terraine, *Douglas Haig: The Educated Soldier* (London: Cassell & Co., 2000), pp. 31; 53.

21 Aron, *Peace and War*, p. 44.

22 J. C. Wylie, *Military Strategy: A General Theory of Power Control* (Annapolis, MD: Naval Institute Press, 1967), p. 66.

23 Basil H. Liddell Hart, *Strategy: The Indirect Approach* (London: Faber and Faber, 1967), pp. 335–6.

24 Edward N. Luttwak, *Strategy: The Logic of War and Peace* (Cambridge, MA: The Belknap Press of Harvard University Press, 1987), p. 69.

25 Michael Howard, 'The Forgotten Dimensions of Strategy', *Foreign Affairs* 57 (1979): 976–86.

26 Gray, *Modern Strategy*, p. 24.

27 Luttwak, *Strategy*, p. 7.

28 Quoted in R. L. DiNardo and Daniel J. Hughes, 'Some Cautionary Thoughts on Information Warfare', *Airpower Journal* 9:4 (1995): 76.

29 Christopher Bassford, 'Primacy of Policy versus the Trinity', paper presented at the Clausewitz in the 21st Century Conference, Oxford Leverhulme Programme on the Changing Character of War (Oxford, 21–3 March 2005).

30 Alan D. Beyerchen, 'Clausewitz and the Nonlinear Nature of Warfare', paper presented at the Clausewitz in the 21st Century Conference, Oxford Leverhulme Programme on the Changing Character of War (Oxford, 21–3 March 2005).

31 Gray, *Modern Strategy*, p. 97.

32 Gray, 'From Principles of Warfare', p. 87.

33 Dwight D. Eisenhower, *Crusade in Europe* (London: William Heinemann, 1948), p. 247.

34 Gray, 'From Principles of Warfare', p. 86.

35 Barry D. Watts, *Clausewitzian Friction and Future War*, McNair Paper 52 (Washington, DC: Institute for National Strategic Studies, National Defense University, October 1996).

36 Luttwak, *Strategy*, p. 14.

37 Gray, *War, Peace, and Victory*, pp. 107–8.

38 J. F. C. Fuller, *Armament and History: A Study of the Influence of Armament on History from the Dawn of Classical Warfare to the Second World War* (London: Eyre and Spottiswoode, 1946), p. v.

39 Charles E. Callwell, *Small Wars: A Tactical Textbook for Imperial Soldiers* (London: Greenhill Books, 1990), p. 23.

40 Gray, *Modern Strategy*, p. 279.

41 Robert Thompson, *Defeating Communist Insurgency: Experiences from Malaya and Vietnam* (London: Macmillan, 1966).

42 Julian Paget, *Counter-Insurgency Compaigning* (London: Faber and Faber, 1967), p. 176.

43 S. Metz and R. Millen, *Insurgency and Counterinsurgency in the 21st Century: Reconceptualising the Threat and Response*, Strategic Studies Institute, US Army War College, PA, November 2004, www.au.af.mil/au/awc/awcgate/ssi/insurgency21c.pdf, p. 5.

44 Williamson Murray, *The Luftwaffe 1933–45: Strategy for Defeat* (Washington, DC: Brassey's, 1996), p. xxiv.

45 John Baylis and John Garnett, 'Introduction', in John Baylis and John Garnett, eds., *Makers of Nuclear Strategy* (New York: St Martin's Press, 1991), pp. 1–2.

46 Williamson Murray and Mark Grimsley, 'Introduction: On Strategy', in Williamson Murray, MacGregor Knox and Alvin Bernstein, eds., *The Making of Strategy: Rulers, States, and War* (Cambridge: Cambridge University Press, 1994), p. 22.

47 Daniel Moran, 'Strategic Theory and the History of War', in John Baylis, *et al.*, eds., *Strategy in the Contemporary World*, p. 17.

48 H. T. Hayden, ed., *Warfighting: Manoeuvre Warfare in the US Marine Corps* (London: Greenhill, 1995), p. 43.

49 Martin van Creveld, *The Transformation of War* (New York: The Free Press, 1991).

50 John Keegan, *A History of Warfare* (London: Pimlico, 1994).

51 Winston S. Churchill, quoted in M. Carver, 'Montgomery', in John Keegan, ed., *Churchill's Generals* (London: Weidenfeld & Nicolson, 1991), p. 148.

52 Gray, *Modern Strategy*, pp. 53; 108.

53 T. N. Dupuy, *A Genius for War: The German Army and General Staff, 1807–1945* (London: MacDonald and Jane's, 1977), p. 307.

54 Robert A. Pape, *Bombing to Win: Air Power and Coercion in War* (Ithaca, NY: Cornell University Press, 1996), p. 275.

55 John Shy, 'Jomini', in Peter Paret, ed., *Makers of Modern Strategy: From Machiavelli to the Nuclear Age* (Oxford: Clarendon Press, 1986), p. 144.

56 Baron Antoine Henri de Jomini, *The Art of War* (London: Greenhill Books, 1996), p. 360.

57 Thomas Cleary, 'Translator's Introduction', in Sun Tzu, *The Art of War*, trans. by Thomas Cleary (Boston, MA: Shambhala, 1988), p. 2.

58 Sun Tzu, *The Art of War*, pp. 77–9.

59 Lawrence Freedman, *The Revolution in Strategic Affairs*, Adelphi Paper 318 (Oxford: Oxford University Press, 1998), p. 60.

60 Colin S. Gray, *Maintaining Effective Deterrence* (Carlisle: Strategic Studies Institute, 2003), p. 25.

61 Lawrence Freedman, *Deterrence* (Cambridge: Polity Press, 2004), p. 5.

62 Gray, *Maintaining Effective Deterrence*, p. 28.

63 Freedman, *Deterrence*, p. 4.

64 Robert J. Art, 'The Four Functions of Force', in Robert J. Art and Robert Jervis, eds., *International Politics: Enduring Concepts and Contemporary Issues* (New York: Longman, 2003), p. 155.

65 Daniel Byman and Matthew Waxman, *The Dynamics of Coercion: American Foreign Policy and the Limits of Military Might* (Cambridge: Cambridge University Press, 2002).

66 Thomas C. Schelling, *Arms and Influence* (New Haven: Yale University Press, 1966), p. 2.

67 *Ibid.*

68 Steven Metz and Donglas V. Johnson II, *Asymmetry and U.S. Military Strategy: Definition, Background, and Strategic Concepts* (Carlisle Barracks, PA: US Army War College, Strategic Studies Institute, 2001), p. 5.

FURTHER READING

Aron, Raymond, *Peace and War: A Theory of International Relations*, trans. by Richard Howard and Annette Baker Fox (New York: Anchor Press/Doubleday, 1973).
One of the best discussions of war and power in international politics.

Baylis, John, Wirtz, James, Gray, Colin S., and Cohen, Eliot eds., *Strategy in the Contemporary World: An Introduction to Strategic Studies* (Oxford: Oxford University Press, 2002).
An excellent introduction to the theory and practice of strategy in the contemporary world.

Beaufre, André, *An Introduction to Strategy: With Particular Reference to the Problems of Defence, Politics, Economics, and Diplomacy in the Nuclear Age* (London: Faber and Faber, 1965).
A classic work of strategic theory from the Cold War, which contains many insights into the complexities of the subject.

Betts, Richard K., 'Should Strategic Studies Survive?', *World Politics* 50 (October 1997): 7–33.
Provides a compelling argument as to why we need to keep the Strategic Studies flame alive.

Brodie, Bernard, 'Strategy as a Science', *World Politics* 1: 4 (July 1949): 467–88.
A vastly important article that outlines the need for an intellectual development of Strategic Studies.

Callwell, Charles E., *Small Wars: A Tactical Textbook for Imperial Soldiers* (London: Greenhill Books, 1990).
An insightful analysis of British imperial strategy, with many pertinent observations for the contemporary environment.

von Clausewitz, Carl, *On War*, trans. by Michael Howard and Peter Paret (London: David Campbell Publishers, 1993).
Quite simply the best work of strategic theory ever written. Clausewitz gets closer than anyone to defining the true nature of war.

Cohen, Eliot A., *Supreme Command: Soldiers, Statesmen, and Leadership in Wartime* (New York: The Free Press, 2002).
An interesting study of the relationship between policy and the military instrument. The work benefits from some good historical case studies.

Gray, Colin S., *Modern Strategy* (Oxford: Oxford University Press, 1999).
Probably the greatest modern work of strategic theory. Gray's analysis is comprehensive and thought-provoking.

Handel, Michael I., *Masters of War: Classical Strategic Thought*, 2nd rev. edn (London: Frank Cass, 1996).
A great introduction to the classic works of strategic theory.

Jablonsky, David, 'Why is Strategy Difficult?', in Joseph R. Cerami and James F. Holcomb, Jr, eds., *US Army War College Guide to Strategy* (February 2001), http://permanent.access.gpo.gov/lps11754/00354.pdf.
This work enables the reader to begin to understand the complexities of strategy.

de Jomini, Baron Antoine Henri, *The Art of War* (London: Greenhill Books, 1996).
A flawed classic; Jomini is still worth reading to see how a 'principles' approach to strategy can underestimate the challenge of complexity.

Liddell Hart, Basil H., *Strategy: The Indirect Approach* (London: Faber and Faber, 1967).
An interesting updating of Sun Tzu's main ideas.

Lonsdale, David J., *Alexander the Great: Lessons in Strategy* (London: Routledge, 2007).
Alexander the Great is still the best example of how to overcome the complexities of strategy and achieve outstanding success.

Luttwak, Edward N., *Strategy: The Logic of War and Peace* (Cambridge, MA: The Belknap Press of Harvard University Press, 1987).
A modern classic which introduces the paradoxical logic and discusses harmonisation of the levels.

Mao Tse-Tung, *Selected Military Writings of Mao Tse-Tung* (Beijing: Foreign Languages Press, 1963).
Mao is arguably one of the most important theorists and practitioners of irregular warfare. He also manages to combine the theories of Clausewitz and Sun Tzu.

Schelling, Thomas C., *Arms and Influence* (New Haven, CT: Yale University Press, 1966).
An outstanding analysis of how military force can be used for strategic effect.

Summers, Harry G., Jr, *On Strategy: A Critical Analysis of the Vietnam War* (Novato, CA: Presidio, 1982).
An insightful and sobering analysis of what happens when strategy is not given its due respect.

Sun Tzu, *The Art of War*, trans. by Samuel B. Griffith (London: Oxford University Press, 1971).
A rich work of strategic theory, which considers military strategy in its grand strategic context.

Watts, Barry D., *Clausewitzian Friction and Future War*, McNair Paper 52 (Washington, DC: Institute for National Strategic Studies, National Defense University, October 1996).
The best analysis of Clausewitzian friction to date.

Wylie, J. C., *Military Strategy: A General Theory of Power Control* (Annapolis, MD: Naval Institute Press, 1967).
Often overlooked, Wylie's little book provides an excellent discussion of strategic theory and introduces the central concept of 'control'.

CHAPTER 2

LAND WARFARE

CONTENTS

KEY THEMES

- The development of modern land warfare is associated with the emergence of a modern system of warfare, a tactical and operational system based on such principles as combined arms, joint operations, depth, and fire-and-manoeuvre.
- Despite debates on the revolutionary impact of such concepts as blitzkrieg, modern land warfare has developed largely through a process of evolution.
- Despite recurring themes in land warfare during the twentieth and twenty-first centuries, there is still no single template for land warfare: the variety in competitive, strategic, political, economic and social contexts means that there are likely to be many different kinds of land warfare in existence at any point in time.
- Despite the contemporary focus on the revolutionary impact of new technology, expressed most prominently in the idea of a Revolution in Military Affairs (RMA), the future form of land warfare is far from certain.

Warfare on land has been pivotal to military outcomes throughout history. This is so because human beings live on land, and therefore the capacity to seize and control territory often carries with it decisive political consequences. As Colin Gray has noted, 'the inherent strength of land warfare is that it carries the promise of achieving decision'.[1] Throughout the twentieth century, and into the twenty-first, land warfare has continued to be pivotal to military outcomes.

This chapter explores the key ideas, concepts, principles and debates associated with conventional, high-intensity land warfare in the twentieth and twenty-first centuries. At the heart of this chapter lies the idea of the so-called modern system of land warfare. During the twentieth century, armies faced a range of problems resulting from the interaction between various forces for change, including the increasing effects of firepower and the problem of moving, feeding and supplying larger armies. Incrementally, armies found potential solutions for these problems by manipulating some of the core areas of continuity in land warfare, not least the nature of the land environment itself and the basic characteristics of armies. These solutions created a dominant set of themes in the conduct of land warfare, such as dispersal, combined arms, fire-and-manoeuvre, depth, and close co-operation with air and maritime forces (joint operations). Collectively, these themes constitute modern-system land warfare.

As with chapters 3 and 4 on maritime and air warfare, this part of the book begins with an exploration of some of the key concepts associated with our particular type of warfare. This provides an essential background to the development of the modern system of land warfare both in terms of explaining the problems facing armies at the beginning of the twentieth century and how important continuities, such as the effect of terrain and the flexibility of armies, have shaped potential solutions. Building on the concepts section, the chapter then explores how and why the modern system evolved during the twentieth century. Whereas the modern system is essentially an evolutionary and adaptive development, more recent debates have often focused on the potential for revolutionary changes in the conduct of land warfare. The final section therefore examines the issues surrounding the application of the idea of a Revolution in Military Affairs (RMA) to the future of land warfare.

Like all warfare, land warfare is shaped by the nature of the environment in which it is fought. Although this may seem like a statement of the obvious, it is important to understand that one of the key differences between warfare on land and the other environments is land itself. The modern system has been shaped decisively by the way that land (in terms of terrain) can be used to mitigate the effects of firepower. The air and sea environments are fundamentally different in this respect. This means that there is no equivalent of a modern system in air and maritime warfare. It also means that, whereas the key developments in land warfare during the period have been (to use the 'levels of strategy' outlined in chapter 1, pp. 24–27) at the tactical and operational level, in the air and maritime environments the focus is much more on the operational and strategic levels.

The land environment

The land environment exhibits a number of attributes, including: its political importance; variety; friction; and opacity.

Political importance

One important attribute of land is its political importance. Human beings live upon land, which gives land a profound tangible and intangible significance. Control of territory is central to the physical capacity and viability of states, and to the credibility and legitimacy of governments. Thus, a capacity to take and hold territory is often a crucial index of success or failure in major combat operations: Adolf Hitler was not defeated until Berlin fell; Saddam Hussein was not defeated until Baghdad was taken; France surrendered in 1940 because it no longer had the capacity to prevent the occupation of its territory.

Variety

Another characteristic of land is its variety. Different combinations of elevation, global position, climate and population density can create great varieties in operating environment even in relatively small areas. Land is therefore a complex environment in which to operate. In jungles, for example, moving and sustaining heavy forces is difficult; problems with visibility and navigation make co-ordination a challenge. In the desert, excessive heat and sand pose problems for the reliability of equipment and the stamina of personnel. With few obvious landmarks, navigation is problematic if access to global positioning systems is unavailable. Snow and sub-zero temperatures can likewise inhibit the capacity of military organisations to function effectively.

Friction

A third characteristic is friction. As has been noted in chapter 1 (pp. 35–36) general friction is inherent in war. The land environment generates additional specific friction in such areas as movement and physical exertion because land is difficult to move over. The simple act of moving is often very wearing on personnel and equipment, even where there is no actual fighting. It is, moreover, relatively difficult to move over land the sort of bulk goods that are often essential for the logistics of an army, such as ammunition and fuel. In land warfare, the problems of actual combat may be dwarfed by the challenges of moving and sustaining troops in the field. Humans have long made attempts to reduce this friction by using rivers and creating such man-made communications routes as roads, canals and railways. Although these can reduce the friction involved in movement, they can also channel movement, reducing flexibility and creating such vulnerabilities as the possible interdiction of transport nodes.

Opacity

A fourth characteristic of land is its opacity. Land is rarely truly flat; as Stephen Biddle notes, even on the 'flat' North German Plain, typically 65 per cent of the terrain within a thousand yards is invisible to an average weapons position.[2] The various obstructions provided by variations in elevation, vegetation and urbanisation can block or inhibit the capacity of firepower and sensors to function. This opacity creates opportunities for cover and concealment. Exploiting terrain gives opportunities to mitigate the effects of sensors and firepower through such techniques as using cover, camouflage and dispersal to reduce the ability of the enemy either to find targets or to apply combat power against them. Guerrilla warfare, for example, is to an extent an exercise in exploiting the cover and concealment provided by land. While the opacity of land can be an important enabler, it also creates challenges. Opacity can make communication and co-operation between friendly forces more difficult, as well as promoting negative psychological effects, such as isolation.

Land is thus a politically vital medium: taking and holding it (or threatening credibly to do so) will often be an end in war as well as a means. The challenges of operating on land are shaped by the variety of different environments and also by the fact that, as an opaque medium, land can be used as a mitigating factor in war. Land shapes, channels, facilitates and mitigates elements in the conduct of warfare. The interaction between the four factors outlined above means that some land matters more than other; varieties in land can create important avenues of advance, fields of fire, points of observation or such obstacles as steep slopes, rivers or towns. Understanding and manipulating 'ground' (the lie of the land) is often crucial to success in land warfare because terrain can provide not only an important obstacle to operations but also a means of reducing the effect of enemy firepower.

The attributes of land forces

Land forces have a number of fundamental attributes. These attributes include: complexity; versatility; persistence; and decisiveness.

Complexity

The first attribute is complexity, not necessarily in terms of technology (which may vary depending upon the army in question) but in terms of numbers of 'moving parts'. Whereas, put crudely, air forces and navies 'man the equipment', armies 'equip the man'. While fighting 'platforms' (such as tanks) have become more important since the First World War, armies still place a premium on having a larger number of smaller combat elements. This is necessary as a means to control ground and also to manipulate the advantages of terrain through dispersal and camouflage. One key expression of this is the continued importance of infantry. This complexity is multiplied by the growing role of specialists in land warfare. Land forces encompass not just combat elements, such as tanks and infantry, but also combat support, combat service support and command support elements. Combat support provides such indirect support as fire support, air defence, reconnaissance and combat engineering, and includes artillery, engineers and air defence units. Combat service support encompasses logistics, supply, administration and medical services. Staff officers, and intelligence and communications personnel provide the command support. While complexity is a functional requirement for armies, it multiplies friction in warfare, particularly in relation to command and control.

Versatility

A second attribute is versatility. Because land forces are complex and personnel-intensive, they are adaptable; they are relatively less dependent on technology than air forces or navies to define capabilities. By refocusing such non-technological variables as training and ethos, armies can solve many military problems through new techniques. One reflection of this is the general utility of land forces across the whole spectrum of war, from peace support operations through to major combat operations. Armies, however, are not infinitely versatile. Land forces are likely to be optimised for particular kinds of warfare and particular physical environments; success or failure in major combat operations are likely to relate in part to the relative capacity of belligerents to adapt to the reality of local conditions.

Persistence

A third attribute is persistence. Land forces can remain in place for long periods of time. This presence allows land forces to provide continuous fire and surveillance. Land forces can hold ground, whereas air and naval forces cannot. General Norman Schwartzkopf has noted that 'There is not a military commander in the entire world who would claim he had taken an objective by flying over it.'[3] Physical presence is often a requirement for political control and for the attainment of such broader objectives as security. There is often no substitute. For example, although precision-guided munitions (PGMs) are effective in delivering firepower, they cannot patrol the streets of a town. While the presence of land forces can be militarily essential and send a powerful political signal, it may also create vulnerabilities. Persistence can make land forces more vulnerable to attack, and the larger political footprint of armies may cause longer-term political problems; for example, it may create friction with the local population.

Decisiveness

A final attribute of land forces is their decisiveness. Stephen Biddle notes that 'where coercion fails, brute force on land has been the final arbiter in disputes'.[4] Air and naval attacks cannot, by themselves, defeat land forces. Land forces may be made irrelevant; for example, in the latter stages of the Pacific campaign in the Second World War sea control allowed the United States to bypass some Japanese island garrisons, simply allowing them to 'wither on the vine'. Firepower delivered from the air or from maritime assets may also inflict considerable damage on and disruption to land forces and their operations. Ultimately, however, only land forces can physically defeat other land forces. Numerous ways exist in which land forces can mitigate the effects of remotely delivered firepower, from greater dispersal and deception through to more effective anti-platform weapons, such as surface-to-air missiles (SAMs).

In combination, the characteristics of the land environment and the attributes of land forces have been fundamental to the development of modern land warfare. The political significance of land means that performance in land warfare matters. Yet there are basic difficulties in the effective conduct of land operations. Armies are difficult to move. They are difficult to sustain. They are problematic both to command and to control. On the other hand, these attributes and characteristics also provide features that provide great utility. Armies can occupy and control; they are flexible and adaptable; terrain can be exploited to great advantage.

Key developments

If the characteristics and attributes outlined above provide a baseline for understanding some of the enduring issues in the conduct of land warfare, the reasons for the evolution of the modern system lie in the interaction between those features and a range of key developments that became of decisive importance in the twentieth century.

Scale

The first development was the growing scale of war. The period from the mid-nineteenth century through to 1914 saw an enormous growth in the size of armies. Reflecting broader political, social and economic changes, the emergence of 'industrialised people's war' led to the massive expansion in the size of armies. By 1914, European armed forces collectively stood at around 20 million men. One consequence was the prospect of war without flanks: war in which the armies disposed by belligerents were so large that the formation of a continuous front across the whole theatre of battle was possible. Unless a victory was won quickly, before enemy forces had been fully deployed, land warfare was likely to become an exercise in frontal assaults. Once this had become the case by 1915, the onus on the military was to develop ways in which to facilitate frontal breakthroughs of the enemy. Another consequence of the increasing scale of war was the increasing irrelevance of what has been termed the 'Napoleonic paradigm of war': the view that war could be won quickly in a single decisive clash between two main armies. With mass armies, the effect of tactical actions was unlikely to be decisive in isolation, because belligerents possessed more than one army. Thus, the means to win wars would focus more and more on the co-ordination and sequencing of multiple tactical actions in order to produce a broader effect.

Firepower

Another key influence on land warfare since 1900 has been the growth in firepower. Between 1900 and 1990, average artillery ranges increased by a factor of more than twenty; small-arms rate of fire increased three or four times; and the weapons payload and un-refuelled range of ground-attack air-craft increased by more than six times.[5] The machine guns, quick-firing artillery and magazine-loaded rifles of the early twentieth century have been augmented by tanks, aircraft and, latterly, PGMs. The growing lethality of firepower challenged the ability of armies to operate in closer formations and in the open. In response, armies moved to consider ways in which to mitigate firepower. Classically, these included recourse to cover and conceal-ment, and to suppressive fire. The extended reach of firepower 'deepened' the battlefield, allowing distinctions to be made between 'deep' and 'close' operations. Depth opened up opportunities to use firepower at extended ranges to attack targets behind the enemy front line – to attack reserves, for example, and such critical infrastructure as transport nodes, command-and-control facilities, and rear artillery positions. Because of the greater range and accuracy of firepower, forces were capable of providing support over greater distances if properly co-ordinated. This permitted additional, if oper-ationally challenging, opportunities for combinations of close and deep attack and also provided a permissive element in allowing greater depth in defence. War is of course adversarial, so these opportunities were also, para-doxically, vulnerabilities, since these developments were open to the enemy as well. For example, during the Cold War the doctrines of NATO and the Warsaw Pact both focused on the use of new technology to add greater range and firepower in the attack, while also attempting to incorporate such meas-ures as greater dispersal to reduce adversaries' vulnerability to one another.

Command and control

Developments have also taken place in the command and control of armies. Command and control is, and always has been, fundamental to the effective performance of armies. Command and control has been com-plicated by a number of developments. One is the growing complexity of modern armies in terms of organisation, specialisation, size, mobility and dispersal. These make forces increasingly hard to control and to co-ordinate. Another is the multiplication in the technological aspects of command and control, such as communications and data acquisition and processing, e.g. television, computers, mobile phones, data links and remote sensors. Taken together, these two problems create the third problem of how these systems should be organised and managed effec-tively, given the increasing volumes of information available.[6] In general, the systems for the command and control of armies have grown in size and complexity over time. 'Personalised' approaches to command and control, which have traditionally placed an emphasis on the activities and deci-sions of a small number of very senior commanders, have been replaced with permanent staff systems with formalised structures and procedures. In addition to being more costly, developments in precision firepower have also made command-and-control systems more vulnerable to enemy attack, not least because headquarters have become larger and command-and-control systems more integrated.

Logistics

Logistics have a crucial impact on the conduct of military operations. Effective logistics are vital to sustaining the tempo, momentum, duration and intensity of land warfare. General Wavell noted that 'It takes little skill or imagination to see *where* you would like your army to be and *when*; it takes much more knowledge and hard work to know where you can place your forces and whether you can maintain them there.'[7] The logistics of land warfare became increasingly complex in the twentieth century. In part, this was because of the growing scale of war. But it has also been a reflection of the growing complexity of military organisations and their increasing consumption of the materiel of war, especially ammunition. By 1918, for example, the German Army was expending 300 million rounds of ammunition a month. Railways provided an imperfect solution, because although they could supply static forces on railheads, they could not support mobile operations. Once forces left their railheads, they continued to rely on horse-drawn supply. Rail supply was thus immobile and inflexible. The internal combustion engine promised to bridge the gap between mobile army and railhead. Yet, as experience during and after the Second World War illustrates, motor transport also created its own logistic problems. Generating, sustaining, maintaining and operating the number of motor transport vehicles required for a modern army was difficult and came with associated costs for the flexibility and mobility of an army as a whole (see figure 2.1).

Logistic constraints impinge on the capacity of modern military systems to realise their theoretical potential in terms of such things as mobility. Paradoxically, modern logistics, which have been a crucial enabler, are also an important source of friction in land warfare. During the 2003 Iraq War, for example, the single longest delay in the Coalition advance towards Baghdad was imposed by logistic problems rather than the actions of Iraqi conventional forces.

Joint operations

Another development has been the introduction of air power and the increasing importance of gaining, maintaining and exploiting the air in land operations. Joint, that is multiservice, operations are not new in land warfare; land operations have often had important riverine or amphibious elements. However, air power has had an increasingly pervasive influence on land warfare. Air power can provide an important means to mass firepower quickly at particular points and at ranges beyond that of land systems. Combinations of air and land forces can produce important synergies, because the means used by enemy forces to escape the effects of air power, such as dispersion, are often those things that make them more

Figure 2.1 RAF bombs explode near a large concentration of German tanks, guns, ammunition limbers and motorised transport advancing towards Paris, 1940. Modern mechanised warfare has created new operational and logistic challenges, not least in relation to the vulnerability of land forces to air power.

vulnerable to land attack. The reverse is also true. Joint operations between land and air forces can be controlled according to a spectrum running from simple de-confliction at one end through to full integration. Historically, however, jointery has often proved to be problematic. In part, this often stems from a difference in perspective: soldiers have a tendency to see air power as a rapid-shock instrument for immediate and visible close air support; airmen take a theatre-wide view – many crucial air power roles are not immediately visible to land forces.

These key developments have raised recurrent problems for the conduct of land warfare. How does one attack successfully in the face of increasing firepower? How does one manoeuvre swiftly, given the complexity of logistics? How does one maintain control over large, complex army organisations under the stress of combat? Fundamentally, how can one win?

The principles of land warfare

The question of how armies should deal with the consequences of the developments outlined above has been a recurrent challenge in the twentieth and twenty-first centuries. Based on an assessment of past experience, armies have developed sets of principles designed to express concepts fundamental to the successful application of military art on land. An indicative selection is provided by the United States' 'principles of war' (actually better termed 'principles of warfare') (see box 2.1). Whatever their theoretical merit, however, applying these principles in the real world is often very difficult. For example, surprise can be a key force enabler and has been used routinely throughout history as a way of multiplying the effectiveness of military operations. However, failed attempts to achieve surprise may leave friendly forces far more vulnerable than they would otherwise have been. In the 1944 Battle of the Bulge, for example, the choice of the difficult terrain of the Ardennes as the avenue of attack contributed to achieving surprise but at a cost of making the subsequent exploitation much more difficult because the lines of advance were narrow and separated and because the terrain created defensive choke-points.

A central problem facing armies in responding to the key agents of change in the modern period has been that land warfare embodies competing demands. Prosecuting land warfare involves important trade-offs, the value of which may be entirely context-specific: techniques that work in one context may invite disaster in another. Some of the key trade-offs during the period in question include those between: attack and defence; manoeuvre and attrition; consolidation and exploitation; concentration and dispersal; forward deployment and depth; and centralisation and decentralisation.

Attack and defence

Victory in land warfare requires offensive operations. Even where an army conducts prolonged defensive operations in order to wear down the opposition, a return to offensive operations is likely to be required in order to exploit this attrition. At the strategic level, the growing scale of war has generated economic and political costs that often place a premium on ending wars as quickly as possible. At the tactical and operational levels, a force that does not attack is likely to cede the initiative to the enemy. In the air and maritime environments, attack is often the stronger form because the physical capacity of air and maritime forces to absorb the effects of modern firepower are limited. This means that victory will often go to the side that finds and attacks the enemy first.

However, traditionally in land warfare it is often more difficult to attack than it is to defend. The frictions associated with such issues as supply, command and control, co-ordination, integration and the application of firepower tend to be magnified in attack because attacking generally requires that forces manoeuvre. Manoeuvre is challenging because armies are complex and because land is difficult to move over and inhibits communication. Defending forces can also use the terrain to multiply the effectiveness of their forces. Defending troops can be concealed or placed in

Box 2.1 The US principles of war

Objectives: Military operations should be directed towards a defined, decisive and attainable objective that contributes to the broader political and military objectives.

Offensive: Military operations should be pro-active rather than reactive. Success in land warfare is more likely if a focus is placed on aggressive operations designed to seize and hold the initiative.

Mass: Military power should be concentrated at the decisive time and place. Success is more likely if a preponderance of force can be gathered for the most significant battles and not dispersed at less important points.

Economy of force: Forces allocated to secondary objectives or positions should be minimised in order to facilitate the concentration of forces at the decisive point.

Manoeuvre: Friendly forces should use movement to place the enemy at a disadvantage. This might involve trying to move onto the enemy's flanks as a way of avoiding a frontal assault, or using combinations of fire-and-manoeuvre to suppress the enemy and advance on a position.

Unity of command: The forces allocated to a specific operation or purpose should be allocated a single overall commander so that the activities of different elements are properly co-ordinated.

Security: Friendly forces should be protected from enemy action that might disrupt or harm them. This principle encompasses a wide range of activities, from providing land forces with adequate anti-aircraft protection through to information-security techniques, such as establishing secure communications and aggressive patrolling to inhibit enemy reconnaissance efforts.

Surprise: Military forces should be used in a manner, time or place that is unexpected by the enemy.

Simplicity: Unnecessary complexity should be avoided in preparing, planning or conducting operations. Those factors that create general friction in warfare, such as human involvement, fear, chance and uncertainty, mean that the more complex a military operation is, the more likely it is that something will go wrong.

prepared positions as ways of reducing the effect of the attack. The problems associated with attacking have been worsened by developments in firepower that have increased the weight and distance of the defensive firepower to which attackers are likely to be exposed. Thus, while armies cannot win without attacking, they are also often most vulnerable when engaging in offensive operations.

Manoeuvre and attrition

Manoeuvre constitutes the movement of forces to achieve an advantageous position. It is sometimes viewed as the opposite of attrition, the process of undermining the enemy by killing personnel and destroying material, because of the association between attrition and static positional warfare, such as that which characterised the First World War. In reality, these are related concepts. High rates of movement do not necessarily translate into effective manoeuvre. Effective manoeuvre involves placing one's forces in positions of advantage relative to the enemy. This relational element has a spatial and a temporal dimension: it is about being in the required place at the appropriate time. Attrition may enable manoeuvre by opening gaps that friendly forces can move through; manoeuvre may enable favourable attrition by placing forces in positions to fire upon the enemy more effectively or as a means of gaining surprise.

The dynamic qualities inherent in manoeuvre give it the potential for decisive results. Classic forms of manoeuvre include those that focus on placing forces, or threatening to place forces, on an enemy's flanks or rear, i.e. turning movements (passing around a flank); envelopments (passing around the flank and threatening to move to the rear); and encirclements (trapping forces by blocking movement to the flanks or rear), creating what the Germans termed a *Kesselschlacht* or 'cauldron battle'.

Some of the developments since 1900 have strengthened the capacity for manoeuvre: the internal combustion engine; air-mobility, which has created the capacity for 'vertical envelopment'; and the shift from such fixed communications as field telephones to wireless radios and digital communications equipment. Against these developments must be set such others as the growing scale of war and, in particular, increases in firepower that have made manoeuvring forces potentially more vulnerable. While methods exist to reduce the effect of firepower on manoeuvring forces, such as dispersal and the use of cover, these measures pose two challenges: first, they reduce the speed of manoeuvre, which may undermine its effectiveness; second, they are demanding techniques in terms of training, motivation, and command and control. Paradoxically, then, while manoeuvre may be the means to avoid unfavourable attrition, it may also, if poorly executed, have entirely the opposite effect by exposing moving forces to the full effect of enemy firepower.

Consolidation and exploitation

A successful operation leads to a choice between exploitation, pushing on to maximise the initial victory, and consolidation, pausing to reconstitute the attacking forces before moving on at a later point in time. Exploitation is a key means of translating local and temporary successes into broader and more significant gains. The initial victory may leave the enemy disorientated and unbalanced. However, the effects of demoralisation, disorder and shock, while powerful, are often temporary. Exploitation is a means to sustain and magnify these effects. It is one enabler for a high tempo of operations. Tempo describes the rate of activity relative to the enemy. This relational component is important. Sustaining a high tempo of operations is an important way of keeping the initiative, maintaining surprise and invalidating much of the enemy's decision-making. Indeed, Richard Simpkin defines initiative as 'constantly creating new situations to be exploited'.[8] Thus, exploitation can be a key way of encouraging the broader systemic collapse of a portion of the enemy forces. While consolidation is a passive activity, exploitation is active.

Despite its apparent effectiveness as a tool, exploitation can be a double-edged sword. First, successful exploitation is challenging and requires, among other things, an ability to identify opportunities and avenues for exploitation. Exploitation requires timely activity. While planned exploitation is important, opportunistic exploitation can be one of the most effective means of exploitation because of its flexibility and speed. Exploitation will often require fresh reserves or echeloned forces. Exploitation can be facilitated by simultaneity: seeking to overload the enemy's decision-making so that the enemy cannot establish effective priorities. This can be achieved through multiple penetrations, or penetrations whose objectives are unclear and that might threaten several targets. However, multiple penetrations will create significant challenges for the command, control and co-ordination of attacking forces.

Second, exploitation can bring risks. One purpose of rapid exploitation is to pre-empt battle and avoid counter-attacks. However, in land warfare the relationship between attack and defence is a fluid one. Generally, one of the purposes of defensive operations will be to create the right conditions for the offensive. Defensive operations can permit economy of force in one area to enable the creation of mass in another; they can allow a pause for the reorganisation or reconstitution of reserves; they can also inflict attrition on the attacking forces and create the conditions for counter-attack. Because exploiting forces will often be advancing rapidly, on a narrow front and without the organised logistic and combat support available for pre-planned assaults, they are vulnerable to aggressive, or 'active', defences, particularly those based upon depth (area defence) or mobile counter-attack (mobile defence). The successful German offensive at Kharkhov in 1943 was a strike at Russian forces over-extended by exploitation. If consolidation is passive, it is a much easier and less risky task to perform than exploitation.

Concentration and dispersal

Concentration can be a crucial positive factor in war. As Clausewitz notes, success in war is supported through being very strong, first in general, and then at the decisive point. Differential concentration, accepting weakness in some areas to mass at the decisive point, is one vehicle to achieve breakthroughs. However, the logic of the dispersed battlefield makes concentration problematic. Progressively greater dispersal has occurred precisely because mass has become increasingly vulnerable to firepower. In 1973, the Syrian attack on the Golan achieved a 6:1 superiority over the Israelis by massing on a narrow front three echelons (or waves) totalling five divisions and four brigades. However, the difference in tactical skill between the two sides stalled the Syrian attack, making the Syrian concentration an effective exercise in Israeli economy of effort.

Forward deployment and depth

Forces can be concentrated forward of or near the front line, or they can be arrayed in a succession of echelons, one behind the other, often with great distances between them. Depth has the advantage that the successive echelons provide uncommitted reserve forces. In the attack, the rear echelons, or 'follow-on forces', provide the means to exploit quickly any initial breakthroughs. They allow success to be reinforced. In defence, multiple echelons give great 'elasticity'. The attackers are worn down as they encounter each defensive echelon, and uncommitted echelons provide the means for the defender to counter-attack and regain lost ground. However, deployment in depth poses real challenges for the command, control and co-ordination of forces, not least because forces arrayed in depth are likely to be more widely separated and because reserve echelons are likely to be used for contingencies dictated by emerging events. Forward deployment maximises the initial combat power available and makes immediate command and control much easier.

Centralisation and decentralisation

Land warfare involves many trade-offs; many of the crucial ones involve time. Hasty attacks, for example, trade mass for time; prepared assaults do the reverse. Rapidity can be a telling force multiplier, magnifying the effects of manoeuvre, surprise and firepower. However, the growing complexity of land warfare, in terms of the nature of armies (size, specialisation, potential mobility) and the volume of information available, creates important trade-offs between time and certainty. For example, co-ordination is crucial in land warfare. Most land warfare involves elements of firepower, movement and decision-making, and intelligence-gathering, processing and dissemination by a multitude of different combat, command and support elements. One way of responding to the uncertainties of complexity is to centralise command and control, concentrating certainty at the top. This allows commanders to impose more unity of effort and co-ordination on armies. However, centralisation often trades certainty and order for time. In particular, centralisation may slow decision-making processes down, as decisions need to be referred upwards, and may reduce the initiative displayed by local commanders. This tension can manifest itself in many ways. The complexity of modern logistics, with the associated premium that is often placed on detailed planning, is also at odds with more modern concepts of opportunistic exploitation and mobility. The ability to exploit local successes with reserves is likely to be undermined by centralised decision-making.

Decentralised decision-making is an obvious alternative. Termed by the Germans *Aufstragstaktik* (mission command), this mode of command and control places an emphasis on instilling in subordinates a clear understanding of what needs to be achieved but giving them latitude as to how it is done. By devolving decision-making downwards, the tempo of operations is increased and the best use can be made of opportunities as they arrive – opportunities for exploitation, for example. Decentralisation accepts less certainty than centralisation but attempts to deal with this by increasing the ability of an army to act faster and thus shape events. Despite its theoretical advantages, however, decentralised command and control carries potential penalties. These include a loss of focus in operations, problems in combined arms and jointery, and over-extension in exploitation operations. Effective decentralisation is a fundamentally demanding mode of command and control that requires excellent training, effective communications, a supporting philosophy of command, and a significant degree of junior initiative. Whatever its theoretical advantages, therefore, decentralised command and control may create risks and simply be inappropriate for many armies.

Modern land warfare has thus been shaped by the existence of a range of interrelated challenges. Some of these have derived from the environment itself, such as the impact of terrain on operations. Some derive from the characteristics of armies, such as their complexity. Others have emerged because of key developments in technology, politics and economics, such as the growing scale of war and the increasing lethality of firepower. Responding to these challenges has been complicated by the wide range of trade-offs that exist in land warfare which allow for the creation of many different and often conflicting responses. In the next part of this chapter, we examine the evolution of the modern system in land warfare as the dominant solution to the challenges of land warfare that have been outlined thus far.

The parameters of how we commonly think about modern warfare were established by developments in the First and Second World Wars. These developments cover the shift from a mode of warfare characterised in the early part of the twentieth century by linear, close battle with a focus on tactics to a kind of warfare characterised towards the end of the twentieth century by a focus on mobile, combined-arms warfare at the operational level. These developments have been identified by Stephen Biddle as constituting the emergence of a definable 'modern system of war'. This modern system comprises 'a tightly interrelated complex of cover, concealment, dispersion, suppression, small-unit independent maneuver, and combined arms at the tactical level, and depth, reserves, and differential concentration at the operational level of war'.[9]

By and large, the basis of the modern tactical system of warfare was established by the end of the First World War as the belligerents struggled to develop the means to cope with the inadequacy of existing tactical concepts in the face of the growing influence of scale, firepower, command and control, and logistics. In the wake of the First World War, this system was refined by belligerents, but the basic precepts informed tactics and operations in the Second World War and after. The operational level of war emerged as a response to the demonstrated challenges of converting the tactical-level successes attainable using modern tactics into broader successes at the higher level of war. The conscious and unconscious focus on operational-level solutions informed Soviet theories on operational art and German blitzkrieg, and formed the basis of operational techniques developed during the Cold War.

The First World War: the emergence of the modern land tactical system

The events of 1914 cruelly exposed the limitations of pre-war concepts on the conduct of land warfare. The severity of the mismatch between the theory and the reality of land warfare in 1914 might encourage the belief that it was the result of incompetence and wilful ignorance with regard to the effects that change, particularly in the scale of war and the increases in firepower, would have on the character of land warfare. This is not true. Pre-war armies were alive to the new, emerging trends in war; debates on the implications of change were widespread, erudite and rational. It was long recognised, for example, that increases in firepower posed a challenge (see figure 2.2). Increasing firepower created a great potential problem in crossing the open ground between two forces, what Colonel (later Marshal) Ferdinand Foch, a key pre-war theorist, referred to as the 'zone of death'. The invention of machine guns, quick-firing artillery, magazine-loaded rifles and smokeless propellants in the late nineteenth century had extended and intensified the 'zone of death' between armies. The solutions discussed were rational and, indeed, form a key part of modern tactics. One was dispersal: allowing troops to spread out and make use of local cover, so making them more difficult targets. Another was a focus on suppressive fire as a way of beating down the defence. However, both carried their own challenges. Dispersed troops were more difficult to command, control and motivate, threatening a loss of momentum in the attack. Suppressive fire was difficult to co-ordinate between units, particularly between the artillery and infantry. These problems were multiplied by a general focus placed upon offensive action. Since industrialised mass warfare was believed to be unsustainable in the long term, success

Figure 2.2 German infantry entrenched during manoeuvres in 1902. European armies acknowledged prior to the First World War that increases in firepower required adjustments in tactics.

would have to be achieved quickly, and this could only be done through attack.

The solution was a focus on the moral component of war as a means of compensating for technology. Victory was to be attained by dominating the battlefield through a focus on will: seizing the initiative and exploiting it through close offensive action to break the enemy spirit. Defensive operations were viewed as a temporary mode in preparation for the attack, or the means of holding in some areas of the battlefield to concentrate the resources for the offensive in the decisive sector. Under such theorists as Foch and Colonel Louis Loyzeau de Grandmaison, offensive action became a cardinal principle in land warfare. Grandmaison, for example, argued that 'the French army, returning to its traditions, no longer knows any other law than the offensive . . . All attacks are to be pushed to the extreme . . . to charge the enemy with the bayonet to destroy him . . . Any other conception ought to be rejected as contrary to the very nature of war.'[10]

The tactical expression of such an approach, however, was more sophisticated: an emphasis was placed on both firepower and shock action. Firepower was essential in order to suppress and weaken the defence; however, decisive results required closing with the enemy. Infantry would thus infiltrate forwards, using cover and concealment to close the distance with the enemy; they would then use firepower, in combination with support from quick-firing artillery and machine guns, to weaken the defence before closing with cold steel. For example, French infantry regulations for 1895 prescribed that the

advance is made by successive rushes followed by a quick fire of short duration. The fighting line reinforced by the reserves . . . gradually reaches to within 150 or 200 metres of the enemy. At this distance magazine fire is commenced, and all available reserves . . . close up for the assault. At a signal from the Colonel the drums beat, the bugles sound the advance and the entire line charges forward with cries of '*en avant, à la baionette*'.[11]

Reflecting the intensity of the debates, the regulations of 1904 placed even more emphasis on dispersion and use of the terrain, although by 1914 doctrine had again returned to the spirit of 1895.

It was recognised that an approach to land warfare that focused on the offensive was likely to be costly. This bloody sacrifice was regarded as being the necessary price to pay for achieving rapid and decisive success. Thus, the lessons learned from the conflicts up to 1914, which were contradictory, tended to be used to reinforce existing orthodoxy. A British observer of the Russo–Japanese War (1904–5), Sir Ian Hamilton (later the British land commander at Gallipoli), noted in 1910 that 'War is essentially the triumph, not of the Chassepot over a needlegun, not of a line of men entrenched behind wire entanglements and fireswept zones over men exposing themselves in the open, but of one will over another weaker will.'[12] By 1914, then, what had emerged was, in a sense, 'anti-modern' warfare, a misinterpretation of some of the implications of social and technological change and a greater focus on enduring human elements of warfare, such as morale, discipline and offensive spirit.

The first year of the war demonstrated the inapplicability of these approaches. Modern firepower made frontal assaults by infantry brutally ineffective. In August 1914, German forces encountered the British Expeditionary Force at Mons. A British soldier noted that the Germans 'advanced in companies of quite 150 men in files five deep . . . The first company were simply blasted away to Heaven by a volley at 700 yards and, in their insane formation, every bullet was bound to find two billets.'[13] The official German account noted that 'Well-entrenched and completely hidden, the enemy opened a murderous fire . . . casualties increased, the rushes became shorter and finally the whole advance stopped. With bloody losses the attack gradually came to an end.'[14] Yet the increasing scale of war resulted in the creation of a continuous front that made the obvious alternative, flanking movements, impossible.

Some important adjustments were made relatively quickly. By March 1915, artillery, not infantry, had become the 'Queen of Battle'; the tactical mantra became 'the artillery conquers, the infantry occupies'. By the Somme offensive, which opened on 1 July 1916, artillery was employed in staggering quantities: 1,437 artillery pieces fired 1.5 million shells over a 7-day period. However, the utility of artillery as an arm of decision was fundamentally undermined by developments in defensive tactical methods – the adoption of the concept of defence in depth – which mitigated the effects of this offensive firepower.

Defence in depth

Attached to a principle of holding ground through forward defence, the German High Command was appalled at the attrition inflicted by the Somme battles on their troops, which seemed to presage the emergence of *die Materialschlacht*, 'the battle of materiel', warfare decided purely by which side could endure attrition the longer. The High Command set about developing the tactical means to counter offensive firepower, and the conclusions were reflected in 'The Principles of Command in the Defensive Battle in Position Warfare', published 1 December 1916. Four pillars underpinned this new approach: depth; firepower; elasticity; and initiative. Depth was achieved by having multiple defensive zones creating a 'web defence'. By 1917, this might consist of up to five successive defensive lines, mixing multiple trench lines, and strong points sited for cover and all-round defence. These would include an 'outpost zone' of 500–1,000 metres, which acted as 'tripwire'; a battle zone of 2 kilometres or more depth; and an artillery protection zone. Ground was used to mitigate enemy firepower; for example, where possible, defensive lines were placed on the reverse slope of hills to make enemy observation and direct fire more difficult. Depth performed a number of functions: it allowed trading space for time; it imposed disorder and attrition on the advancing enemy; and it allowed the forward zone, which was the zone that would saturated by enemy artillery, to be lightly held. Firepower allowed fewer forces to be deployed in the forward areas and yet still allowed them to impose meaningful costs on the advancing enemy. Firepower was enhanced by deploying new technology, including light machine guns, by utilising smaller, more flexible sub-units using fire-and-manoeuvre to utilise the advantages of cover, and by improved integration of the artillery into the defence plan. Elasticity expressed the focus on rapid counter-attacks as the means of re-taking ground lost and defeating the enemy assault. Defensive units were echeloned for counter-attack; using terrain, firepower and strong points to provide economy of force allowed a large portion of defensive manpower to be allocated to counter-attack roles. In order to work effectively, all of these ideas required initiative, achieved by devolving responsibility and decision-making downwards. Local commanders were given command over all of the forces in their area. Isolated forces in the outpost zones needed to have the initiative and motivation to keep on fighting even when cut off; counter-attacks needed to be

Table 2.1 Late First World War German defence in depth

═══════════════	0m
△ △ △ △ △ △	**Security line**
□ ■ □ ■ □	**Resistance line**
■ □ ■ ■ □	**Main line of resistance**
	2,000m

(Diagram: units arranged in depth from Enemy front line (0m) through Security line, Resistance line, Main line of resistance (2,000m), BATTLE ZONE (Counter-attack companies at ~2,000m and battalions at 4,000m–6,000m), and REAR ZONE (battalions at 6,000m–8,000m).)

BATTLE

4,000m

ZONE

6,000m

REAR

8,000m

ZONE

KEY

═══ Enemy front line	⁝□ Gruppe	□ Counter-attack unit
△ Sentry group	·□ Company	■ Static garrison
·□ Truppe	⊞ Battalion	

Source: Martin Samuels, *Doctrine and Dogma: German and British Infantry Tactics in the First World War* (London: Greenwood Press, 1992), p. 79.

launched quickly to take full advantage of the disorganisation inflicted on the enemy through the depth and firepower of the defence.

The development of defence in depth worsened already existing challenges to create a fundamental problem: exploitation. The central problem for much of the First World War was not that tactical success was impossible. Far from it: in general, when supported by effective artillery, infantry tended to succeed in taking the first line of enemy defences. However, a focus on extended artillery barrages could deliver only limited gains. Extended bombardments destroyed the ground over which advances would have to take place; they gave away the point of attack; and they allowed the enemy to mass reserves. Moreover, once troops had achieved initial success, other problems manifested themselves. Communications relied on field telephones connected by cables. These were static. It therefore proved difficult to co-ordinate the activities of assaulting troops once they had left their trenches (usually disorganised and enervated by the attack), with their reserves, with other friendly forces on their flanks and with artillery support. Difficulties in communication also meant that higher headquarters often had a very imperfect grasp of how an attack was developing – even of as basic an issue as where the front line of the advance might be. Once defence-in-depth techniques became disseminated among the other belligerents, however imperfectly, this problem worsened.

Infiltration techniques

The answer to the predominance of the tactical defence did not lie in new technology. For example, while both aircraft and tanks assumed greater significance during the war, the technology of both was still too immature to exert a decisive influence on the conduct of operations; light payloads and command-and-control difficulties mitigated the effect of the former, unreliability and vulnerability the latter. Instead, solutions were found in the use of new tactical techniques. Again, it was the German Army that innovated more comprehensively, reflecting, among other things, the need in 1917 to find the tactical means to exploit the transient strategic advantage provided by the surrender of Russia that allowed the transfer of German troops to the West.

Published on 1 January 1918 as 'The Attack in Position Warfare', German techniques placed a priority on two things. First, the objective of offensive operations was to be the disruption, rather than the destruction, of enemy forces. By focusing on the disruption of the enemy military system, the offensive would paralyse the enemy's ability to respond appropriately. Second, the revised German methods were based upon flexible infiltration. Referred to as *Flachen und Lücken*, or 'surfaces and gaps', attacking forces would avoid enemy strength (surfaces) and instead seek to flow through gaps in the defence.

Achieving these two effects depended upon realising a number of principles. One was neutralisation of the enemy. For example, rather than extended, destructive artillery barrages the focus was on heavy, but sudden and unexpected, attacks facilitated by more scientific gunnery techniques, such as pre-registering fire by map. The technique of 'map shooting' had been developed on the Eastern front by Colonel Georg Bruchmüller. Targeting focused less on enemy entrenchments than on the broader infrastructure required for the enemy to function and respond, including headquarters, command posts, transport nodes and enemy artillery positions. As Bruchmüller noted, 'We desired only to break the morale of the enemy, pin him to his position.' A second requirement was depth in the attack. The assault required multiple echelons. The first echelon would bypass centres of resistance, leaving them to be mopped up by follow-on forces. The first echelon would ignore flanks and push on, following routes of tactical success. They would not halt to be relieved. This facilitated continuous offensive action. The speed of offensive action and the depth in the assault maximised the shock against the enemy, provided protection to the vulnerable flanks of the attack and helped to ensure that the defenders did not regain the initiative. Jointery was also a feature, with aircraft used to help interdict the enemy rear areas, adding more depth to the attack. Another important principle was effective combined arms. Although, in general, the control of heavy artillery was centralised, pyrotechnics were used to control a creeping artillery barrage, the *Feuerwalze* or 'fire wall', which would facilitate more flexible artillery support for the infantry.

A further means was a focus on independently manoeuvring small-unit infantry teams. Infantry tactics eschewed a rigid and inflexible linear advance in favour of greater flexibility and a focus on initiative at lower levels. Specialist 'storm battalions' were organised around assault teams with light machine guns, mortars, flamethrowers and light artillery. These units were used as the cutting-edge of the attack. The basic infantry sub-unit became much smaller: the *Gruppe*, a section with riflemen and a light machine gun. The section manoeuvred around the light machine gun, which acted as a firebase. To enable these changes required improved training and small-unit leadership. In January 1917, for example, the Germans established an infantry division whose sole purpose was to experiment with, and to train in, the new tactics. The first major use of these tactics on the Western front occurred in March 1918 as part of the German spring offensive. They achieved impressive tactical successes, and the techniques were adapted by the Allies. In the last year of the war, these techniques allowed the offensive to obtain significant successes: the Germans overran Allied defences three times – at the second battle of the Somme, the battle of Lys River and at the Chemin des Dames. The Allies used similar techniques in their later offensives that ended the war, including the second battle of the Marne in July, Amiens in August and the 100 Days' offensive of September to November 1918. That mobility did not depend upon tanks was illustrated by the great success of General Allenby in Palestine: at Megiddo in 1918, Allenby achieved both breakthrough and exploitation with cavalry in concert with air power. It is important to note, however, that these offensives still involved attrition. The 1918 offensives cost the Germans a million men. British losses from August to November 1918 were greater than in the Passchendaele offensives of 1917. Still, by the end of the war, these new 'modern' techniques of land warfare had restored an element of manoeuvre to the battlefield and had established the basis of techniques that would later be used in the Second World War.

Figure 2.3 A derelict tank trapped in mud, 1917. Early tanks were unreliable, slow and vulnerable. New methods, not new technology, would be the key to ending the stalemate caused by industrial-age firepower.

Thus, the period from 1900 to 1918 saw a shift from what can crudely be termed 'anti-modern' warfare to a form of land warfare that was recognisably modern. In 1900, the response to the material conditions of land warfare had been to place undue emphasis on the moral component of war, expressed through a concentration on linear, close shock action. By 1918, the response was to place more emphasis on the conceptual dimension of warfare, finding new ways to use existing resources, not least combined arms, flexible sub-unit manoeuvre, infiltration tactics and tactical depth. The German Army pioneered these techniques, but they spread rapidly, if with varying degrees of success, to the other combatants through a 'bloody process of mutual education'. The war had produced, as Stephen Biddle notes, a 'stable and essentially transnational body of ideas on the methods needed to operate effectively in the face of radically lethal modern weaponry'.[15]

The Second World War and after: the operational level of war

The period after the First World War is commonly perceived as one dominated by the development and execution of blitzkrieg warfare, a form of war that constituted a definable military revolution. This view would argue that while states other than Germany were mired in First World War thinking, German techniques represented a 'paradigm shift', providing the bridge between the static attrition of that conflict and 'modern' mobile land warfare. The reality is more complex. As the preceding discussion has demonstrated, warfare had already become more mobile by the end of the First World War, and infiltration tactics provided the basis of tactics during the Second World War and after. New technology, such as mines and anti-tank guns, would complicate, but not change, the basic tactical principles developed in 1917 and 1918. This observation is significant, because it illustrates that the German successes of 1939 and 1940 did not derive from a revolutionary tactical superiority but from operational-level advantages. The problem experienced in 1918 was how to translate the success of tactical actions into something broader and more decisive. The German spring offensive of that year, for example, had mauled two British armies, but this tactical success had not resulted in broader operational and strategic success: the offensive could not be sustained logistically, and the German High Command lost control over the offensive after five or six days.

Traditional military thought had identified two levels of war: strategy and tactics. Strategy encompassed all those activities to bring forces to the battlefield with maximum advantage; tactics covered the conduct of forces on the battlefield itself. What was most significant about the period after 1918 was not blitzkrieg but the conscious and unconscious reflection of the importance of an intermediate level of war, the operational level, between strategy and tactics, of which the ideas and practices that informed what later became known as blitzkrieg were a manifestation. The emergence of the operational level resulted from material and cognitive developments. In material terms, the growing scale of war meant that strategic success could not be delivered through a single decisive battle, but only through the co-ordination in time and space of multiple tactical actions. As noted in chapter 1, at a cognitive level some recognition of this had already begun to occur: Jomini, for example, used the term 'grand tactics' to refer to this intermediate level. The pre-First World War military mindset, with its focus on decisive battle, was not conducive to more systematic thinking about the subject. Von Schlieffen, for example, envisaged his plan for war in 1914 as a giant Cannae, and his attempt to treat the whole massive operation of one and a half million men as a single choreographed tactical action exceeded the command and logistic realities of the time.[16]

Operational-level mobile warfare

The most systematic thinking in the interwar period regarding operational art emerged not from the Germans but from the Red Army. Concluding that, in modern war, one could not defeat the enemy with one blow, Soviet thinkers began to develop the conceptual framework for a mode of war that would allow the delivery of co-ordinated, successive blows against the enemy that would enable local tactical successes to be exploited to produce a larger effect. This focused on operational art: the theory and practice of preparing for and conducting combined and independent operations by large units (armies and groups of armies). As A. A. Svechin, one of the key Soviet theorists noted, 'tactics make the steps from which operational leaps are assembled; strategy points out the path'. The Soviet perspective focused on even greater depth in battle. Experiences in the Russian Civil War (1918–24) had demonstrated how cavalry corps and cavalry armies could be used for deep penetration of the enemy. As the technologies for mechanisation came of age after the First World War, these seemed to provide new means to realise this principle. Mobile forces would allow 'deep battle' and 'deep operations'. 'Deep battle' was penetration of the enemy to their rear artillery line. This would be followed by 'deep operations': exploitation beyond an individual battlefield into the depth of a theatre. Enshrined in the Field Service Regulations of 1936, this doctrine envisaged infantry, cavalry and mechanised forces operating with air support in a two-part battle. First, using artillery fire to suppress the enemy, an echeloned, combined-arms attack would be launched on a narrow front to penetrate the enemy line. Second, 'mobile groups' consisting of cavalry and mechanised forces would exploit, striking deep and outflanking the enemy defences. These mobile groups would encircle the enemy to a depth of 200 or 300 kilometres. Also enshrined in this doctrine was the importance of simultaneity: influencing at the same time the entire depth of the enemy positions by using smoke, deception and air attack. The aim, according to the regulations, was the 'violent development of tactical success into operational success with the aim of the complete encirclement and destruction of the enemy'.

The possibilities of the new technology were also recognised by other armies. In May 1918, J. F. C. Fuller, a British staff officer, conceived 'Plan 1919', a massive armoured offensive that he hoped would end the war. Plan 1919 combined tanks and aircraft in a massive joint effort on a narrow front that would rupture the enemy line. Using the mobility of armour and the reach of aircraft, this force would then engage in what was in effect a 'deep battle', exploiting quickly, overrunning enemy command and control, and completely paralysing the German capacity to respond. Another British military theorist, Basil H. Liddell Hart, argued for a future similar to that of Fuller's; however, whereas Fuller focused exclusively on tanks, Liddell Hart saw the need for a force of accompanying mobile infantry – in effect, mechanised infantry. In 1927, Britain created the Experimental Mechanised Force (EMF), consisting of a mixed force of tanks, motorised infantry and artillery with air support. By 1939, the United Kingdom had the only fully motorised army in the world. The United States also recognised the possibilities. In 1928–9, the United States created the Experimental Armoured Force, which included small tanks and lorried infantry.

However, only Germany was as comprehensive in its focus on combined-arms exploitation as the Soviets. Moreover, since the Red Army was thrown

Table 2.2 Deep operations, as envisaged in Soviet Field Service Regulations, 1936

KEY

1 Army boundary (Soviet symbol); bulge
   is to include/exclude certain objectives
2 Front boundary (Soviet symbol)
3 Fortified area (Soviet symbol)
4 Armour (Soviet symbol)
5 Parachute landing (airborne brigade)
6 Air attacks
A Army

A(FR) Army (Front Reserve)
AC Airborne Corps
IO Immediate objective
MG Mobile Group (prototype OMG)
FA Front aviation
RC Reserve corps
SA Shock army
SO Subsequent objective

Source: Christopher Bellamy, *The Evolution of Modern Land Warfare: Theory and Practice*
(London: Routledge, 1990), p. 90.

into turmoil by political purges in 1937–8, the German Army was left as the
pre-eminent exponent of a form of operational art, even if they did not for-
mally recognise the operational level of war in their doctrine. Under the
direction from 1919 to 1926 of the Commander of the Army, Hans von
Seeckt, the German Army sought to compensate for the restrictions placed
upon it by the Versailles Treaty through superior mobility and flexibility.
Despite the tendency to focus on the 'revolutionary' character of blitzkrieg
(see box 2.2), the principles from which it was derived stemmed from those

Box 2.2 The reality of blitzkrieg

The term 'blitzkrieg' provides a convenient short-hand for operational-level mobile, combined-arms warfare. It is important to note, however, that blitzkrieg never existed as a formal part of German doctrine. The term blitzkrieg was rarely used in the German Army; indeed, in November 1941, when Hitler first heard it, he referred to it as 'a very stupid word'. Moreover, the German principles for mobile combined-arms warfare were not regarded by the German Army as revolutionary. The scale of the success experienced in France in 1940 was thus wholly unexpected, Hitler referring to the result as 'a miracle, an absolute miracle'.

The ideas that we commonly associate with blitzkrieg continued to be resisted by significant elements in the German Army and Luftwaffe. Even in the Polish campaign in 1939, tensions existed between such radicals as Heinz Guderian (author of *Achtung – Panzer!)* and conservatives over the proper use of armour and mobile forces. Many in the German Army continued to view armour as primarily an infantry-support weapon. Thus, as late as 1937 and 1938 scarce tanks were allocated to form two infantry-support tank brigades. The Luftwaffe continued to prioritise tasks other than close air support. Not until 1940 did the German Army's regulations focus on the operational-level use of armour. Even afterwards it remained far from being a template that was applied consistently throughout the army.

extant at the end of the First World War. German approaches applied technologies for mobile warfare through a conscious adaptation of the concepts developed in the latter stages of that war. Thus, the 1924 and 1932 German regulations *Die Truppenführung*, or 'troop leadership', married the infantry assault unit tactics and effective artillery doctrines of the First World War with close air support and the use of tanks. It continued to stress flexibility, initiative and exploitation, with a focus on either narrow breakthroughs or encirclement. The essence of the German techniques used in the early part of the war was a surprise attack on a narrow front designed to ensure a penetration. The focus of the attack was then on demoralisation as well as destruction: multiple columns would exploit the initial penetration by moving to the rear of the enemy, bypassing concentrations and acting as pincers to encircle the enemy. Aircraft would act as flying artillery and, in concert with rapidly moving panzer divisions, would deepen the battle, helping to create operational-scale systemic shock.

Despite the apparent importance of panzer divisions, blitzkrieg was not a tank phenomenon. By 1941, the German Army was reducing the amount of armour in panzer divisions and trying to increase the allocation of motorised and mechanised infantry. Combined arms, rather than tanks, was one of the keys to success. For example, anti-tank guns would protect the vulnerable flanks of the breakthrough. Engineers would be on hand to increase mobility. Combined arms was facilitated by a flexible structure combining the use of all-arms battlegroups with flexible command and control and a capacity to vary the tactics to suit the situation. Blitzkrieg was thus the result of training and doctrine in combined arms, tied to a focus on penetration and manoeuvre.

A key enabler was the recognition of the importance of radio communications in land warfare. Widespread use of wireless radios enabled the effective command and control of more complex, mobile and dispersed forces. From the mid-1920s, for example, the German Army fitted new vehicles with radio mounts, and efforts were made to develop a full range of radios including short-range sets for vehicles and high-power/low-frequency sets for headquarters. There was also recognition of the importance of joint operations. Even before the re-creation of the Luftwaffe in 1933, the German Army maintained a doctrine on co-operation with the air. This co-operation was reflected also in the development of specific joint assets, especially the JU-87 Stuka dive bomber. The practical reflection of these ideas was the creation of panzer divisions – mobile all-arms formations, focused around the tank but including infantry, artillery and other supporting arms. By 1939, two-thirds of the German tank force was concentrated in six panzer divisions.

The German Army achieved startling successes in France and Poland and in the first stages of the attack on Russia. In the battles against France, at least, the operational-level application of concepts of deep battle seemed vindicated.[17] Five days into the attack, for example, German forces were already conducting deep penetrations and exploitation, wreaking havoc on Allied command and control and morale. Deep operations, realised through such principles as combined arms, mobility, rapidity, fire-and-manoeuvre, massing at decisive points, decentralised command and control, and rapid exploitation, seemed to have restored the capacity to deliver decisive outcomes in land warfare, even if these principles were still being applied in a rather ad hoc fashion.

Operational defence in depth

Yet, despite these extraordinary successes, the Second World War came to exhibit a progressively more positional and attritional character. One reason for this was that, to an extent, the early opposition facing the German Army provided a 'best-case' test for operational-level mobile warfare, because armies such as those of the Poles and French were badly deployed and had inadequate reserves. Operation Barbarossa was launched against a Russian opponent suffering from the mutually reinforcing problems of political purges, reorganisation, expansion and inexperienced commanders. Moreover, the Soviet leadership forced ill-chosen offensive and defensive operations on Russian commanders. If Barbarossa had been launched four years earlier, or one year later, it might well have been much less successful.

Logistics posed other emerging limitations. Mobile armoured warfare may have helped solve some tactical problems, but it created new logistic ones.

Operational-level mobile warfare required heavy, complex, mobile logistic support if it were not quickly to lose momentum. Whereas a 1914 infantry division required 100 tons of supplies a day, a panzer division required 300 tons and a US division by 1944 required 600 tons. In the Polish campaign of 1939, no German unit advanced more than 150 miles into Poland, yet it still proved difficult to keep front-line units in supply. In Russia, with supply lines extending up to 900 miles, the problems of supplying the needs of high-intensity mobile warfare often proved insurmountable. Even operating the rail lines was problematic, given freezing weather conditions and incompatible rail gauges; linking railheads to mobile forces was even more difficult, with the dearth of motor transport and the severe operating conditions. For example, by November 1941 some of the lead German infantry divisions were operating 90 miles from their railheads, a distance twice that from which they could be supplied effectively.

Exploitation posed a related challenge. In 1940, only one-tenth of the German Army was made up of panzer or mechanised divisions. The rest was reliant on horses for its transport; indeed, the German Army used nearly twice as many horses in the Second World War (some 2.7 million) as it did in the First. Panzer exploitation could often only take place once infantry and logistics had caught up. It is notable that the average daily rate of advance for panzer divisions in Poland was only 11 miles. Quick 'leaps' forward were accompanied by long pauses while the means to consolidate gains caught up. In Russia, this 'mobility gap' imposed delays that reduced the tempo of advance and provided opportunities for Russian counter-attacks. Operational-level mobile warfare also therefore required broad-based mechanisation if effective mobile combined arms was to be achieved. In that sense, the German Army of the Second World War was only 'semi-modern'.

Another difficulty was vulnerability. Operational-level mobile warfare relied on causing the systemic collapse of the enemy as a key to prevent the launching of counter-attacks against vulnerable exploitation forces. If the enemy did not collapse quickly, then the costs of a risk-based exploitation approach were likely to mount. Thus, the cutting-edge of blitzkrieg, the panzer divisions, suffered heavy attrition even in the early stages of the campaign in Russia. In the Polish campaign, German tank losses amounted to 10 per cent of the initial force. Many units also lost up to 50 per cent of their motor vehicles. In Russia, from June to November 1941 the German Army lost two-thirds of its motor vehicles and 65 per cent of its tanks. The attrition in motor vehicles compounded the logistic problems. From November 1941 to March 1942, the German Army lost another 75,000 vehicles but could only find 7,500 replacements.

In addition to these challenges, we must add another: the response. The essence of blitzkrieg was to get a mechanised combined-arms force through the enemy front line so that it could penetrate the enemy, causing their systemic collapse. One of the key answers to this was a rational development of concepts developed in the First World War, in this case the principle of 'defence in depth', applied at an operational and not just a tactical level. This was not a new idea. The Russian deployment prior to Barbarossa was in essence a defence in depth, but it was poorly executed. By the middle of the Second World War, as combatants became more experienced, defence in depth had reasserted the strength of the defence. New technology, such as anti-tank guns, complicated combined arms, but it also made defence in depth potentially more effective by improving the effectiveness of non-tank forces in fighting armour. At Kursk, for example, the Soviet defences were in places 110 miles deep. Defences this deep were designed not just to inflict losses on the attacker but to disorganise them and to break down the capacity for combined arms by separating armour from supporting infantry. At points of expected German attack, the defences might have 1,500 to 2,000 mines and 25 to 30 anti-tank guns per kilometre of frontage. The defence-in-depth concept also harnessed armoured and mechanised forces. The Soviets held the Steppe Front of five armies in reserve for counter-attack. Depth helped to mitigate surprise and gave opportunities for counter-attack. The Germans themselves elevated the mobile counter-attack to an art form through the use of 'manoeuvre on interior lines', using mobile forces based on a central position to counter-attack enemy encirclement attempts, defeating them sequentially in detail.

This did not mean that the tactical and operational offensive concepts developed since 1917 were irrelevant; far from it. Offensive successes were still possible. For example, in Operation Bagration, which began in June 1944, the Russians smashed the German Army Group Centre, destroying seventeen divisions and reducing another fifty to below half strength. The offensive pushed the Germans back 350 miles. Soviet concepts developed from 1943 were illustrative of the techniques elaborated in an attempt to overcome defence in depth. Reconnaissance elements were strengthened in order to promote the chances of a breakthrough, transforming time-consuming reconnaissance into the first echelon of the attack designed to seize outposts and 'recce' by fire. Attack groups were made more flexible by dividing them into reconnaissance, blocking, fire and attack sub-groups to promote greater flexibility in combined arms. Use was made of tailored assault groups and specialist formations, such as combat engineers. Great emphasis was put on deception to promote surprise and to facilitate massing at critical points. In order to increase the pace of exploitation, the Soviets promoted decentralised command and control: relatively junior officers were encouraged to use initiative and seize targets of opportunity. The size of forward elements and their distance from the main body was increased: by 1944, forward elements for a tank corps might operate some 50 miles in front of parent corps, and might include a tank brigade and field and anti-aircraft artillery, assault guns and engineers. For important points of exploitation, forward air controllers would accompany lead elements, and dedicated air assets would be allocated for close air support to speed the advance.

Nevertheless, neither Bagration nor other examples of rapid advances, such as General Patton's advance in the Normandy campaign of 400 miles in 26 days, induced the general systemic collapse of the enemy forces as blitzkrieg had in 1940. These were not the victories envisaged by Fuller and Liddell Hart. Operations from late 1942 onwards were, in some respects, reminiscent of the First World War, for example in their focus on set-piece attacks, particularly those used by Britain and the Soviets. Eventual Allied success depended upon broad, protracted attrition at the strategic level, in which elements of more mobile warfare were interspersed with long periods of positional fighting. In a general sense, this could still be decisive: in two and half years of war, the Soviets drove the Germans from the Volga to the Elbe. However, breakthroughs depended to an extent on attrition first rather than lightning breakthroughs, and this attrition might be as bad or worse than that of the First World War. The combined casualties at Verdun in that war were 750,000 suffered over a period of 10 months; in Normandy, 637,000 casualties were suffered in 80 days. The breakout from Normandy was enabled by two months of heavy, static fighting that had inflicted significant losses on the Germans. For example, most German infantry units suffered more than 100 per cent casualties during the campaign.[18]

AirLand and land–air battle

The essentially evolutionary nature of the development of modern land warfare was sustained during the Cold War despite the great uncertainty caused by the impact of such new technology as nuclear weapons, helicopters and PGMs and by such new strategic ideas as deterrence and limited wars. Operational techniques were developed from ideas extant in the latter stages of the Second World War. The basic 'pieces' of land warfare remained the same – the tanks, artillery and vehicles were recognisably similar – and most discourse on conventional land warfare remained rooted in such theorists as von Seeckt and Fuller.

Nuclear weapons posed a fundamental challenge to existing concepts of land warfare. As the eminent civilian strategist Bernard Brodie noted, 'Thus far the chief purposes of our [the United States'] military establishment has been to win wars. From now on its chief purpose must be to avert them.'[19] In the Soviet Union, less emphasis was placed on operational art; in the United States, the solution was to focus on nuclear armed units, emphasising firepower over manoeuvre. Changes in ethos took place, with a focus on technology and 'managerialism': land warfare became increasingly associated with 'futurism, technological innovation and bureaucratic procedures'.[20] By the 1960s, however, it was clear that nuclear war was not inevitable, and that conventional land warfare might still have a crucial role to play in future conflict.

In the period from the 1960s through to the 1980s, Soviet military doctrine returned to an emphasis on familiar themes of operational art, albeit modified to take into account developments in technology and US doctrine. Soviet doctrine noted that 'the possibilities of defeating the enemy in the entire depth of his operation combat formations have increased. Motorized rifle and tank forces, in coordination with other types of armed forces and branches of forces, can perform very complicated combat tasks with decisive aims, at a great depth and at a high tempo.'[21] Soviet doctrine stressed the need for: surprise; attacking the enemy throughout its depth; superiority in numbers and firepower at decisive points; mobility; and continuous operations, pushing forward at 50–70 kilometres a day. Flexibility remained crucial; this was achieved through keeping powerful reserves to exploit initial successes and by placing maximum forces under the control of the operational-level commander. New technology provided the means to supplement ground operations in 'land–air' battle with a 'vertical echelon' delivered by air-mobile forces. PGMs could add more depth to the attack but also made massed echelons more vulnerable to counter-strikes. New weapons gave greater scope for *aktivnost* – drive, activity and aggression. Because nuclear weapons and PGMs increased the vulnerability of massed forces, Soviet doctrine emphasised rather different means to realise traditional principles. Instead of penetration and envelopment operations by deeply echeloned forces along a limited number of axes, Soviet doctrine identified that the assault would instead consist of 'numerous operational and tactical cutting blows delivered along numerous axes, by vertical *desants* [drops or landings], and by strikes against the enemy rear area by ground and air-delivered forces'.[22] The second echelon was replaced by 'operational manoeuvre groups', based on the older mobile-group concept, which would pass through the first echelon and exploit quickly. Manoeuvre and ranged firepower were used to realise the effects of concentration rather than mass itself.

In the United States, the 1970s and 1980s were notable for the formal recognition of the importance of the operational level of war, contained in a new US Army publication, *FM 100-5 Operations* (see box 2.3). Defeat in Vietnam prompted a reassessment of US doctrine. One conclusion was that US defeat was partly attributable to an over-reliance on firepower and a managerial approach to war that focused on systems and technology. Other factors also influenced this reassessment. For example, the Arab–Israeli Yom Kippur/Ramadan War of 1973 demonstrated the impact of PGMs: in three weeks of fighting, the losses of armour and artillery exceeded in numbers the entire US inventory at the time. Modern war appeared to be fought at a high tempo in a fast-moving, complex, all-arms environment which required excellent command and control. The results of these debates was

Box 2.3 The operational level

At the operational level of war, joint and combined operational forces within a theater of operations perform subordinate campaigns and major operations and plan, conduct, and sustain to accomplish the strategic objectives of the unified commander or higher authority.
US Army Field Manual *FM 100-5 Operations*, p. 6–2.

The focus of the operational *level* is the campaign, a series of tactical actions that should be linked by time, geography and a common purpose, so that they serve broader military and grand strategic objectives. Operational *art* is the employment of military forces at this level.

the emergence of a new concept, 'AirLand battle', introduced in a new edition of *FM 100-5* in 1982 and refined in 1986. The concept brought together, and tried to weave into a whole, close operational interaction between air–ground forces, combined arms, fire support, electronic warfare, deception intelligence and manoeuvre. AirLand battle tried to marry firepower with manoeuvre by attaching importance to four concepts: initiative, depth, agility and synchronisation. The essence of AirLand battle was 'deep battle' and developing the capacity to slow Soviet second-echelon forces while pinning down and destroying the first-echelon forces. Manoeuvre and firepower were treated as inseparable elements.

Thus, developments in modern land warfare after the Second World War reinforced already established themes: the need for operational-level thinking to focus tactical effort; depth; manoeuvre; combined arms; joint warfare; mobility; tempo; and initiative. For example, AirLand battle was underpinned by the explicit adoption among Western armies of a philosophy of 'manoeuvre warfare'. The manoeuvrist approach is an indirect approach that places the emphasis on attacking the enemy's conceptual and moral component of fighting power rather than the physical (see box 2.4). This involves a focus on undermining the enemy's will, cohesion and decision-making capacity, rather than destruction in a crude 'force-on-force' struggle. Manoeuvre warfare has been characterised as the capacity to cycle through OODA loops (Observe, Orientate, Decide, Act) faster than the opponent, thus invalidating their decision-making, robbing them of the initiative and promoting systemic collapse (the OODA loop concept is discussed in more depth in chapter 4, p. 201). As exponents of the manoeuvrist approach acknowledge, there is nothing new in this; instead, it is a systematisation of historical 'best practice'. This evolutionary approach was reflected in a resurgence in Western armies of a study of Soviet methods of 1943–5 and also of German operational art. Some of the key tools associated with manoeuvre warfare draw on German approaches

Box 2.4 Manoeuvre warfare

Maneuver warfare is a warfighting philosophy that seeks to shatter the enemy's cohesion through a variety of rapid, focused, and unexpected actions which create a turbulent and rapidly deteriorating situation with which the enemy cannot cope.
US Marine Corps publication *MCDP1 Warfighting*, p. 73.

Manoeuvre warfare places an emphasis on speed, focus, surprise, disruption and exploitation. It is a demanding philosophy that requires of armies initiative, flexibility, lateral thinking and an ability to cope well with uncertainty.

adopted and utilised before and during the Second World War, including *Aufstragstaktik* ('mission command'), *Schwerpunkt* ('focus of effort'), and *Flachen und Lücken* ('surfaces and gaps').

Modern land warfare in the twentieth century therefore emerged from the evolutionary development of tactical and operational methods embodying such principles as depth, combined arms, joint operations and high-tempo operations. In relation to the trade-offs identified at the beginning of this chapter, the tendency has been to focus on offensive operations, manoeuvre, exploitation, dispersal, depth and decentralisation. From this perspective, 'modern' land warfare has evolved as a means to cope with broader developments in warfare, such as firepower and the growing scale of war. Successful mastery of modern land warfare has enabled armies to mitigate some of the consequences of industrialised people's war, such as firepower, and to harness others, such as new weapons platforms and means of mobility. The use of this system explains why casualty rates have not expanded in relation to theoretical lethality or the speed of modern weapons. Despite increases in firepower technology, in the period between 1900 and 1990 average casualty rates decreased by more than 60 per cent. It also explains why, despite the power of the defence demonstrated in the initial part of the First World War, modern armies have been able to conduct successful offensive operations. From this perspective, the outcome of the 1991 Gulf War can be explained in the same way as the outcome of Germany's attack on France in 1940. In both, the clash involved armies plentifully supplied with the equipment of modern land warfare. In both, there was a marked difference in the ability of the two sides to use that equipment in modern ways.

Context and variation

Thus far, the discussion has implicitly conflated 'modern land warfare' and 'Western land warfare'. This association is defensible insofar as the nineteenth century saw an emerging dominance of Western models of government and military organisation. In twentieth-century militaries, 'modernisation' and 'Westernisation' appeared coterminous, states as diverse as Turkey, Japan, India and Egypt 'modernising' their forces in ways that seemed to reflect accepted Western norms.

At one level, this should not be surprising. Logically, there should be an important imitative dynamic in warfare. War is a serious business. Failure can often be catastrophic for a state. There should be every incentive, there-fore, for armies to imitate the structures, values and practices of other armies that have a demonstrated history of effectiveness. Even where states are not actually at war, examining the experiences of other states that are at war may provide important lessons. Over time, particular armies, through noted success in war, may acquire the status of 'paradigm armies': armies that appear to embody so many of the standards of military effectiveness that they are widely copied. 'Modern war' is therefore 'Western war' because in the twentieth and twenty-first centuries the Western way of warfare, the key tactical and operational features of which have been outlined in the pre-ceding discussion, appears to be uniquely effective, at least in terms of the prosecution of major conventional high-intensity land combat.

However, the processes that have shaped the way states develop and use military power on land (and in other environments, for that matter) are complex. The range of responses to military change is potentially broad: inno-vation, or the introduction of new techniques or ideas; resuscitation, or the repair of existing institutions that have fallen into decay; adaptation, or the contextualisation of imported values/ideas; imitation, or the importation and recreation of values and ideas; or no change at all. The last of these may be a perfectly rational option, given that, as identified in the previous chapter, the reasons for defeat are often not self-evident and may lie outside issues relating to the effectiveness of an army itself, such as poor political choices or mistaken grand strategy. Crucially, direct imitation is rarer than might be imagined, even among European armies. Generally, context is crucial in determining whether, when and how states respond to the perceived lessons of the battlefield. Context is also crucial in determining fundamental benchmarks in land warfare, such as a state's judgement regarding what 'effectiveness' means. This context may include a state's factor endowments (such as resources, demographics or geography), its polit-ical culture, civil–military relations, the organisational culture of its armed forces, the desired goals of the government, the outlook of its people and so on. This context, rather than strict military necessity, may play a decisive role in shaping how states fight land warfare. For example, the issue of whether or not a state has a professional or a conscript army may have an important bearing on how it conducts land warfare; yet the choice between the two may have as much to do with broader political and ideational objectives, such as nation-building, as with military-centred definitions of efficiency.

The conclusion that can be drawn from this is that, even if the modern system has proved to be effective for Western militaries fighting in Europe, at any point in time during the twentieth century there have been many different forms of land warfare in existence. First, even within states that appear to be adhering to the same broad paradigm there are likely to be different responses to change. Second, even if armies focus upon one central paradigm of land warfare, geopolitical conditions may force armies to wage land warfare in ways that diverge from this. Third, local conditions may decisively shape the available ways and means of land warfare, making certain options difficult or impossible to implement. The remainder of this section examines each of these propositions in turn, examining their consequences for notions of modern land warfare.

Same paradigm, different responses

Despite the development and diffusion of some common military practices during the First World War, the interwar period was marked by significant differences in approaches to land warfare. There were many generic challenges to the 'modernisation' of armies during the period leading up to the Second World War. There was a strong anti-war bias in the politics of many countries during the period, which tended to marginalise the military; economic conditions were often unfavourable to heavy military investment; additional calls on those resources that were available were made by air forces. There was also the effect of peace; notwithstanding the Spanish Civil War (1936–9), new concepts and new technology could not be extensively tested and validated. Institutional factors also shaped views on modern warfare; for example, the 'cavalry outlook' that had a strong representation in some armies tended to shape the view on the potential uses of mobile forces. Political ideologies, from the revanchism of Nazism to the modernist outlook of Marxism, were also relevant. The point is that these generic political, economic, historical and bureaucratic conditions differed in each country. The evidence demonstrates that even where countries have close military interaction, there may still be significant differences in the way in which they organise and practise land warfare. Even during wartime, these differences may persist. During the First and Second World Wars, for example, Britain consistently adopted a more centralised and methodical approach to operations than Germany. Centralisation was seen as a route to ensuring effective concentration and avoiding over-extension, ensuring what Montgomery called 'balance' in military operations.

Divergent realities

A second reason modern land warfare is a more heterogeneous concept is that political necessity may force armies to fight in conditions that are unexpected and/or not conducive to the application of assumed norms of land warfare. As Lord Kitchener commented, 'We make war as we must, not as we would like.' There is often a tendency for armies to focus on the needs of symmetrical, high-intensity war, because these wars pose the greatest risk to the state and because this task may reinforce accepted norms of military professionalism. As the costs of such wars have grown (and bearing in mind the potential, in some cases, for nuclear escalation), the probability of their occurrence has diminished. After 1945, the number of interstate conflicts declined and the number of intrastate conflicts increased. The need to adapt techniques to meet what, from a Western military point of view, might be regarded as 'peripheral' tasks is complicated by the inherently asymmetric nature of warfare: opponents will tend to adapt their techniques to mitigate their own weaknesses and exploit their strengths. Martin van Creveld notes, for example, that an inverse relationship often seems to exist between the modernity of an army (defined in terms of technology and organisation) and its effectiveness at unconventional operations.[23]

The French experience in Indo-China provides us with an example of the complex realities of land warfare. The problem for the French was that the techniques suitable for modern land warfare in Europe were not wholly suitable for the conditions of Indo-China. The challenge was to develop a method for mitigating French weaknesses and allowing French strengths to come to bear. The French response, used most famously at Dien Bien Phu in 1954, was the concept of the *base aéro-terrestre*: establishing air-supplied fortified camps on Viet Minh supply routes. These bases would provide a jumping-off point for offensive sorties and bastions against attack. This was a means to try to make unconventional war more conventional. Featuring the use of carefully laid networks of prepared defences and supported by artillery and aircraft, this concept appeared to be a way of forcing the Viet Minh to fight on French terms. Established and supplied by air drop and air landings, these bases overcame the traditional vulnerability of modern army logistics to irregular attack. The concept deliberately eschewed mobile warfare which, because of the jungle terrain, huge size of the theatre, mobile nature of the enemy and lack of resources, would not work. The French deliberately embraced static, positional attrition warfare because it was believed, erroneously as it transpired, that French firepower would ensure that that attrition would be one-sided.

The challenges posed by the potential variety of land warfare were also evident during the Korean War of 1950–3. There, UN forces operated under conditions that required adaptation to techniques used during the Second World War. These conditions included a shortage of troops, difficult terrain and enemy tactics that often focused on the use of light forces to bypass and cut off UN troops. UN commanders needed to come to terms with the problems of operating far from roads and with the possibility of being isolated and threatened in flanks and rear. Thus, the most common UN defensive position became a dispersed defence with company positions entrenched in all-round defence with hundreds, sometimes thousands, of yards between positions. The UN dropped defence in depth in favour of a

Figure 2.4 Modern logistics? The Korean War: rations are sent to Australian forces holding positions in hilly terrain in Central Korea. Local context, such as terrain, may force 'modern' land warfare to be conducted in decidedly 'unmodern' ways. Adaptability is often one of the keys to success.

thin line of discontinuous strong points on high ground. To support these positions required active patrolling and excellent fire support – sometimes the whole corps artillery would be used to support a single outpost. On one occasion, 40,000 artillery rounds were fired in support of a single infantry company.

Another example of this variety is provided by Russian experiences after the end of the Cold War. The doctrinal focus of the Russian Army in the 1990s was conventional warfare, rooted in the Soviet thinking of the Cold War. Even in 2000, the focus of doctrine was still on high-technology war against external threats. Yet the major combat experience of the Russian Army consisted of urban operations in Grozny in 1994–5 and 1999–2000 as part of the war in Chechnya. The Russian experience reinforced the lesson that sustained urban operations are extremely demanding. Buildings make target acquisition more difficult: they obstruct navigation and communications; and they channel movement, making manoeuvre more restricted. All of these things make armoured vehicles more vulnerable, impede the use of indirect firepower, create problems in combining arms and make urban warfare a particularly demanding psychological environment in which fear, isolation and the prospect of sudden, close encounters with the enemy can quickly erode the morale of troops. Thus, the kind of warfare that the Russians planned to fight was the not the sort of war they had to fight.

Even if we were to assume, then, that many armies make similar general assumptions about the way to conduct land warfare, we can conclude that there are still likely to be important differences in how operations are actually conducted, not least because political necessity and adaptive enemies may force armies to fight according to unfamiliar rules.

Multiple paradigms

Variety in forms of land warfare is also likely because land warfare, like all warfare, cannot be divorced from its wider context. The modern system is difficult to implement because it carries with it a variety of political, social and economic trade-offs. Effective combined-arms and joint capabilities are expensive and may be beyond the abilities of states to procure. Devolved command and control may be at odds with more authoritarian political systems. This means that states may have modern equipment but not conduct 'modern' warfare, at least by the definition of contemporary Western militaries. This contingent effect of varying context has been extended by some writers into the realms of culture. For example, Victor Davis Hanson argues that the 'Western Way of War' has demonstrable superiority and that, at its heart, this superiority stems from Western culture. Features of this culture, such as individualism, consensual government and civic militarism, provide the foundation for specific military advantages like organisation, discipline, morale, initiative and flexibility. Williamson Murray identifies a 'Western Way of War' built on 'finance, technology, eclecticism, and discipline'.[24] However, cultural explanations for military behaviour remain controversial, not least because of the difficulty of defining culture and identifying exactly how it shapes actions.

It is not difficult to find evidence of the way that local context has shaped the ability of states to fight land warfare. One example would be the Iran–Iraq War of 1980–8, in which the character of the fighting was reminiscent of the middle element of the First World War, with a focus on artillery and infantry assaults in the context of static, attritional warfare. Both sides laboured under great difficulties. Command, control and intelligence were a recurring challenge. In part, this stemmed from difficulties at the grand strategic level that cascaded downwards. In Iran, military operations were subject to interference from the mullahs, and serious divisions existed between the army proper and the *Pasdaran*, or Revolutionary Guards. In Iraq, a climate of fear and a focus by Saddam Hussein on loyalty rather than competence stifled enterprise and initiative. There were also basic technical, doctrinal and organisational problems: major failings in intelligence-gathering; a lack of effective and secure communications; and rigid and slow command chains. There was also a lack of training, leadership and organisation for combined-arms warfare. Reliance on conscripts and high attrition of combat-effective elements reduced the capacity of both sides to formulate, disseminate and implement demanding alternatives. Neither side had the logistic capacity to sustain large-scale mobile warfare; even small increases in logistic lines or relatively minor movements of forces often resulted in disorganisation and disruption.

However, we should resist the tendency to see local context and efficiency as automatic trade-offs. There is a political context. The purposes of armies vary. Some are not designed to fight major combat operations. For example, although Latin American armies have acquired much of the panoply of war for modern major combat operations, in the period we are examining they have been deployed predominantly on internal operations. In other states, considerations of military effectiveness may be traded off deliberately against domestic political priorities; in Saudi Arabia, for example, parallel military structures, consisting of an army and a national guard, have been created to help forestall coups. Jeremy Black argues that Western attempts to develop taxonomies of military change fail to understand the role played by social and political circumstances in shaping the development of armed forces. Many of the things that we regard as essential for military efficiency, such as a focus on professional officers, discipline and training, are culturally conditioned. Thus, Black comments that: 'Modernity, defined in a Western fashion and as a Westernising project, emerged in large part through military forces operating under Western systems of control and discipline.' As he goes on to argue, even where organisation and weapons might converge with Western practices, this does not imply 'convergence in terms of the cultural suppositions affecting war, especially understandings of victory, suffering and loss.'[25] Cultural perspectives argue that the legitimacy of a particular paradigm of land warfare cannot be defined solely in terms of military efficiency or organisational interests.

For example, the Yom Kippur/Ramadan War of 1973 might be construed as the victory of a Western-style army, the Israeli Defence Force (IDF), featuring a military system based on integration, trust and professionalism, over fundamentally less competent, Soviet-orientated Arab opposition. In reality, the IDF had developed a style of land warfare that was somewhat at odds with Western norms of war, not least because the IDF placed an emphasis on offensive air and armour operations at the expense of true combined arms because this had worked in previous Arab–Israeli wars. In fact, in the early part of the 1973 war, the IDF forces were often poorly handled, an Egyptian general noting that 'their sole tactic remains the cavalry charge'. The Syrian and Egyptian Armies certainly suffered from recognised challenges relating to the poor performance of junior officers, problems with combined arms, improvisation and a lack of flexibility. Many of these problems were deeply embedded in a culture of conformity, deference and an avoidance of shame that often resulted in passivity and a lack of initiative. Recognising these challenges, Egypt deliberately set out to compensate, its President, Anwar Sadat, noting 'We will simply have to use our talents and our planning to compensate.' The improvement in the effectiveness of the Egyptian Army in 1973 came from methods that might be regarded as 'anti-modern' in terms of the conduct of contemporary land warfare: rigid planning; the exhaustive practicing of a very limited number of missions; a focus on consolidation, not exploitation; and an emphasis on defence, not attack. From an Egyptian perspective, the 1973 war was far from being a defeat, and in the sense that Egypt achieved its political objectives it was indeed a successful use of military power.

Another example was the methods used by the Chinese People's Liberation Army (PLA) forces in Korea. The PLA response to encountering the conventional forces of the United Nations encompassed elements of adaptation and compensation. Adaptation stemmed from a basic lesson: large-scale modern land warfare could not be fought against UN forces without adequate logistics and firepower. The Korean War saw the evolution of the PLA from a light, guerrilla war-orientated army to a mirror in some ways of the US Army, with an emphasis on firepower, especially artillery, and on air power, professionalism and logistics. Where they could not adapt, the Chinese compensated tactically. The Chinese often advanced at night, using low ground to bypass strong points and infiltrate. This allowed the Chinese to attack from unexpected directions and to threaten the artillery positions to the rear that were so vital for the support of company positions. If assaults had to be made on positions, the Chinese rarely used crude human-wave tactics. Instead, they would use machine guns and mortars to suppress and pin down the defenders before assault groups crept forward searching for weak points. In order to counter US air and artillery support, Chinese forces would try and 'hug' US positions.

The history of land warfare in the twentieth century is filled with examples that combine elements of continuity and important elements of variation. The war between Somalia and Ethiopia from 1977 to 1978 over the Ogaden involved tanks, armoured personnel carriers and heavy artillery, and featured the use of tank spearheads, combined arms and air-mobile operations. Yet it was also conditioned by the local context, such as the interaction between guerrilla and conventional warfare, between foreign advisors and indigenous forces, and between regular forces and militias, into something very different from the Western European experience of war. Similarly, the 1987 war between Chad and Libya featured Chadian 'Toyota War', using light vehicles to inflict heavy losses on the heavier and less mobile Libyans. The Indo–Pakistan war of 1971 has been characterised by Robert M. Citino as 'high-tempo manoeuvre warfare' but under South Asian conditions.[26] Victory was achieved very quickly by an Indian army lacking a significant degree of mechanisation; and rapidity was achieved by capitalising on local advantages, such as support from the population in East Pakistan (who provided intelligence and logistic support), by the use of infiltration tactics and by exploiting the passivity of the Pakistan defences. In the Sino–Vietnam War of 1979, the Vietnamese engaged the Chinese with local and regional forces, manipulating the difficulties in terrain and the Chinese reliance on roads to launch infantry-based irregular attacks while main-force regular units were generally held in reserve.

The idea, then, that modern land warfare exists as a single template is false, as is the idea that only one approach can be effective. Land warfare is a human, as well as a competitive, activity, and responses to the challenges posed by major combat operations have often varied. War is, after all, relational; one does not have to meet some abstract 'gold standard' in land warfare – one only has to be sufficiently better than one's opponent or sufficiently good in order to meet the desired political objectives. Adaptation is often more prevalent than wholesale imitation, because local context will shape the compatibility, practicality and suitability of techniques. If there are recurrent themes in the conduct of land warfare, such as the importance of logistics, combined arms, and fire-and-monoeuvre, they are not always realised in the same way. Moreover, there may be ways open for states to compensate for weaknesses in some areas through processes of operational or strategic substitution – compensating for weaknesses in conventional high-intensity capabilities, for example, by focusing on political will or mixing in unconventional techniques.

In contrast to the evolutionary underpinnings of the modern system approach, the 1990s saw the debates on military revolutions move to centre stage, proponents arguing that developments in warfare, particularly in the realms of information systems and precision firepower, were creating a Revolution in Military Affairs (RMA), a change of proportions as groundbreaking as the introduction of gunpowder. From this point of view, the modern systems perspective was representative of a form of land warfare, industrial land warfare, that was being rendered progressively less valid by broader changes in globalising, information-based societies and economies. There were, in particular, two related views on how these changes might shape land warfare: one that focused on the relative importance of land warfare, and the other focusing on the form that land warfare might take. This discussion considers both of these views before exploring some of the challenges and implications of these ideas.

Land warfare: changing roles?

The Gulf War of 1991 cast a long shadow over subsequent debates on the character and future of land warfare. One of the most significant lines of argument was that the Gulf War, reinforced by subsequent conflicts in Kosovo in 1999 and in Afghanistan in 2001, illustrated the subsidiary nature of land warfare as against the devastating new capabilities demonstrated by air power. To paraphrase an old adage, this argument took the line that 'Air power conquers, land forces occupy.'

As Daryl Press notes, the assumption that the Gulf War was emblematic of an emerging revolution is understandable to the extent that the war was so one-sided.[27] Extreme one-sided outcomes do occur in battles: in the battle of Omdurman in 1898, for example, Anglo-Egyptian forces inflicted one hundred casualties for every one that they lost. These outcomes could be explained by massive disparities in firepower technology and by assumptions that these battles pitted 'primitive' military systems against 'modern' ones. The Iraqi Army, however, was reasonably well equipped and large, and had experience from the Iran–Iraq War to draw on. Notwithstanding the developments in US land warfare doctrine, structures and training associated with AirLand battle, the expectation on the part of US planners was for friendly casualties of around 10,000.

The reality was very different. On 17 January 1991, the Coalition commenced a 38-day campaign of air strikes against Iraqi forces. The land campaign, when it began on 24 February, lasted only 4 days. Coalition casualties were far smaller than expected; estimates of Iraqi dead ranged from 20 to 22,000. More significant was the scale of the victory. The Iraqi army appeared to have collapsed: the frontal assault by two Marine divisions on the Iraqi positions, which was intended as a pinning operation, for example, broke through with relative ease. Where fighting did occur, the outcomes were also disproportionate. In the nine major ground engagements, Coalition force ratios varied from at best 1.5:1 to at worst 1:1.5, well short of accepted norms for success. Yet the Iraqis suffered catastrophic casualty exchange rates. In five major battles on 26 February, the Iraqis lost 350 armoured vehicles and hundreds dead. US losses amounted to only thirteen dead, of which only one was killed by the Iraqis.

In the immediate aftermath of the war, many were convinced that the reason for the decisive military victory won in 1991 was air power, proponents of this view asserting that 'Simply (if boldly) stated, air power won the Gulf War' and that 'air power was the decisive factor'.[28] Advocates of the decisive influence of air power argued that it had eviscerated Iraqi land forces. Air power, it was asserted, had established the conditions under which the Coalition's ground campaign could not lose: through attacks on Iraqi command and control, communications and intelligence facilities; the interdiction of Iraqi supply lines; constraining the capacity of Iraqi forces to manoeuvre in the open; inflicting attrition on Iraqi forces; and undermining morale.

The lessons relating to the decisive effect of air power were reinforced by conflicts in Kosovo and Afghanistan. In 1999, NATO air attacks were launched in response to evidence of the ethnic cleansing by Serbs of Albanians in the region of Kosovo. The acceptance by the Serbs of a peace agreement was achieved without the intervention of conventional ground forces, although special forces and irregulars of the Kosovo Liberation Army (KLA) were involved. Air power, it was argued, had been able to destroy around one-third of Serbian holdings of armour, artillery and mechanised equipment, and this, in concert with attacks on political targets, had been sufficient to coerce the Serbs into a political settlement. Further validation of the ability of air power to deliver decisive results appeared to be provided by the war in Afghanistan in 2001. Regime change, ousting the Taliban, was effected by what was from a Western perspective an extremely cost-efficient triumvirate: special forces; air power; and indigenous allied forces provided by the Northern Alliance. Air power provided the primary capacity to pin, destroy and disrupt, delivering devastating precision strikes against the Taliban at long ranges; special forces identified the targets for air power; indigenous forces mopped up and provided occupation forces.

The significance of the experiences in Afghanistan, building upon the apparent lessons of Kosovo and the 1991 Gulf War, was that land warfare was no longer the decisive element in war. Indeed, the lesson of the so-called 'Afghan Model' of war was that land forces needed to be configured in a completely different way in the future. If the RMA had given air power the capacity to deliver very heavy, precise and rapid firepower at long or short range, then it provided a low-risk destructive or coercive tool that could also perform the functions of armour and artillery. The role of land forces would therefore be two-fold: small, elite units to assist in target identification and to help co-ordinate air attacks; and larger 'constabulary' forces whose job it would be to secure the ground. While such an approach reinforced some of the long-running themes in land warfare, such as the importance of air–ground co-operation, the potential implications of the 'Afghan Model' for existing land warfare doctrine, structures and training was profound, not least that techniques and structures of combined-arms co-ordination that had proved a foundation for success in land warfare in the past would be marginalised.

Land warfare: changing forms?

An alternative line of argument on the future of land warfare was that, even if land warfare capabilities continued to be of central importance, the traditional tenets of land warfare might no longer be relevant.

Again, the 1991 Gulf War was an important catalyst for this debate. The then US Secretary of Defense, Richard ('Dick') Cheney, argued that the Gulf War 'demonstrated dramatically the new possibilities of what has been called the "military–technical revolution in warfare"'. The rapid, decisive victory achieved in 1991 at minimal cost strengthened the hand of those who argued that the developments of the 1970s and 1980s could be taken further: that in the post-Cold War period, the United States had a unique opportunity to leverage the possibilities inherent in emerging technologies to produce a dramatic leap forward in military effectiveness. US thinking in the early and mid-1990s was led by the Pentagon's Office of Net Assessment and by such individuals within the military as Admiral William Owens, who became the Vice Chairman of the Joint Chiefs of Staff. The fruits of this new thinking were evident in a number of key Pentagon and Congressional documents, including *Joint Vision 2010*, produced in 1997, *Joint Vision 2020*, produced in 2000, and the Quadrennial Defense Reviews of 1997 and 2001. The basis of this thinking was founded on the perception that technology was providing new means for the conduct of war: improved precision; improved means for delivering firepower; and, crucially, new systems for collecting and processing information. Through greater integration and the creation of a 'system of systems' (see box 2.5), theorists argued that the US military would be able to achieve 'dominant battlespace awareness': a decisive information advantage that would allow the United States to manoeuvre and to apply massive force, rapidly and with great precision, while preventing the enemy from doing so. This would allow the United States to attain 'full-spectrum dominance': a decisive superiority in military effectiveness at every level of war. Later developed under the broader heading of 'Military Transformation', the implementation of these new ideas was accelerated under the Bush Administration. Full-spectrum dominance would be achieved by 'network-centric warfare' in order to realise 'effects-based warfare'; war would be conducted by a fully integrated military system directed not towards crude destruction but instead towards causing systemic shock and the consequent collapse of the enemy. For example, advances in technology allowed 'nodal targeting': the identification and precision destruction of the sorts of discrete targets that would have an effect throughout the enemy system, such as communications centres and headquarters.

The potential implications of these concepts for the way in which land warfare was conducted were profound. President George W. Bush asserted that 'Military Transformation' was a blueprint for an armed force that was 'defined less by size and more by mobility and swiftness, one that is easier to deploy and sustain, one that relies more heavily on stealth, precision weaponry and information technologies'. For the US Army, this meant land forces that were expeditionary in outlook. Organisationally, the focus was 'modularisation': the creation of modular, combined-arms manoeuvre brigade combat teams. Modularisation would allow greater flexibility and integration, a focus on smaller, more agile forces would improve sustainability and command and control. Underpinning this idea was the perception that new technology would enable new concepts and structures to

Box 2.5 The army as a system

Generically, a system is a set of interrelated elements that collectively form a whole. Armies are made up of many different systems: myriad units; organisations; command arrangements; multiple commmunications nets; logistic structures, and so on. Co-operation between these elements is required for effective command and control, movement, fighting and supply. Contemporary thinking about armies as systems has led to the emergence of two concepts: the 'system of systems' and 'systemic shock'.

A 'system of systems' is created through intense networking between systems, utilising new technology (especially digital communications) and associated procedures to create a more unified whole out of the distinct elements. This allows information to flow much more quickly and efficiently, which, in theory, dramatically increases the speed at which decisions can be made and the tempo at which operations can be conducted.

Conversely, it is possible to render enemy forces ineffective by destroying their capacity to function as a system, even if the enemy combat elements are still intact. This can be done by inducing 'systemic shock' in the enemy: paralysing the ability of the individual elements in an army to function together. This can be achieved through a variety of related means, including: disrupting enemy communications; attacking command-and-control infrastructure; undermining enemy decision-making through high-tempo operations; denying the enemy information; and undermining their morale.

allow smaller forces to deliver greater effects. 'Transformed' future land warfare would take established concepts in land warfare even further. Land warfare would be decisively joint: the battlefield would be a 'battlespace' marked by ground, sea, air, space and electro-magnetic environments; there would be even more effective combined-arms integration; mobility, digitalisation and information superiority would facilitate 'dominant manoeuvre', allowing smaller, more articulated land forces to manoeuvre coherently and at a high tempo, despite being more dispersed, against enemy vulnerabilities. Thus, a traditional focus in land warfare on mass and sequential operations would be replaced by simultaneity and an emphasis on effects. This kind of approach struck at the *raison d'être* of heavy armoured and mechanised forces.

These debates were driven by the United States, but the ideas had wider application. While it is unsurprising to note, for example, that such close US allies as the United Kingdom took on board many of these ideas, developing its own version of network-centric warfare, the influence of US debates on information warfare went much further a field. The magnitude of US victories in the 1991 Gulf War and in Afghanistan led the Chinese military to focus on improving their capabilities in those aspects of warfare that were perceived to lie at the heart of US success, notably joint operations and information warfare. The global influence of 'transformation' appeared illustrated by a US Government Accounting Report of 1997 indicating that over 100 nations were then planning 'modernisation', including states as diverse as Poland and Malaysia. Significantly, 'modernisation' seemed to be defined according to a set of common themes, including electronic warfare, professionalisation and precision technologies. The dominant paradigm for 'modern' armies appeared to be an RMA paradigm in which armies strove for five characteristics: doctrinal flexibility; strategic mobility; tailoring and modularity; joint and international connectivity; and the versatility to operate over the whole spectrum of war.

An RMA future?

Despite these debates, prognostications that an evolutionary, imitative land warfare past might be giving way to a revolutionary, innovative future remain far from forming a consensus. Advocates of the RMA as the new standard of modern land warfare are open to several important criticisms.

The continuing role of land power

It is symptomatic of the difficulties associated with learning relevant lessons from past conflicts that early assumptions about the reduced role of land power in future warfare have since been contested and that the assertions of a revolutionary relationship between land and air power have been replaced with more evolutionary conclusions. The 1991 Gulf War is a case in point. Air power made an important contribution to victory. For example, Coalition air superiority reduced Iraqi road traffic into Kuwait by 90 per cent; it may have inflicted up to 40 per cent attrition on Iraqi armoured vehicles; it disrupted Iraqi command, control and supply; and it undermined Iraqi morale. Despite this, key elements of the Iraqi Army were able to move and did fight. Only six hours after the Coalition flanking operation began, Iraqi heavy forces manoeuvred into blocking positions. In the nine set-piece battles facing the Coalition flanking forces, the Iraqis displayed a willingness to fight, had the ammunition and supply to do so, had favourable force ratios by current doctrinal standards and were often deployed in prepared positions. Yet they were still annihilated: in the nine battles, the Iraqis lost more than 600 vehicles and killed only 2 US soldiers. Although technology was an important enabler, it is worth noting that even less well-quipped units, such as the Marines, scored equivalent success. Victory in the Gulf War thus still required potentially very costly ground battles; that these ground battles were so one-sided reflected not just the enabling effects of air power and technology, but fundamentally more effective techniques in land warfare

Table 2.3 The RMA system-of-systems argument

Battlespace awareness

INTELLIGENCE
SURVEILLANCE
RECONNAISSANCE

Near-perfect battle
assessment

Dominant battlespace
knowledge

ACCURATE
PRECISE
APPLICATION

COMMAND
CONTROL
COMMUNICATIONS
COMPUTERS
INTELLIGENCE

Precision force

Nodal targeting,
communication

Near-perfect mission
assignment

Source: James R. Blaker, *Understanding the Revolution in Military Affairs (RMA): A Guide to America's 21st Century Defense* (Washington, DC: Progressive Policy Institute Report, 1997), p. 10.

founded upon effective combined-arms warfare: dispersal; co-ordination; fire-and-manoeuvre; and mission command.

Similar conclusions can be drawn regarding the experiences in Afghanistan. Early successes against inexperienced Taliban fighters progressively gave way to tougher fights against more experienced al-Qaeda personnel. Learning their vulnerability to US air power, al-Qaeda fighters began to emphasise successfully techniques designed to counter the effects of air power, including the use of cover, dispersal, camouflage, deception and 'hugging' Coalition forces. By mitigating the effects of air power, al-Qaeda forced the Coalition forces to re-emphasise the use of larger quantities of better-quality ground forces with a stress on such traditional skills as fire-and-manoeuvre. Kosovo, too, was illustrative more of conventional wisdom than of a revolution in the relationship between land and air power. Without the pressing need to concentrate their forces to meet a ground threat, the Serbs were able to take steps to counter NATO air power. Dispersal, camouflage and the use of dummies meant that the physical damage done to Serb forces was minimal; assessments after the war placed the actual number of tanks, armoured personnel carriers and artillery pieces destroyed at fewer than fifty. Eventual NATO success resulted from the growing threat of a ground war: the concentration of forces by the Serbs required to meet this threat would undoubtedly have dramatically increased the efficacy of NATO air power, illustrating the synergistic effect of having effective air and land capabilities.

Continuities in warfare

The broader debate on the form that land warfare might take has also been subject to important critiques. One obvious point is that many of the precepts of 'post-modern' land warfare are hardly new: jointery, combined arms, manoeuvre, dispersal, surprise, flexibility, disruption, simultaneity and tempo, for example, are core themes in the evolution of modern warfare. The 1991 Gulf War and the 2003 Iraq War were both very conventional victories in this sense. In the end, even the latter war was a twentieth-century fight, albeit with improved jointery, tempo, precision firepower and intelligence. This was made even more the case by the fact that many of the key 'transformative' systems relating to command, communications and logistics did not work effectively when subjected to the friction of real combat. One might pose the question, then, whether successes in conventional operations against Iraq in 1991 and 2003 were because of the application of a new paradigm in warfare or whether, to parallel the German experiences of 1939 and 1940, the one-sided victories reflected the proper application of evolutionary techniques against poor-quality opposition.

Ethnocentrism and future warfare

Current debates on the future of land warfare have also been criticised as essentially ethnocentric: they fail to recognise the extent to which Western views on future land warfare may be an expression of unspoken assumptions or desires on the part of Western states regarding how they would *like* war to be fought. Western debates on the future of warfare often stress the role of technological solutions to political and social problems; this 'technism' or 'cyborgism' has led to the argument that post-modern war is as much a cultural phenomenon or an ideology as it is an objective reflection of reality. US strategic culture, for example, has a tendency to emphasise technology, decisiveness and efficiency. Thus, future war has been seen as 'virtual war' or 'post-heroic war', in which warfare can be conducted at a distance without much of its traditional savagery. This is a 'de-bellicisation' of war, in essence 'victimless war', with an emphasis on disruption rather than destruction. As part of this, Jeremy Black detects an RAM, a Revolution in Attitudes to the Military,[29] that includes not just unwillingness to accept military casualties but an unease at causing enemy casualties (reflected in the hand-wringing over Kosovo in 1999) and even unease at causing enemy military casualties (evidenced by the disquiet caused by images of the 'Road of Death' during the 1991 Gulf War).

It may be, then, that contemporary debates on land warfare, with their focus on the rapid application of overwhelming military power, on manoeuvre rather than attrition and on disruption rather than destruction are expressions of the sorts of war the West would like to fight, rather than those it is likely to face. Robert R. Tomes, for example, ponders the existence of a 'rapid dominance *zeitgeist*' in Western strategic culture, an

Figure 2.5 M1 Abrams Main Battle Tank during a cordon-and-search operation in Biaj, Iraq, 2006. Even 'low-intensity' operations can have high-intensity components, especially at the tactical level.

affinity for 'temporal escalation' and decisiveness that leads Western militaries to focus on sudden brilliance as the acme of military skill rather than such concepts as protraction or attrition.[30] There may be a real danger that armies that focus on manoeuvre warfare solutions fail to understand a lesson from the Second World War: unless the disparity between the quality of the protagonists is very marked (and the war is therefore won very quickly), modern warfare has a tendency to return to attrition.

The present as future

A related challenge is the argument that RMA enthusiasts may too often be unable to distinguish what is transient from that which constitutes long-term change. This is reflected in the tendency to take current, specifically Western experiences and extrapolate them forward and generally as the 'nature of future land warfare', ignoring the 'contingent character of warfare' outlined in chapter 1. The challenges of Western land warfare in terms of the political problems associated with deployments, an aversion to casualties (on either side) and a desire for ever-greater precision are related in part to Western policies, particularly the use of land forces in 'wars of choice'. Thus, there is a tendency to conflate the 'nature of land warfare' with the 'character of contemporary Western land warfare'. Yet the two are very different. As noted in chapter 1, the nature of warfare does not change; its character does. But there is far from being a consensus on the character of future warfare. Since 1945, 90 per cent of conflicts have been civil wars fought with relatively simple weapons. Arguments have been made on this basis that land warfare is, in some senses, moving backwards, and that high-intensity conventional land warfare is much less relevant. In this 'neo-medieval' or 'Fourth-Generation' future (see box 2.6), local savagery, terrorism and non-state actors may be key. Then again, other commentators, such as Colin Gray, have made equally plausible arguments that conventional high-intensity warfare between states is far from obsolete.[31] Certainly, such states as India or China continue to regard conventional land warfare capabilities as crucial.

Future warfare and military culture

In relation to this uncertain future, the attachment of many contemporary armies to a model of a modern army that reflects the RMA ideal may stem from institutional cultures rather than objective reality. One pessimistic conclusion might be that the RMA debate is illustrative of a 'rhetoric–reality disconnect', in that the core concepts of 'post-modern' land warfare, with its emphasis on rapidity and decisiveness, do not fit with the broader Global War on Terror and low-intensity operations. The RMA military has become the 'paradigm army' of the twenty-first century: a model of a 'modern' army that serves to legitimise militaries in their own eyes and in the eyes of others. The fact that so many diverse states have accepted this model does not automatically mean that it is related to objective conditions (or indeed that it is militarily effective); rather, it may say more about how military professionals see themselves and how they want others to see them. In a sense, RMA land warfare may actually reduce military effectiveness, particularly by ignoring the importance of numbers and over-stating the importance of information and integration. One lesson from Afghanistan, reinforced by the 2003 Iraq War, is that winning the conventional battle is not enough: securing the peace is crucial if conventional success is to have any meaning. However, securing the peace has often required far more troops than winning the battle. In fact, this is an old lesson: in April 1941, Germany defeated Yugoslavia in a week, losing only 151 men. Three years later, 350,000 German troops and their allies were still there trying to pacify the country. Similarly, a focus on the importance of information is fine as far as it goes, but information is not intelligence. Intelligence is what is produced from the analysis of information. Good intelligence is related as much to *how* information is analysed as it is to the volume of information available. Moreover, a system designed to produce near-perfect knowledge is likely to create so much information that it may result in information overload and decision-making paralysis.

Box 2.6 Fourth-Generation Warfare (4GW)

In his book *The Sling and the Stone*, Colonel Thomas X. Hammes argues that the contemporary conflicts in Iraq and Afghanistan are symptomatic of a new 'Fourth Generation' in warfare. First-Generation Warfare was horse-and-musket warfare, exemplified by the Napoleonic Wars. Second-Generation Warfare was the rifle-and-railway warfare that evolved from the American Civil War to the First World War. Third-Generation Warfare encompassed blitzkrieg and manoeuvre warfare.

Fourth-Generation Warfare (4GW), however, represents an evolution in insurgency. Fourth-Generation Warfare is marked by a focus on the higher-level political decision-making of the enemy. Using political, economic and social networks, as well as military action, Fourth-Generation Warfare seeks to undermine the enemy's political will to fight.

The premium placed upon ever-greater integration may be equally problematic. Integration can create vulnerability: a highly integrated military system may suffer if one or more parts cannot perform as expected; for example, if terrain prevents the deployment of heavy equipment, or if terrain, weather or enemy counter-measures undermine communications. The very complexity of highly integrated systems ensures that shocks are transferred quickly. Thus, the more integrated a system an army is, the more likely it may be that it will itself be systemically shocked if the conditions of battle do not conform to expected parameters. This challenge is also reflected in the broader trade-offs in land warfare between efficiency and effectiveness: the means used to promote technological efficiency does not necessarily improve military effectiveness. This problem goes to the heart of criticism of the adoption of some business practices in land warfare, such as the contemporary focus on new ideas of 'just-in-time logistics', in which digitalisation of logistics leads to the integration of the entire logistics organisation into one large synchronised system, which is designed to reduce the logistic footprints of armies. However applicable this concept may be to business, it requires a reliable, predictable environment; in other words, an environment that, as the preceding chapter has demonstrated, is fundamentally at odds with the nature of warfare. However 'inefficient' the holding of large logistic stocks may be, it also insulates a logistics system from unexpected shocks. Since, as noted in the preceding chapter, war is the realm of uncertainty, 'inefficient' practices may help to sustain effectiveness. Another example is provided by air support: greater efficiency, in terms of such measurables as sortie rates, is best achieved through attacks on pre-planned targets. However, this reduces the flexibility and the effectiveness of what the air power can deliver in response to unfolding events.

In the end, then, the future of conventional land warfare is far from certain. Conventional land warfare may currently be overshadowed by the demands of irregular warfare. But this may simply be a Western perspective shaped by operations in Iraq and Afghanistan rather than a general assumption shared by such other states as India or China. Even if this perspective were true, we cannot guarantee that it will remain so in the medium to long term. It may be that future land warfare will be dominated by the revolutionary impact of new technologies and their application, through innovative new concepts that will produce a dramatically more effective form of land warfare. As the discussion has noted, however, there is far from being a consensus that the RMA paradigm will be the dominant future context for land warfare, or even if it will be relevant. At the beginning of this century, one only needs to look back at the beginning of the last to determine the challenges of predicting the future of land warfare and the potential consequences of flawed assumptions.

The preceding discussion demonstrates, first, that there would appear to be a strong evolutionary dynamic in the way in which land warfare has developed over time. In this respect, there are strong parallels between developments on land and those in the air and maritime environments, even if, on land, most change has been at the tactical and operational levels. The infiltration tactics of 1917–18, blitzkrieg and manoeuvre warfare form much more of a continuum of development than they do radical discontinuities. The recurrence of such themes as combined arms, joint warfare, fire-and-manoeuvre, flexibility, decentralisation and depth suggests that, all other things being equal, a greater proficiency in these things relative to the enemy is likely to promote the chances of military success.

Second, however, all other things are rarely equal. Traditional Western 'meta-narratives' on the development of warfare often focus on such tangibles as technology and weapons systems. However, the adaptive nature of warfare generates varied responses conditioned by broader political, economic, cultural and societal factors. For many states, the assumed norms of Western land warfare may be irrelevant, unsuitable or impossible to implement. These states may adapt elements of Western techniques or compensate through political or unconventional strategies. Even in Western states, land warfare has been marked by the parallel existence of different approaches. This divergence may worsen in the future if the United States moves further down the RMA road.

Third, we should be suspicious of a focus on decisive success and the idea that there is one conventional military doctrine that can guarantee victory. Military effectiveness may lie more with intangibles, such as the capacity to adapt relative to the opponent, than with technological tangibles, such as information systems or precision firepower. We should also not forget that military effectiveness, in terms of the capacity to defeat an enemy's conventional capabilities, does not relate in a linear fashion to overall political success, which, after all, is what counts in the final analysis. Success in land warfare is contingent; it is dependent, among other things, upon the broader political context. In the Suez Crisis of 1956, for example, actual combat operations demonstrated the superiority of the British and French military system against the Egyptians'; but the operation still failed to achieve its political objectives. It is not irrelevant that the German Army, widely studied for the quality of its tactical and operational techniques, lost two world wars. Equally, North Vietnam was roundly beaten in 1968 and 1972 when it resorted to conventional operations, but it won the war just the same.

NOTES

1 *Land Warfare Doctrine 1: The Fundamentals of Land Warfare* (Australian Army, 2002), chapter 1, p. 1. www.defence.gov.au/army/LWD/.htm.
2 Stephen Biddle, *Military Power: Explaining Victory and Defeat in Modern Battle* (Princeton, NJ: Princeton University Press, 2004), p. 36.
3 Quoted in David Lonsdale, *The Nature of War in the Information Age: Clausewitzian Future* (London: Frank Cass, 2004), p. 50.
4 *Ibid.*, p. 69.
5 Biddle, *Military Power*, p. 30.
6 Martin van Creveld, *Command in War* (London: Harvard University Press, 1985), pp. 1–10.
7 *Ibid.*, pp. 231–2.
8 Quoted in J. P. Kiszely, 'The Contribution of Originality to Military Success', in Brian Holden Reid, ed., *The Science of War: Back to First Principles* (London: Routledge, 1993), p. 26.
9 Biddle, *Military Power*, p. 3.
10 Quoted in Jay Luvaas, *The Military Legacy of the Civil War: The European Inheritance* (Kansas, KS: University Press of Kansas, 1988), p. 167.
11 *Ibid.*, p. 167.
12 Colin McInnes, *Men, Machines and the Emergence of Modern Warfare, 1914–1945* (Camberely: Strategic and Combat Studies Institute, 1992), p. 8.
13 Michael Glover, *Warfare from Waterloo to Mons* (London: Book Club Associates, 1980), p. 248.
14 *Ibid.*
15 Biddle, *Military Power*, p. 28.
16 It was at Cannae that Hannibal achieved a successful, and since widely studied, envelopment of a Roman army in 216 BC. See also chapter 1 above, p. 28.
17 There is still debate as to whether the Polish campaign was really blitzkrieg at all, given that the use of mobile armoured forces was still overwhelmingly tactical in conception.

18 Total casualties (including replacements) as compared with initial strength.

19 Quoted in Michael Evans, *The Primacy of Doctrine: The United States Army and Military Innovation and Reforms, 1945–1995* (Canberra: Directorate of Army Research and Analysis, Dept of Defence, 1996), p. 3.

20 *Ibid.*, p. 9.

21 David Glantz, *Soviet Military Operational Art: In Pursuit of Deep Battle* (London: Frank Cass, 1991), p. 38.

22 *Ibid.*

23 Martin van Creveld, 'Technology and War II: Postmodern War?', in Charles Townshend, ed., *The Oxford Illustrated History of Modern War* (Oxford: Oxford University Press, 1997), pp. 311–12.

24 Victor Davis Hanson, *Why the West Has Won* (New York: Faber and Faber, 2002); Williamson Murray, 'The Future of Western Warfare', in Geoffrey Parker, ed., *The Cambridge History of Warfare* (Cambridge: Cambridge University Press, 2005), p. 417.

25 Jeremy Black, 'Military Organisations and Military Change in Historical Perspective', *The Journal of Military History* 62:4 (October 1998): 886.

26 Robert M. Citino, *Blitzkrieg to Desert Storm: The Evolution of Operational Warfare* (Lawrence, KS: University of Kansas, 2004), pp. 209–11.

27 Daryl G. Press, 'The Myth of Air Power in the Persian Gulf War and the Future of Warfare', *International Security* 26:2 (Fall 2001): 37.

28 Richard Hallion and the Gulf War Air Power Survey respectively, quoted in Press, 'The Myth of Air Power', 10.

29 Jeremy Black, *War: Past, Present, and Future* (New York: St Martin's Press, 2000), pp. 245–6.

30 Robert R. Tomes, 'Schlock and Blah: Counter-Insurgency Realities in a Rapid Dominance Era', *Small Wars and Insurgencies* INFO: 16:1 (March 2005): 41.

31 Colin S. Gray, *Another Bloody Century: Future Warfare* (London: Weidenfeld & Nicolson, 2005), pp. 170–211.

FURTHER READING

Adams, Thomas K., *The Army after Next: The First Post-Industrial Army* (London: Praeger, 2006).
A critical analysis of the application of the concepts of Military Transformation and the RMA.

Biddle, Stephen, *Military Power: Explaining Victory and Defeat in Modern Battle* (Princeton, NJ: Princeton University Press, 2004).
A compelling analysis of the nature and development of the modern system of warfare.

Black, Jeremy, *War since 1945* (London: Reaktion, 2004).
An antidote to Eurocentric, Cold War-focused analyses of warfare.

van Creveld, Martin, *Supplying War: Logistics from Wallenstein to Patton* (Cambridge: Cambridge University Press, 1977).
A thought-provoking book on a subject that is often ignored in accounts of land warfare.

Freiser, Karl-Heinz, *The Blitzkrieg Legend: The 1940 Campaign in the West* (Annapolis, MD: Naval Institute Press, 2005).
Discusses the essentially evolutionary origins of German doctrines for operational-level mobile warfare.

Glantz, David, *Soviet Military Operational Art: In Pursuit of Deep Battle* (London: Frank Cass, 1991).
Charts the development of Soviet thinking on operational art from its origins in the 1920s to the doctrines of the Cold War.

Griffiths, Paddy, *Forward into Battle: Fighting Tactics from Waterloo to the Near Future* (Swindon: Crowood, 1990).
Focuses on the evolutionary nature of modern battle tactics.

House, Jonathan, *Combined Arms Warfare in the Twentieth Century* (Lawrence, KS: Kansas University Press, 2001).
A detailed survey of developments in land warfare from the late nineteenth century to the 1990s.

Leonhard, Robert, *The Art of Maneuver: Maneuver-Warfare Theory and AirLand Battle* (New York: Ballantine, 1991).
An introduction to US operational art and manoeuvre warfare and its application to the doctrine of AirLand Battle.

Lupfer, Timothy, *The Dynamics of Doctrine: The Changes in German Tactical Doctrine during the First World War* (Kansas, KS: Combat Studies Institute, July 1981).
Explains the development of German infiltration tactics.

Pollack, Kenneth M., *Arabs at War: Military Effectiveness, 1948–1991* (Lincoln, NE: University of Nebraska, 2002).
A fascinating case study of the challenges of absorbing Western norms in land warfare.

Scales, Robert H., Jr., *Yellow Smoke: The Future of Land Warfare for America's Military* (Lanham, MD: Rowman and Littlefield, 2006).
A Western-centric, RMA-inspired view on the future character of land warfare.

Shambaugh, David, *Modernizing China's Military: Progress, Problems, and Prospects* (Berkeley, CA: University of Califonia, 2004).
An important study of how China views the challenges of modern warfare.

Sheffield, Gary, *Forgotten Victory: The First World War – Myths and Realities* (London: Headline, 2001).
Highlights convincingly how far land warfare had developed by 1918.

Sondhaus, Lawrence, *Strategic Culture and Ways of War* (London: Routledge, 2006).
Explores cultural contexts and their impact on militaries.

Strachan, Hew, *European Armies and the Conduct of War* (London: Allen & Unwin, 1983).
An excellent overview of European warfare from the eighteenth century through to 1945.

CHAPTER 3

NAVAL WARFARE

CONTENTS

KEY THEMES

- Naval warfare revolves around the use, or the denial of the use, of the sea.
- Navies attempt to use the sea in order to influence events on land.
- The maritime environment offers a potential for manoeuvre that can be exploited by navies to provide military advantage and to generate leverage.
- Many of the concepts and theories pertaining to military operations on land do not apply at sea. In order to understand naval warfare, one must address a distinct body of thought known as maritime strategy.
- While naval tactics change over time, there is a considerable amount of continuity in the strategic and operational roles fulfilled by navies.
- An examination of the history of modern naval warfare suggests that today navies have an enhanced ability directly to influence events ashore as compared with the past, but that they continue to face a range of serious military challenges when seeking to do so.

Success in naval warfare provides one of the most important keys to success in war. Indeed, there is a remarkable correlation between strength at sea and success in modern war that defies explanation as coincidence. According to one eminent commentator, 'great sea powers or maritime coalitions have either won or, occasionally, drawn every major conflict in modern history'.[1] That they have been able to achieve this remarkable run of success reflects upon the strategic leverage that navies can generate, and this, in turn, is a result of the operational and tactical possibilities inherent in naval and wider maritime activity.

This chapter will examine the ideas, concepts and principles that are required to develop an understanding of naval warfare in the twentieth and twenty-first centuries. Given their unique working environment, navies operate in a very different manner from both armies and air forces, as discussed in chapters 2 and 4. Put simply, war at sea is different from war on land: many of the concepts and principles pertaining on land apply either differently or not at all at sea, notwithstanding some continuity between the use of land- and sea-based aircraft. To understand naval warfare and to comprehend the terms within which debates about such warfare have been expressed, one needs to address a particular set of concepts and principles relating to maritime strategy. Defined in 1911 by Sir Julian Corbett as 'the principles which govern a war in which the sea is a substantial factor',[2] such strategy goes beyond the activity of navies, setting naval activity within the broader national strategy. Naval warfare is therefore a sub-set of maritime strategy and can only be properly under-

Box 3.1 Definition of 'naval' and 'maritime'

Naval: refers to dedicated seaborne military forces, such as warships, submarines, auxiliaries and aircraft operating from ships. It can also be used in reference to land-based infrastructure and administration devoted to the support of these systems. In essence, 'naval' refers to the activities of navies.

Maritime: an overarching subject that encompasses the full range of mankind's relationship to the seas and oceans. The notion of maritime power therefore encompasses all naval forces and activity in addition to all non-military uses of the sea, such as merchant shipping and fishing. It also refers to all other assets and capabilities that directly influence the ability of a state or organisation to use the sea. This might include land-based aircraft, coastal artillery and missiles, space-based systems, such as communications and surveillance satellites, a facility for effective maritime insurance and a variety of other factors that are not necessarily naval in origin.

stood within this context. To put this into terms that Clausewitz might have recognised (see chapter 1), naval warfare may have a certain 'grammar', but maritime strategy provides the 'logic', by integrating narrow naval concerns into national strategy.

This chapter will address the grammar of naval warfare and the logic that is provided by maritime strategy. In common with chapters 2 and 4 on land and air operations, it will begin with a discussion of the key concepts relating to naval warfare. As with the other chapters, this will include an examination of the particular nature of the operating environment, in addition to a discussion of the attributes of naval forces. It will also include an appraisal of the ideas and theories of traditional maritime strategists, as this provides a necessary starting-point for an examination of the principles and concepts of naval warfare that they espoused and that continue to influence thinking about naval warfare today. The final part of this chapter is devoted to an examination of the development of naval warfare from 1900 until the present day in which it will be argued that, despite changes at the tactical and technological levels of naval activity, these long-established concepts continue to provide a useful means of understanding naval warfare, and that navies continue to provide one of the most important keys to success in war and armed conflict.

Naval warfare is profoundly shaped by the nature of the maritime environment. It is the nature of this environment that gives the forces that operate within it their particular characteristics. An understanding of the maritime environment and of the particular attributes of naval forces is therefore a basic prerequisite for understanding naval warfare.

The particular characteristics of the sea, and of naval forces, have led to the development of a series of concepts and principles peculiar to naval warfare. This is not to suggest that the traditional principles of war, as noted in chapter 2, do not apply at sea. In most respects they do, and this point is emphasised in current US naval doctrine.[3] However, it might be suggested that this is, at least in part, because the principles of war themselves are so anodyne as to make them applicable, in some way or another, to almost any situation. They say little about the way in which war is actually conducted at sea. In order to understand naval warfare and, in particular, to understand the thought processes that lie behind much modern naval activity, it is necessary to be conversant with distinctly naval concepts and principles. This, in turn, requires a familiarity with the work of the traditional maritime strategists who first articulated and popularised such concepts. The impact of the most notable of these, Alfred Thayer Mahan (1840–1914), was reflected in the 1940s by the former US Secretary of War, Henry Stimson, when he complained that the Navy Department frequently 'seemed to retire from the realm of logic into a dim religious world in which Neptune was God, Mahan his prophet and the United States Navy the only true Church'.[4]

Of course, it could be suggested that a conceptual approach derived primarily from an analysis of naval warfare during the age of sail, as was that of Mahan and many of his contemporaries, might find itself increasingly outdated, given the dramatic changes in ship design and armament and in the tactical conduct of naval operations that have occurred since the nineteenth century. The contention of this chapter is that, while change is a recurring feature at the tactical level of naval warfare, at the strategic and operational levels the established concepts and principles retain much utility. This point will be examined later (pp. 166–70) and returned to in the chapter conclusion (pp. 173–74).

The maritime environment

There are three obvious features of the maritime environment, namely the sea: it is vast; it is featureless; and, for the most part, it is empty. In combination, these simple facts have a profound influence on naval warfare.

Size and connectivity

The sea covers 70 per cent of the earth's surface. This may be 30 per cent less coverage than is provided by air (see chapter 4), but, in stark contrast to the land and the air above it, which are criss-crossed by innumerable physical and political barriers, the sea provides a medium for transportation that is freely available to all in peacetime and is difficult to deny to a superior navy in war. By using the medium of the sea, ships provide a means of bulk transportation greatly superior to their land- and air-based alternatives. With over 90 per cent of global trade (by weight and volume) carried by ships, this is as true today as it has always been. The importance of the sea to trade and the importance of trade to national and international prosperity have made attacks on, and defence of, trade a key feature of naval warfare over the centuries. Maintaining the free flow of international trade remains one of the most important objectives of US naval policy today.

With the exception of such inland seas as the Caspian and the Aral, the different oceans and seas of the world in effect represent a single continuous world ocean. Distant lands that are bounded by the sea are thus connected by what is, in essence, a broad highway or, more accurately, a series of highways. In the words of current Indian maritime doctrine, naval forces can therefore exploit the maritime environment to 'provide a spatial interconnectivity between every country that has a coastline'.[5] As Colin Gray emphasises, the connectivity provided by the sea has frequently allowed dominant sea powers to knit together maritime coalitions with a total strategic weight greatly in excess of those secured by dominant continental powers.[6] If one controls the seas, one controls access to most of the world's resources. Furthermore, the ability to make use of the access provided by these ocean highways offers navies a potential for manoeuvre on a global scale, and in wartime their use can be decisive. Conversely, to those unable to use it the sea can act as an impenetrable barrier. The German intention to invade Britain in 1940 and Communist China's ambitions towards Taiwan in the 1950s were thwarted owing to the aggressors' inability to exploit maritime communications.

Emptiness

With the exception of the ships that traverse them, and of a small number of offshore oil platforms and the like, the seas are empty. They do not have a permanent resident human population. There is no one to comment on the passing of enemy vessels, and ships do not leave footprints in the ground. This, in conjunction with the size of the seas and the ability of ships to travel hundreds of miles each day, makes it generally much harder for naval forces to find each other than is the case with armies on land. Given that the sea is empty, and that there is no resident population, industry or agriculture to defend, the consequences of declining battle at sea are less severe than on land. This makes it easier for an inferior maritime force to avoid a superior opponent. The enemy cannot occupy the deserted battlefield in any meaningful way. Naval warfare therefore focuses on the use, or the denial of the use, of the sea rather than the physical control of something that can be neither occupied nor fortified.

The lack of a resident population also means that combat at sea can often occur without the threat of the collateral damage that is a feature of most land operations. This may imply that the use of military force at sea has fewer political complications than its equivalent on land. During the Cold War, this led to speculation that the use of tactical nuclear weapons at sea would be more permissible and therefore more likely than their use against targets ashore. However, in reality, most maritime activity occurs in relative proximity to the shore in what is frequently referred to as the 'littoral' region. The littorals are often a focus for civilian shipping and are also traversed by commercial airline routes. Far from being free from the threat of collateral damage, they may be relatively cluttered, offering great potential for mishap. The events of 3 July 1988, when the American cruiser USS *Vincennes* shot down an Iran Air Airbus A300 with the loss of 290 innocent civilian lives in the mistaken belief that it was a hostile Iranian F-14 fighter, illustrate the dangers and the challenges facing commanders who may have seconds to decide whether a radar contact is benign or signifies an attack in progress. The *Vincennes* acted as if it was the latter, and the result was a tragedy. The previous year, an American frigate, the USS *Stark*, had chosen an alternative course of action and suffered an attack from an Iraqi fighter-bomber, resulting in the death of thirty-seven US personnel.

Physical features

Geographical factors are important in naval warfare. The particular features of a coastline, the existence of inlets or fjords, and the presence or otherwise of offshore islands, rocks and shoals all have an impact on inshore operations. Geographical and topographical factors can also have a broader impact on the ability to gain access to the sea, as, for example, narrow straits may cause choke-points that inhibit access to the high seas. The presence, or otherwise, of bases and supporting infrastructure ashore can also affect a navy's ability to operate in a given region. Physical factors are also important in operations below the surface. The depth, warmth, ambient noise levels and salinity of sea areas vary according to circumstances, and this can significantly complicate the process of detecting enemy submarines. A good understanding of hydrographic conditions is thus important in modern warfare and can give local forces an advantage over opponents unused to a particular area. However, in comparison with the land, the sea itself is featureless. There is no terrain that can be exploited to the advantage of the defence. A weaker naval force has less ability to mitigate qualitative or quantitative inferiority than its equivalent on land, another factor that inclines such forces to avoid battle.

Platforms

Because one cannot live on or travel across the sea without recourse to some form of vessel, activity at sea is necessarily focused on platforms, the people that operate these platforms and what one can do with them. Without such platforms, one cannot survive at sea, and the sea itself can sometimes pose a deadly threat to them. It is fair to say that at sea one must fight and survive the environment before fighting the enemy. Naval warfare is therefore more 'platform-centric' than its equivalent on land. These platforms tend to be expensive, meaning that they are generally few in number when compared with their equivalents on land or in the air. Naval warfare is thus characterised by engagements between relatively few high-value assets. These assets are difficult to replace, and impossible to replace quickly, yet may be sunk within minutes of engaging an opponent. While ships may have built into their design specifications the ability to absorb considerable punishment, they lack the recuperative qualities of, say, an armoured division that may be shattered in combat yet still be able to withdraw, re-equip and take in replacement personnel. Unlike the armoured division, the fighting power of the ship is not disaggregated into smaller units many of which will survive all but the most disastrous engagement. This brings us to another feature of naval warfare: it is deadly and decisive. The major naval battles of the twentieth century were decided in hours, or even minutes, whereas on land they tended to last days, weeks and even months. The potential for catastrophic defeat within a short space of time is yet another feature of naval warfare that inclines many commanders towards caution.

Attributes of naval forces

It is often claimed that naval forces have distinctive operational attributes that are derived from the forces themselves and from the medium in which they operate. In contemporary British maritime doctrine these attributes are identified as: access; mobility; versatility; sustained reach; resilience; lift capacity; poise; and leverage. Each of these is discussed below.

Access

This attribute is directly connected with the nature of the sea itself. As much of the world is covered by water and most of this area is accessible to maritime forces, the ability to use the sea can be exploited to provide access to areas of interest. A range of physical, military or political factors might limit access, but such limitations tend to affect maritime forces far less than their land-based alternatives.

Mobility

Maritime forces are by their very nature mobile. In stark contrast to its land-based counterparts, a modern ship or task force can easily sail 400 miles a day, every day, for thousands of miles with no ill-effects, and it can be ready to fight throughout this journey. This mobility provides a potential for manoeuvre that can be exploited at the strategic, operational and tactical levels.

Versatility

Maritime forces can be very versatile. Warships can be designed to fulfil a wide range of functions, from disaster relief to high-intensity warfighting, and can move from role to role without the need to be re-equipped. Naval task forces, comprised of ships with different capabilities, are even more flexible and adaptable.

Sustained reach

Some ships, such as the triremes of Ancient Greece or the motor torpedo boats of the 1940s, were designed to operate relatively close to land and were not intended for oceanic voyages. Other vessels, including most large warships today, have impressive endurance and offer the ability to project forces at great distances for a long period of time, particularly when supported by a network of overseas bases or by an ability to conduct supply and replenishment afloat.

Resilience

Ships can be designed to take a considerable amount of damage before they become non-operational. Even in the missile age, it is not necessarily the case that a hit equates to a kill. In any case, resilience is not simply a function of the survival of an individual vessel, any more than in land warfare it reflects the survival of an individual unit. Resilience reflects the ability of the maritime force overall to survive and to complete its mission. Well-equipped and well-balanced fleets have proven to be extremely resilient despite the loss of individual and sometimes multiple units.

Lift capacity

Ships can carry and transport large and bulky items much more effectively than alternative means of transportation can. For example, the US Lockheed C-5 Galaxy heavy-lift aircraft can carry a single main battle tank or similar heavy vehicle. One Bay class landing ship, operated by the British Royal Fleet Auxiliary, can embark 32 main battle tanks or 150 light trucks in addition to 356 troops and 3 landing craft.

Poise

Once maritime forces have been deployed to a theatre, they can remain on station for an extended period of time. The endurance of individual vessels may allow them to remain deployed for weeks or months, particularly if they are supported by an ability to conduct replenishment at sea. Of equal importance is the fact that, by operating on the sea, they can remain in international waters without the need to negotiate basing rights and without infringing the sovereignty of any third party. By choosing to remain out of sight of land they can also, if they wish, take tangible steps to reduce their profile without reducing their capabilities in any

Figure 3.1 The Nimitz class aircraft carrier USS *Dwight D. Eisenhower* sails in formation with two Arleigh Burke class destroyers and a Ticonderoga class cruiser. Together these vessels represent a formidable combination of naval power that can be exerted at sea or against the shore using guns, missiles or aircraft.

way. They can remain poised for action without actually being committed to anything.

Leverage

It is posited that maritime forces can generate a disproportionate amount of leverage ashore by using suitable positioning and force packaging to exploit access.

In many respects, the first six attributes in this list relate to the ability of a maritime force to establish and maintain access to a particular region at the time and place of choice. This access can then be translated into leverage, depending, of course, on circumstances. Leverage might therefore more properly be described as a potential result of these attributes rather than an attribute itself. Nevertheless, the claim in British doctrine that '[m]aritime forces can maintain presence without occupation; coercion without embroilment' reflects a central tenet of much contemporary writing about maritime power.[7]

The particular utility of maritime power is, therefore, founded upon an ability for sustained manoeuvre that navies can exploit because of the nature of the environment that they operate in. This can provide useful options in wartime. It also has important political consequences in situations short of all-out war. It means that ships can be deployed overseas without having to cross any territorial boundaries. They can poise in international waters without infringing any state's sovereignty and without the need to negotiate basing rights. While at sea they are far less visible than their land-based equivalents, both in a literal and a figurative sense. This means that the deployment of naval forces can be less provocative than that of air forces or armies. The routine deployment of individual ships, task groups or even entire fleets into particular regions is generally less likely to excite adverse comment than the deployment of a squadron of land-based aircraft or of ground forces, both of which require a footprint ashore that can become the focus for political dissent. All of these factors mean that maritime forces can have a particular diplomatic utility, reflected in the Indian Navy's claim that 'navies are the only legitimate, non-provocative trans-border military capability'.[8] Recently there have been political and legal developments that appear to some to have threatened that freedom of manoeuvre, including the extension of 'territorial seas' out to 12 nautical miles from the shoreline. However, to date, such moves have not seriously undermined the ability of navies to exploit the traditional freedom of the sea. And the US Navy, among others, has been pro-active in asserting its rights of passage.

Principles of naval warfare

Maritime strategy

The ability to generate maritime power and to take advantage of these operational attributes does not come automatically with proximity to the sea. It depends upon an ability to exploit the maritime environment. Naturally, much of the literature relating to naval warfare is focused on the ways and means to achieve such exploitation. Historically, there has been a paucity of material emanating from countries in the Asia-Pacific region that is puzzling, given the importance that naval warfare and maritime trade has played in that region. There is, however, a rich tradition of European and Arab writing on the subject, of which King Alfonso X of Castile's *Of the War That Is Made on the Sea* (1270), the writings of Ahmad bin Majid in Julfar two hundred years later and the Omani Suleiman al Malin's *Fundamentals of the Mastery of Naval Science* (1511) are just three examples.[9]

Modern, professional naval history and the principles and concepts that dominated thinking about naval warfare throughout the twentieth century have their origins in pioneering work undertaken in Britain from the 1860s by John and Philip Colomb and by John Knox Laughton. Laughton, in particular, played an important role in establishing the credentials of modern naval history. His impact was not limited to his homeland: he influenced Admiral Stephen B. Luce, who was instrumental in the establishment of the US Naval War College, an institution that Andrew Lambert identifies as the first naval educational (as opposed to training) establishment in the world.[10] In 1884 Alfred Thayer Mahan joined the faculty of that college.

Born in 1840 at West Point, the son of a professor of civil and military engineering at the US Military Academy, Mahan was to become one of the most prolific and certainly the most influential writers on maritime strategy of his time. In 1856, he joined the US Naval Academy at Annapolis, Maryland, and remained a naval officer until 1896, when he retired with the rank of captain. Unusually for his time and profession, he was not keen on service at sea, writing when in command of the protected cruiser USS *Chicago* in the 1890s, that 'I had forgotten what a beastly thing a ship is, and what a fool a man is who frequents one.'[11] He is remembered not for his exploits as a commander but rather for a written output that amounted to 20 books and 137 articles before he succumbed to heart failure in December 1914. The key point of Mahan's work was that maritime power had played a decisive role in the course of history and that strength at sea was key to a state's material prosperity and success in war. His work was timely, coming at a period of increased interest in naval affairs. It was read widely and had an impact beyond his home country, notably in Britain, Germany and Japan. One may question the degree to which his views changed the policies of any of the major navies, but at the very least he was important in articulating and popularising views that were already held. His impact was to prove enduring. In Geoffrey Till's 2004 publication, *Seapower: A Guide for the Twenty-First Century*, the first word in the main body of the text is 'Mahan'.

Mahan sought to demonstrate the influence of 'sea power' upon history and to affirm that there were enduring principles of maritime strategy that remained valid despite changing technology. Such principles could be discovered through an examination of the past, which revealed them in 'successes and failures, the same from age to age'. He believed that the past showed that maritime preponderance was key to prosperity and success as a great power, focusing in particular on the experience of the British since the seventeenth century. To Mahan, maritime power had played a decisive role in international relations. National prosperity, and through it the means to wage war, was dependent on seaborne trade. Such trade required the protection of a navy. There was therefore a close and beneficial relationship between trade and naval strength. Maritime trade encouraged the development of a navy to protect it and also provided the raw materials (trained manpower, ship-building and repair facilities etc) to support such a navy. A strong navy could lead to dominance at sea, at the expense of rival countries, which in turn encouraged more trade.

Mahan identified particular conditions that affected the ability of a country to develop 'sea power'. These were: geographical position; physical conformation; extent of territory; population size; the character of the people; and the character of the government and national institutions. The detail of his argument in this respect now appears rather dated and has been subjected to much criticism. Indeed, the list, transparently derived from the British experience, seems designed principally to illustrate American potential to develop maritime power. In essence, Mahan was suggesting that countries with favourable geography, sufficient resources, and an appropriate national culture and political structures were more likely to be able to develop and sustain maritime power than those that lacked these conditions. In this respect, his conclusions may retain considerable validity and provide a useful counter to the idea that economic strength alone is the key determinant. Nevertheless, it should be remembered that Mahan's examination of the past could be rather biased. His interpretation often lacked the accuracy or detachment of an impartial historian. He wrote to promote the education and instruction of fellow naval officers, and his focus on principles must be seen within this context.

After Mahan, the most influential writer of this period was Sir Julian Corbett. Born in 1854 and trained as a lawyer, Corbett taught at the Royal Naval War College at Greenwich from 1900. That he did not always find this a rewarding task was reflected in his complaint about the difficulty of presenting theory to the 'unused organs of naval officers'.[12] Like Mahan, Corbett used an examination of the past to identify the important role that maritime power had played in British military and economic success, although his historical method was more professional than his American counterpart's. While recognising the strengths of maritime power, Corbett placed a greater emphasis than Mahan on its limitations. In contrast to Mahan, whose focus tended to be on activity at sea, Corbett emphasised the importance of joint operations involving the co-ordination of land and sea forces. In 1911 in his most famous work, *Some Principles of Maritime Strategy*, he articulated this in the following way:

Since men live upon the land and not upon the sea, great issues between nations at war have always been decided – except in the rarest cases – either by what your army can do against your enemy's territory and national life, or else by fear of what the fleet makes it possible for your army to do.[13]

That this now seems to be a statement of the obvious is a reflection both of the perspicacity of Corbett's work but also the degree to which his ideas continue to influence modern naval thinking (*Some Principles* is listed as recommended reading in current US naval doctrine). Such views as these were discomfiting for a naval audience in the 1900s whose preferred focus was on battle at sea.

Corbett and Mahan were the most prominent writers on maritime strategy of their day, but they were not the only ones. In Britain, in particular, there were a considerable number of individuals who wrote on maritime strategy and history and who may, despite their various differences, be said to have formed something of a 'blue-water' school of thought regarding the use of major navies. There were also a number of individuals who focused on joint operations and amphibious warfare, most notably Charles Callwell, although these tended to lack the profile and impact of their blue-water counterparts.[14] Writing about maritime power was not exclusive to Britain and America. Contemporaries of Mahan's included the Frenchmen Richard Grivel, Théophile Aube and Gabriel Darrieus, the Russian Stephan Makarov and the Italian Domenico Bonamico. In the twentieth century, Raoul Castex, Wolfgang Wegener and Sergei Gorshkov offered interpretations of maritime strategy from a French, German and Soviet Russian perspective.[15] Some of these individuals, including Darrieus and Gorshkov, worked within a framework similar to that of Mahan and Corbett. Others, most notably Aube, did not, seeking instead to tailor an approach to maritime strategy suited to a particular set of circumstances. Such differences raise the question of whether it is possible to define a set of enduring principles that determine the nature of naval warfare or whether such factors are, indeed, dependent on particular circumstances. These issues are explored in more detail below in an examination of the traditional concepts of naval warfare.

Command of the sea

The key to naval warfare is an ability to use the sea and to deny that use to the enemy. The ability to do this is frequently defined as command of the sea. The requirement to gain such command, and the various means of doing so, lies at the heart of traditional approaches to naval warfare. Mahan laid a particular emphasis on the importance of gaining command and believed that its achievement was the first responsibility of a navy. The best means to achieve it was to concentrate forces and to defeat the main strength of the enemy in battle. Once this was achieved, the way would then be open to exploit the command that had been gained. In his historical examinations of the Anglo-French struggle for mastery at sea in the eighteenth and nineteenth centuries, he castigated the French for neglecting this basic point and instead for subordinating the fleet to 'particular operations' designed to meet limited temporary needs without directly challenging British command. Mahan believed that the enemy's fleet was the controlling factor in a campaign and that its destruction was the true objective for one's forces. He focused upon the enemy's means of fighting more than the frustration of their plans. The best way to secure ulterior objectives was first to remove the force that threatened them. The degree of command that was achieved might vary. Philip Colomb wrote of levels that ranged from 'indifference' to 'disputed command' and then 'assured command'.[16] More recently, Colin Gray has identified that command can differ in range, being either local or general, and that it also varies in degree. It can be disputed, it can shift between protagonists, but it cannot be shared.[17] Gaining command of the sea denies it to the enemy.

The particular ways in which command can be achieved, disputed or exploited are usually defined using the following terms:

- Decisive battle: For Mahan and those like him, the favoured means of achieving command of the sea was through a 'decisive battle' in which the main enemy fleet was defeated or, better still, destroyed. Examples of such battles might be Trafalgar (1805), Navarino (1827), Tsushima (1905) or Leyte Gulf (1944), all of which, to a greater or lesser degree, removed the main threat posed by the enemy fleet. In truth, however, it is relatively rare for a single battle to be decisive. Often identified as the shinning example of a decisive battle, Trafalgar was actually just one of a series of British victories over their French (in this case Franco-Spanish) opponents. Similarly, at Leyte Gulf the US Navy virtually extinguished the threat posed by the Japanese surface fleet, but this was only the last of a series of impressive American victories. Most frequently, decision is the result of a series of encounters.

- Fleet in being: One of the main problems with a policy that revolves around seeking out and destroying the enemy in main battle is the fact that weaker opponents are usually loath to let this happen, preferring instead to husband their resources and in so doing act as a constraint on their superior opponent. This is known as maintaining a 'fleet in being'. In the age before strike aircraft and long-range missiles, weaker fleets could seek the safety of protected harbours where they were difficult to get at. Even when at sea, they might still be able to avoid engaging on unfavourable terms, retreating from rather than facing a superior foe. Forcing battle on a reluctant opponent is more difficult at sea than on land. This approach does not represent an immediate attempt to gain command of the sea but rather represents an appreciation that more limited objectives might be achieved by maintaining one's forces intact.

- Guerre de course: Seaborne trade is vulnerable to attack from organised military forces, from irregular vessels such as privateers operating with state sanction and from the criminal activity of pirates. A combination of privateers and naval vessels could be employed as part of a 'guerre de course', an attack on enemy merchant shipping. This strategy was generally employed by the weaker maritime power against an opponent reliant on seaborne trade, since it does not require command of the sea. The approach has been characterised as the policy of a land power raiding at sea.

- Economic blockade: There are two basic types of blockade: economic and fleet. Economic blockade involves cutting enemy maritime communications, driving their trade from the seas and halting, or at least reducing, the import and export of goods by sea. Traditional maritime strategists tended to stress the importance of such blockades in bringing steady pressure to bear on an opponent over a period of time. Mahan emphasised that blockade, based on the foundation provided by command of the sea, was a far more effective tool of economic warfare than a guerre de course.

- Fleet blockade: This represents the usual response to an enemy who adopts a fleet-in-being strategy, and there are two basic sub-sets: close blockade and distant blockade. A close blockade involves ships or craft staying close outside the enemy harbour, able to react quickly in the event of any ships trying to put to sea. In this way, the enemy fleet is effectively neutralised, and command of the sea can be maintained. Unfortunately, such blockades are very difficult to maintain, particularly since the introduction of mines, submarines, long-range coastal artillery, small fast-attack craft and aircraft have all made the areas close to the enemy shore an unhealthy place to be. A distant blockade requires one to accept that enemy ships will be able to put to sea, but that they will be denied access to particular areas. Blockades are usually very wearing on both ships and personnel, and tie down assets that might be employed more usefully elsewhere. This point helps to explain the preference for decisive battle on the part of dominant navies and the value of a fleet-in-being approach to their weaker opponents.

Sea control

Command of the sea is often portrayed in rather absolute terms. Australian maritime doctrine defines it as 'the possession of such a degree of superiority that one's own operations are unchallenged by the adversary, while the latter is incapable of utilising the sea to any degree'.[18] Such an ability is rare. It is usually limited in time, place, extent and consequence. There may be some circumstances when positive use of the sea can be achieved without meeting such exacting requirements. Equally to the point, one cannot actually 'command' the sea in the same way that one can control land: it is not open to territorial conquest. In truth, gaining command of the sea simply means gaining control of sea communications. Defeating an enemy fleet is not an end in itself but rather a means of dominating the use of those communications.

Corbett recognised that it might be difficult to force battle upon a weaker opponent and that there might be other things that your forces could be doing before command of the sea was achieved. He recognised the value of such activity as amphibious raids as one way of reducing enemy maritime power and, also, of forcing a weaker fleet to give battle. He provided a more sophisticated appreciation of the role of battle and command of the sea than most naval officers of his time had got from their reading of Mahan. This was not always well received. His refusal to espouse an offensive doctrine of battle at all costs led to criticism that he had undermined the fighting spirit of the Royal Navy in the First World War. The crowning insult, albeit one that came after his death, was the insertion by the Admiralty of a disclaimer into volume III of the *Official History of the Navy in the First World War*, written by Corbett, to the effect that they did not agree with his tendency to 'minimise the importance of seeking battle'. A dispassionate analysis of the performance of that navy in the war might suggest that they had indeed been well placed to secure command of the seas but, despite Corbett's efforts, displayed a limited grasp of what to do with that command once they had it.

Corbett's emphasis on command of the sea as an enabling factor and his overt recognition that it was liable to be limited in time, space and degree lie behind the modern concept of sea control. This can be defined as the 'condition that exists when one has freedom of action to use an area of sea for one's own purposes for a period of time and, if necessary, deny its use to an opponent'.[19] This reflects a more realistic understanding of the degree of control that can be achieved and of the role of sea control as an enabler and not an end in itself. The modern American concept of battlespace dominance fits within this tradition. It encompasses the entire battlespace on, under and above the water, and reflects 'zones of superiority' surrounding deployed forces. These zones are regions within which the Americans aim to maintain superiority during their operations. The zones will be shifted as the situation requires.[20] The degree of control that is established within that zone may be more complete than other navies could aspire to, but, in essence, the result is sea control providing the freedom to use the seas for their own purposes and denying that use to the enemy. The requirement to control the battlespace above the surface, of course, means that sea control cannot be achieved unless one also gains a measure of air superiority. It should be noted that an important function of sea control in one region might be to provide cover to weaker forces or detached units to enable them to conduct their operations unhindered by the main force of the enemy. In this sense, the main function of a powerful naval force in one region might be to enable friendly activity hundreds or even thousands of miles away by providing the appropriate cover.

Sea denial

The principles outlined above are derived from an Anglo-American tradition, primarily built upon an examination of the history of the Royal Navy and largely focused on the challenges and opportunities facing 'sea powers'. This body of thought influenced, and continues to influence, thinking about maritime strategy and naval warfare across the globe. However, it could be argued that it was not particularly well suited to countries that had an inferior navy or that were ill placed to exploit maritime power in the traditional way. In such situations, it might make more sense to devote limited resources to denying the enemy the unfettered use of the sea rather than seek to gain positive use for oneself. This is particularly true as sea denial, as it is known, can often be achieved with small and relatively unsophisticated forces that might typically include mines, submarines, fast-attack craft and land-based aircraft.

Even as Mahan was formulating his ideas, an alternative school of thought in France was articulating the utility of a strategy of sea denial in any future war with Britain. Known as the *Jeune École* (Young School), this group enjoyed influence beyond France, and it had an impact upon all of the major European navies in the 1880s and 1890s, raising important questions about the utility of traditional strategies based upon securing command of the sea with large, expensive battleships. The School advocated adopting an asymmetric response to British sea control. Abandoning any attempt to match the British battleship for battleship, they argued instead for relying on small, fast and inexpensive torpedo launches to deny the British the ability to institute a close blockade, releasing fast, steam-driven cruisers into the Atlantic to prey on British trade in a ruthless guerre de course.

The *Jeune École* had fallen from favour in France by the end of the nineteenth century, not least because the strategy that they advocated was unlikely to offer any useful military options in a war against their most likely future opponent, Germany. In any case, the technological developments that made big ships vulnerable to small craft were soon matched by counter-measures that somewhat evened the balance, including the provision of more small craft to defend the battleships. The *Jeune École* may have been eclipsed, but this did not necessarily invalidate their central argument. Within a few years, a new form of technology, that of the submarine, offered a different means of achieving the same result. The unrestricted U-boat (submarine) campaigns undertaken by Germany in both world wars was grounded in the same logic as that expressed by the *Jeune École*. Rather than attempting to gain positive use of the sea, the U-boat campaigns sought to exploit a particular technology in order to deny the use of the sea to Britain and its allies. That both campaigns ultimately failed does not mean that the idea was not well grounded. For a country able to devote only limited resources to maritime power and facing an opponent reliant on using the sea, a strategy that focuses on sea denial rather than sea control may indeed make more sense.

An emphasis on local sea denial was also apparent in the coastal defence theories developed by the Soviet New School that emerged in the Soviet Union in the late 1920s and early 1930s. Reacting to the paucity of traditional maritime assets and in light of the experience of maritime power projection being applied against the nascent Soviet state in 1919, this school of thought advocated an integrated system of minefields, coastal artillery, submarines and motor torpedo boats instead of a more traditional, balanced fleet. This approach was, however, abandoned by the Soviet Union in the 1930s, when greater resources and increased ambition led the navy to emphasise a more traditional approach to maritime power that could extend beyond coastal waters. Communist China went through a similar process, emphasising the value of 'mosquito fleets' of small defensive coastal craft in the 1950s before moving towards a more traditional interpretation of the role of the fleet once greater resources became available. Some Western navies, including those of Denmark and Norway, emphasised coastal defence during the Cold War. The removal of the threat from the Soviet Union has seen both navies changing their policies and exploring ways of making more positive use of the sea. This does not mean that writings on coastal defence by, for example, Jacob Borresen, do not still have utility for other small navies who may face a threat from the sea.[21]

Continental theories

While achieving, maintaining and exploiting sea control might represent the main aim of dominant maritime powers, and coastal defence and guerre de course might be the favoured option of their weaker opponents, it is not immediately clear whether either approach is suitable for a major navy that is still inferior to its main opponent. Mahan criticised eighteenth-century France for misusing its frequently quite substantial maritime power. He particularly criticised what he saw as a failure to establish an appropriate hierarchy of objectives which should have emphasised the long-term objective of securing command of the sea by the destruction of the British battle fleet instead of focusing on short- and medium-term objectives. In the first half of the twentieth century, it was the German Navy that found itself in a position analogous to that of France in the eighteenth. What could be done with a navy of the second rank once Tirpitz's 'Risk Fleet' had failed to deter Britain? The German belief that the Royal Navy would institute a close blockade and could thus be worn down to the point at which it could be faced in decisive battle proved to be illusory. Tirpitz has been criticised for an undue focus on battle for its own sake and a failure to realise that command of the sea meant, in reality, command of seaborne communications. By closing off the exits from the North Sea, Britain could dominate these communications without seeking battle and without needing to institute a close blockade.

One notable German critic of his navy's policy in this war was Wolfgang Wegener.[22] Wegener served in the navy throughout the war and retired in 1926 as a vice admiral. He argued that deference to the German Army's ingrained concepts of land warfare had led the navy to prepare for battle without thinking enough about strategy and, in particular, the importance of geography and maritime communications. To Wegener, maritime power was about a combination of fleet and position. Bottled up in the Helgoland Bight, Germany had the former but not the latter. It was therefore not possible to engage the Royal Navy on anything like favourable terms. He favoured the seizure of Denmark (he later added Norway) as one means of improving the navy's strategic position. It is ironic that in the Second World War, when Germany achieved all of this and more, it had the position but lacked a fleet able to exploit it.

In contrast to Wegener, Captain von Waldeyer-Harte and Ernst Wilhelm Kruse argued along similar lines to those of the *Jeune École* that Germany should not again seek to challenge for command of the sea but instead focus on attacking enemy trade. Kruse noted that the stronger sea power was more dependent on sea communications and could be forced onto the defensive by a weaker power not so encumbered.[23] These ideas, and those of Wegener, were attacked by another German, Herbert Rosinski, who held a position on the faculty of the German Naval Staff College until he fled that country in 1936. Rosinski adopted a more traditional position, criticising von Waldeyer-Harte and Kruse for believing that an attack on trade could be successful without a complementary challenge for sea control. He criticised Wegener for placing too much emphasis on geography and for failing to appreciate the importance of a significant material superiority. At the heart of his work was a very Mahanian belief in the utility of command of the sea and the difficulty of achieving anything of great value without it. He was pessimistic about the prospects of an outnumbered fleet, writing of the 'strategic helplessness of a decisively inferior fleet, which is the outstanding characteristic of war at sea and distinguishes it most sharply from war on land'.[24]

In contrast to Rosinski, the French naval officer Raoul Castex identified a range of activities that an inferior fleet might usefully engage in. Castex was a prolific writer, publishing eighteen major works and over fifty journal articles. His major contribution was the enormous, five-volume *Théories Stratégiques* ('Strategic Theories') published between 1929 and 1935.[25] He recognised the value of gaining what he called 'mastery of the sea', defined as control of sea communications. He also recognised the centrality of battle to its achievement. He was, however, very aware of the problem of achieving this with inferior forces. For those not yet in a favourable position of strength, there were a range of things that one could do to improve the situation. At the heart of his theory was the concept of 'strategic manoeuvre'. Such manoeuvre implied exploiting the possibilities of such activity as attacks on commerce, naval raids, amphibious operations or blockades to force an opponent to divert resources. This also implied a diversion of friendly resources, something that Mahan warned against. However, Castex suggested that it was possible to use space and distance to concentrate more rapidly than an opponent, thereby using strategic manoeuvre as a vehicle

Box 3.2 Features of naval warfare at the tactical level

- Naval forces tend to be disaggregated into fewer independent units than is the case in land and air operations.
- Battles usually occur in proximity to the land. This is true of all the major naval battles of the twentieth century.
- Given the existence of efficient ship-killing weapons, the ability to land the first effective strike can often prove critical.
- Scouting (to find the enemy) and screening (to deal with enemy scouts) is a vital prerequisite to landing, or avoiding, the first effective strike.
- The potential for manoeuvre is inherent within naval forces and plays an important role in naval combat. This was particularly true of the battleship era, when the ability to manoeuvre a fleet into a superior firing position was the acme of skill at the tactical level.
- Notwithstanding the above, position and manoeuvre are not as critical as they are in land warfare. Naval warfare revolves around the destruction of units rather than the seizure of territory.
- Naval warfare tends to be attritional, even if that attrition is often applied in a very one-sided fashion. Enemy fleets are defeated by the destruction of their constituent parts rather than by being out-flanked or encircled, as is often the case on land.
- Concentration has traditionally mattered even more at sea than on land, given the need to mass offensive and defensive firepower and the inability to exploit terrain. It is also more attainable than on land.
- Given the above, and the speed with which naval combat can be decided, there is rarely any point in maintaining a reserve in battle.
- Naval warfare can be deadly and decisive. Battles at sea are often decided within hours or even minutes. Naval campaigns, however, can last months or even years.
- Many of the factors that make 'mission command' attractive in land warfare do not apply at sea, where a commander must try to fight his ship as a cohesive unit. Command and control therefore tends to be rather more centralised at sea than on land.

for creating local superiority of numbers and thus the conditions under which battle might be successfully entertained. The main target remained the enemy fleet, and the chance of defeating a fleet with inferior numbers was 'almost nil', but one need not passively accept an inferior position. To Castex, the guerre de course, including submarine operations, could be a useful way of diverting enemy forces, but it could not be decisive on its own. Rather, it had to be integrated into a system of operations whose eventual aim was to contest mastery of the sea.

Naval tactics

The ideas and concepts above examine issues relating to the strategic and operational employment of navies. These have a direct bearing on naval tactics, for, as Wayne Hughes points out, unrestrained by the need to hold ground, battle tactics at sea are determined by national strategy in a way that is not necessarily true on land.[26] Upon encountering another, a fleet that is seeking to achieve command of the sea is likely to proceed in an entirely different fashion from one that has adopted a fleet-in-being approach. The tactics adopted by Admirals Jellicoe and Scheer at Jutland in 1916, for example, were the result of their national maritime strategies. Scheer withdrew and Jellicoe pursued, cautiously. However, had Scheer decided to engage the British Grand Fleet with the German High Seas Fleet, both sides would have been operating within the confines of a tactical system that revolved around maximising the impact of fire from the big guns of their battleships and, if possible, using destroyers to launch torpedo attacks on the enemy. Within twenty-five years of Jutland, the battleship had been replaced as the key arbiter of naval combat by the aircraft carrier, and tactics changed accordingly. Within another twenty-five years the development of anti-ship cruise missiles brought further changes. The propensity for tactics to change in line with changing technology is more apparent at sea than on land, as the various factors that mitigate the impact of technological change ashore are largely absent at sea. It was for this reason that Mahan concluded that it was difficult to establish enduring principles of naval tactics. Despite this difficulty, there are some enduring features of naval warfare at the tactical level (see box 3.2).

Defining the timescale that should be encompassed in a discussion of 'modern' naval warfare is not easy. The principles of maritime strategy addressed above were founded upon an historical examination of war at sea from the sixteenth century. It was around this time that navies, as permanent fighting services made up of ships designed for war, manned by professionals and supported by an administrative and technical infrastructure, had begun to replace the more temporary and ad hoc organisations that had previously existed. It was also in the sixteenth century that the wooden sailing ship finally replaced the oared galley as the dominant vessel in naval warfare. The battle of Lepanto in 1571 was the last major engagement between fleets of oared vessels. One could therefore make a good case that 'modern' naval warfare originated in the age of sail. On the other hand, in the century that separates the 'decisive' battles of Trafalgar (1805) and Tsushima (1905), numerous technological and organisational developments transformed the way in which navies were equipped and structured and how they fought, even if, as Mahan *et al.* suggested, the roles they fulfilled and the strategies that they employed changed little. One might even argue that Tsushima itself does not belong to the era of 'modern' warfare, coming as it did before the employment of aircraft or submarines in war at sea and bearing in mind that, in the following year, the new British battleship HMS *Dreadnought* would render obsolescent all existing battleships, including those of the Japanese victors in that battle. Nevertheless, given the emergence in the first years of the twentieth century of a variety of new factors (the first effective submarines, aircraft, the use of wireless telegraphy at sea, dreadnought-type battleships) that affected the character of naval warfare, it may be best to focus this enquiry on the period since 1900.

We have already noted that the study of naval warfare implies a particular focus on platforms and, by extension, on technology. In naval warfare, technology matters; it also changes. These changes have a significant impact on tactics, to the extent that Mahan believed that one could not identify enduring tactical principles for war at sea: they would change with changing technology. At sea, there is no counterpart to the so-called 'modern system' of land warfare discussed in chapter 2. In particular, the factors that have enabled land forces to mitigate the impact of increased firepower (cover, concealment, dispersal) are absent from war at sea. The tactics required to prevail in the battleship encounters of the First World War were different from those that dominated the aircraft carrier battles of the Pacific War twenty-five years later and bear little relation to the way that navies operated in the era of anti-ship cruise missiles that followed. In this sense, naval warfare may be different from its equivalent on land. An examination of modern naval warfare is thus less about the evolution of a modern system and more about the way in which navies adapted to meet and exploit a variety of challenges and opportunities that include, but are by no means limited to, technological change.

From fighting sail to dreadnought

In the century between Trafalgar and Tsushima there were dramatic changes in the conduct of naval warfare at the tactical level. Most obviously these revolved around the transformation of warships from wooden sailing vessels armed with short-range cannon firing solid shot to armoured steel vessels powered by triple-expansion steam engines and equipped with much longer-ranged heavy weapons firing armour-piercing shells. The adoption of steam propulsion was particularly significant, and brought costs and benefits. It provided for greater speed and offered ships the ability to manoeuvre without relying on the vagaries of the wind. This was particularly useful when operating in rivers or inshore areas, places where sailing ships had been loath to go. Steam power also increased the potential to provide reliable logistic support to overseas expeditions. On the other hand, whereas sailing ships had enjoyed almost unlimited endurance, steam power relied on coal (later oil), and the requirement to restock with this fuel limited the endurance of warships, making possession of overseas coaling stations of particular importance. This factor favoured the British, who possessed a string of bases at key points throughout the world. Strategic direction from London was made possible by a series of undersea telegraph cables that connected these bases.

Inevitably in a period of technological change, the second half of the nineteenth century saw a considerable degree of experimentation in ship design and also in tactics. However, by the end of the century the position of the battleship as the 'capital ship', the most important naval vessel and the main determinant of relative naval strength, was well established. War at sea would be decided by gunfire, and in such circumstances large, heavily armoured battleships equipped with large-calibre guns mounted in traversable turrets and powered only by steam were the ultimate expression of power at sea. Increases in the range and accuracy of naval gunfire that occurred in the first years of the new century served to reinforce the ascendancy of ships equipped with the heaviest guns and able to trade blows with their counterparts.

Despite this, a number of developments promised to threaten the ascendancy of these behemoths and to change the character of naval warfare. These included the explosive sea mine, first employed during the Crimean War (1854–5) and used to good effect in the US Civil War (1861–5). These weapons posed a serious threat to even the most powerful warships, accounting for the loss of three battleships and a number of cruisers in the Russo–Japanese War (1904–5). The self-propelled torpedo, first developed in the 1870s by Robert Whitehead, was another relatively cheap weapon that could sink the mightiest warship if it could be delivered accurately. The threat posed to big ships by these weapons and by the small, fast torpedo boats that carried them led to the development of a new kind of ship, the torpedo boat destroyer (later known simply as destroyers), designed to protect the bigger ships and, if possible, to launch their own torpedo strikes. Most radical of all, perhaps, was the progress made towards the development of an effective submarine. During the US Civil War the Confederacy had employed a hand-cranked submarine, the CSA *Hunley*. This vessel had succeeded in sinking a Union sloop with a spar torpedo (an explosive fitted to a long pole) but sank with all hands in the process. It was not until the development of the gyro-compass and periscope enabled underwater navigation, electric batteries provided a means of propulsion when submerged, and diesel engines provided propulsion and recharged the electric batteries on the surface that the submarine's potential for war could begin to be realised. The British commissioned their first submarine in 1902. The following year, the Wright brothers' first flight saw the start of a process that would, eventually, revolutionise naval warfare.

Therefore, while battleships may have dominated naval warfare at the turn of the century, they were not the only vessels that navies required. Fleets were made up of numerous different vessels that can be differentiated into three general groups:

1 battleships designed to secure control of the sea by engaging and defeating other warships
2 cruisers able to support the battle fleet by scouting for enemy ships and by screening their own fleet from the effects of enemy scouting. Such ships also provided a means of exercising sea control by protecting or attacking trade and projecting power ashore through gunfire or naval landing parties
3 flotilla craft, such as destroyers, required to conduct inshore work, carry despatches, land troops and, increasingly, protect larger vessels from attack by other flotilla craft.

Successful fleet tactics involved co-ordinating the activity of multiple ships of different types and could be considered to be analogous to the combined-arms tactics of land warfare described in chapter 2. Unfortunately, the difficulties of command and control facing commanders remained considerable, particularly as they might not be able to see both ends of their fleet once deployed for battle. Command and control was dependent on flag signalling until the 1900s, when wireless telegraphy began to be deployed at sea. The latter did not solve the problem, and in some senses it served to compound it, tempting commanders to centralise too much control in their own hands and stifling initiative among their subordinates. Use of radio did provide a means for dispersed ships to communicate, greatly assisting the process of scouting and providing shore-based admiralties with a means to support (or interfere with) commanders at sea. Unfortunately, however, radio transmissions could be detected, betraying the presence of enemy vessels, and, if your codes were broken, much useful information might be gathered by the enemy. For this reason, ships at sea often maintained radio silence, continuing to communicate by flag signals and searchlight flashes.

The Russo-Japanese War provides a valuable case study of naval warfare at this time. In a strategic sense, the war, which revolved around control of Port Arthur and its hinterland in Manchuria (present-day China), represents a classic case of a land power (Russia) being defeated by a maritime opponent (Japan) not least because of the superior access to and support within the theatre available to Japanese land forces because of the ability of the Imperial Japanese Navy to achieve sea control. The war began with a pre-emptive attack by Japanese destroyers on the Russian Pacific fleet at Port Arthur in which two Russian battleships and a cruiser were badly damaged by torpedoes. Minefields subsequently accounted for one Russian and two Japanese battleships sunk, with a further Russian battleship badly damaged. It is significant that the first major fleet engagement, the battle of the Yellow Sea (10 August 1904), occurred because the Russian commander had been ordered to relocate his fleet from Port Arthur to Vladivostok as Japanese troops advanced to threaten the former. After the resulting Japanese victory, most of the major Russian ships returned to Port Arthur, where they were eventually destroyed by land-based howitzers. From the Japanese perspective, this was a truly joint campaign. The second major battle, Tsushima (27 May 1905), occurred after the Russian Baltic fleet had made an epic voyage around the world, overcoming enormous logistic challenges in an attempt to challenge Japanese sea control. Despite having more armoured ships than their opponents (eleven battleships, three armoured cruisers and five protected cruisers, compared with four battleships and eight armoured cruisers), the Russian ships were older than their rivals and arrived in theatre in a poor material condition and with disheartened crews to face a fresh, experienced, well-motivated and well-led enemy.

The Russian fleet was sighted at first light by a Japanese auxiliary cruiser and, with his fleet in a conventional line-ahead formation, Admiral Togo deployed across the Russian line of advance to Vladivostok. He succeeded in crossing the Russian T twice (see box 3.3) before both fleets ran on parallel courses as the Russians sought to escape to the northeast. The Japanese ships held a speed advantage over their opponents that facilitated more effective tactical manoeuvre and, with superior fire control and gunnery, they shattered the Russian fleet, sinking six battleships and two cruisers, with a further four battleships surrendering and one battleship and three cruisers scuttled to avoid capture. Fire was initiated at ranges in excess of 6,000 yards. The Japanese lost three torpedo boats. Tsushima was the largest naval battle since Trafalgar and appeared to confirm the central role within naval warfare of the battle fleet and of decisive battle.

The position of the battleship as the main determinant of relative naval strength was therefore already well established by 1906, when HMS *Dreadnought* was launched, lending its name to the new generation of battleships that followed. Heavily armed and armoured, the 21,850-ton *Dreadnought* was notable for steam turbines that provided an impressive speed of 21 knots and for an all-big gun main armament of ten 12-inch guns. Pre-dreadnought battleships had carried a mixed battery of weapons of different calibre, many optimised for fire at short range. Tsushima demonstrated that heavy guns could be decisive at ranges far beyond the distance at which small- and medium-calibre weapons could be effective. Improvements in the range and accuracy of torpedoes provided an additional incentive for battleships to carry guns that enabled them to conduct engagements beyond the effective range of such weapons. Long-range fire from guns of different calibres made the task of spotting the fall of shot and correcting fire extremely difficult. Fire control was much easier if all

Box 3.3 Crossing the T

Crossing the T was a tactic in naval warfare where one fleet manoeuvred to cross in front of the line of enemy vessels, allowing its ships to concentrate fire from guns at the front and the rear of the vessel while receiving fire from only the forward guns of the enemy ships. This was achieved by the Japanese at Tsushima (1905) and twice by the British at Jutland (1916). In the last ever battleship-versus-battleship engagement, the battle of the Surigao Strait (1944), US battleships crossed the Japanese T and devastated their opponents with accurate, radar-guided fire at long range.

the guns were the same calibre, firing in salvoes that could be corrected until the enemy ship was straddled and then hit by shell fire. The all-big gun concept was adopted by all the major navies, and the dreadnought-type battleship became accepted as the true measure of naval power. By 1910, continuous-aim fire and director control had replaced local gun-laying, further improving long-range accuracy.

The number and quality of dreadnought battleships was the measure by which navies judged themselves prior to 1914, and rival dreadnought construction set the terms for the pre-war Anglo-German naval race. The prestige associated with the possession of such ships, and their potential to dominate any battle at sea, led to the construction or purchase of dreadnoughts by all the major navies and by many navies of second or third rank, including those of Argentina, Brazil and Chile. At the same time, the British developed a new kind of ship, the battle cruiser. These vessels, exemplified by the three *Invincible* class ships that entered service in 1908, were similar in size to battleships and carried an equivalent main armament but, by reducing their armour protection, could boast superior speed. Their sponsor, Admiral Sir John Fisher, hoped that speed and manoeuvrability would compensate for lack of protection. In the First World War, they proved well suited to their intended role, that of chasing down and destroying enemy cruisers and squadrons raiding the sea lanes beyond Europe. They were, however, ill-suited to engage battleships or even other battle cruisers, as their armour was not designed to withstand fire from heavy guns. The loss of three British battle cruisers at Jutland in 1916 highlighted their vulnerability. German battle cruisers, built with better armour protection, proved to be more resilient.

Although state of the art in 1906, the *Dreadnought* was outclassed by bigger, faster, better-armed and more heavily armoured rivals by 1914. The 'super-dreadnought' USS *Pennsylvania*, on which work began in 1913, had roughly double the displacement of the first US dreadnought, the USS *Michigan*, commissioned just three years earlier. Super-dreadnoughts such as *Pennsylvania* or its contemporary, HMS *Queen Elizabeth*, would prove to have enduring utility: both vessels served in both world wars. In the short term, the time that it took to build these ships, their huge expense and the considerable prestige associated with their possession made them extremely valuable as symbols of national strength. It also made navies very wary of risking them, as was evident throughout the First World War. Naval combat during that war illustrated the continued importance of the battleship and the big gun, but also their limitations.

From dreadnought to Scapa Flow, 1906–18

On 21 November 1918, nine battleships, five battle cruisers, seven light cruisers and forty-nine destroyers of the German High Seas fleet supinely made their way to captivity at Scapa Flow, led by the cruiser HMS *Cardiff* and escorted on either flank by a massive armada that included twenty-eight British and five US battleships. Two days earlier, 176 German U-boats had surrendered to the Royal Navy at Harwich. Seven months later, the Germans scuttled the fleet in the deep waters of Scapa Flow, where it remains to this day as a fascinating, if rather chilly, attraction for visiting scuba divers. This is not the fate that Kaiser Wilhelm II had envisaged for his navy. The Kaiser's fleet, built at vast expense to challenge the British, had not been defeated in any major battle. Its demise was the result of the national defeat of Imperial Germany. Nevertheless, the battleships, cruisers and destroyers had failed totally in their role as a deterrent to the British, just as they also failed to offer any particularly useful military options during the course of the First World War. In retrospect, even the name given to the main German naval force, the High Seas fleet, seems unintentionally ironic, given that fleet's imprisonment within the North Sea for the duration of the war. The ultimate impotence of the German surface navy can be contrasted with the activity of their U-boats, which conducted a campaign that brought the British to the brink of defeat without ever challenging the might of the Royal Navy's Grand Fleet.

Maritime power made a vital contribution to Allied victory in the First World War. Allied sea control allowed the deployment of British forces to France in 1914 and the subsequent mobilisation of the global resources of the French and British empires, of the United States and of neutral countries. It also enabled the Allies to initiate and maintain campaigns beyond the main theatre, albeit with mixed results. The dangers facing battleships in enemy coastal waters led the Royal Navy to adopt a distant, rather than a close, blockade of Germany once war broke out in 1914. This robbed the Germans of the chance that they had been counting on to whittle down British battleship strength to the point at which the smaller German fleet might engage them with some prospect of success. As a result, the High Seas fleet spent the war imprisoned in the North Sea. On occasion, it was able to bombard towns on the east coast of England and to threaten the

Scandinavian convoys and, once, at Jutland in May 1916, to assault its jailor. The realisation of how close the High Seas fleet had come to annihilation in the latter case led its leadership to be more circumspect in future, to the point of inactivity. In the meantime, the British blockade cut off German trade, isolated its colonies and slowly strangled its economy. By 1916, there were food riots in German cities. By neutering the High Seas fleet the dreadnoughts of the British Grand Fleet set the conditions for Allied sea control beyond the North Sea. The cautious way in which these vessels were employed should not be allowed to hide the importance of this role. The control provided by the Grand Fleet allowed other vessels to engage in trade protection, amphibious operations and a variety of other tasks unmolested, and, by setting the conditions that enabled Britain and France to maintain access to the resources of their worldwide empires and of the United States while denying them to the enemy, it made a necessary contribution to Allied victory.

Although Allied sea control was vital to eventual victory, the limited ability of navies directly to influence events on land became very apparent. The German guerre de course failed, and the Allied blockade, while significant, took years to become effective and did not, on its own, force Germany to sue for peace. German bombardment of towns on the east coast of England were significant in the context of the war at sea, as they were attempts to lure a portion of the British fleet into an ambush, and British attacks on German territory using sea planes can be viewed within the same context. Neither were there very significant examples of maritime power projection from the sea against the shore. The one way that maritime forces could directly influence events on shore was through amphibious operations. A number of these were attempted, most notably at Gallipoli, where an Anglo-French force sought to seize that peninsula in April 1915 in support of a naval campaign to force access through the Dardanelles Straits. The troops succeeded in establishing themselves ashore, despite heavy casualties. However, they became pinned down within their beachheads and were unable to break out, even after an additional landing at Suvla Bay in August 1915. The eventual failure of the campaign, and the associated loss of life, did something to undermine faith in such operations in the interwar period. The campaign itself had been prompted by the earlier failure of the fleet to force its way through minefields and past fixed batteries and mobile howitzers during the initial phase of the Dardanelles campaign. The Dardanelles/Gallipoli campaign illustrated that it was very difficult for navies to deploy decisive power from the sea to the shore.

There were a number of naval battles during the war: at Helgoland Bight (28 August 1914), Coronel (1 November 1914), the Falkland Islands (8 December 1914) and Dogger Bank (24 January 1915). However, the caution exercised by both sides in the use of their big ships and their equal reluctance to fight when outnumbered meant that the main fleets clashed only once, at the battle of Jutland, on 31 May 1916. Typically, the battle occurred as a result of a German attempt to coax out and then ambush a detachment of the British fleet. Forewarned by signals intelligence, the British, on the other hand, sought to exploit a rare opportunity to engage the main enemy force. With 250 vessels employed and no significant contribution from either submarines or aircraft, the resulting engagement stands as the largest, surface-only engagement of modern times and the only major battle of the dreadnought era. The much-anticipated battle proved to be an unsatisfactory experience for the British, who suffered a greater material loss than the Germans.

At Jutland, deficiencies were apparent in the British use of intelligence, command and control, and signalling. British gunnery was less accurate than the Germans' and their shells and armour protection were both less effective. For the first time in centuries, the Royal Navy faced an opponent in battle who was, ship for ship, better than it was. The numerical advantage possessed by the Royal Navy (twenty-eight battleships and nine battle cruisers at the start of the battle, compared with sixteen battleships plus six pre-dreadnoughts and six battle cruisers) meant that, provided the Grand Fleet remained concentrated and took no risks, they would not be defeated. Admiral Jellicoe's decision not to pursue the Germans vigorously and to turn away from his enemy when threatened by torpedoes from their destroyers must be viewed within this context. Anything other than a German victory would still leave Britain able to dominate the vital seaborne communications. In this context, Jutland was a British victory and a German defeat, a fact recognised tacitly by the German commander, Admiral Scheer, in his advocacy of a resumption of unrestricted submarine attacks on Allied shipping. Perhaps the submarines could achieve what his battleships could not.

The widespread use of submarines was the most obvious way in which the war at sea differed from previous conflicts. Although still rather primitive, with limited speed and endurance when submerged, such vessels posed a danger to shipping through their covert nature and an ability to attack with either torpedoes or (against unarmed vessels) a gun mounted on the deck. That they posed a deadly threat to unwary warships was illustrated on 22 September 1914, when one U-boat sank three old British armoured cruisers in quick succession in the English Channel. Submarines lacked the speed to keep up with a surface warship at sea, and communication with friendly surface vessels was problematic, and impossible when submerged. It was therefore possible to try to use them to ambush ships passing through particular areas, but they could not be used in a co-ordinated fashion with the fleet, and attempts to use them in this way generally failed. Nevertheless, the existence of these vessels forced all of the combatants to be circumspect in their use of ships, particularly in coastal waters. For example, the threat posed by submarines forced the British to move their fleet from Scapa Flow to the west coast of Scotland, and even Ireland, until they had provided appropriate anti-submarine defences for the main base. Similarly, the arrival of German U-boats off Gallipoli in 1915 forced the British to reassess their use of heavy vessels in support of ground forces on that peninsula. However, and despite occasional successes against major warships, it was in their role as commerce raiders that submarines were to have their greatest impact on the war.

The use of seaborne communications was a key enabler for Allied victory in the war. It did, however, represent a critical vulnerability for Britain, a country whose industry was dependent on the import of raw materials and whose people would starve without the import of foodstuffs. The Germans, like the French and Americans before them, recognised this vulnerability. Pre-war plans had envisaged the use of surface ships in a traditional guerre de course. In the event, a small number of German light cruisers and converted merchant ships attacked Allied trade before being sunk or interned in neutral ports. Despite causing considerable alarm and disruption, their effect on the Allied war effort was limited. The submarine campaign against shipping heading towards British ports had a far greater impact. Once German U-boats were released by their government from the requirement to operate within the bounds of international law, and were allowed to sink ships without warning and with no consideration for the safety of non-combatant passengers and crew, British losses mounted alarmingly. Given the primitive state of submarine-detection equipment and anti-submarine weapons, it was fortunate that the first such exercise of unrestricted U-boat warfare, in 1915–16, was curtailed owing to the international outrage that it caused. The second attempt, begun in February 1917, came close to success, sinking up to 600,000 tons of allied shipping a month before the British adopted suitable counter-measures. Unfortunately for Germany, the campaign contributed to the US decision to declare war in 1917, adding the American fleet to the Allied inventory and freeing up for Allied use a large number of German ships interned in American ports.

Traditional approaches to trade defence could be divided into two basic sub-sets: direct and indirect. Direct defence involved protecting the key assets, ships, in the vicinity of each ship. To an extent, this could be catered for by equipping merchant vessels with some means of self-defence. It also involved the provision of armed escorts for merchant vessels gathered together to form a convoy. Such convoys travel together, at the speed of the slowest member, and may be escorted for some or all of their journey. This was the favoured British method of protecting merchant shipping in the age of sail, and its success bolstered Mahan's views on the inefficacy of a guerre de course. Unfortunately, the use of convoys had, and still has, some serious drawbacks. The physical problems associated with assembling and organising a fleet of merchant ships can cause delay and congestion around the ports at either end of the journey. Convoys represent a very inefficient way of delivering cargo. Naval officers frequently doubted whether merchant ships and their crews had the ability to maintain station in a convoy on a long ocean journey. Given the requirement to station destroyers with the Grand Fleet, it would also be difficult to provide sufficient escorts to protect such convoys, raising the risk that, by collecting a large number of ill-protected ships in one place, one had put 'too many eggs in one basket'. One could add to this list a naval aversion to adopting such 'defensive' measures as convoy protection rather than taking a more 'offensive' approach.

Offensive-minded naval officers tended to prefer sweeps and hunting groups to find submarines and protect the sea lanes. This was reflected in British policy in the early stages of the First World War. It was far from successful. In the face of unsustainable losses at the hands of German submarines, and reinforced by the addition of the US Navy to the Allied inventory, the Admiralty introduced a system of convoys from April 1917, after which losses fell significantly. In retrospect, it is clear that the policy of protecting the sea lanes was flawed, not least because such lanes do not really exist in a physical sense. Ships, on the other hand, do exist and can be protected. The creation of convoys collected vessels together, thus emptying vast areas of ocean of shipping. This made it harder for enemy submarines to find targets. If a convoy was detected, it might be attacked and an individual vessel sunk, but the remaining shipping was liable to escape and could not be picked off one by one. It also became clear that the best place to find submarines was near their prey. Rather than conducting fruitless searches of empty ocean for enemy raiders, one could escort convoys through the most vulnerable stages of their journey and wait for the submarines to come to oneself. Nevertheless, the U-boat campaign came close to forcing the British to sue for peace, demonstrating the vulnerability of a state dependent on seaborne communications to a sea-denial strategy.

Naval arms control and emerging capabilities, 1918–39

The end of the war in 1918 and the scuttling of the German High Seas fleet did not bring an end to naval rivalry. In the years that followed there were attempts to manage this rivalry through arms control agreements that sought to limit the size and number of major warships. The Washington Treaty of 1922 was successful in halting, or at least delaying, a potential British, American and Japanese naval arms race, but this, and the later London Treaties of 1930 and 1936, could not long remove the root causes of naval rivalry. By the limits that they set, the treaties influenced the design and construction of warships and led to the creation of a new type of vessel, the heavy cruiser of up to 10,000 tons. The 'building holiday' that was imposed on capital-ship construction hit the British hardest, as the Royal Navy was generally equipped with older vessels than its rivals. Limits on battleship size and armament also worked against the British, who, unlike their future adversaries, did not cheat during construction. The 1930 London Treaty established limits on the numbers of cruisers that were determined by the relative strength of the major navies and not by their likely tasks, again disadvantaging the British, who had a global empire to protect. Limitations on the use of submarines against merchant ships, contained in the London Treaties and also in the 1936 Anglo-German Naval Agreement, proved to be worthless in wartime.

Despite the attempts at arms control, navies continued to try to adapt techniques and technologies for future conflict. Notable technological advances included the development of ASDIC (now called sonar), a device that used sound waves to detect submerged submarines, and also of radar, which, when deployed at sea, could be used to detect enemy vessels and assist in fire control, in addition to providing crucial early warning of air attack. These contributed to the process where, from the 1940s, combat at sea was increasingly directed from the operations room within the ship based on information provided by such surveillance devices rather than from the bridge.

Despite the relative lack of success of amphibious operations during the First World War, the Japanese, Americans and British all studied ways of undertaking such operations in the future. A lack of priority retarded British progress, although much useful theoretical work was undertaken and prototype landing craft developed. The chastening experience of Gallipoli in 1915, when assaulting troops had established themselves against opposition fire only after heavy casualties, may have inhibited British interest, although not to the extent that is commonly supposed. It was simply the case that, prior to the defeat of France in 1940, there was no apparent requirement for a major amphibious capability in any future war in Europe. With more obvious use for amphibious forces in a conflict between themselves, the Japanese and Americans made more progress. Japanese capabilities were in advance of all others', prompted by the use of amphibious forces in their war with China. However, it was to be British and American techniques and capabilities that would, during the Second World War, solve the problems of conducting landings on an enemy-held shore and by 1943–4 offer the Allies the ability to land hundreds of thousands of men, plus all of their supporting equipment and logistics, over open beaches in the face of enemy opposition. Amphibious forces had finally come of age, significantly increasing the offensive potential of maritime forces.

One other area where capabilities developed significantly was in the provision of aircraft at sea. The potential for aircraft to have an impact on war at sea was evident even prior to the First World War. During that conflict, both fixed-wing, heavier-than-air aircraft and lighter-than-air, rigid and

Figure 3.2 The battleships HMS *Duke of York*, *Nelson* and *Renown*, the aircraft carrier HMS *Formidable* and the cruiser HMS *Argonaut* sail in line ahead in support of the Allied landings in North Africa, November 1942. By this time the battleship was losing its dominant position in naval warfare but still had a role to play, particularly in providing fire support for amphibious operations.

non-rigid airships played a role in reconnaissance, anti-submarine operations and bombing. In September 1918, the Royal Navy commissioned HMS *Argus*, the first aircraft carrier to be fitted with a full flight deck from bow to stern, and a hangar below deck for the carriage and maintenance of aircraft. The Royal Navy was planning to launch a major strike by carrier-based aircraft against the German High Seas fleet in harbour, although the end of the war brought the cancellation of such plans. Twenty-two years later, the British would demonstrate the ability of carrier-based aircraft to strike at ships in harbour when just twenty-one Swordfish biplanes flying from HMS *Illustrious* sank one Italian battleship and damaged two others at Taranto on the night of 11–12 November 1940. A year later, on 7 December 1941, the Imperial Japanese Navy went one better, sinking four battleships and damaging many other warships in a pre-emptive strike on the US Pacific Fleet at Pearl Harbor.

Although expected initially to play a supportive role subordinate to the fleet's big guns, in the Second World War carrier-based aircraft were to prove themselves to be the decisive arm in naval warfare. Carrier-based aircraft and, when in range, land-based aircraft could fulfil a variety of roles at sea, including reconnaissance, spotting for gunfire, bombing and torpedo attack, air defence and anti-submarine operations. They could act in support of traditional surface-orientated action, as at the battle of Cape Matapan in the Mediterranean in March 1941. They could also threaten naval vessels independently. Allied experience off the coast of Norway and at Dunkirk in 1940 and in the Mediterranean from 1941 demonstrated the vulnerability of warships to attack by land-based aircraft and showed the need for appropriate anti-aircraft weapons, tactics and, above all else, fighter cover. The most radical developments occurred in the Pacific War, where the true potential of carrier-based aircraft was shown in the attack on Pearl Harbor and in subsequent operations. At the battles of the Coral Sea in May 1942 and again, on a greater scale, at the battle of Midway in June that year, the US Navy and the Imperial Japanese Navy fought major battles in which their surface vessels were never within sight of each other or within range of their big guns. The outcome was decided in both cases by the action of carrier-based aircraft resulting, at Midway, in a major defeat for the Japanese. The last encounter between battleships decided by gunfire alone occurred in October 1944 at the battle of Surigao Strait off the coast of the Philippines. It is noteworthy that the two Japanese battleships *Yamato* and *Musashi*, the largest and most powerful battleships ever constructed, were both sunk by US carrier-based aircraft. The third vessel in the class was converted during construction into an aircraft carrier, demonstrating Japanese recognition that the aircraft carrier, not the battleship, would be the capital ship of the future.

Naval warfare and the Second World War, 1939–45

In contrast to the First World War, where the vital contribution of maritime power to Allied success was overshadowed by the dramatic events on land, during the Second World War the struggle at sea was obviously central to the eventual outcome. Within Europe, Allied naval power set the limits to Axis expansion, sustained Britain during the dark days of 1940–1 and, eventually, provided the means for a counter-offensive across the Mediterranean, into Italy and France and then the Third Reich itself. Once again, German surface raiders and U-boats attempted to cut Allied seaborne communications, this time aided by long-range aircraft and German possession of French Atlantic ports. Once again, the Allies were able to overcome the threat, with a combination of convoys, escorts and, of increasing importance, air support. Aircraft, either shore- or sea-based, proved to be one of the most effective means of defeating the U-boats. The anti-submarine campaign in the Atlantic also illustrated the importance of intelligence and of good operational analysis. On the other side of the world, from 1942 the United States initiated a submarine campaign against Japanese shipping that was as ruthless as its

German counterpart but that, given woeful Japanese counter-measures, had, by 1945, destroyed Japan's merchant fleet.

It should be noted, of course, that the war in Europe was not won at sea but, as Corbett would have been quick to comment, by armies on land. In the case of the Western Allies, these armies were landed from the sea and, given their continued reliance on seaborne supplies, may justly be regarded as an expression of maritime power. In the east, the Soviet Union absorbed, contained and then destroyed the main German armies. They were aided in this process by the diversionary effect of Allied maritime power, ensuring that the Germans could never concentrate their entire strength against them, and also by the provision of vital supplies by convoys fighting their way through to Murmansk. In particular, the deep operations conducted so successfully by the Soviets from 1944 would not have been possible without the mobility provided by American trucks delivered in this way.

The Pacific War, fought over a vast expanse of ocean, was, of course, primarily maritime in nature, notwithstanding land campaigns in China and Burma that depleted Japanese strength. There were more naval battles in that war and more major warships sunk than in all other wars of the twentieth century combined. After an initial surge of success that was halted at Midway in June 1942 (see box 3.4), the progressive destruction of the Japanese fleet, and in particular its aircraft carriers and naval aviators, set the conditions for Allied victory. In the process, the US Navy grew into a force of unprecedented size and capability, dwarfing all of its rivals and relegating its British counterpart, for the first time in centuries, to a navy of the second rank. In a series of engagements fought across the Central Pacific between 1942 and 1944, the US Navy shattered the Imperial Japanese Navy, opening up Japanese-held islands to assault by ground forces, primarily the US Marine Corps. In the course of this campaign, the Navy–Marines combination was to develop powerful new amphibious capabilities able to overcome the heavily fortified islands that they faced. The campaign was enabled by a new capability to support and supply the main fleet at sea and from extemporised forward bases, without requiring an established base in theatre. To the south, naval forces supported operations by US and Australian troops that liberated New Guinea and the Philippines. By 1944, the Japanese position had become so desperate that they resorted to using kamikaze attacks, attempting to fly explosives-laden aircraft directly into ships. This seriously complicated the problems of air defence, as it was now no longer enough to distract or deter a pilot: the aircraft had to be destroyed. In this sense, the kamikazes presaged the problems that would face navies during the missile era. In any case, US maritime power had, by summer 1945, brought Japan to its knees. The atomic attacks on Hiroshima and Nagasaki, with bombs transported by sea and dropped by aircraft operating from islands seized from the sea, forced the Japanese leadership to

Box 3.4 The battles of the Coral Sea (May 1942) and Midway (June 1942)

The battle of the Coral Sea is significant because it was the first engagement between fleets at sea decided entirely by air power. Indeed, the surface ships of both sides were never even close to being within visual or weapons range of each other. The battle resulted in one US aircraft carrier sunk and another damaged in exchange for one small Japanese carrier sunk and two others damaged. In all cases the damage was inflicted by enemy carrier aviation. Although tactically indecisive, the battle resulted in the Japanese abandoning an attempted invasion of Port Moresby in New Guinea.

The battle of Midway resulted from a Japanese attempt to draw out and destroy the remaining US carriers by attacking the US base at Midway atoll. Forewarned by Ultra signals intelligence, and assisted by a degree of luck, the US fleet was able to surprise the larger Japanese force, sinking all four Japanese carriers present for the loss of only one of their own. Once again, neither fleet was ever within range of the other's guns. Despite their losses, the Japanese still possessed a large superiority of gun-armed surface forces but, in the face of US control of the skies, were compelled to withdraw. The battles illustrated the growing importance of aircraft carriers in naval warfare.

accept this fact. They also threatened to pose a fresh set of problems for navies.

Kamikaze aircraft and nuclear weapons were new challenges for navies, while the enhanced potential of amphibious forces and aircraft carrier aviation and the extended reach provided by a modern fleet train presented new opportunities. In battle, the virtue of the traditional focus on concentrating one's fleet was not always apparent. The US Navy chose not to concentrate its carrier force at Midway, reducing the danger that all three of its carriers could be destroyed in a single strike but limiting the chances of mutual support and the co-ordination of their air group's activities. The Japanese adopted a different approach, although in that battle they still believed that the decisive blow would be struck by their concentrated surface force once their carriers had set the conditions for victory. They were to be disappointed. Later in the war, the United States returned to the notion of a concentrated force, buoyed up by their confidence in the ability of their carriers' fighters to ward off enemy air attack and by the enhanced potential for air defence provided by the concentrated fire of hundreds of anti-aircraft guns firing shells armed with new proximity fuses. They were not disappointed by the results.

The Japanese fleet did not cease to threaten US activities with the defeat at Midway. They still possessed a powerful navy that was particularly dangerous in night actions, for which they were well trained and in which aircraft were unable to play a role. In particular, the Japanese inflicted a number of defeats on US forces in the series of night engagements that characterised the six-month campaign for Guadalcanal in the Solomon islands (August 1942 to February 1943). It was not until the US Navy learnt appropriate procedures to counteract Japanese strengths, particularly their remarkably effective 'long lance' torpedoes, that they began to dominate the sea both day and night. Once this was achieved (around the time of the third battle of Savo Island in November 1942), the way was open for the United States to exploit sea control in a sustained counter-offensive. They adopted an innovative policy of 'island-hopping', using the manoeuvre potential of maritime forces to bypass enemy strongholds, seizing only those islands required to support the advance towards the Japanese home islands and using aircraft to neutralise those bases that had been bypassed. The campaign involved a sophisticated combination of air, land and naval assets, and it would not be going too far to suggest that this successful approach represented a maritime equivalent of operational art, as discussed in chapter 2.

The battle of the Philippine Sea (19–20 June 1944) provides a good example of the defensive potential of a concentrated fleet. The battle resulted from a Japanese attempt to respond to the US invasion of the island of Saipan. The First Japanese Mobile Fleet under Admiral Ozawa sought to attack the US Fifth fleet with land-based aircraft and submarines before launching a devastating strike with carrier-based aircraft. Forewarned by intelligence reports, the US Admiral Spruance had been able to neutralise the land-based airfields prior to the battle and had succeeded in sinking seventeen of the twenty-five Japanese submarines deployed. Ozawa detected the US fleet first and was able to launch an air strike beyond the range of his US counterparts (owing to the greater endurance of his aircraft and the presence of land bases for refuelling etc). Spruance refused to be drawn towards his enemy as Ozawa had hoped and instead relied on his own fighter aircraft to destroy the incoming wave. The resulting air battle, nicknamed the 'Great Marianas Turkey Shoot', saw the incoming Japanese aircraft devastated by the more experienced US pilots, guided to their targets by radar and radio intelligence. To compound Ozawa's problems, he lost two carriers to US submarines and another to a counter-strike by American aircraft. In this case, the first strike did not prove to be the first *effective* strike. Controversially, Spruance decided not to pursue the retreating Japanese foe, instead remaining in the vicinity of the amphibious forces at Saipan. He was to receive some criticism for this failure to focus on the enemy fleet and to secure its destruction.

Spruance's 'failure' at the Philippine Sea can be put into perspective by an examination of the last major naval battle of the war, at Leyte Gulf (23–6 October 1944). Often described as the largest naval battle in history, Leyte Gulf represents a series of interconnected battles. Once again, the Japanese were responding to a US amphibious assault, this time on the island of

Leyte in the Philippines. In the kind of complex plan that they favoured during this war, the Japanese Navy sought to entice the US carrier force to the north with bait provided by their remaining aircraft carriers, vessels that, in the absence of trained aircrew, were now of limited fighting value. Meanwhile, two traditional surface forces would close in on the amphibious fleet in a pincer movement to destroy it and its escort while the carriers were away. Admiral Halsey, in command of the US Third fleet (including sixteen carriers), took the bait. Maintaining his focus on the enemy fleet, he pursued the carriers to achieve a decisive victory. This provided the Japanese with a significant opportunity to attack the US amphibious group off Leyte and to secure their own victory against the odds. In the event, both prongs of the Japanese pincer were defeated by US surface forces and the small escort carriers that were with them at the battles of the Surigao Strait and the San Bernadino Strait. However, in both cases, and particularly the latter, the Japanese had been presented with a significant opportunity that would not have existed if Halsey had remained concentrated in the vicinity of the amphibious force, as had Spruance at the Philippine Sea. It is by no means clear that maintaining a focus on the destruction of the enemy fleet is always the best option.

The battle of Leyte Gulf also provides an interesting insight into the problems facing an inferior navy. The Japanese naval command was fully aware that the battle would probably result in very heavy losses to their own forces but reasoned that if the amphibious invasion proceeded unhindered and the Philippines fell, then their strategic position would become untenable, particularly regarding the supply of fuel oil from the Dutch East Indies. In such circumstances, there would be no point in maintaining a fleet in being, and thus it was better to chance the fleet in a desperate gamble. By posing a threat to their vital interests, the United States had forced their hand.

Naval warfare and the Cold War, 1945–89

In the years after 1945, navies continued to fulfil their traditional roles. However, the devastating potential of nuclear weapons posed challenges that were both tactical and strategic. At the tactical level, the destructive potential of such weapons posed serious question marks over the future viability of concentrated naval forces. Navies could, and did, point to their potential for manoeuvre and also dispersal as effective defensive countermeasures, in addition to the value of the air defence and counter-strike potential provided by their aircraft carriers. Unfortunately, some maritime operations required a degree of concentration that would render them highly vulnerable. These included important activities that had been central to Allied success in the Second World War, such as large-scale amphibious operations and also the delivery of convoys to congested ports.

Over time, warship design adapted to make these vessels and their crew less vulnerable to the side-effects of nuclear attack and also to attack by chemical and biological weapons. By design, ships remain less vulnerable to attack by weapons of mass destruction (WMDs) than their land-based counterparts. The deployment of nuclear weapons at sea from the 1960s, in the form of bombs, missiles and depth charges, offered navies great potential for land-attack and anti-submarine warfare. Navies developed new approaches for the conduct of operations in an environment where nuclear exchange was possible and continued to see a role for themselves in major war situations, particularly after NATO placed a renewed emphasis on conventional warfighting under its policy of Flexible Response adopted in the late 1960s. A notable example of this came with the US *Maritime Strategy* of the 1980s, whereby the US Navy planned to place its aircraft carrier battle groups deliberately in harm's way, posing a challenge to Soviet nuclear submarine 'bastions' in northern waters in a bold attempt to seize the initiative in a future war at sea. Nevertheless, the widespread use of nuclear weapons against naval forces and their supporting infrastructure would have posed serious questions as to their ability to perform traditional duties, or indeed any co-ordinated role. The same, of course, applied to armies and air forces, and was denied as vociferously by generals and air marshals as it was by admirals. These issues are discussed in greater depth in chapter 6.

At a broader level, the proliferation of nuclear weapons posed a serious challenge to the credibility of navies that lacked an obvious role in a future conflict, which was expected by many to be characterised by an early and massive nuclear exchange. In the 1940s, the US Navy sought to develop a role in that nuclear exchange for its aircraft carriers, while in the 1950s the British Royal Navy stressed its utility in the 'broken-backed' warfare that might follow such an exchange. Neither was particularly convincing to policy-makers. Both navies did, however, develop an important role in the provision of flexible military options in situations short of all-out war, focusing in particular on the power-projection potential of their aircraft carriers and a regenerated amphibious capability.

Western naval forces fulfilled a variety of useful roles in the various crises and conflicts beyond Europe that characterised the Cold War and that accompanied the decolonisation of Africa and Asia. That the traditional roles of power projection and naval diplomacy remained as important as ever was demonstrated in a series of conflicts and crises from the Korean War that began in 1950 to the Falklands Conflict of 1982 and the Gulf War of 1991. Somewhat belatedly, the Soviet Union came to recognise the value of this role and, from the late 1960s, developed both the size and reach of its navy.

With the end of the Cold War, and the demise of the Soviet threat, most Western navies moved away from strategies designed to cater for a major war in Europe to more limited contingencies. These ranged from crisis response, sanctions enforcement and peace-support operations through to expeditionary warfare and maritime power projection. This change in priorities was reflected in the policy of the US Navy, in medium-sized navies such as the French and British, and even, on a smaller scale, in the coastal navies of Norway and Denmark. It also tended to be accompanied by an increasing emphasis on joint (interservice) operations. Sea control now tended to be viewed more as a local problem within littoral regions in the context of forward presence and expeditionary warfare rather than a worldwide assault on seaborne communications.

The years after 1945 saw changes in the size and structure of navies, including the final demise of the battleship, most of which had been retired from active service by the 1960s. A handful of battleships remained in periodic service with the US Navy until 1992, providing shore bombardment with their 16-inch guns and, after a refit in the 1980s, with Tomahawk cruise missiles. Cruisers, destroyers and frigates remained important surface combatants, although by the 1970s the gun was being replaced as the primary weapon system by missiles for anti-air and anti-surface warfare, in addition to improved torpedoes, depth charges, rockets and mortars for anti-submarine warfare. The deployment of helicopters at sea, en masse on specialist amphibious ships and aircraft carriers, and also individually on frigates, destroyers and cruisers, enhanced the flexibility and potency of surface warships, particularly in the fields of amphibious warfare and anti-submarine operations, for which helicopters proved particularly well suited.

We have already seen that even before 1945 aircraft carriers had replaced the battleship in its role as capital ship. Aircraft carriers provided a more flexible platform and more effective options for air defence, sea control and land attack than did the battleship and now represented the most potent, and therefore the most desirable, symbols of naval power. Unfortunately, they, and their associated air complements, were also more expensive to operate, making it harder for second- and third-rank navies to afford them. A number of navies deployed small carriers with limited air groups, but only the US Navy was able to develop 'super carriers', such as the USS *Nimitz*, a 100,000-ton nuclear-powered vessel capable of operating around 90 fixed- and rotary-wing aircraft. These vessels, supported by an array of destroyers and cruisers, represent the ultimate expression of naval power and are capable of exerting force both at sea and deep inland.

As ever, while some navies focused on sea control and power projection, others focused primarily on sea denial. Existing weaponry, such as mines, torpedoes, coastal artillery and land-based aircraft, was subjected to incremental improvements and in the 1960s was supplemented by anti-ship missiles. The potency of these missiles was demonstrated in 1967 when the Israeli destroyer *Eilat* was sunk by Soviet-built Styx missiles fired from an

Egyptian missile boat. The dangers that they posed were demonstrated again during the 1971 Indo–Pakistan War, when the Indian Navy launched successful attacks against the port of Karachi using Osa class missile boats, sinking a destroyer and a minesweeper in the initial strike and destroying most of the Pakistan Navy's fuel reserves in a follow-up attack. The 1973 Yom Kippur/Ramadan War included engagements between Israeli missile-armed craft and (separately) their Syrian and Egyptian opponents. The Israelis' Gabriel missile lacked the range of the Styx missiles deployed by their enemies, but they overcame this disadvantage by adopting a tactic whereby they tempted their opponent to fire at long range, where chaff (metallic strips designed to confuse the missile's radar) and electronic counter-measures (e.g. jamming the missiles' guidance systems) ensured that the missiles were ineffective. Then, once the enemy had exhausted their limited supply of missiles, the Israelis closed the range and launched their own counter-strikes, sinking numerous Syrian and Egyptian vessels with no loss to their own forces. Experience during this war further illustrated that, while technology is an important factor in naval warfare, the impact that it has depends on the way in which it is used. It is not an independent variable.

There were a small number of naval engagements at sea during the Cold War and a large number of times when navies projected force against the shore, but there were no large naval battles equivalent to those fought in the Second World War. The victims of naval force projection could often do little to protect themselves at sea, as they usually did not possess a navy capable of challenging enemy sea control. In 1982, the Argentine Navy did have a mix of capabilities, including missile-armed surface ships, submarines and even an old aircraft carrier, with which to challenge the British in their attempt to repossess the Falkland Islands. However, the ease with which the British nuclear-powered submarine HMS *Conqueror* sank the cruiser ARA *General Belgrano* illustrated the danger facing Argentine ships at sea and caused that navy to withdraw its vessels, adopting a very passive fleet-in-being approach for the remainder of the conflict. Notwithstanding failed Argentine attempts to use their own submarines against the British task force, the remainder of the battle for sea control/denial revolved around a contest between land-based aircraft flying from Argentina and British surface ships and carrier aviation. The latter played a key role but was always in short supply and was hampered by a lack of airborne early warning. Eventually, the British lost one destroyer and a merchant ship sunk and another destroyer damaged by sea-skimming Exocet missiles. They lost a further four ships sunk and ten damaged by conventional bombs dropped by land-based aircraft. In the process, they inflicted heavy losses on the Argentine Air Force and were able to gain a sufficiently favourable air situation in order to maintain enough sea control to blockade the islands, conduct an amphibious

Figure 3.3 The nuclear-powered attack submarine HMS *Conqueror* in the South Atlantic, 26 April 1982, with HMS *Antrim* and *Plymouth* in the background. *Conqueror* is transferring an SBS special forces party to *Plymouth*. One week later, operating in its more traditional role, *Conqueror* would sink the Argentine cruiser ARA *General Belgrano*, demonstrating the potency of submarines in naval warfare.

landing at San Carlos and support the land campaign that defeated the occupying Argentine Army.

The Falklands Conflict illustrated that the most potent challenge to sea control would often come from land-based systems. It also illustrated that old weapons as well as new could challenge navies at sea. Notably during the 1991 Gulf War, it was a very old weapon, traditional sea mines, that posed the greatest threat to Coalition activity at sea, badly damaging the cruiser USS *Princeton* and the amphibious assault ship USS *Tripoli*. Ironically, *Tripoli* was at the time acting as flagship for the minesweeping operations taking place in the northern Gulf. The requirement for an effective mine counter-measures capability was reinforced. The timely provision of such a capability in expeditionary operations is complicated by the limited size and speed of most mine counter-measures vessels. In the 1991 Gulf War, Coalition naval forces blockaded Iraq, contributed to the land-based air effort with carrier aviation, conducted strikes against land targets with missiles and guns, and destroyed with ease the small Iraqi Navy. A US Marine Corps force embarked in amphibious shipping threatened to conduct a landing on the Iraqis' flank in Kuwait, forcing them to divert forces to meet this threat. In the broadest sense, the entire war was enabled by Coalition sea control, for without this it would have been impossible to build up the land forces in Saudi Arabia. Over 90 per cent of equipment and supplies employed by US forces during Operation Desert Storm arrived by sea. Given this, it was fortunate that Iraq did not possess any submarines capable of attacking reinforcement shipping en route to the Gulf.

Submarines only really reached maturity after the Second World War. By the end of that conflict, the Germans had introduced snorkel equipment that allowed their boats to run on diesel engines without having to surface, greatly reducing their vulnerability to air attack. More recently, the development of Air-Independent Propulsion (AIP) systems for diesel-electric submarines (SSKs) has further reduced the vulnerability of these boats, making them more like true submarines than the submersibles of the two world wars. Advances in submarine technology made SSKs quieter and thus more difficult to detect, significantly enhancing their potential, particularly in shallow water where large, nuclear-powered boats are at a disadvantage. The US Navy developed the first nuclear-powered submarines (SSNs) in the 1950s. Such vessels boast high speed and unlimited endurance, and have no requirement to surface in order to replenish batteries. Equipped with torpedoes, anti-ship missiles and, in some cases, land-attack cruise missiles, they are extremely potent weapons platforms. It is significant that the British have given their SSNs old battleship names. However, being larger and noisier than SSKs, they are less well suited to shallow coastal waters. They are also more expensive and technologically demanding than SSKs, meaning that, unlike diesel-electric boats which are now widely available, only the most advanced navies currently possess this capability. When equipped with ballistic missiles, such boats (SSBNs) have proved to be an ideal means of deploying a nuclear deterrent, owing to their relative invulnerability to a pre-emptive strike. The presence, or potential presence, of submarines in a war zone continues to force navies to be circumspect in their activities.

Thus far this chapter has identified continuing change at the tactical level of naval warfare and a considerable degree of continuity in the roles that navies fulfilled. It is not necessarily true that this will always remain the case. It is possible that naval roles might change to reflect political or strategic developments and that, even if the roles do remain, navies might be forced to change their forms dramatically in order to meet future challenges. The notion that enhancements in information systems and precision firepower have engendered a Revolution in Military Affairs (RMA) has had as much an impact on naval warfare as on land and air operations. Similarly, the trend towards joint operations has affected operations at sea as well as on land. Navies, like their counterparts in armies, have also suffered from the claims of air power enthusiasts that air forces have made other forms of military power either less relevant or less viable in conditions of modern warfare. Navies are particularly vulnerable to the latter claim, given their oft-stated (but rarely proved) vulnerability to air attack. This section will address the challenges and implications posed by such ideas.

Naval warfare: changing roles?

Contemporary Western navies continue to emphasise power projection from the sea, and none more so than the US Navy. In the absence of a peer rival, the US Navy does not currently have to contend with a sustained global challenge to sea control such as occurred during both world wars and was anticipated during the Cold War. This has allowed them to refocus attention away from such contingencies and to focus on the positive use of maritime power. This in turn has brought an increased emphasis on joint operations, with a conscious focus on operations within a joint battlespace that contains, but is not limited to, the maritime environment.

This switch in US naval strategy was articulated in a series of policy statements, including: *From the sea* (1992), *Forward . . . from the sea* (1994), and, for the US Marine Corps, *Operational Maneuver from the Sea* (1996). The Department of the Navy's vision for the twenty-first century was expressed in *Naval Power 21* (2002) and the Navy and Marine Corps' strategies in *Sea Power 21* and *Marine Corps Strategy 21*. The latter, under the concept of 'expeditionary maneuver warfare', seeks to harness advances in technology allied to concepts of manoeuvre warfare (see chapter 2) greatly to enhance the ability to project, support and, if necessary, sustain military force ashore. Similarly, *Sea Power 21* stresses that the sea will provide 'a vast maneuver area from which to project direct and decisive power around the globe'. Under this strategy, the Navy is defined in terms of three fundamental concepts of Sea Strike, Sea Shield and Sea Basing. Sea Strike is defined as the ability to project precise and persistent offensive power from the sea. Sea Shield is the ability to use sea-based systems not only to defend naval task forces but also to provide theatre and strategic defences, and to contribute to homeland defence. Sea Basing, as the name suggests, involves basing military forces and their support at sea. It is intended to provide 'operational maneuver and assured access to the joint force while significantly reducing our footprint ashore and minimizing the permissions required to operate from host nations'.

Sea Basing is identified as a vital enabling capability for both Sea Strike and Sea Shield, as it will allow forces to be deployed and sustained without undue reliance on land facilities, providing flexibility, supporting manoeuvre potential and reducing vulnerability to political and military challenges. It is not relevant just to high-intensity warfighting. An associated concept is that of the Global Fleet Station (GFS), a persistent sea base of operations from which to co-ordinate and employ adaptive force packages within a regional area of interest. Through the provision of persistent presence, the GFS concept is intended to enable maritime security activities and the building of regional partnerships in support of regional stability and global maritime awareness. Sea Basing thus has utility at all levels of conflict, from diplomatic 'presence' missions, through low-intensity security and counter-terrorist activities, to maritime strike and expeditionary operations such as those that characterised US and allied operations in Afghanistan (2001) and Iraq (2003). It provides another way of maintaining presence without occupation and, potentially, coercion without embroilment.

Such approaches are beyond the means of most navies. Medium-sized navies will experience difficulties matching these capabilities, even on a reduced scale. Most navies, of course, will not try. They will continue to focus on their particular requirements, whether they be constabulary, local sea control or sea denial. *Sea Power 21* will have little relevance to navies like the Irish Naval Service, whose main roles are protecting national security (defined as the ability to deter or resist aggression, surveillance of the Exclusive Economic Zone and upholding neutrality) in addition to fishery protection, aid to the civil power, maritime safety, diving operations, pollution control and support to overseas UN missions. These roles, and the forces available to support them (eight patrol vessels), will more closely reflect the experience of many Western navies than the US example does. One should note that they are enabled by the benign maritime environment in which the Irish Naval Service operates and to which the US Navy contributes.

Non-Western navies are designed to fulfil a wide range of roles, from largely constabulary navies, such as those of Fiji or Ghana, to those with an overt focus on sea denial in local waters, such as the Iranian Navy. The Russian Navy has suffered from years of neglect since the fall of the Soviet Union, apparently confirming Mahan's views on the difficulties of maintaining a first-rank navy when lacking the characteristics of a 'sea power'. The navy still has a capable submarine arm and the potential to be a powerful sea-denial force with some capacity for sea control and power projection at a regional level. In the Pacific theatre, China's People's Liberation Army (Navy) represents a regional force optimised for coastal defence, local sea control and small, well-defined campaigns to enforce sovereignty claims against Taiwan and in the South China Seas. It is intended to prevail

Figure 3.4 The guided-missile cruiser USS *Bunker Hill* fires a Tomahawk cruise missile towards Iraq, March 2003. Such missiles, also deployed in submarines, provide modern navies with an ability to strike targets deep inland with great accuracy.

Figure 3.5 The Singapore Navy frigate RSS *Formidable* (foreground) and the Indian Navy frigate INS *Brahmaputra* conducting exercises in the Bay of Bengal, September 2007, as part of a multinational exercise that also included American, Australian and Japanese vessels. Such exercises provide valuable training in multinational operations and also serve a useful diplomatic purpose.

out to what is known as the First Island Chain (running from the Kurile Islands, through Japan, Taiwan, the Philippines and Borneo) but has a very limited capacity to project force beyond this, and, despite occasional claims to the contrary, there seem to be no serious plans to develop large, blue-water capabilities in the near future. These are all fairly traditional roles for inferior navies. The Indian Navy is slightly different. It has pretensions to be the major navy within the Indian Ocean and has sought to develop a traditional balanced fleet, including aircraft carriers, that will enable it to conduct the full range of naval tasks, including sea denial, sea control and power projection.

In the 1970s, Ken Booth borrowed an analogy from Clausewitz (see chapter 1) and described the functions of navies as a trinity. The 'one-ness' of the trinity was provided by the idea of the 'use of the sea' and its character was defined by three characteristic modes of action by which navies carried out their purposes: the military, the diplomatic and the policing function.[27] Ten

Box 3.5 The functions of navies

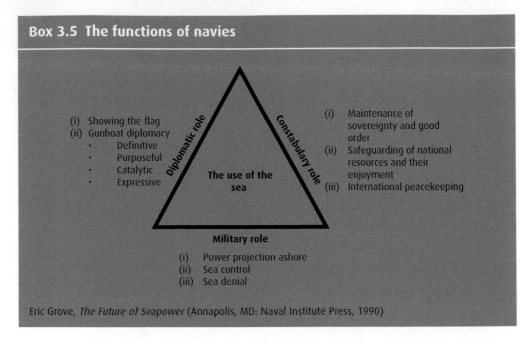

Eric Grove, *The Future of Seapower* (Annapolis, MD: Naval Institute Press, 1990)

years later, Eric Grove adopted a similar approach, although he preferred to use the term 'constabulary' in preference to 'policing' when describing that role (see box 3.5).[28] The military role lies at the base of the trinity, because it is a navy's ultimate ability to threaten or use violence that gives meaning to the other modes of action. It is also this that distinguishes them from coastguards.

An examination of current and planned future naval activity suggests that the trinity is as valid in the twenty-first century as it was in the Cold War. Navies continue to fulfil these functions, although different navies place varying emphases on each depending on their particular circumstances. This in turn calls for a different mix of capabilities, according to what the particular navy is designed to achieve. It makes little sense for a navy that focuses on constabulary duties, as do many, to attempt to provide a scaled-down version of a navy optimised for global power projection. Within the military function, it remains the case that some navies focus on gaining and exploiting sea control while others emphasise sea denial in one form of another. This is nothing new. The means of achieving these ends has changed, but the basic functions or roles appear enduring.

Naval warfare: changing forms?

Given the widespread availability of sea-denial weapons, many of which do not require one to be particularly proficient at sea, questions have been raised as to the survivability of naval forces, and particularly surface vessels, in conditions of modern warfare. The successful attack on the Israeli corvette INS *Hanit* by Hezbollah militia using a radar-guided C-802 missile in July 2006 demonstrates that even sub-state actors may have access to such weapons. Small, cheap, fast-attack craft armed with such weapons have sometimes appeared likely to fulfil the prophesies of the *Jeune École*, prompting two American writers, commenting on the US Navy's continued emphasis on large surface ships, to suggest that '[t]he US is making a few well-armoured knights and they will face a forest full of peasants armed with longbows'.[29] Missile-armed fast-attack craft pack a powerful punch but are, like nineteenth-century torpedo boats, vulnerable to enemy counter-measures. The fate of Iraqi fast-attack craft in 1991, destroyed with ease by Coalition aircraft, may be instructive.

Land-based missiles and air forces are likely to continue to pose a threat, although they are also vulnerable to pre-emptive missile or air attack from the sea. Mines will continue to offer a relatively cheap means of denying access in coastal waters. SSKs, available 'off-the-shelf' to any state capable of affording them, will pose additional problems. Concerns about the survivability of large surface vessels, particularly in congested littoral waters, have reinforced the desire of the most advanced navies to develop the ability to project military force into the littoral while remaining further offshore, 'over the horizon', where they may be better able to deal with the threats that they face. They have also prompted such developments as the US 'littoral combat ship', smaller combatants optimised for the challenging littoral environment. It is worth noting that, while the threats facing navies have increased in recent decades, so has the ability of modern navies to deal with such threats. To date, claims that advances in missile, submarine or aircraft technology will make surface vessels obsolete have proved unfounded. A balanced naval task force, containing a mix of anti-submarine, anti-surface and anti-air assets, represents a powerful offensive and defensive force. It is by no means clear that any air force could hope to achieve much success against a US task force centred upon one or more aircraft carriers and supported by the advanced AEGIS missile defence system. The surface ship remains the only maritime instrument that operates simultaneously on, under and above the surface of the sea, making it by far the most flexible and useful platform, albeit one that requires support from a range of other forces if it is to operate effectively in a high-threat environment. It is unlikely to disappear from naval inventories in the near future.

A different line of reasoning has suggested that navies are less relevant than armies or air forces in the type of asymmetric, low-intensity conflicts in which Western states are most likely to engage in the future. This rather underestimates the range of support that naval forces can provide to a land force using their own aircraft, missiles, artillery and sensors. It also neglects the key role that navies played in the initial Coalition attacks on

Afghanistan (2001) and Iraq (2003), where sea-based missiles, aircraft and (in the case of Iraq) amphibious troops played an important part in the initial military response. In the aftermath of these operations, it is possible that Western governments may once again be very wary of deploying troops on foreign soil, where they become a target for local discontent and terrorist attack. In such circumstances, the ability to keep military forces at sea, available for use but not actually deployed on foreign soil, may be seen as increasingly useful, and this underlies the US concept of Sea Basing discussed above. In any case, the deployment of forces overseas to fight limited wars, and their subsequent support within theatre, depends upon an ability to use the seas to transport most of their heavy equipment and support; in short, it depends on the assured access provided by sea control. That this is not always contested should not hide its importance. Should that sea control be challenged by the emergence of a serious rival to the US Navy, it is likely that there will be a shift in attention away from fighting from the sea towards fighting at sea, as sea control remains the vital prerequisite for all positive use of the sea.

The future of naval warfare

In the first decade of the twenty-first century the US Navy is without peer. Rather like the Royal Navy at times during the nineteenth century, it is both larger and more capable than any other navy or even any likely combination of navies. In terms of a capacity for sustained operations on a global scale, the next most capable navies, those of Britain and France, are much smaller and, in any case, belong to countries that are linked to the United States through formal alliances and shared interests. Future challenges to US hegemony may come from a growth in Chinese, Indian, Japanese and Russian maritime capabilities. The Chinese People's Liberation Army (Navy) may increase its somewhat limited capability for blue-water operations if China fulfils its potential to become an economic and military superpower in the decades ahead. Chapter 2 has already discussed alternative discourses over the future of land warfare. It is just as difficult to predict with certainty the threats that will emerge at sea in the future. Suffice to say, just as a return to large-scale, high-intensity warfighting on land and in the air is not impossible, the same is true at sea. It would be dangerous to assume that navies will never again have to fight to maintain sea control beyond littoral waters. Indeed, the suggestion seems to confuse the relatively benign international environment of today for a shift in the nature of naval warfare.

By focusing on sea control and power projection (albeit under different names), current US policy differs little from traditional ideas about the use of maritime forces. It is likely that Mahan would be comfortable with current US doctrine, Corbett even more so. If the US Navy is able to fulfil the promises contained within current doctrine, then in the twenty-first century the most powerful navy will have a greatly enhanced ability directly to influence events on land than had its counterpart one hundred years ago. However, the vision of naval warfare advocated in these policy statements is technologically demanding, relying on the apparently transforming ability of so-called network-centric operations to deliver information dominance and to 'glue' together troops, sensors, command and control, platforms and weapons into 'a networked, distributed combat force'. The result may indeed be transforming. In the past, there was a cost associated with translating strength at sea into strength ashore; naval gunfire had limited reach, aircraft carriers carried limited numbers of aircraft, and amphibious forces were often short of heavy equipment and transport. In the future portrayed by the US Navy, there will be a premium associated with sea-based forces as the old limitations of the past are overcome and the strategic manoeuvre potential of maritime forces is retained at the operational and tactical levels through Sea Basing. Indeed, new technologies and the techniques that they enable may significantly enhance the ability of navies to exploit access to project power ashore, enabling new approaches to amphibious operations and providing for precision-strike at extended range. New hull forms may increase speed of transit, reducing the reaction time for strategic sealift, further enhancing the manoeuvre potential of maritime forces. It is not possible to foresee the future, but it seems likely that navies will continue to adapt and to provide useful military options in a variety of circumstances.

The discussion above seems to confirm that, while the tactics and technology of naval warfare have changed and will continue to change over time, navies continue to fulfil their traditional roles and that these remain focused upon achieving, exploiting or denying sea control in order to influence events on land. The ability to utilise the manoeuvre potential of the sea will remain as important in the future as it was in the past. The globalised world economy is entirely dependent on the free passage of seaborne trade, providing all responsible states with a stake in maintaining its flow. This shared interest and also shared vulnerability underlie US aspirations to create a '1,000-ship navy' in which numerous states would collaborate in policing and protecting 'the maritime commons'. Protecting the 'maritime system' from various challenges, whether they be from terrorism, piracy, the actions of rogue states or accidental damage caused by sloppy practice at sea, represents, in a sense, a new form of sea control that all navies, large and small, may contribute towards in co-operation rather than conflict. This apparent shared interest should not blind one to the fact that the sea also remains an important avenue for military endeavours. This was illustrated by US and Allied activity in Afghanistan and Iraq, where maritime forces played an important role in both campaigns, projecting power deep inland from platforms offshore. It was also demonstrated, on a smaller scale, by the activities of the Israeli Navy, conducting blockade and bombardment operations in support of the Israeli campaign in Lebanon in 2006. The ability of naval forces to exploit their inherent attributes, and those of the medium in which they operate, in order to provide access that can be turned into leverage is central to current US policy. The denial of such access will figure prominently in the minds of potential opponents. While sustained conflict at sea on a global scale appears highly unlikely at present, it would be naive to assume that this will always remain the case. An understanding of naval warfare will be as important in the twenty-first century as it was in the twentieth, and, indeed, as it has been for centuries.

NOTES

1 Colin S. Gray, *The Leverage of Seapower: The Strategic Advantage of Navies in War* (New York: The Free Press, 1992), p. ix.
2 Julian Corbett, *Some Principles of Maritime Strategy* (Annapolis, MD: Naval Institute Press, 1988 [first publ. 1911]), p. 13.
3 *Naval Doctrine Publication 1. Naval Warfare* (Washington, DC: US Govt. Printing Office, 1994).
4 Philip Crowl, 'Alfred Thayer Mahan: The Naval Historian', in Peter Paret, ed., *Makers of Modern Strategy from Machiavelli to the Nuclear Age* (Princeton, NJ: Princeton University Press, 1986), p. 444.
5 *Indian Maritime Doctrine* (India: Ministry of Defence (Navy), 2004), p. 43.
6 See Gray, *The Leverage of Seapower*, passim.
7 *BR1806, British Maritime Doctrine*, 3rd edn (London: The Stationery Office, 2004), p. 35.
8 *Indian Maritime Doctrine*, p. 69.
9 See Geoffrey Till, *Seapower: A Guide for the Twenty-First Century* (London: Frank Cass, 2004), pp. 35–6.
10 Andrew Lambert, 'The Development of Education in the Royal Navy: 1854–1914', in Geoffrey Till, ed., *The Development of British Naval Thinking: Essays in Memory of Bryan Ranft* (London: Routledge, 2006), p. 47.
11 Philip Crowl, 'Alfred Thayer Mahan: The Naval Historian', in Paret, ed., *Makers of Modern Strategy*, p. 445.
12 Geoffrey Till, 'Sir Julian Corbett and the Twenty-First Century: Ten Maritime Commandments', in Andrew Dorman, Mike Smith and Mathew Uttley, eds., *The Changing Face of Maritime Power* (Basingstoke: Macmillan, 1999), p. 19.
13 Corbett, *Some Principles*, p. 14.

14 Sir Charles Callwell, *The Effect of Maritime Command on Land Campaigns since Waterloo* (London: Blackwood, 1897) and *Military Operations and Maritime Preponderance: Their Relations and Interdependence* (London: Blackwood, 1905). Also see Sir George Aston, *Letters on Amphibious Wars* (London: John Murray, 1911) and George Furse, *Military Expeditions beyond the Seas*, 2 vols. (London: William Clowes, 1897).

15 For a discussion of these see Till, *Seapower*, ch. 2 and also his *Maritime Strategy and the Nuclear Age* (London: Macmillan, 1982).

16 See Philip Colomb, *Naval Warfare: Its Ruling Principles and Practice Historically Treated* (Annapolis, MD: Naval Institute Press, 1990 [first publ. 1891]), pp. 204–12.

17 Colin Gray, *The Navy in the Post-Cold War World: The Uses and Value of Strategic Sea Power* (Pennsylvania, PA: Pennsylvania State University Press, 2004), pp. 14–15.

18 *Australian Maritime Doctrine. RAN Doctrine 1*, ch. 5. Available online at www.navy.gov.nu/spc/amd/amdintro.html.

19 *British Maritime Doctrine*, p. 289.

20 *Naval Doctrine Publication 1. Naval Warfare*, pp. 63–4.

21 See Jacob Borresen, 'Coastal Power: The Sea Power of the Coastal State and the Management of Maritime Resources', in Rolf Hobson and Tom Kristiansen, eds., *Navies in Northern Waters, 1722–2000* (London: Frank Cass, 2004), pp. 249–75.

22 Wolfgang Wegener, *The Naval Strategy of the World War* (Annapolis, MD: Naval Institute Press, 1989 [first publ. 1929]).

23 B. Mitchell Simpson III, ed., *The Development of Naval Thought: Essays by Herbert Roskinski* (Newport, RI: Naval War College Press, 1977), pp. 15–17.

24 *Ibid.*, pp. 78–9.

25 See Raoul Castex, *Strategic Theories*, ed. and trans. by Eugenia Kiesling (Annapolis, MD: Naval Institute Press, 1994).

26 Wayne Hughes, *Fleet Tactics and Coastal Combat*, 2nd edn (Annapolis, MD: Naval Institute Press, 2000).

27 Ken Booth, *Navies and Foreign Policy* (London: Croom Helm, 1977), p. 15.

28 Eric Grove, *The Future of Sea Power* (Annapolis, MD: Naval Institute Press, 1990), pp. 232–6.

29 Joseph Gattuso and Lori Tanner, 'Set and Drift Naval Force in the New Century', in *Naval War College Review* (Winter 2001).

FURTHER READING

Cable, James, *Navies in Violent Peace* (New York: St. Martin's Press, 1989).
Offers a valuable introduction to the use of navies in situations short of war.

Callwell, Charles, *Military Operations and Maritime Preponderance: Their Relations and Interdependence* (Annapolis, MD: Naval Institute Press, 1996 [first publ. 1905]).
A classic examination of the interrelationship between operations on land and at sea and of the utility of amphibious operations.

Castex, Raoul, *Strategic Theories* (Annapolis, MD: Naval Institute Press, 1994).
An abridged translation of the French admiral's theories on the use of navies. Of particular interest for his theory of strategic manoeuvre and the employment of navies of the second rank.

Corbett, Julian, *Some Principles of Maritime Strategy* (Annapolis, MD: Naval Institute Press, 1988 [first publ. 1911]).
This volume outlines Corbett's views on maritime strategy. No serious student of the subject can afford to ignore this work.

Friedman, Norman, *Seapower as Strategy: Navies and National Interests* (Annapolis, MD: Naval Institute Press, 2001).
An examination of the role of navies in the twenty-first century, supported by a range of historical case studies.

Gorshkov, S., *The Sea Power of the State* (Annapolis, MD: Naval institute Press, 1979).
An examination of the subject from a Soviet perspective by the then commander-in-chief of the Soviet Navy.

Gray, Colin, *The Leverage of Seapower: The Strategic Advantage of Navies in War* (New York: The Free Press, 1992).
One of the most influential contemporary commentators on strategic issues provides an examination of the strategic impact of maritime power from ancient times through to the present day.

Grove, Eric, *The Future of Sea Power* (Annapolis, MD: Naval Institute Press, 1990).
Slightly dated now, but still a useful examination of maritime power and the role of navies.

     and Hore, Peter, eds., *Dimensions of Sea Power* (Hull: University of Hull Press, 1998).
Provides a collection of good short essays that examine different aspects of maritime power at the end of the twentieth century.

Hughes, Wayne, *Fleet Tactics and Coastal Combat* (Annapolis, MD: Naval Institute Press, 2000).
A detailed examination of the evolution of modern naval tactics.

Mahan, Alfred Thayer, *The Influence of Sea Power upon History, 1660–1783* (Boston, MA: Little Brown, 1890).
Mahan's best-known book, and a useful introduction to his ideas.

Sumida, Jon, *Inventing Grand Strategy and Teaching Command: The Classic Works of Alfred Thayer Mahan* (Baltimore, MD: Johns Hopkins University Press, 1997).
A valuable introduction to and examination of Mahan's work.

Till, Geoffrey, *Seapower: A Guide for the Twenty-First Century* (London: Frank Cass, 2004).
Written by one of the most respected authorities on maritime power and strategy, this book provides an excellent introduction to the subject.

Uhlig, Frank, Jnr., *How Navies Fight: The US Navy and its Allies* (Annapolis, MD: US Naval Institute Press, 1994).
Provides an examination of naval history and warfare since the eighteenth century with a particular, but not exclusive, emphasis on US experience.

CHAPTER 4

AIR AND SPACE WARFARE

CONTENTS

KEY THEMES

- The air and space environments are very complex. This complexity is reflected in the sustained and vigorous debates on the roles, use, and utility of air and space power.
- Air power is important. Some form of control of the air is required for armies or navies to perform effectively. Air power creates powerful synergies in combination with surface forces. Nevertheless, air power should be seen as an enabler rather than an end in itself.
- The 'strategic effect' that air power can deliver is much broader than the simple delivery of firepower against targets beyond the battlefield. Air power is a flexible tool, although this flexibility can be undermined by trying to impose its use on a single conceptual model.

This chapter examines the key concepts of air warfare, introducing the basic principles of air power. It seeks to provide the reader with insights into some of the concepts of air warfare and the challenges presented by an operating environment stretching from a few yards above the ground to the outer reaches of the earth's atmosphere. It then considers space power, which, while relevant to all military operating environments, has some notable synergies with air power concepts.

Despite the perception that air power is a form of warfare that originated with the development of the aeroplane, some of the key aspects of modern aerial warfare can be traced to the late eighteenth century. They illustrate not only that some of the premises regarding modern air power had their origins in concepts that remained within the institutional memory of armies and navies (even if the memories were rather dim) but also that some of the basic notions underpinning modern air power thinking are closely related to long-standing principles of war itself, rather than being revolutionary and unrelated to conflicts of centuries past. The First World War saw a pronounced quickening of aviation technology, and by the conclusion of the conflict in 1918 the fundamental roles and missions of air services had been established. The success of aircraft in the conflict also led to deeper thinking about military aviation, and from this stemmed a range of controversies and disputes over the fundamental purpose of air power, many of which remain relevant today.

These debates illustrate that, despite its relative youth compared with the history of conflict within the land and maritime environments, the nature of air power is a contested area. It swiftly became the subject of intense debate as to its precise utility and its political, ethical and technological dimensions, a discourse complicated by contending perspectives regarding the degree of subservience or otherwise of air services to surface forces. This was further complicated by arguments between air power theorists propounding the notion that air forces can be the decisive factor in conflict with little or no involvement of the other services and those who thought such ideas ludicrous. The picture was further complicated by subtle variations in the views of the leading air power theorists and the fact that some nations – notably France and Germany – took different views from these theorists with regard to their own air services.

As will be seen, while the controversies began in the immediate aftermath of the First World War, they have not all been resolved, in spite of technological advances and different perceptions about the nature of war itself. Debate – often heated – has ebbed and flowed over the ensuing decades, frequently as practitioners, politicians and analysts use the most recent conflict to espouse a particular view of air power and the 'right way' to use it. Such contentions are influenced by service loyalties and the dictates of the prevalent fiscal climate – often inextricably linked factors as armed services fight for limited funding. Endeavouring to understand air power in modern war can, therefore, sometimes be a challenge, and comprehension can be made more difficult unless conceptual debates of air power's early years are recognised. Inherent in any assessment of the evolution of air power is the constant of technological development. From the start, this has driven air power theorists to postulate views of revolutionary or near-revolutionary changes to the nature of warfare, sometimes despite the fact that their calculations have depended on nascent technology working perfectly from the outset, something that has rarely occurred.

Notions that the rise of modern air power and its associated technology has rendered the views of Carl von Clausewitz obsolete have all too frequently been disproved when subjected to Clausewitz's ideas of 'friction' and 'the fog of war'. This, in turn, has meant that cynics have been far too willing to criticise the quality of advocacy for air power, reducing often complex issues to simplistic sound bites. This chapter examines the development and refinement of the basic principles established by interwar theorists and the imperatives underpinning their ideas. The association of bombing with strategic air power has become so entrenched within air forces that some of the other strategic applications of air power have been overlooked, and the chapter addresses some of the areas where air action other than that by bombers has been of importance. Air power has been vital when employed in conjunction with surface forces (used in this chapter as shorthand for armies and navies). It could be argued, therefore, that the views of the theorists regarding the strategic application of air power have been disproved by the successful application of air power in the land and maritime environments, but such contentions have often been based on a simplistic analysis of events and do not prove that air power is always subordinate to land and naval units, as some observers might suggest.

While the major concepts of control of the air (and space), strategic air operations and operations in conjunction with other forces remain valid, there has been much evolution in both theory and practice, which has made air power a particularly dynamic environment in its short history.

The air environment

The air is perhaps the most challenging environment in which humans can fight. As altitude increases, thinner air means that the supply of oxygen decreases to the point where the ability of a human being to function declines progressively until unconsciousness and then death ensue. The drastic fall in temperature as altitude increases adds to the problems of survival. Aircrew in the First World War operated aeroplanes that could, at the end of the conflict, reach heights of approximately 20,000 feet. The bitter cold experienced even at relatively low altitudes could be partially overcome by wearing heavy clothing, but this hampered movement and dexterity, making the aircraft more difficult to fly. The cold and a lack of oxygen meant that operating at above 10,000 feet was a deeply fatiguing experience.

These physiological effects were soon recognised by doctors; by the outbreak of the Second World War, most – although by no means all – military aircraft were provisioned with an oxygen system, with the aircrew supplied through a face-mask. As technology advanced, pressurisation systems were developed for certain military aircraft to keep the pressure experienced in the cockpit or passenger area at that experienced several thousand feet lower than the actual altitude at which the aircraft flew. A further challenge facing aircrew, and one not regularly encountered by sailors or soldiers, is that of gravitational force. As an aircraft manoeuvres, g-forces may increase. Blood drains from the pilot's head, increasing the risk of unconsciousness. If g is sustained for any length of time, 'black-out' may follow. If the pilot fails to recover quickly, the aircraft can depart from controlled flight and crash. In combat, a semi- or unconscious pilot is highly vulnerable to attack. The crews of high-performance military aircraft are at risk of so-called G-Induced Loss of Consciousness (GLOC). This factor has led to the need to provide aircrew with equipment to mitigate the effect of g, in the form of garments that inflate as g-force increases, compressing the lower limbs to restrict the flow of blood away from the head and reducing the onset of the loss of consciousness.

Physiological challenges presented by temperature and altitude are not the only issue. Platforms that aircrew operate need to be designed to meet the challenges of operating at a variety of altitudes and speed ranges. As a generalisation, it may be said that basic physics and aerodynamic principles complicate the design process for military aircraft rather more than for the equipment to be found in the other two environments. A further consideration for military aircraft designers is the need to provide the crew with the means of escape should their aircraft be fatally damaged or suffer a mechanical failure. After the First World War, air forces began to issue their pilots with parachutes to provide them with a chance of escaping from a fatally damaged aeroplane. The jet age added further complications to crew-escape for designers. The increasing speeds of aircraft made escape more difficult, leading to the development of the ejector seat – but even this presented challenges, since the force required to expel the seat from the aircraft is such that it can cause spinal compression, while there is a risk of traumatic limb amputation caused by wind blast should the pilot be compelled to eject at particularly high speeds.

While these factors may not appear, at first glance, to have a great deal of relevance to understanding modern air warfare, they are in fact important. Unlike sailors and soldiers, military aviators operating combat aircraft that operate at altitude require an array of personal survival equipment simply to ensure that they stay alive whether or not they encounter the enemy.

Attributes of air power

The challenges of operating in the air environment are not air power's only distinct characteristic. Proponents of maritime power sometimes note that 70 per cent of the earth's surface is covered by water. Airmen are not averse to responding that *all* the earth's surface is covered by their operating environment. Air forces can, at least in theory, range across the entire globe, giving air power one of its main characteristics – reach.

Reach

The movement of armies can be hindered by terrain, while navies have historically been unable to attack deep into the heart of enemy territory, constrained by the need for navigable waterways for their warships. Aircraft are unaffected by such vagaries and can engage the enemy at depth, through strikes against rear-echelon forces or by attacking war industries or communications infrastructure. This characteristic has influenced much thinking about air power. It underpinned the concept that strategic bombardment could win wars without surface forces and played a broader part in the consideration of operational art – perhaps best evinced by the examples of Soviet thoughts on air power's part in deep battle, the German use of air power with land forces in blitzkrieg and NATO's development of AirLand battle doctrine in the 1970s and 1980s.

Rapidity

In addition to the reach that aircraft enjoy, they can generally deploy more quickly than ships or vehicles. In cases where a swift response to a crisis is required, aircraft enable the deployment of troops and equipment, while in certain scenarios the ability to engage a desired target within a matter of hours as opposed to a matter of days may be necessary. Cases in point include the rapid reinforcement of Saudi Arabia in 1990 after Iraq's invasion of Kuwait. Following the formal issuing of a request for assistance by the Saudi king, Operation Desert Shield was launched. The vanguard of the deployment came in the form of American fighter and attack aircraft, followed by warplanes from other nations. Desert Shield also saw the delivery of large numbers of troops and equipment, increasing the strength of the defences in Saudi Arabia within the space of a few days. However, despite the deployment, had Saddam Hussein decided to invade, his numerical superiority in terms both of troops and aircraft would have made defence difficult. Only when shipping carrying heavy armour and other equipment too large to be carried in any numbers by air arrived in Saudi Arabia did the balance swing decisively in favour of the defences.

It is important to note that the concepts of reach and rapidity of action do not apply exclusively to land-based air power, since the ability to project air power from the sea has been a significant factor in warfare. Initial aircraft carrier operations began in the First World War, but carrier-based air power came into its own during the Second World War, most notably in the Pacific theatre. The Pacific War began with the projection of Japanese air power from its carrier fleet and ended with targets in Japan being attacked from American carrier-based aircraft. More recent examples of the importance of combining ships and aircraft have been seen in the Falklands Conflict of 1982. Long-range air power from land bases in the form of transport operations, air-to-air refuelling and reconnaissance played a significant, if often underrated, part in that operation, while the carrier-based Sea Harriers of the Royal Navy provided the fleet with the necessary measure of protection against Argentine attacks on shipping, and a small number of Royal Air Force (RAF) Harriers aboard the carriers provided air support for British forces once they had landed upon the islands. Without the carriers, it would have been impossible for fighter aircraft to cover the fleet and support the landings, since there were no land bases within range that could be used for this purpose. The difficulties facing the use of land-based air power were demonstrated in attacks by a single Vulcan bomber against the runway and Argentine positions around Port Stanley airfield. While the attacks achieved the desired effects of inflicting some damage and communicating intent to the Argentines, it took more than a dozen air-to-air refuellings to get a single aircraft to and from its base at Ascension Island. Operating fighter aircraft in such a fashion would have been impossible.

Figure 4.1 Originally designed as a means of delivering nuclear weapons during the Cold War, the USAF's B-1B bomber fleet is now employed delivering precision munitions in the on-going conflict against insurgent groups in Afghanistan and Iraq.

Despite demonstrating the fact that there are limits to air power's reach, even with air-to-air refuelling, the Falklands illustrated the flexibility of air power, which could be turned to a variety of different tasks, and the importance of air power to the success of joint operations; as will be discussed below, events have consistently illustrated that surface forces benefit immeasurably from having air power available to support their operations. The flexibility of air assets, combined with the rapidity with which they can reach the required part of the battle area, enables commanders to concentrate air power and exploit the synergies from co-ordinating air and surface units to maximise the psychological and material impact upon the enemy.

While air power can operate independently, history tends to suggest that independent air operations, while often contributing a great deal to the conduct of a particular war or campaign, do not have the same potency as when they are synergised with land and/or maritime forces. This conflicts with the views of the classic air power theorists and raises considerable debate among commentators. Those such as John A. Warden III (see p. 200) contend that the development of precision weapons and the technological advances in air power that have occurred since 1945 mean that air power can now achieve a strategic effect against the enemy to the point where the opponent may be compelled to surrender swiftly (see figure 4.1). This approach involves following the classic air power notion that air power should be used to attack targets critical to the functioning of the enemy government, such as command-and-control facilities, or critical infra-structure items that prevent the opponent from waging war correctly. If the enemy nation is viewed as a system, its critical vulnerabilities can be targeted in parallel rather than sequentially. Instead of first aiming to destroy the enemy's fielded forces, then moving on to attack – for instance – communications targets, identifying those targets that are vital to the enemy's ability to function and then striking them offers the tantalising prospect of bringing about the enemy's collapse without the need for surface forces to fight against those of the opponent and without the scale of casualties that would be concomitant with such an approach. In this vision, the application of technology, combined with air power's speed and reach, allows the opposition's swift defeat. Critics contend that this view is too optimistic and that, for all the evolution of technology, attacks against supposedly strategic enemy targets have not, to date, brought about the effects that Warden and others have suggested.

Impermanence

Despite the potential offered by air power, there are limitations. Aircraft are incapable of occupying ground, and this means that troops will always be required, unless a campaign is being fought in which the seizure of enemy-held territory is not necessary. Aircraft cannot stay aloft perma-nently, despite the development of air-to-air refuelling, giving rise to another notable characteristic, that of impermanence. Impermanence gives the enemy the opportunity to gain respite from attack as aircraft return to base to rearm. Given the likelihood that it will be impossible to provide sufficient aircraft numbers to keep an aerial presence overhead, such lacunae in the presence of aircraft overhead may minimise the shock effect of an air attack. This can, however, be offset by closely co-ordinated action with the other components to ensure that the effect upon the enemy achieved by air action, be it physical or psychological, is exploited to the full. During the Normandy campaign of the Second World War, for instance, air attacks against German positions caused considerable psy-chological disturbance to German troops, frequently leading to the aban-donment of vehicles and emplacements as the air attack was followed up by the advance of ground forces.

Environmental characteristics, therefore, have significant implications for the effectiveness of air power in warfare. Some of the limiting or adverse characteristics can be mitigated by design, technological development and close co-ordination with the other services, while the positive characteris-tics, such as reach, speed and flexibility, allow air power to be employed to telling effect. The best means of exploiting these characteristics are, however, a source of controversy. Consequently, it is necessary to explore the early developments in air power. Although conceptual thought was often lacking in rigour, with a broad-brush appreciation that exploiting the ability to put man in the air over the battlefield would be useful, the early use of air power for military purposes offers several examples that still have resonance today.

Control of the air

Perhaps the most important aspect of air power is the need to ensure that air forces have the freedom to operate in the face of hostile activity. Without having at least some degree of freedom of action, air forces are unable to function properly, and this has serious effects upon surface forces. In the absence of air defence, enemy aircraft are able to attack targets almost at will.

As shown above, the first role that air power undertook came in the form of reconnaissance and observing for artillery. Both these functions were of critical importance in the First World War, and it was rapidly proved that there was a need for these functions to be carried out if armies were to function effectively, particularly once the war bogged down into static, trench warfare. It then became necessary for the warring sides to attempt to deny their opponent the ability to utilise their air assets effectively, which led to the development of air fighting.

Stories abound of aviators from opposing sides flying past one another on their way to and from the area they were reconnoitring, waving to one another in a fraternal manner. This friendly approach did not last for long. As had been predicted well before the war, it soon became clear that denying the enemy the ability to conduct aerial reconnaissance missions was desirable. By the end of 1914, all the air services engaged in the war in France and Belgium were convinced that it was not a question of whether fighting between aircraft would occur, but when and on what scale, since it was clearly necessary to attempt to deny the enemy the ability to operate effectively. The difficulty, at least initially, was being able to achieve this. Aircraft were not routinely fitted with weapons with which they might attempt to bring down hostile machines, so pilots and observers armed themselves with a variety of weapons in an improvised attempt to provide them with the means of doing that. Such steps proved to be generally ineffective, since aiming pistols and rifles from the cockpit of an aircraft was not an easy task.

The ability of aircraft to manoeuvre in three dimensions at some speed complicated aiming weapons. The need to take account of the speed and angle through which the opposing aircraft was moving when engaged required whoever was firing the weapon in the aircraft to take account of such issues as deflection of aim and making necessary adjustments as the enemy aircraft manoeuvred. It soon became clear that the most effective way of attacking an enemy aircraft was with a machine gun. The rate of fire from this type of weapon increased the probability of obtaining hits on a manoeuvring enemy, but the best means of aiming the machine gun involved pointing the aircraft at the opponent. This, in turn, demanded that the gun be fitted to the centreline of the aircraft, but overwing mountings that fired above the propeller were unwieldy, and mounting machine guns outside the propeller arc meant that they could not be attended to by the pilot if the weapons jammed. This was a common failing with First World War machine guns, which had not been designed to function in the freezing air encountered even at relatively low altitudes.

The initial answer, from the French aviator Roland Garos, came in the form of fitting deflector plates to the propeller blades, but this was an interim solution. The development of interrupter gear by the Dutch designer Anthony Fokker and his team was a far more elegant answer, preventing the gun from firing when the propeller passed in front.

Fokker fitted the device to one of his own aircraft designs, the Fokker Eindekker, and a small number of these aircraft were sent to the Western front in a special fighting unit which inflicted heavy casualties on the French and British. Such was the success of the Fokkers that the period from June 1915 through to early 1916 became known as 'the Fokker Scourge'. By January 1915, the British Royal Flying Corps (RFC) found its operations badly hindered as a result of the threat posed by the Fokkers. This demonstrated one of the effects of gaining some form of control of the air, namely that of compromising the ability of the opponent to conduct aerial missions. The development of new British and French designs, all using their own interrupter gear after mid-1916, tipped the balance in favour of the Allies again – but the period of the Eindekker's dominance marked the point at which control of the air could be thought of as a proper dynamic contest with implications for the success or failure of air operations, and potentially of those operations on the ground that aircraft were trying to support.

The early experiences of the First World War have been replicated ever since. A nation or coalition that has been at a serious disadvantage in the air has never found itself enjoying particular success in the conflict as a whole. Without establishing some form of control of the air, the operations of surface forces become ever more difficult. The Second World War further demonstrated the point. In the opening rounds of the war, the Luftwaffe enjoyed considerable success against Allied forces, and their role contributed significantly to both the attack in the West and, in June 1941, the invasion of the Soviet Union. However, there were already warning signs for the Germans that they could not guarantee that they would maintain control of the air: in 1940 at Dunkirk, the RAF managed to wrest some degree of control from the Germans, which prevented full-scale attacks on the evacuation beaches and the ships that were withdrawing the remnants of the British Expeditionary Force and those elements of the French Army that were in a position to leave so that they might continue the struggle against Hitler elsewhere. The presence of the English Channel then played a further part in undermining the image of the Luftwaffe as invincible, since it was absolutely essential for any invasion of the United Kingdom to be conducted with the Luftwaffe providing air support to the invasion fleet. The Royal Navy presented an enormous threat to any invasion attempt, and it was essential that the Germans destroy as much of the fleet as possible. This was not a realisable goal in terms of the traditional naval battle, since the German Navy simply did not have the numbers to engage the Royal Navy with any reasonable prospect of success. This demanded that the British fleet be attacked from the air, which in turn meant that it was necessary for the Luftwaffe fighter force to engage and destroy the RAF's fighters. Supremacy over the RAF was required, since if the British managed to muster sufficient strength to gain localised or temporary control of the airspace above the Royal Navy or in which the German bombers were operating, this would be enough potentially to lead to disaster for the bombers.

The resulting battle of Britain ended in failure for the Luftwaffe. Although the battle was a close-run affair, the RAF suffering heavy pilot casualties, a combination of skilful defence, based around an integrated air defence network exploiting radar and effective nodes of communication, and German errors in failing to maintain their aim meant that the British never lost control of the air, rendering the prospect of an invasion unappealing.

Conversely, the fact that losing control of the air over the homeland could be disastrous was demonstrated to its fullest extent by the Germans in the face of the Allied strategic air offensive. Hermann Goering had initially informed the German public that no enemy aircraft would fly over the Reich, but this prediction was soon proved incorrect. While the British bomber offensive switched to operating at night because of the heavy losses sustained in daylight, the American approach to strategic bombing meant that large-scale air battles developed. Initially, the Germans gained the upper hand, but the introduction of escort fighters and a shift in emphasis by the Americans, which saw the inflicting of attrition upon the Luftwaffe fighter force as important as the actual bombing of key targets in Germany and occupied Europe, had a profound effect. The Germans could not ignore the challenge posed by the escorted bomber formations and were forced to engage. This meant that the focus of German fighter efforts was over Germany itself as far as fighting the Western Allies was concerned. This militated against the deployment of large numbers of fighter aircraft to the occupied territories in Western Europe, and the pressure imposed by fighting against the numerically superior Soviet air forces in the East meant that the Luftwaffe was unable effectively to oppose Anglo-American air operations in Northwest Europe from June 1944 onwards. By late 1944, Hitler's planning had to take account of Allied air superiority, prompting his decision to conduct the build-up for the Ardennes offensive (the 'battle of the Bulge') in heavily forested terrain so that Allied reconnaissance aircraft, by now operating with near impunity over many areas, could not reveal his plans, while the attack itself was to take place in a period of predicted bad weather to deny the Americans – the main target of the offensive – any air support. Although it is something of an oversimplification to suggest that the lifting of the bad weather that afflicted the Ardennes region until just after Christmas 1944 was the sole reason for the German defeat in this campaign, the fact that the planning process had to rely upon meteorological conditions to offset Allied air power is instructive.

Being able to control the air was also decisive in the Pacific War. Initial Japanese successes were achieved thanks to the destruction of American, British and Commonwealth air assets, notably in the cases of the Philippines and Malaya and Singapore. This was not to last. The ability of the United States to produce vast numbers of aircraft and the men to fly them meant that it was enormously difficult for the Japanese to maintain their position. The destruction of the majority of the Japanese aircraft carrier fleet at the battle of Midway coast the Japanese both some of their most experienced pilots and the ability to challenge American carrier-based air power. Aircraft operating from American carriers were able to inflict heavy and on-going attrition upon the Japanese, as were long-range US Army Air Force fighters. The nadir for the Japanese came in June 1944 with the American assault on the Marianas Islands, in which the Japanese air forces suffered crushing losses in what became known as the 'Great Marianas Turkey Shoot'. The inability to provide effective air support to the army from this point onwards meant that the Japanese were placed at a grave disadvantage during the last year of the war. Allied aircraft, by con-trast, became particularly important in adding to the striking power of land forces, while gaining control of the air enabled the use of transport aircraft to support advancing Allied forces, particularly in Burma, where General Sir William Slim commented that the ability to resupply troops in the jungle had been a critical factor in the defeat of the Japanese in this theatre.

Once the Americans had captured island bases from which their B-29 bomber force could attack the Japanese home islands, the importance of defending the homeland from air attack was brought home to the Japanese leadership, just as it had been to the Nazi regime in Germany. Although the Japanese made a robust defence of their territory, they were unable to stem the raids. As a result, the B-29s inflicted massive damage. The ultimate demonstration of what could occur with the loss of control of the air over the homeland came in August 1945, when the Americans delivered two atomic weapons against Hiroshima and Nagasaki: both attacks occurred without the interference of Japanese defending aircraft, illustrating how utterly defeated the Japanese air services had been. While the importance of control of the air had been established beyond any doubt by 1945, the development of nuclear weapons had an interesting effect upon conceptions of air superiority during the Cold War. Initially, it was clear that the only means of delivering nuclear weapons was from aircraft. This prompted both sides in the Cold War to invest in their air defence assets. In the United States, this led towards a concentration upon fighter aircraft that could engage the enemy at long range using guided missiles, and the traditional fighter aircraft, designed to win control of the air over the battlefield, fell out of favour. The limitations of such a policy were seen in Vietnam and, most notably, in the Middle East. The success of the Israeli pre-emptive strike on Egyptian airfields in the 1967 Six Day War and the subsequent freedom of operational manoeuvre this granted the Israeli Defence Force (IDF) highlighted the fact that being able to fight and win against enemy fighters that were designed for combat with similar types remained as important as it had always been. The Israelis went on to demonstrate this again in 1982 in their invasion of Lebanon, ensuring that they destroyed the Syrian integrated air defence system in the Bekka Valley as a precursor to operations.

The evolution of the concept

Despite the constant reminders that maintaining control of the air is important, recent developments have led to a debate about the concept. The success of Coalition operations against the Iraqi Air Force in 1991 highlighted the possibility that lesser powers might adopt an asymmetric approach towards control of the air. Asymmetric responses were not new. The North Vietnamese made extensive use of surface-to-air missiles (SAMs) and anti-aircraft artillery (AAA), and the 1973 Arab–Israeli Yom Kippur/ Ramadan War had a clear strand of asymmetric thinking by the Egyptians, who had chosen to rely upon SAMs against the Israelis to offset enemy air superiority. Although the Israelis successfully drove back the Egyptian attack once the Egyptian Army moved beyond the protection of its SAM coverage, the war suggested that the nature of control of the air had changed: the enemy would no longer seek to engage simply in a series of attritional air battles but would use a variety of different techniques to achieve the desired aim. The Iraqi example of making a limited air effort against the enemy before falling back on the use of SAMs highlighted the importance of adding a new dimension to the concept of controlling the air, namely that of suppressing the enemy's air defences (SEAD). The Americans had made a start in Vietnam with the 'Wild Weasel' project, which saw fighter bombers fitted with additional electronic equipment and anti-radar missiles duelling with SAM sites in a bid to protect strike packages.

The altered enemy response has been given fullest exposition since 1999, in the operation by NATO to enforce Yugoslavian (in effect, Serbian) acceptance of a solution to the Kosovo crisis. The Yugoslav Air Force initially opposed the NATO air attack, but losses during the opening phases of the operation suggested that the only outcome of flying was likely to be the destruction of most Yugoslav air assets. The leadership in Belgrade increased its reliance upon SAMs and reduced flying to a bare minimum. In 2003, the Iraqi Air Force chose not to fly at all in the face of the invasion by the US-led Coalition, prompting suggestions that air forces would be better off investing in aircraft of more utility to the type of operations that have emerged since the end of the Cold War. The conflict in Afghanistan that broke out following the terrorist attacks on New York on 11 September 2001 (9/11) added to such notions, since the Afghan Air Force had been in a state of almost complete disrepair for some years, and none of the warring factions, least of all the Taliban government, was able to operate any aircraft in the face of overwhelming American supremacy. Although such suggestions appear tempting at first sight, it is worth noting that the fundamental unpredictability of war suggests that this would be an unwise move. In 1919, the prospect of a major state-on-state war seemed incredibly remote, yet within twenty years it had become a reality. Without control of the air, the success of operations both in the air and on the surface cannot be guaranteed, and the likelihood of failure is dramatically increased.

Strategic air operations

The notion that air power can have an effect at the strategic level of conflict may have been first mooted in the nineteenth century, but it remains a source of considerable debate today. The matter is complicated by the fact that the term 'strategic air power' is open to many interpretations, most of which revolve around the use of aircraft to bomb targets that are generally not to be found on the battlefield or at sea but within the enemy homeland. The use of bombers in an attempt to affect the strategic levels of war during both the First and Second World Wars has created an over-generalised concept of what strategic air power is. It does not simply include attack against key targets in enemy territory but should be seen in its broadest context, namely the employment of air power to achieve an effect against the opponent. This may not involve fighting at all and in fact may *prevent* conflict. Complicating the picture even further is the fact that some of the thought about strategic air power owes much to initial concepts underpinning notions of control of the air, particularly the offensive use of air power, which expanded in broader theories of the use of air power for direct attack at the strategic level of war.

Offensive air power and morale bombing

Although the Italo-Turkish War (1911–12) saw the first use of air power in an offensive manner, the concept was not fully articulated until September 1916, by the commander of the RFC in France, Brigadier-General Hugh Trenchard. Trenchard produced a memorandum entitled 'Future Policy in the Air', in which he laid down the key principles for gaining and maintaining control of the air.

Trenchard set out to address concerns from ground units that they should enjoy direct protection from their air service, friendly aircraft remaining overhead at all times. This concern remained a factor throughout the twentieth century, and, as will be discussed below, air forces have been subjected to complaints that they pay inadequate attention to the demands of the army and navy in pursuit of operations well beyond the immediate battle area. For Trenchard, such complaints ignored the fact that it was much better to prevent enemy aircraft from reaching friendly forces in the first place than having to seek to engage them while they were in the process of attacking or, worse still, after they had completed their attack. Trenchard argued: '[A]n aeroplane is an offensive and not a defensive weapon . . . The aeroplane is not a defence against the aeroplane; but it is the opinion of those most competent to judge that the aeroplane, as a weapon of attack, cannot be too highly estimated.'[1]

This not only underpinned the approach that Trenchard and the RFC (and its successor, the RAF) would employ for the remainder of the war but helped to form wider views upon the way in which air power could be best exploited. As well as taking the view that air power was best employed offensively, Trenchard added his voice to those who had suggested that one of the effects of air power might be psychological:

The mere presence of a hostile machine in the air inspires those on the ground with exaggerated forebodings with regard to what the machine is capable of doing . . .

The sound policy then which should guide all warfare in the air would seem to be this: to exploit this moral effect of the aeroplane on the enemy, but not to let him exploit it on ourselves. Now this can only be done by attacking and continuing to attack.[2]

Two strands of thought emerged from this line of thinking (which was not unique to Trenchard). The first was that of using aircraft to attack the enemy more widely through hitting targets beyond the front line, and possibly in the enemy homeland; the second was that of the psychological effects of air power that could be exploited to bring about the collapse of enemy morale, thus bringing about the end of the war. When Trenchard was called upon to put such theories into action with his appointment in spring 1918 to command the so-called Independent Force that was specifically tasked with bombing Germany, he was singularly unimpressed, believing that this was a diversion of effort away from the crucial arena of war, the Western front itself. However, as Chief of the Air Staff from 1919 to 1929. Trenchard took the idea of carrying air power to the enemy's homeland as the core building-block that would maintain the RAF's independence from the other two services. Trenchard offered the British government two distinct reasons for maintaining the RAF as an independent force. The first was that of policing the British empire, which he claimed – correctly, as it transpired – could be done at less cost if aircraft were employed in some regions to support locally raised forces instead of garrisons of British troops. The second reason was the role of strategic bombardment of the enemy in a major conflict. Both relied upon exploiting the offensive nature of air power to bring about moral collapse on the part of the opposition through bombardment.

Interwar thought

The promise of a new arm bringing about a rapid victory proved enticing in the interwar era. The sheer scale of death and destruction caused by the static warfare between 1914 and 1918 led to a determination that the experience should not be repeated, and this in turn led to the notion of exploiting the potential reach of bombers to carry the war to the enemy's homeland, the aim of attempting to bring about a rapid surrender becoming not just the purview of those speculating about air power's potential, but also a matter of serious consideration by those involved in running air services, as will be discussed in the section below on strategic air power. The move towards the dominance of the bomber aircraft created a number of interesting issues for air power thinkers with regard to controlling the air. The very title of Italian theorist Giulio Douhet's most famous publication, *Command of the Air*, demonstrates his view that it was necessary to control the air, but his vision of how this should be achieved relied not upon the fighters of the First World War but upon heavily armed 'battleplanes'. Douhet's thought relied upon the assumptions that bombing population centres would shatter the will of the enemy, and that this could be achieved with relative ease because it was impossible to envisage any effective defence against attacking aircraft. He saw control of the air being won through attacking the logistic and manufacturing centres for enemy air power, with this enabling the attack on population centres to be conducted. The battleplanes would be capable of defending themselves against any enemy attempts at interception, and destroying the opposing air force's ability to fight at the outset of a war would ensure that a counter-stroke by the opponent would not be possible. Possessing a sufficiently large arsenal of battleplanes would obviate the requirement for fighter aircraft to defend the homeland against enemy attack. The employment of an offensive doctrine would bring about utter defeat, particularly if the social cohesion of the enemy's society was undermined by the use of a full array of weaponry, including poison gas. Douhet's apocalyptic vision of aerial bombardment was, however, flawed. His considerations assumed that every aeroplane reached its target, that every bomb dropped hit the target beneath and that every direct hit would explode. Given the technological standards of the time, this was an unrealistic projection of what air power could achieve.

In contrast to Douhet, Trenchard did not feel that directly targeting enemy civilians was justifiable, the moral component of aerial bombardment resulting not from direct targeting of the people themselves but of their nation's 'vital centres', such as the factories that employed them and the transport network that took them to and from work. Trenchard's tenure as Chief of the Air Staff saw the production of several doctrine manuals, the most important of which was Air Publication 1300 (AP1300) *Royal Air Force War Manual*. AP1300 suggested that: 'Objectives should be selected the bombardment of which will have the greatest effect in weakening the enemy resistance and his power to continue war.'[3] As Philip Meilinger observes, the manual noted that it was important there was a full understanding of the enemy country.[4] Although not clearly stated, the inference is clear. Without such a knowledge, it would be difficult to identify the key targets that would need to be struck: it might be that the British conception of what was an enemy 'vital centre' was not the same as that of the opponent, and striking something that the enemy did not value would not be effective. This fundamental point lies at the heart of current air power thought about strategic attack. Such intelligence may be difficult to obtain and can lead to problems in seeking out the correct set of targets, but it is vital if air power is to have any effect at the strategic level of war.

While Trenchard's outlook on air power was dominated by considerations of the offensive, he conceded that it was necessary to retain a small fleet of air defence aircraft largely to maintain the morale of the civilian population, even if the majority of funding for the RAF should be spent on bomber aircraft. Over-investment in fighters would be 'rather like putting two teams to play each other at football and telling one team they must only defend their own goal . . . the defending team would certainly not be beaten, but they would certainly not win, nor would they stop the attack on their goal from continuing'.[5]

This was entirely in keeping with the notion that air power could not have a truly strategic effect if used purely for defensive purposes. However, It missed the fact that air defence itself could be of strategic importance, as was demonstrated in the battle of Britain, when the ability to conduct defensive operations was critical to success.

The debate was no less heated in the United States, where Colonel William 'Billy' Mitchell and later the US Army Air Corps (USAAC) Tactical School that took forward US air doctrine changed their perceptions regarding control of the air. In the immediate aftermath of the First World War, 'pursuit' [fighter] aviation was seen as the main effort of the USAAC, since its duty was to maintain air superiority. From about 1926, however, the USAAC began to see bombardment as its most important task. Pursuit aviation remained significant, as fighter aircraft could be employed to escort friendly bombers or to carry out sweeps against the enemy fighter force. By the early 1930s, the position had changed yet again. The appearance of high-speed bombers in the USAAC inventory convinced air officers that notions that the bomber would be impossible to intercept in a future conflict were correct. Advocates of pursuit aviation, most notably Captain Claire L Chennault, felt that the inevitability of the bomber reaching its target was not as clear cut as some colleagues thought. They were ignored. As Robert Hurley observed, 'on the crucial issue of what happened when a bomber formation was opposed by hostile pursuit, it can only be concluded that there was some sketchy thinking'.[6]

The issue of whether the bomber would really be able to get through did not deter the USAAC from developing a concept of precisely targeting key elements in the enemy's war economy. The required precision would come through the use of sophisticated bombsights, while careful understanding of the enemy would allow a list of targets to be drawn up. This was the 'key-node' approach through which the USAAC (later renamed the US Army Air Force) developed thoughts about strategic air power. Although the stress upon the precise targeting of industry was notable, there were elements of the moral component of air power present in American thinking. Thus, when the Second World War broke out, thoughts about strategic air power saw it as being the use of bombing rapidly to paralyse the enemy, crippling industrial output and undermining the morale of the civilian population. Yet strategic air power did not deliver in the way in which the interwar theorists had envisioned.

Theory, practice and controversy

The nature of strategic air bombardment in the Second World War has been the source of much controversy. The extensive historical coverage has produced much debate, which can obscure some of the key issues when it comes to understanding strategic air power; certainly, it can suggest that strategic air power is only that delivered by bombers. Although there are dangers in compressing the analysis of such a voluminous corpus of literature into a few short sentences, some key conclusions regarding the strategic bombing campaign between 1939 and 1945 can be made. First, the *nature* of the Second World War did meet theorists' expectations. Surface forces were heavily engaged from the outset, while the financial constraints upon the British armed services in the interwar years meant that the bomber fleet needed to conduct the sort of strategic bombing campaign Trenchard envisaged simply did not exist. The early years of the war were marked by a distinct lack of navigational and bombing accuracy, which drove the RAF to its 'area' policy of attacking German cities, on the basis that they would stand a greater chance of striking industrial targets; the corollary of this, of course, was that no discrimination could be made between civilian housing and industrial areas. Despite the introduction of an array of navigation devices and improved bombsights, the commander of RAF Bomber Command, Sir Arthur Harris, remained convinced that area bombing would bring success and resolutely refused to change target sets. Bomber Command did strike targets other than cities in the latter part of the war, but the Air Staff found it extremely difficult to persuade Harris to launch his forces against these alternative targets.

The US Army Air Force's daylight bombing policy gave some precision, but despite the technology of the Norden bombsight, which was designed to achieve the destruction of the key nodes, the degree of accuracy desired could not be achieved. There were several reasons for this, including the depredations of German fighters and anti-aircraft fire, and – more simply – the weather, which meant that bombardiers in American bombers found it impossible to see the targets beneath through heavy cloud and had to release their bombs using radar targeting, which was inaccurate and made realising the clean theory of key-node targeting impossible to achieve in Europe. In the Pacific, weather conditions were better, but the dispersal of Japanese industry was such that firebombing of area targets – with enormous civilian casualties – resulted; the bombing campaign concluded with the use of two nuclear weapons, which could hardly be said to fit in with the notion of precise targeting of key nodes. The US Army Air Force remained committed to the notion that it should seek to target key elements of the enemy's warmaking capability, perhaps best exemplified by the dispute that arose in 1944 over the employment of the bomber forces in the run-up to the invasion of Europe. While General Eisenhower, as Supreme Allied Commander, supported the concept of targeting German transportation put forward by his senior airmen, General Carl Spaatz, the commander of the American bombing forces, argued vehemently in favour of attacking oil production, in the knowledge that the Germans had always been painfully aware of their limited access to oil resources, their conquest of much of the continent of Europe notwithstanding. Spaatz was overruled, with the proviso that oil might become a major target once Allied forces were established ashore. The end result was to intensify the debate regarding 'strategic' air power.

The failure of the bomber offensive to achieve what had been promised by the interwar theorists damaged the credibility of air power in the eyes of many observers, who felt that their view that air power was better used in direct support of ground and naval forces had been vindicated. However, the atomic bomb meant that conceptions of air power operating in a strategic role had to be rethought. The Americans and Soviets established large forces of bomber aircraft to carry nuclear weapons, while the British and

French developed their strategic bomber forces to carry their own nuclear deterrent. The appearance of nuclear weapons was particularly important in the United States, since it helped convince the Truman Administration that while the US Army should still have its own air power, the bulk of American combat aircraft should be under the auspices of an independent air force, and so the US Air Force was created in 1947. The US Air Force remained wedded to the notion that air power could win wars alone, and this perspective was articulated through the refinement of two concepts that defined the nature of considering strategic air power, but which remain controversial. Building upon theories pertaining to nuclear strategy, air power thinkers developed the concept of employing air power for coercive purposes; this was then followed by attempting to take the oft-expressed idea that strategic air power had 'effect' and defining what, exactly, constituted effect at the strategic level, and the means by which it could be achieved.

Coercive air power

The debate over the nature of coercion is complex and multilayered (as described in chapter 6 of this book), but Robert A. Pape – drawing upon Thomas Schelling and Robert J. Art – provides an appropriate definition for the purposes of this chapter: 'Coercion is like deterrence in that both focus on influencing the adversary's decision calculus. However, coercion differs from deterrence in that deterrence is concerned with maintaining the status quo by discouraging an opponent from changing his behaviour, while coercion seeks exactly the opposite: to force change in the opponent's behaviour.'[7]

This was demonstrated in the attempts by the Johnson Administration in the 1960s to apply air power against North Vietnam, with the intent of coercing the Hanoi government into ending its support of the insurgency in South Vietnam conducted by the National Liberation Front (more commonly known as the Viet Cong). However, the attempt at coercion, an aerial bombing campaign known as Operation 'Rolling Thunder', failed, the North Vietnamese remaining resolute in their defiance of American efforts. There were several reasons for this: most notably, the way in which air power was employed, and, most critically, a misunderstanding of the enemy. The American approach was to apply air power in an incremental fashion, underpinned by the notion that coercion of the enemy could be achieved through an escalation of attacks to the point where the North Vietnamese would modify their behaviour as desired.[8] This did not take into account the determination of the government in Hanoi and the insurgents in the south of the country to bring about the unification of their nation. They were quite prepared to wait until the United States tired of the conflict, no matter how long this might take, a stance which in turn meant that their resilience against coercive air attack was greater than the

Americans anticipated. The American attacks, although relatively limited, were exploited by the Hanoi government to bolster national unity, while the scale of the attacks allowed the North Vietnamese to reduce the vulnerability of some target sets by dispersing oil supplies.

The Americans failed to take account of the nature of the conflict: notions of strategic air power were based upon attacks against significant military, political or industrial targets, yet the first phase of American involvement in the conflict was in a guerrilla war, in which the key targets were those against which air power could not be employed effectively. Both military and civilian leaders in the United States thought that targeting North Vietnamese industry would prove an effective means of coercion, failing to appreciate that the only vital target was the transportation system, which could sustain considerable damage without having a major effect on supplies to forces in South Vietnam, whose logistic requirements were low. The North Vietnamese exploited bombing pauses to re-equip, drawing heavily upon supplies from the Soviet Union and China, yet the key importation routes, both overland and by sea, were not targeted; for instance, mining Haiphong harbour was prohibited by the US Administration because of fears of escalation of the conflict if a Soviet ship were to be sunk.

Failed conception

The combination of incorrect target selection and self-imposed constraints meant that Rolling Thunder was unlikely to succeed. This was in contrast to the use of air power in 1972, when the Americans began Operation Linebacker, a much less restrained employment of bombing against targets throughout the North. The culmination of Operation Linebacker II, a short, brief assault against key targets in December 1972, came with the signing of the Paris Peace Accords enabling the United States to disengage from the war. Air power proponents contend that Linebacker demonstrated that if air power was employed against key targets without the political constraints and gradual escalation seen in Rolling Thunder, then it could be decisive; indeed, they argued, if Rolling Thunder had been conducted in the same manner, the result of the conflict might have been different. However, an alternative view suggests that the nature of the war had changed by the time that Operations Linebacker I and II were conducted. The Tet offensive of 1968 had led to enormous losses for the Viet Cong, compelling the Hanoi government to use North Vietnamese Army (NVA) troops to pursue the goal of Vietnamese unification. This meant that while the war retained many characteristics of a guerrilla conflict, the NVA pursued a more conventional approach. This, in turn, made them vulnerable to air power, as demonstrated by the telling effect of air attack on their forces during the invasion of the South during spring 1972. Targets chosen for attack in the Linebacker campaigns were important to the sustenance of a conventional army and had a notable effect. Mining Haiphong harbour ensured that the NVA began to run short of supplies. As Clodfelter notes: 'Linebacker II, combined with mining, threatened to paralyze [the NVA] by preventing necessary materiel from flowing to it.'[9]

The debate over the nature of the employment of air power in Vietnam served to demonstrate a number of tenets regarding the use of air attack for coercive purposes. Perhaps the most important was the need to understand the enemy, in particular to know which targets were of importance to the enemy's will and which were critical to his ability to continue resisting. Without this comprehension, success was impossible. A vital consideration was that of public opinion, both national and international. One of the legacies of the air campaign of the Second World War was awareness of air attack's destructive capacity, creating aversion within Western societies towards anything that had the appearance of targeting civilians. This was a particular source of contention throughout the Vietnam War, the micro-management of target selection from the White House notwithstanding. In the context of the Cold War, allegations of targeting civilians in North Vietnam gave the Soviet Union a useful propaganda weapon that was exploited in their wide-ranging campaign to undermine the legitimacy of American action in Southeast Asia.

The imperfect nature of the air campaign in Vietnam led to further development in thought about strategic air power. The Cold War paradigm in which 'strategic' was taken to refer to the use of air power in the nuclear role began to unravel as the US Air Force undertook a fundamental review of its business. The association with nuclear bombing meant that Strategic Air Command (SAC) all but handed the task of conventional bombing to Tactical Air Command (TAC), suggesting that the parameters for 'strategic' air power needed reconsideration. The introduction of AirLand battle doctrine during the mid-1970s led to a brief period during which the view that air power was a supporting arm to surface forces returned; this did not last long, as new perceptions of strategic air power developed. The new thinking drew heavily upon ideas postulated by a retired US Air Force officer, Colonel John Boyd, and taken to a new level by Colonel John A. Warden III.

John Boyd and John A. Warden III

Boyd's thought covered a wide range of subjects, and his major contribution to the development of strategic air doctrine was not designed with air power alone in mind. Boyd developed the notion that conflict could be won though 'decision cycle dominance'. The decision cycle laid out by Boyd of 'Observe – Orient – Decide – Act' became known as the 'OODA loop', the aim of decision cycle dominance being to 'get inside the opponent's OODA loop'.

Box 4.1 Boyd's OODA loop

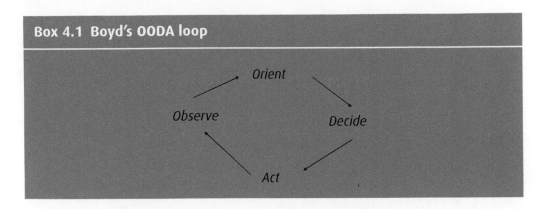

Conducting the decision cycle more quickly than the adversary meant that the opponent would lose situational awareness, becoming more confused as to what was being done to him; as confusion mounted, the enemy would become paralysed and unable to resist. Warden built upon these ideas during the 1980s and was presented with an opportunity to articulate them following the Iraqi invasion of Kuwait in August 1990. Warden's concept of strategic air power envisaged the use of air forces to attack targets vital to the enemy's ability to prosecute war without having to engage the enemy army, a concept that Mitchell and Douhet would have recognised. Warden did not consider the enemy's fielded forces completely irrelevant, since they formed one of the five key target sets in his conception. The target sets were represented visually by a series of concentric rings. Leadership lay in the centre of the rings, moving outward through key production, infrastructure and the population to the outer ring, military forces. This representation demonstrated Warden's view that the enemy state could be regarded as a system – or a 'system of systems' – all aspects of which were equally vulnerable to attack by air power at any time.

While Warden's vision might at first sight appear to be a simple refinement of earlier thinking, his concept of air power was enabled by technological developments. The visions of destruction held by the early theorists had fallen foul of the apparently insuperable problems of accurate weapons delivery and navigation to the target, particularly in poor weather. The problems of navigation and poor-weather flight were substantially overcome by technological development by the 1960s, but despite much-improved bombsight technology, striking targets remained problematic. The solution came through guided weapons. Their development began in the 1920s, and there had been limited use of guided bombs during the Second World War, although they had not enjoyed a high success rate. Further work in the United States led to the creation of the Paveway series of laser-guided bombs and electro-optically guided ordnance. These demonstrated their worth in the Vietnam War, notably in attacking bridges in North Vietnam. By the late 1980s, the range of precision-guided

Box 4.2 Warden's 'five ring' model

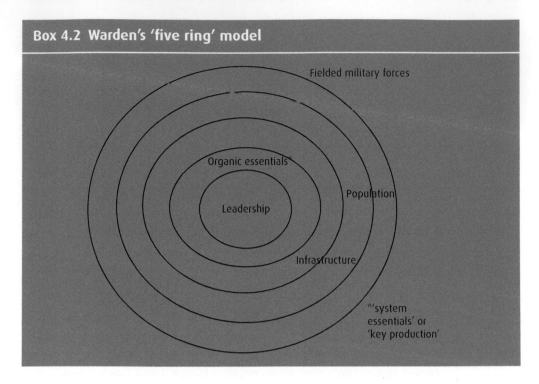

munitions (PGMs) available meant that it was possible for such theorists as
Warden to have confidence in the ability of a relatively small number of aircraft not only to locate their targets but also to be able to attack them with
a high probability of success. With the need to send large bomber fleets
against individual key targets obviated by technological advances, a range
of targets could be attacked simultaneously, giving air power the ability to
cause the strategic paralysis that Boyd and Warden advocated. The 'parallel
warfare' that simultaneity of targeting through the use of PGMs permitted
appeared to offer the tantalising prospect that the long-held vision of air
power bringing about swift victory without the need to engage hostile
fielded forces might be realised.

Theory into practice

Warden had the opportunity to put his ideas to the test in the 1991 Gulf
War. When Iraq invaded Kuwait in August 1990, Warden was a member of
the US Air Force's Air Staff Plans Directorate. He established an informal
planning cell known as 'Checkmate' and, on his own initiative, began to
draw up plans for an American aerial response to the invasion. General
Norman Schwarzkopf, commanding US Central Command (CENTOM, the
American command leading the anti-Saddam Coalition) and tasked with
preventing an Iraqi invasion of Saudi Arabia, asked that the air force
develop plans for an aerial response to such an eventuality. This brought
Warden's planning team and its ideas to the fore. The Checkmate plan,

Instant Thunder, was designed to be the antithesis of Rolling Thunder, bringing air power to bear in a decisive fashion against the Iraqis. Warden envisaged an air campaign against Saddam Hussein's ability to fight by attacking command-and-control facilities in Iraq itself, including power stations and communications infrastructure. This would be made possible by gaining control of the air through attacking the sophisticated Iraqi air defence system. Iraqi forces in Kuwait would be struck only if it appeared that they were on the verge of invading Saudi Arabia.

Schwarzkopf was initially enthusiastic about the plan, but as the task of the Coalition assembled in response to the invasion of Kuwait evolved from one of defence of Saudi Arabia to that of removing Saddam Hussein's troops from Kuwait by force if necessary, Instant Thunder came under closer scrutiny. The air component commander, Lieutenant Charles Horner, was not convinced that Warden's approach to the air campaign was practical, with its focus upon targets in Iraq rather than upon the Iraqi units occupying Kuwait. The end result was a modification of Instant Thunder. The plan that emerged involved four key phases: attacking strategic targets; a campaign against Iraqi air forces in Kuwait; neutralising the Iraqi Republican Guard and cutting off Iraqi forces in Kuwait; and supporting the ground assault into Kuwait to evict the Iraqis. All of these phases were to be enabled by winning air superiority, and the ground offensive would begin only when Iraqi forces in Kuwait were reduced to 50 per cent combat effectiveness by air attack.

The air campaign that resulted was a spectacular success. The first three phases of the campaign occurred simultaneously, in keeping with the concept of parallel air operations. The Iraqis ceased to contest control of the air, and Coalition air forces conducted an effective campaign that enabled a short and decisive ground war. The effectiveness of precision munitions, particularly when employed in combination with the F-117 'stealth' aircraft that were almost impossible for Iraqi radar to detect, gave rise to the argument that the strategic air campaign had worked as planned. However, some observers contended that the attack against Saddam Hussein's command-and-control system had not worked as planned, despite the fact that it had a considerable effect on dislocating the ability of the Iraqi dictator to effect command and control. John Andreas Olsen contends that the Coalition failed fully to comprehend the nature of the Iraqi regime, which meant that targeting its command-and-control system to fullest effect could not be achieved, although he makes the important point that air power still achieved a great deal.[10] Furthermore, there was an unexpected element to the air campaign that could be said to have been of the greatest strategic significance, namely what became known as 'the great Scud hunt' in the Iraqi western desert. Saddam Hussein endeavoured to destroy the Coalition ranged against him by detaching its Arab members; he sought to do this by bringing Israel into the war. To achieve this goal, he began to fire

SS-1 Scud intermediate-range missiles (and Iraqi-built derivatives) into Israel. To prevent the Israelis from entering the war, a large proportion of the Coalition air effort was diverted to the difficult task of attempting to locate the mobile missile launchers being used to fire the weapons. Although this diversion reduced the weight of attack upon other targets, the degree of Coalition air superiority was such that the overall effect was barely deleterious to the overall air campaign. The most serious difficulty facing the campaign came with an attack on the al-Firdos bunker, which was being used as a shelter rather than in its designed capacity as a command-and-control facility. Several hundred civilian deaths resulted, with extremely negative media coverage. To ensure that a similarly damaging event did not happen again and risk undermining public support in Coalition nations, the US Joint Chiefs of Staff reviewed targeting, a process which dramatically reduced the number of attacks against targets in Baghdad. This revisiting of targets suggested that the notion of effects, which did not necessarily demand the destruction of a target, merely rendering it inoperable or ineffective for the duration of the conflict, had not fully entered the planning process.

While the 1991 Gulf campaign demonstrated the efficacy of air power against strategic targets, it helped further to demonstrate that the notion that strategic air power meant only the destruction of targets vital to the prosecution of the enemy's war effort was an unsatisfactory concept.

The application of air power against the Scuds represented the strategic use of air power, even though the number of Scuds destroyed was minimal. Prior to the war starting, the effort to deter an Iraqi invasion of Saudi Arabia had been bolstered by the rapid reinforcement of the Kingdom by air: as well as providing a greatly increased air strength ranged against the Iraqis, the use of airlift to bring forces into theatre swiftly – even if sealift was required to bring in the heavy forces necessary fully to guarantee a successful defence and to mount an invasion of Kuwait – was of strategic significance. The use of air transport in a strategic role had been demonstrated many years previously, strategic effect being achieved in the Berlin Airlift of 1948–9, where keeping Berlin resupplied by air frustrated Soviet ambitions to bring the entire city under Communist control. Not a bomb was dropped, but the air power employed was decidedly strategic in nature.

While such examples demonstrate that the strategic applicability of air power is far broader than that envisaged by the early air power theorists, this is not to say that strategic attack should be disregarded as a concept. The Kosovo campaign demonstrated again how careful targeting, exploiting the accuracy provided by PGMs, could have the sort of effect envisaged by air power theorists for decades. Without the presence of a credible ground threat to Slobodan Milosevic's regime, air power shaped the political conditions by which Milosevic felt it necessary to capitulate to NATO's demands to end ethnic cleansing in Kosovo. However, this took far longer to achieve

Figure 4.2 Tornado GR4 strike aircraft of 12 Squadron, RAF. Developed as part of a trinational project, the Tornado has been in service since 1981 and has seen operational use in Iraq and Kosovo.

than had been expected; the air campaign was hindered by initial confusion over targeting and bad weather which militated against the use of laser-guided weapons. NATO's Supreme Allied Commander Europe (SACEUR), General Wesley K. Clark, argued that the air campaign should be conducted against fielded forces in Kosovo itself. His air component commander, Lieutenant General Michael Short, disagreed, contending that air power should 'go for the head of the snake', in keeping with classic strategic air attack theory. Clark's view prevailed initially, and the combination of bad weather and poor results from targeting forces in Kosovo led to a re-evaluation of the campaign. The strategic target sets that Short had advocated began to be attacked, particularly targets that were of significance to supporters of the Milosevic regime. This 'crony attack' approach undermined support for Milosevic, while the apparent ability of NATO air assets to attack almost at will created an impression within the Serbian regime that the weight of bombing could leave Serbia utterly devastated if the government failed to comply with the demands of the international community. Combined with the realisation that expected support from Russia would not be forthcoming, Milosevic chose to capitulate. The perceived success of air power in Kosovo enhanced consideration of the use of air attack to bring about rapid victory. In the United States, the concept of Rapid Dominance was developed, in which air power would play a key part in overwhelming the enemy with great rapidity. The authors of the Rapid Dominance concept presaged the final version of their study with a pamphlet called *Shock and Awe*, a title closely associated with air power in Operation Iraqi Freedom (OIF) – the invasion of Iraq – in 2003. Warden's ideas of targeting the enemy leadership were taken a stage further in OIF, with time-sensitive intelligence information used to launch an attack on a building in which it was thought Saddam Hussein was dining. Saddam was not killed in the attack, but the conflict was marked with a number of time-critical air attacks against enemy command-and-control systems with the aim of quickly achieving the desired level of dominance over the Iraqi regime. The 'shock and awe' concept was poorly articulated, however, and television coverage of attacks on leadership targets in the middle of Baghdad were taken – erroneously – by some sources as a sign that air power was being used in an indiscriminate fashion. In a further parallel with the earlier conflict against Saddam, the air campaign plan was modified to take account of changing conditions on the battlefield, demonstrating that the adage 'no plan survives first contact with the enemy' remains just as relevant to strategic air attack as to other forms of warfare.

Air power in joint operations

The final aspect of air power that requires consideration is its employment in conjunction with the other two components. As noted earlier, air power theorists have been loath to concentrate upon the utility of air power in support of the surface battle, often for fear of the implications that this might be perceived to have on the validity of the existence of independent air forces. This has led to practical problems, air forces and armies almost wilfully choosing not to co-operate as closely as they might (while complaining about the attitude of the other service) when the two services have been required to co-operate in wartime.

Nevertheless, air power has been of critical importance when used alongside both armies and navies almost from the outset of the creation of organised air arms. In the First World War, even with the limited aviation technology at hand, air power came to be seen as vital. Aerial reconnaissance was credited, for instance, with providing the critical information needed to stop the German advance at the Marne in 1914. The move to static warfare meant that artillery came to dominate the battlefield, and aircraft were employed to direct fire and to locate the positions of enemy guns. By 1916, the British Expeditionary Force saw aircraft as an essential tool for providing information and for the correction of artillery fire. However, while information-gathering and surveillance were the cornerstones of air operations in the First World War, these were not the only tasks performed. It became evident that the use of aircraft in an attacking role in support of ground troops would be of utility, and this led to the development of ground attack operations. Ground attack took two forms: close support to troops in contact with the enemy, and interdiction of enemy forces behind the battle area, with the aim of interfering with the flow of men and supplies to the front line. Both roles proved effective, although there were differing philosophies between the Allies and the Germans, the latter developing dedicated aircraft for the attack role, while the British and French preferred to fit fighter aircraft with light bombs. The most significant employment of air power in support of land operations came first during the German spring offensives of 1918, where air power played a vital role in disrupting and dislocating the German advance, particularly in attacks against supply convoys and reinforcements moving up to the front, and then in the period of 'the Hundred Days' that began with the Allied offensives in July and August. While the Germans enjoyed some success with their dedicated attack aircraft (notably at Cambrai in 1917 when countering the British offensive), the lack of air superiority meant that their battle flights were unable to achieve the effect that they hoped for.

The loss of joint effort

Although the Allies began to invest in their own dedicated attack as the war drew to a close, the Armistice came into force before these aircraft could be employed. As noted earlier, the RAF then moved away from stressing the importance of close support to the army in its doctrine publications for reasons of service politics. In reality, the RAF provided considerable support to the army during colonial policing campaigns. The same applied to the French air service, which remained dedicated to supporting the land component, while the Americans moved towards a position whereby support for ground forces took on less importance. The Soviets and Germans took a different position. The Russian approach to air power saw aeroplanes as an integral part of the land battle, notions of independent air action being replaced by the use of air power for deep attack. The Germans, assessing the reasons for defeat in 1918, concluded that it was impossible for land forces to function against a serious opponent without air power; they set about developing aerial doctrine that laid great store by the support of ground forces, even if suggestions that they abandoned notions of strategic bombardment entirely are inaccurate.

The lessons of the First World War were demonstrated conclusively in the Second. One of the keys to German success in the early part of the war resulted from the close integration of air and land assets. The failure of the French and British to develop an effective counter to this, not least because of an inability to gain control of the air, led to disaster in 1940. Complaints by the British Army regarding the inadequacy of air support grew louder in the face of defeats by the German Afrika Korps in the desert campaigns, but by this point steps were in hand to overcome the difficulties. The RAF, largely through an ad hoc approach by local commanders, rather than as a result of centrally formulated doctrine generated by the recently formed Army Co-Operation Command, fell back on the lessons learned in 1914–18. The quality of air–land integration improved immeasurably as close liaison was developed between air and ground formations at all levels, most notably between senior commanders. Similar improvements occurred as the US Army Air Force developed and refined its own doctrine for air support. The Afrika Korps commander, Erwin Rommel, complained that his forces could not compete in the face of co-ordinated action by enemy air and land forces. Lessons from North Africa were taken to the Italian campaign, and then to Western Europe after D-Day.

While there were difficulties caused by a breakdown in relations between Field Marshal Montgomery and his air commanders, the system of air–land support was particularly significant. The effect of air attack on the morale of soldiers was notable. This had been observed in the First World War by both the British and the Germans and was seen again in Normandy; it was not uncommon for advancing Allied troops to encounter German tanks that were completely intact but had been abandoned by their crews in the face of air attack. Furthermore, the campaign to interdict German supplies was highly effective, thus denying the Germans the ability to respond as rapidly to the Normandy invasion as might otherwise have been the case, while attempted counter-attacks were often brought to a standstill before the necessary units had reached their starting-point for the attack.

A similar situation pertained on the Eastern front, where the Soviet use of air power on a massive scale to support land operations proved increasingly difficult for the Germans to resist. Careful co-ordination of air attacks in support of the objectives of the various Red Army Fronts as they advanced meant that a combination of firepower from both land and air assets, combined with sheer weight of numbers, first rebuffed the Germans and then forced them into retreat. In the Far East, the use of transport aircraft was critical to success in the China–Burma–India (CBI) theatre of operations. The lack of communications infrastructure in many of the locations in which campaigning was conducted meant that aerial resupply was the only means by which rapid transport of men and supplies could be guaranteed, particularly given the considerable geographical area that the CBI theatre covered. Air supply was essential during the battles of Kohima and Imphal, for although the Japanese successfully cut off the British positions there, the regular delivery of supplies from the air and evacuation of casualties meant that controlling the land communications links was not as significant as it might have been; in the absence of control of the air, the Japanese were unable to prevent supplies from getting through. The commander of the British XIVth

Army, Viscount Slim, observed that the victory in Burma belonged as much to the air forces involved as to the troops who had fought on the ground.

In the maritime environment, the importance of combined air–maritime interaction was demonstrated on numerous occasions. The use of air power from carriers and land bases to provide cover for convoys in conjunction with groups of naval vessels dedicated to hunting for German U-boats (submarines) was of critical importance to victory in the battle of the Atlantic; constant air cover forced German submarines to remain underwater for considerable periods of time, reducing their endurance on patrol and their overall effectiveness. The Royal Navy's air attack on Taranto in 1940 played a significant part in the maritime campaign in the Mediterranean, the greatest challenge in the theatre arguably arising from punishing German and Italian air attacks against British shipping and against the island of Malta, which was a critical base. While the Pacific War was a maritime campaign, it depended throughout on effective air–maritime synergy. The Japanese attack on Pearl Harbor in December 1941 failed to destroy American aircraft carriers, and this gave the Americans the opportunity to strike a devastating blow against the Japanese six months later at Midway, a naval battle won through the employment of air power. The defeat at Midway cost the Japanese their carriers and most of their experienced aircrew, who proved impossible to replace. The Americans went on to employ their maritime air power to telling effect in the advance on the Japanese home islands, notably in the destruction of the last real vestiges of Japanese air power during the Marianas campaign in June 1944 and in the provision of close air support to invasion forces as the 'island-hopping' campaign progressed.

Joint air power in the nuclear age

Although the post-war period was dominated by nuclear weapons and the creation of the strategic air forces that would employ them in a Third World War, it became clear that air–surface co-operation remained an essential part of modern warfare. The Korean campaign (1950–3) was notable for the 'hard slogging' of the troops on the ground, reliant upon air support to contain the North Koreans and then to offset the numerical superiority of Chinese forces. Marshal of the Royal Air Force Sir John Slessor (Chief of the Air Staff 1950–2) observed that there would be 'more Koreas', implying that visions of air power winning wars swiftly and independently were misplaced.[11] The Vietnam War strengthened the notion that air power was inextricably linked with land and maritime power, a combination of American air-mobile tactics, aerial resupply and close air support by US Air Force, US Naval and US Marine Corps aircraft playing a critical part in the conflict, even if historians later tended to concentrate upon Rolling Thunder and Linebacker as exemplars of the air war.

The reassessment of the Vietnam experience by the Americans led, as we have seen, to AirLand battle doctrine and subsequent developments whereby the lines between tactical and strategic air power have become blurred. When Operation Desert Storm began on 16 January 1991, air–land synergy was essential to the success of the ground operation to liberate Kuwait; however, since attacks on Iraqi fielded forces were part of what would have traditionally been considered the strategic air campaign, it may appear difficult to judge whether or not the air action was an example of air–land synergy or independent air action. Furthermore, since attacking command-and-control facilities had implications for the land battle by degrading Saddam Hussein's ability to direct his army, it could be contended that even attacks that were envisaged as strategic in purpose were also of tactical significance. When combat was joined by the land component, the use of overwhelming air support certainly enabled success at lower cost than might otherwise have been expected against what was then the fourth largest army in the world. Similarly, air–land synergy in 2003's Operation Iraqi Freedom played a significant role in reducing the fighting power of the Iraqi forces, although there is evidence that the potency of air power displayed in 1991, coupled with an aggressive Information Operations campaign, dissuaded many Iraqi units from fighting at all; the Iraqi Air Force chose not to contest the air battle in the face of overwhelming American supremacy, ensuring that coalition ground forces did not come under air attack. In both conflicts, the role of air–maritime co-operation has been rather underplayed, but the use of air and naval forces to interdict supplies to Iraq was successfully conducted during both Desert Storm and Iraqi Freedom, while in the earlier conflict maritime air power destroyed the majority of the Iraqi Navy.

Air power and insurgencies

There has been one further area in which air–surface synergy has been important, namely in combating insurgencies. The role of air power in this type of conflict has been an outgrowth from the colonial policing role of the 1920s and 1930s, but with some notable alterations. In the interwar period, air power was used for coercive and destructive effects. In the British model, recalcitrant indigenous groupings were threatened with attack if they did not modify their behaviour. If it was considered necessary to carry out the threat, warning leaflets were dropped, and the village in which the rebels lived attacked. This approach was criticised by some on ethical grounds, notably that air power was being employed to create terror. The use of transport aircraft by counter-insurgents for the deployment of troops and evacuation of the wounded and civilians was largely overlooked. After the Second World War, air power was used in a number of counter-insurgency campaigns. The use of transport aircraft and helicopters – as the technical capabilities of these machines increased – was of considerable importance, particularly in such campaigns as those fought in Malaya (in the 1950s) and Algeria (in the 1960s). The value of aircraft for transport has remained

Figure 4.3 A US Air Force A-10 attack aircraft releases defensive flares, used to prevent infra-red homing missiles from locking on to the aircraft.

constant, particularly in fighting insurgencies in areas with limited communications – as seen in the importance placed on such activity by the Soviets and then the anti-al-Qaeda/Taliban Coalition in Afghanistan, with air transport used for the swift deployment of troops to areas almost inaccessible by land.

Aerial reconnaissance was particularly valuable for the French when fighting the Front de Libération Nationale (FLN) in the Algerian countryside, but once the insurgency moved into the cities its value lessened as the insurgents exploited the cover provided by an urban environment. Subsequent advances in technology have facilitated better observation, even in urban areas, and the use of aircraft to exploit the electromagnetic spectrum – also used by insurgent groups – has become important, notably in the on-going conflict in Iraq following the 2003 invasion. The use of unmanned aerial vehicles (UAVs) has been of value and may be said to be transformational, in that their ability to remain on station for hours at a time has mitigated the negative air power characteristic of impermanence. The ability of some UAVs to carry weapons adds to their potency, since these platforms can make the transition from providing information to attacking key targets, should they be detected during the course of their mission.

The use of air power to attack insurgent targets has remained important, but there have been difficulties: in jungle environments, seeing the enemy to strike them is problematic. Ethical considerations are also an issue, and the mantra of 'winning hearts and minds' means that air attacks need to be targeted precisely to ensure that the effect is not to garner support for the insurgents as a result of casualties inflicted upon civilians by such attacks. The development of PGMs has lessened this problem, but it still remains an issue, as demonstrated with the employment of air attack in the assault by the Americans and Iraqi National Government forces on the insurgent stronghold of Fallujah. In Afghanistan, Soviet units placed considerable value upon air support when in contact with the Mujahadeen, and air support has played a vital part in operations against the Taliban and al-Qaeda forces since 2001. Precision weapons have increased the effectiveness of air support in such confrontations, but concerns over the effect of air attack on civilians in proximity to the fighting remain. Thus, while the full range of air power capabilities is an important factor in combating insurgencies, it must be employed carefully. Views that air power is best used in a subordinate role in counter-insurgency are perhaps overstated, since the psychological value of air power needs to be considered. As Trenchard noted in 1916, the mere presence of an aircraft has a psychological effect, and there is evidence that the presence of aircraft overhead deters insurgents, even in environments where they may be prepared to launch suicide attacks. Whether air power has been used for transportation, reconnaissance, attack or its psychological effect, the evidence suggests that it enhances the ability of the land component to conduct counter-insurgency operations if careful planning as the result of close liaison between air force and army is undertaken.

Space power is very much a nascent form of military power, yet it is of considerable significance in modern war. Furthermore, its importance to operations by major powers has given rise to a ready stream of doctrinal thinking as to how space power may be exploited in the future. There is some debate as to whether space power should be considered an adjunct of air power or whether it should be regarded as a completely separate entity altogether. Attempting to produce a universal definition of space power is as difficult as endeavouring to produce one for air power, although the following premise put forward by David E. Lupton in his book *On Space Warfare: A Spacepower Doctrine* is worth considering: 'Spacepower [*sic*] is the ability of a nation to exploit the space environment in pursuit of national goals and purposes and includes the entire astronautical capabilities of the nation.'[12]

It is worth noting that air and space power share certain general characteristics which make it worth addressing some of the factors relating to space in this chapter. Like air power, space offers height, speed and reach, although at different orders of magnitude. While conventional aircraft operating at up to 20 miles above the earth's surface enjoy a considerable vantage point, this pales into insignificance in comparison with the field of vision that can be obtained from 100 miles above the earth. Also, the speed at which space-based assets move is far greater than that of conventional aircraft. Depending on the nature of a space platform's orbit and/or propulsion system, it is possible for it to travel around the world several times in twenty-four hours, thus providing regular coverage of an area of interest, or for the space asset to be moved above such an area from its extant orbit. Space power has become an increasingly important aspect of military planning and operations, and the potential of the operating environment is considerable. It does, perhaps, suffer from problems of perception, since notions of military operations from space seem to be almost inevitably coloured by perceptions drawn from the *Star Trek* television series (and associated franchises) and George Lucas' *Star Wars* series of films. This perhaps obscures the fact that space technology, while not as advanced as portrayed on screen, is evolving rapidly and cannot be divorced from the military operations conducted by major industrialised powers today.

The development of space power

Space power's origins lay very much in the Cold War, the so-called 'space race' between the United States and the Soviet Union being a display of the two nations' rivalry as each sought to demonstrate the superiority of its technology – and perhaps subliminally the supremacy of the political system that had developed it. The success of the Soviets in placing the satellite Sputnik in orbit in 1957 caused uproar in the United States, the public fearing that the Soviet Union might be able to place nuclear weapons in space, rendering America vulnerable to attack. While such visions were far-fetched at the time, they inspired vast investment in the American space programme, the 'race' culminating with the landing of Apollo 11 on the moon in July 1969. The manned space programmes obscured major developments in satellite technology, much of which was of considerable utility to the armed services of both major powers and their allies.

After Sputnik, the Americans developed similar technology. From the early 1960s, both the Soviets and the Americans placed satellites in orbit to obtain information about their adversary. For the Americans, this was particularly desirable, since the use of a space platform meant that it was possible to obtain photographic evidence of military installations within the Soviet Union without recourse to dangerous (and potentially embarrassing) over-flights by manned aircraft. Although scientists and engineers recognised that satellites could be placed in a geostationary orbit (that is to say, remaining over a fixed point, rotating at the same speed as the earth), early satellites could not provide the twenty-four-hour coverage given by this approach, because they recorded their information on film cartridges which had to be jettisoned over friendly territory for subsequent analysis by intelligence services. This demanded a geosynchronous orbit pattern, the satellite circling the earth frequently and giving coverage of a wide area of the earth's surface as it did so. As satellite technology improved, it became possible to use recording devices which transmitted their information to an operating centre, where the images could be interpreted and disseminated to the agencies that required them. Throughout the Cold War, increasingly sophisticated reconnaissance satellites were developed. These employed a range of imaging capabilities, including radar, infra-red and photography, while the resolution and clarity of images obtained became almost legendary.

However, while the satellites provided large amounts of information about the disposition of opposing forces, such information was carefully controlled. The information gathered was of relatively little significance to the wider military, since it was highly classified and disseminated to a relatively small number of agencies, with the aim of supporting the deterrence strategy in place between the two rival superpower blocks. This meant that the wider military application of space power was relatively limited in scope, if not in scale. During the Vietnam War, satellites were predominantly used for the purpose of weather forecasting and communications, with some navigational information transmitted in addition. Although the utility of space platforms became widely recognised, the high-security classifications applied to their use meant that the potential was not fully understood, nor was it integrated effectively into the wider military environment. By the late 1980s, the United States held a commanding lead in military space power – but much of the American military remained unaware of the capabilities that were on offer. The American interventions in Grenada (1983) and Panama (1989) saw the exploitation of information from satellites being used to inform military operations, even though the high levels of classification pertaining to the intelligence product obtained from space again meant that there were difficulties in ensuring that information gained from space assets was provided to those who needed to know about it.

The expansion of space power

The end of the Cold War and the Iraqi invasion of Kuwait changed the way in which the United States exploited space power; with the latter being the leading nation in the exploitation of space for military purposes at this point, the events of the early 1990s informed perceptions of space power generally around the world. When Operation Desert Shield began in August 1990, the Americans were notably unprepared to use space power to full effect. Although some doctrine regarding the effective integration between space assets and terrestrial-based forces existed, there were areas in which the command and control of space assets, hampered by the previously mentioned over-classification of information product, did not function as well as they might. While national command authorities were provided with much useful information from space platforms, General Norman Schwarzkopf, as theatre commander, did not receive information that would have been extremely useful.

Nevertheless, space power did play a vital role in operations in the Persian Gulf in 1990 and 1991. Approximately 80 per cent of communications to and from CENTCOM was transmitted by space-based communications assets. The Global Positioning System (GPS), a relatively new piece of technology, proved an essential asset to the Coalition, giving precise navigational co-ordinates to army formations manoeuvring across featureless deserts, while aircrews purchased hand-held GPS terminals designed to assist civilians in such leisure pursuits as sailing and attached them in their cockpits with velcro, preferring to trust to these than to the often unreliable navigational equipment fitted to their aircraft.

Multispectral sensor information (that is to say, using radar, infra-red and electro-optical sensors) provided an array of highly detailed images that aided in battle damage assessment (BDA), although there were complaints from within the theatre of operations that BDA information that would have been of considerable utility in planning had not reached the units that required the information the most. Perhaps most importantly, space power's most dramatic contribution to Desert Storm came with its use in the campaign against the Iraqi Scud missile attacks against Israel. Satellites with infra-red sensors were employed to detect the heat 'bloom' generated by the firing of the Scuds' rocket motors. From this information, which provided the co-ordinates of the launch site, it was possible to make a rough calculation as to where the missile was heading. This information was then sent to the US Air Force's Space Command in the United States, which then sent the information directly to the crews manning Patriot SAMs based in Israel and Saudi Arabia, bringing them to alert so that they could use their own radar systems to search for and detect the incoming missile. As Gregory Billman observes, the 1991 Gulf War 'provided space power with its first large-scale opportunity to demonstrate its capabilities'.[13] The Americans reflected deeply upon the use of space power in Desert Storm and made amendments to the way in which space assets were tasked and information disseminated. The significance of GPS increased dramatically after Desert Storm as the US Air Force pursued the development of GPS-guided munitions, notably with the Joint Direct Attack Munition (JDAM) series of weapons, where a GPS guidance kit is fitted to standard unguided bombs. JDAM is not as precise as laser-guided weapons, but its accuracy is impressive, bombs usually landing within 30 feet or less of their designated aim point. The need for such a system was illustrated during the NATO operation against Slobodan Milosevic's regime in 1999, when many aircraft sorties had to be aborted because bad weather prevented aircrew from seeing the ground, preventing them from designating targets for their laser-guided weapons.

Space vulnerabilities

The increasing importance of space power during the 1990s both in terms of GPS and information-gathering created new concerns about the exploitation of space. These are particularly acute in the United States, which relies upon space assets like no other nation; in turn, many of America's allies are dependent upon US space systems for their militaries – for instance, the RAF now employs the 'Enhanced Paveway' series of bombs, which combine laser and GPS guidance to make the weapons employable in all weathers. The concern stems from the fact that it is evident that an adversary may seek to deny the Americans (and thus their allies) the use of space assets in future conflict. It is possible for GPS signals to be jammed. Indeed, in Operation Iraqi Freedom in 2003, the Iraqis employed GPS jamming systems purchased from Russia; in this case, the investment proved unsound, since the Americans destroyed the jammers – ironically, using JDAMs – but the point that an enemy may seek to mitigate American space superiority was well made.

The potential for adversaries to make use of the widely available commercial satellite systems has also become an issue. In Operation Desert Storm, the coalition made sure that the Iraqis were unable to make use of the French commercial SPOT imaging satellite system (*Système, Probatoire pour l'Observation de la Terre*), which might have given Saddam information about the disposition of Coalition forces; in the insurgency in Iraq after Saddam's deposition, and in the intervention in Afghanistan, concerns have been expressed about the ability of insurgents to use packages such as Google Earth to gain images of the layout of Coalition bases, enabling them to make effective indirect fire attacks on the most vulnerable parts of those facilities. To an extent, this was addressed by Google Earth responding positively to requests to obscure the imagery of bases, but commercial concerns offering similar services may not be so accommodating in future. Furthermore, it is possible that adversaries with access to suitable technology may seek to 'blind' satellites with the use of ground-based laser systems that dazzle the satellite's equipment. A US Army test in 1997 employing a low-powered laser blinded a US Air Force satellite flying 300 miles above the earth's surface.

Subsequently, there have been suggestions that the Chinese, embarking upon a space programme of their own, may have utilised similar low-powered laser blinding devices to deny the United States intelligence information about sites of interest in Chinese territory. Another threat may emanate from adversaries launching a cyber attack on space-based platforms, interrupting communication between the control room and the platform itself. Such an attack could be used to render the space asset useless, either by sending it tumbling out of orbit or shutting down key systems.

Space control and force application

American concerns about such developments have increased discussion of the concept of space control. Like control of the air, this seeks to ensure freedom of action of friendly assets without interference from the enemy, while denying the opposition access to the benefits provided by space. This represents a horrendously complex issue for the United States, since blinding or destroying a civilian-owned, -launched and -operated satellite system if the owner refuses to ensure that either information product or communications facilitation provided by their space asset is unavailable for enemy exploitation is fraught with legal difficulties. The Americans developed an air-launched anti-satellite (ASAT) weapon in the 1980s which was successfully tested before the project was cancelled over concerns that it violated international treaties; a Chinese test of an ASAT in 2007 caused considerable consternation, particularly in the United States. US military war games have illustrated the threat posed by an adversary capable of employing ASAT or blinding technologies. As a participant noted at the end of one such war game, '[the enemy] took out most of our space-based capabilities. Our military forces just ground to a halt.'[14] Observers suggest that the only means by which the United States can guarantee space control is not only to invest in anti-satellite capabilities deployed from earth-based locations but also actively to fight for control in space itself; the US Space Commission report of 2001 concluded that the threat to American space capability was a 'virtual certainty', making the need to invest in some form of space control technology seem even more important. The degree of space control considered necessary by some proponents would involve placing weapons in space, an issue of considerable political sensitivity. Weaponisation of space, even for defensive purposes, is controversial; the Soviets fitted a 30mm cannon to the Salyut-3 space station in the 1970s, with the aim of protecting the station from a possible attack by an American platform, but such was the sensitivity about placing weapons in

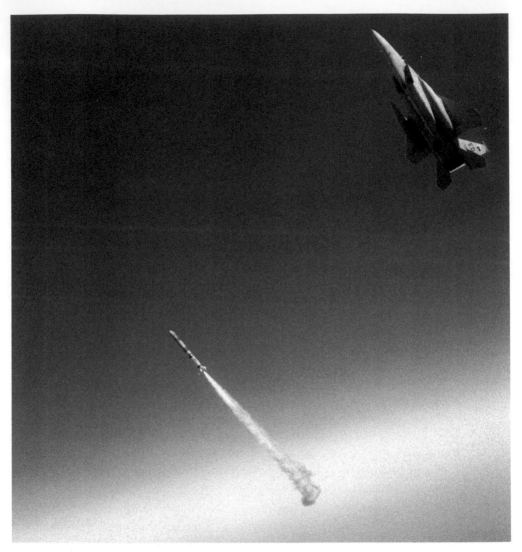

Figure 4.4 An F-15 Eagle launching an ASM-135 Anti-Satellite Missile (ASAT). The ASAT was cancelled by Congress prior to service introduction for fear that it would breach international laws regarding the weaponisation of space. The importance of space assets to American military power means that such weapons systems are once again under consideration.

orbit that this was not revealed at the time, details emerging only as the result of information provided from those who served aboard Salyut-3. This makes another potential space concept, that of Force Application, an even more controversial area.

The concept of Space Force Application takes the possibility of weaponising space a stage further, in that it would see the development and use of weapons systems against terrestrial targets. Such a step would involve the use of directed-energy and kinetic-energy weapons (that is to say, lasers and ultra-high-speed projectiles that destroy the target through their kinetic energy rather than with a warhead) against both missiles and enemy ground targets; enemy targets on earth might also be attacked using space-based conventional weapons. The value of the kinetic-energy weapon from space against such targets as hardened bunkers would be that the energy inherent in such a weapon descending from space would be far greater than anything that could be obtained by a conventional weapon launched from within the earth's atmosphere.

The ultimate frontier

While space power is still, in many ways, a nascent form of warfare, the critical nature of space-based platforms means that there is a widespread belief that issues of space control and the weaponisation of space will need to be addressed, even if not in the short term.[15] Space power shares many features of air power, notably in the way in which it is a key enabler for operations. The former Commander-in-Chief of both North American Aerospace Defense Command and the USAF's Air Force Space Command, General Howell M. Estes III, has observed: 'The potential of aircraft was not recognised immediately. Their initial use was confined to observation . . . until one day, the full advantage of applying force from the air was realised, and the rest was history. So too with the business of space.'[16]

While Estes' view may involve too linear a description of the way in which the utility of using air power for the projection of military force was realised, the comparison with air power (and arguably land and naval power) is valid. As soon as the value of the operating environment was realised, it became clear that future conflict between powers of roughly comparable technical proficiencies would involve the struggle for control of that environment. This has become the underpinning rationale of air power, and it appears that space power will increasingly be subjected to the same dynamics, albeit only as long as the competing powers possess an approximately symmetrical degree of technical advancement and aptitude. For asymmetric operations, where one power enjoys overwhelming technological overmatch against the opponent, the value of space power as a key enabler remains unchallenged, hence the notion that 'space superiority has joined air superiority as a *sine qua non* of global reach and power'.[17]

As has been shown, air power is a complex operating environment that has been subjected to considerable debate as the result of visions of what can be achieved by air attack against targets at the strategic level. Nevertheless, despite the on-going debate as to where air power is best employed, a few general observations can be made. It is clear that no army or navy can operate effectively in the absence of some form of control of the air. It may be that having control of the air for a limited period of time or in a limited area is all that is required for the success of a particular operation, but prolonged activity in the face of enemy air superiority makes the achievement of success increasingly unlikely. However, control of the air should be seen as an enabler for operations rather than an end in itself.

A second key point is to note how important air power is to surface operations. The Second World War demonstrated that surface forces could not function to full effect in the face of enemy air superiority and that the efficacy of their operations was greatly enhanced by being able exploit the key characteristics of air power discussed in the first section of this chapter so as to project power beyond the range of the surface forces. Synergy between air and surface units greatly enhances the effect of what can be achieved, particularly in an era when precision weaponry enables targets to be attacked with considerable discrimination. This is also of importance in the application of air power for strategic attack. There is a further complication regarding the use of air power alone to achieve victory, since to do so requires in-depth knowledge of the adversary at the political, cultural and societal levels, and this may be difficult to obtain. For instance, the failure of the United States to comprehend the nature of the North Vietnamese leadership, their conduct of the war and their desired political end state made it extremely unlikely that Rolling Thunder would succeed; in many ways, the Americans struck targets that would have undoubtedly had an effect within the American political system but that made little impact upon the North Vietnamese. Similarly, there is anecdotal evidence that the targeting in Operation Iraqi Freedom achieved effect, but not always those effects intended of it by the planners, efforts to comprehend the ideal target sets notwithstanding.

As suggested, the term 'strategic air power' causes much confusion, since it is synonymous with bombing targets away from the battlefront. While it is true that air attacks against targets that are of importance to the adversary's ability or willingness to continue to fight undoubtedly merit the application of the term 'strategic', it is important to recognise that air power can have considerable effect at the strategic level without being employed to attack targets within the enemy homeland. The ability to deploy troops rapidly, to render fielded forces ineffective and unable to operate so that the enemy's goals can no longer be achieved, or to protect sea lanes may all have implications at the strategic level and can thus be said to fall under the categorisation of 'strategic air power'. If such qualifications appear confusing, this may be a further result of perhaps the most important aspect of comprehending modern air power. Air power's attributes make it essential to conducting modern conflict. It is a vital enabler for operations by surface forces in terms of providing security from enemy air attack and rapid mobility that cannot be attained through any other medium; the psychological effect of air attack is particularly potent, although historical examples suggest that it is more powerful against enemy troops, in direct contradiction to the views of early air power thinkers who presumed that it would be the civilian population who suffered most. While there is no denying that attacks against targets in enemy heartlands can be of importance, attempting to harness air power to a particular model of operation risks robbing it of its flexibility and versatility. Air power is a particularly adaptable form of military power, and the greatest challenge faced by commanders is to ensure that they use it to best effect. If they become entangled in the long-running debate over whether air power is decisive and whether it renders surface forces less relevant, they are likely to misemploy their air power.

The historiography of modern conflict suggests that the side that fails to employ its air power to best effect tends to be the side that is defeated, hence the need to understand what air power can and cannot achieve. To ignore this important requirement is to court disaster. The same is increasingly true of the arena of space power; now that the veil of secrecy of the Cold War era has been lifted and some of the mystique of what space-based assets can achieve, it is clear that air and space are critical enablers to the prosecution of modern war. While the time has perhaps not yet arrived for air and space to be blended seamlessly into a concept of 'aerospace power', it is evident that the synergies of air and space power, and the way in which these contribute to modern war, make them vital to the business of war, their relative immaturity in respect of the land and maritime environments notwithstanding.

NOTES

1 The National Archives (TNA), Air 1/718/29/1, 'Future Policy in the Air' 22 September 1916.
2 *Ibid.*
3 Phillip S. Meilinger, 'Trenchard and Morale Bombing', in Phillip S. Meilinger, *Air War: Theory and Practice* (London: Frank Cass, 2003), p. 49.
4 *Ibid.*
5 TNA, AIR 19/92, Minutes of a Meeting in Chief of the Air Staff's Room, 19 July 1923.
6 *Ibid.*, p. 78.
7 Robert A. Pape, 'Coercive Air Power in the Vietnam War', *International Security* 15:2 (Fall 1990): 106.
8 Mark Clodfelter, *The Limits of Air Power* (New York: Free Press, 1989), pp. 45–72.
9 *Ibid.*, p. 196.

10 John Andreas Olsen, *Strategic Air Power in Desert Storm* (London: Frank Cass, 2003), pp. 269–74.

11 Quoted in David MacIssac, 'Voices from the Central Blue: The Air Power Theorists', in Peter Paret, ed., *Makers of Modern Strategy: From Machiavelli to the Nuclear Age* (Princeton, NJ: Princeton University Press, 1986), p. 644.

12 David E. Lupton, *On Space Warfare: A Spacepower Doctrine* (Maxwell, AL: Air University Press, 1988), p. 7.

13 Gregory Billman, 'The Inherent Limitations of Space Power: Fact or Fiction?', in Bruce M. DeBlois, ed., *Beyond the Paths of Heaven: The Emergence of Space Power Thought* (Maxwell, AL: Air University Press, 1999), p. 511.

14 Benjamin S. Lambeth, *Mastering the Ultimate High Ground: Next Steps in the Military Uses of Space* (Santa Monica, CA: RAND, 2003), p. 101.

15 *Ibid.*, p. 118.

16 *Ibid.*

17 Department of the (US) Air Force, *Global Reach – Global Power* (Washington, DC: Department of the Air Force, 1992), p. 8.

FURTHER READING

Biddle, Tami Davis, *Rhetoric and Reality in Air Warfare: The Evolution of British and American Ideas about Strategic Bombing 1914–1945* (Princeton, NJ: Princeton University Press, 2002).
An excellent analysis of the development of air power strategy and doctrine during the interwar period and the results of the application of this doctrine during the Second World War.

Buckley, John, *Air Power in the Age of Total War* (London: UCL Press, 1999).
An interesting overview of the use of air power in conflict during the twentieth century.

Clodfelter, Mark, *The Limits of Air Power* (New York: Free Press, 1989).
Probably the most important book on the American application of air power during the Vietnam War.

Corum, James S. and Johnson, Wray R., *Airpower in Small Wars: Fighting Insurgents and Terrorists* (Lawrence, KS: University of Kansas, 2003).
A survey of the employment of air power in small wars, insurgencies and low-intensity conflict.

Davis, Richard G., *On Target: Organising and Executing the Strategic Air Campaign against Iraq* (Washington, DC: Air Force History and Museums Program, 2002).
A useful and highly detailed analysis of the strategic air campaign against Iraq during the 1991 Gulf War.

Douhet, Giulio, *The Command of the Air* (Washington, DC: Office of Air Force History, 1983 [reprint]).
The seminal work from one of the leading air power theorists. Essential reading for anyone wishing to gain a deeper understanding of the development of thought about strategic bombardment, despite some flaws in reasoning.

Gray, Peter W. and Cox, Sebastian, eds., *Air Power Leadership: Theory and Practice* (London: The Stationery Office, 2003).
As the title suggests, a collection of essays examining the way in which various personalities and air forces have approached the issue of commanding and utilising air forces.

Air Power History: Turning Points, from Kitty Hawk to Kosovo (London: Frank Cass, 2003).
An excellent collection of essays on a variety of air power subjects.

Gooch, John, ed., *Airpower: Theory and Practice* (London: Frank Cass, 1995).
A useful collection of essays dealing with air power thought, doctrine, legal issues and the use of military air power in conflict.

Hallion, Richard, *Strike from the Sky: A History of Battlefield Air Attack* (Washington, DC: Smithsonian Institution Press, 1989).
A survey of the way in which air power has been employed in support of land operations since the earliest days of military air power.

Storm over Iraq: Air Power and the Gulf War (Washington, DC: Smithsonian Institution Press, 1992).
One of the first books to deal in detail with the 1991 Gulf War, and still one of the most useful sources on this conflict.

Lambeth, Benjamin S., *Mastering the Ultimate High Ground: Next Steps in the Military Uses of Space* (Santa Monica, CA: RAND, 2003).
A survey of the nascent field of space power and possible future developments.

Mason, Tony, Air Vice-Marshal, *Air Power: A Centennial Appraisal* (London: Brassey's, 1994).
An extremely useful survey of air power and air power thought from the last years of the nineteenth century until the end of the Cold War.

Meilinger, Phillip S., *Paths of Heaven: The Evolution of Air Power Theory* (Maxwell, AL: Air University Press, 1997).
An edited collection of essays by a variety of leading air power historians addressing the development of air power doctrine in a variety of nations.

Air War: Theory and Practice (London: Frank Cass, 2003).
A collection of insightful essays addressing a variety of aspects of air power.

Mitchell, William S., *Winged Defense: The Development and Possibilities of Modern Air Power* (New York: Putnam, 1925).
The key work by the leading American air power theorist of the interwar period.

Warden III, John A., *The Air Campaign: Planning for Combat* (Washington, DC: National Defense University, 1988).
The main work by the leading American air power theorist of recent times and essential for an understanding of the principles that underpinned the air campaign in the 1991 Gulf War.

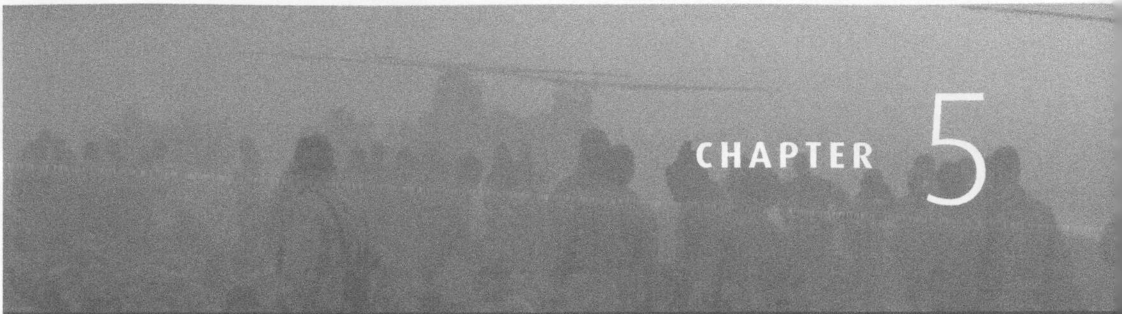

CHAPTER 5

IRREGULAR WARFARE

CONTENTS

KEY THEMES

- Irregular warfare is primarily about politics and organisation. Violence plays a role in irregular warfare, as in all forms of war, for political purposes. The immediate purpose of violence is to demonstrate the political ineptitude of the ruling government and as a tool to intimidate and coerce populations. The ultimate goal of irregular warfare is political power for the purposes of political, social, economic and/or religious change.
- The character of irregular warfare is dynamic, but its nature, outlined above, is not. This character is shaped by social, environmental and technological factors. Insurgents, terrorists and revolutionaries have adopted irregular warfare methods for a key pragmatic reason: to offset their military and organisational weaknesses.
- Irregular warfare is a complex phenomenon that is difficult to understand, as different types of violence can be used individually or simultaneously. This can lead to confusing the method or tactics of irregular warfare for its strategy or its purpose. Fixating on the tactics of violence, as opposed to its organisation and rationale, can lead only to frustration and failure.
- Understanding the continuity of and differences between historical rationale and practice, and not just the most recent era of lessons learned, is the key to success in current and future irregular wars.

In order to achieve victory in warfare, most political leaders have relied historically upon their military leaders to use their various armed forces – armies, navies and, later, air forces – as effectively and as efficiently as possible. As has been discussed in preceding chapters, the destruction of enough of an adversary's armed forces in a decisive operational campaign is the traditional manner of convincing enemy leaders to seek an end to hostilities. By any historical measure, the initial phase of Operation Iraqi Freedom from March to April 2003 is the epitome of how to fight a joint military campaign. Planners at US Central Command (CENTCOM) adapted quickly to changing political circumstances. Operation Iraqi Freedom was launched with only one-third of the ground forces originally planned and despite denial of Turkish ports of entry and overflight rights.[1] CENTCOM joint commanders, including Lieutenant-Generals David McKiernan and T. Michael Moseley, made use of available land, sea, air, space, cyberspace and special operations capabilities in an integrated manner to unbalance and unhinge anticipated Iraqi counter-strokes to the invasion. The manoeuvre of US Army V Corps and I Marine Expeditionary Force (I MEF) towards Baghdad, conducted in conjunction with Coalition air dominance and the use of special operations forces in the west and north of Iraq, was, with few exceptions, a textbook example of the operational art of war conducted jointly along multiple axes of approach.[2] The net result of this joint application of military power was the toppling of Saddam Hussein's regime and the seizure of Iraq's undamaged oil infrastructure in a mere twenty-one days.

Despite this demonstrated conventional military prowess, Coalition forces in Iraq and Afghanistan seem unable to deal effectively or efficiently with the irregular threats that have prevailed in both countries since the ruling regimes were removed. The perceived failure of Coalition forces led by the United States to come to grips with irregular threats, which have been characterised as terrorism, insurgency, sectarian violence and civil war, has led a number of scholars and observers to draw analogies or explanations from a range of disciplines, including history, sociology and political science. One explanation suggests that culture or religion is the crucial factor. In particular, an inability or unwillingness on the part of the US military to understand or value Iraqi tribal language or culture, or the Afghan tribal code of Pushtunwali, suggests that any potential responses to irregular threats cannot succeed.[3] Another cultural explanation offered relates to how organisations innovate and adapt. Other military cultures are apt to look at the different problems through the lens of available military forces and capabilities. According to the old adage, when the only tool that you have is a hammer, all of your problems start to look like nails. Established military bureaucracies may be unwilling to reform or unable to innovate against a highly flexible and adaptive irregular opponent, as the American experience in Vietnam suggests (see Figure 5.1).[4]

Other writers suggest that irregular warfare will prevail not despite Western military prowess but rather because of it. Adversaries looking to challenge the United States and its allies understand their ability to dominate militarily almost every operational environment, including land, sea, air, space and cyberspace. One potential response to superior conventional military power, discussed in chapter 6 on weapons of mass destruction, involves significantly raising the potential stakes of conflict. The other option is to challenge established militaries using irregular forces such as terrorists, insurgents or other paramilitary forces. In such struggles conventional military power cannot be used to achieve a swift, decisive victory on the battlefield. When confronted with superior military force, irregular adversaries can disperse, choose where and when to attack, and then melt back into the population. Proponents suggest that the next, fourth generation of warfare (4GW) is already upon us. 4GW involves asymmetric tactics, enabled by information and other commercially available technologies, used against the political, social and economic weaknesses of post-industrial status and, the author suggests, represents a change in the nature of war itself.[5] The more often that modern militaries use their blunt instruments of conventional military power to achieve decisive results, and ultimately fail to do so, the greater the likelihood that the local population

Figure 5.1 American military interest in and efforts to understand irregular warfare have historically tended to wax and wane. Here, two military instructors discuss primitive weapons from Latin America as part of a counter-insurgency course conducted at the US Air Force's Air University Institute of Professional Development during the 1960s.

and domestic or even international constituencies will increasingly withdraw their support for the conflict. The United States is not alone in its frustration in dealing with irregular threats. The campaign in the summer of 2006 in Lebanon, in which Israeli forces failed to rescue two of their kidnapped soldiers or disarm the armed group Hezbollah, while incurring military losses in the air, on the ground and at sea, is proof positive to 4GW supporters that the clash of conventional armies is increasingly becoming an anachronism.

Do the conflicts in Lebanon, Iraq and Afghanistan herald a fundamental change in the nature of war? Is irregular warfare the only form of war that will be waged in the twenty-first century? Why are the armed forces of democracies, which have a well-demonstrated ability to project combat power, seemingly powerless in the face of irregular adversaries? This chapter suggests that there is nothing mystical or even uniquely new about the rationale for adopting irregular warfare.

In order to demystify irregular warfare, this chapter first defines and distinguishes between its key terms of reference. This straightforward task is much more difficult than it appears at first glance. Indeed, much of the confusion relating to irregular warfare results from the misunderstanding and misapplication of its core terminology. With the core terms and concepts firmly in hand, this chapter next surveys various theories of irregular warfare from the perspective of those who seek to exploit insurgent and terrorist violence. The key theme of this review is that irregular warfare methods themselves have rarely been sufficient to achieve meaningful change. Historically, insurgents and terrorists have taken one of two approaches, depending on the specific context of the conflict. The first approach is simply to outlast and force the eventual withdrawal of an occupying adversary, often after the latter has experienced considerable political frustration or exhaustion. The second approach has been to translate internal support from the population, as well as external support from sponsors, into political and military capabilities that overwhelm the forces of an adversary. From this perspective on irregular warfare this chapter switches sides and looks next at the challenges confronting those who seek to defeat insurgent and terrorist groups. The 'science' of countering insurgents and terrorists has been established historically through a number of well-known and, some might argue, self-evident principles. Difficulties in counter-insurgency and counter-terrorism, as in all other forms of warfare, lie largely in attempting to apply such principles thoughtlessly without accounting for the unique context and changing circumstances of the conflict – in other words, failing to grasp the 'art' of strategy.

Irregular warfare

Defining irregular warfare, much less its component elements, is no easy task. A number of problems plague attempts to define irregular warfare clearly and concisely. In some cases, authors are inclined to lump everything together under a concept to the point where a term describes everything but explains nothing. Examples include 'insurgency' and 'asymmetric warfare'. At the other end of the spectrum are scholars and soldiers who create categorical definitions as they try to separate the terminology of irregular warfare with mechanical precision. Such definitions suit the purposes of specialised disciplines but have little recognition or application outside their individual communities. In addition, new terms are created or revived in an attempt to capture the realities of the most recent manifestations of violence. According to US doctrine, the preferred term has changed from 'counter-guerrilla operations' through to 'counter-insurgency'[6] and 'foreign internal defence'.[7] On the surface there appears to be little that distinguishes them apart. The term 'foreign internal defence', however, was coined in the wake of Vietnam, and it captures two essential realities associated with US involvement in dealing with insurgencies:

military operations play a secondary role in countering insurgents, and US actions are restricted largely to training, advising and equipping host nation forces; and US freedom of action and ability to direct the course of operations are not only subject to domestic political considerations but are likely to be subordinated to those of the leaders of the nation trying to defeat the insurgents. Organisations, professional communities and influential individuals potentially become wedded to terms that describe their understanding of a phenomenon and reflect their particular functional focus or biases. As a result, seemingly innocuous language can either lead to vociferous disagreement in policy and planning circles or confusion among allied nations.

Language, and in particular specific terms, presents other challenges in attempting to define irregular warfare. The two most daunting obstacles are the changing connotations of specific terms and the subjective and often emotional qualities associated with them. For example, Bruce Hoffman has charted the evolution in meaning behind the term 'terrorism' from 'state violence against the population' to 'violence used by sub-state groups for political purposes'.[8] 'Insurgency' was first used to describe insurrections or violence with limited aims and duration, but the term now conveys motivation, organisation and a degree of popular support. Although this might appear to be an exercise in intellectual hair-splitting, words have meanings that can in turn influence how and what actions are taken. For several months after the fall of Baghdad in 2003, senior leaders within the Office of the US Secretary of Defense forbade the use of the term 'insurgency' to describe the violence, lest it appear to be anything more threatening than the last vestiges of a dead regime. Many opportunities were lost in Iraq from June 2003 to July 2004 by failing to understand the character and source of the violence, label it accordingly and take corrective action as early as possible while it was still at this stage. The subjective value associated with specific terms can also lead to misunderstandings and disagreement over collective action that should be taken between governments or agencies. Differences of opinion over what should be labelled 'terrorism' have nothing to do with the form of violence employed. What colours perceptions is the fact that innocent civilians are often the victims of indiscriminate violence, which strikes an emotional chord. In addition, scholars and decision-makers are likely to disagree over whether such violence should be rationalised and legitimised. One consequence has been an inability to forge a meaningful consensus on what constitutes terrorism, which, in turn, has impeded attempts to proscribe it internationally.[9]

One method of defining irregular warfare and its associated concepts relates to the purpose for which the violence, regardless of its form, is used. Ultimately, irregular warfare has at its core a cause based on grievances. The range of potential grievances and the motivations behind them is wide and can include ethnic and religious persecution, foreign occupation or

Table 5.1 Types of insurgency[10]

Anarchist	Egalitarian	Traditionalist
Apocalyptic-Utopian	Pluralist	Secessionist
Reformist	Preservationist	Commercialist

domination, economic disparity and other forms of injustice that are real or merely perceived. Bard O'Neill has offered a comprehensive categorisation of types of causes for which groups are willing to commit violence (see table 5.1).

As table 5.1 suggests, some groups conduct irregular warfare to weaken the existing order and destroy it (anarchist), or profit from chaos (commercialist) or prefer to break away from the existing order and establish one of their own (secessionist). Others believe the existing order can be saved (reformist) or changed to serve traditional norms (traditionalist) or privileges (preservationist) better. Still others believe a more just and equitable society (egalitarian) can be created, while some believe that they are anointed to mete out religious rewards or punishments (apocalyptic-utopian). Groups can espouse a single cause, blend together one or more of the above or shift from one to another over time. Almost all groups seek to change the existing system, whether on a national, regional or global scale. The only way for most groups to change the status quo is to establish their own territory, or seize control of the existing system by some means and redistribute power, or remake society according to their ideology. For the Taliban in Afghanistan, control means enacting Sharia law along strict Wahhabist lines and replacing Pushtunwali and other tribal codes. Power and control are ultimately political objectives. The violence within irregular warfare is far from random in nature. Instead, it is suborned to a political purpose, as other forms of warfare should be.

Another trait that irregular warfare has in common with other forms of warfare is the idea of a dynamic created as a result of the struggle between adversaries. On a theoretical level, each adversary is seeking to impose its will upon the other while avoiding having another will imposed upon them. What distinguishes war in theory from war in practice is the dynamic that exists within and between adversaries and other actors, and the level of information available to each. The interaction between adversaries, in turn, creates friction, chance and uncertainty that influence the outcome of events and disrupt even the soundest and most elegant strategy.[11] Within irregular warfare, the role played by friction, chance and uncertainty is magnified owing to the political nature of the struggle, the character of the violence and the resources involved.

The key distinction between irregular and other forms of warfare, and different types of irregular warfare, rests on resources and the ability to translate them into effective capabilities. Groups conducting irregular warfare are attempting to defeat or overcome adversaries that possess significantly more powerful and numerous resources. Most often, sub-state groups are fighting against a state that not only possesses superior resources but also has a legitimate monopoly on violence within its borders. In order to have a reasonable chance of success in any type of irregular warfare, groups must keep their activities hidden from their adversary for as long as possible, so as not to be detected, tracked and destroyed.[12] Those who conduct irregular warfare rarely do so as a matter of preference or because they find a semi-clandestine and potentially dangerous lifestyle appealing. Most groups adopt irregular warfare because other, more decisive, forms of political violence are unavailable to them. If given a choice, some insurgent or terrorist leaders would prefer to have the nuclear or conventional resources and capabilities of their adversary in order to achieve their objectives without the need for prolonged struggle.[13] To some extent, the appeal of a group's cause for and the access to a particular population base determines the resources it has available to it. Groups can also forge alliances with others to pool together their resources and seek out state sponsors who are willing and able to finance, train, equip and support them.[14] Yet few groups are co-ordinated, sophisticated or competent enough, at least in the early stages, to turn resources into capabilities that can overwhelm their adversary. Due to the nature of their cause or the extremism of their views, other groups are unable to translate their call for social justice into anything more than a handful of zealous or fanatical supporters. The quality and quantity of resources that a group enjoys have a significant bearing on the type of irregular warfare it can wage and the time it takes to achieve its objectives. To sum up, *irregular warfare* is defined as the use of violence by sub-state actors or groups within states for political purposes of achieving power, control and legitimacy, using unorthodox or unconventional approaches to warfare owing to a fundamental weakness in resources or capabilities. Other definitions of irregular warfare are contained in box 5.1.

Types of irregular warfare

The types of irregular warfare dictated by resources can be broken down into five main categories or forms: coup d'état, terrorism, revolution, insurgency and civil war. Each will be explored briefly on the basis of their centre of gravity, mechanism for success, strategic and tactical orientation, and duration. Table 5.2 summarises the key attributes of the different types of irregular warfare.

Coup d'état

As a form of irregular warfare, coups d'état are conducted to change the system by overthrowing key facilities of government as quickly and with as

Box 5.1 Definitions of irregular warfare

The term 'irregular warfare' is only one of many coined to describe conflict between those fielding conventional forces and capabilities against an opponent who refuses battle, uses hit-and-run tactics and even targets non-combatants indiscriminately in order to achieve their objectives. W. E. D. Allen wrote on the subject of irregular war prior to the Second World War, and his definition is shaped and limited by his studies and experience gained while serving with Lieutenant-Colonel Orde Wingate in 1941. Wingate and Allen advised, trained, equipped and fought with Abyssinian irregulars against occupying Italian regulars. The other definition of irregular warfare below was in response to guidance from the 2006 Quadrennial Defense Review to develop an 'umbrella' term within the US Department of Defense and other agencies for all their activities that captures both the use of and defence against irregular opponents.

Irregular war is in fact as old as the hills which offer it its best terrain; older, clearly, than 'regular' war which has grown out of it, as the city grew out of the village. It would be difficult to define precisely where irregular war ends and regular war begins. It would be possible to say that irregular war is warfare carried out by forces other than the regular armies of a belligerent power. But this definition is not exact . . . Irregular and regular war are clearly two aspects of the same activity, but it should be taken as axiomatic that irregular action in the field should always be ancillary to parallel regular action . . . In no instance have guerrilla operations proved ultimately successful without the regular forces of a friendly power.

W. E. D. Allen, *Guerrilla War in Abyssinia*
(New York: Penguin, 1943), p. 18.

IRREGULAR WARFARE (IW): A violent struggle among state and non-state actors for legitimacy and influence over the relevant populations. IW favors indirect and asymmetric approaches, though it may employ the full range of military and other capabilities, in order to erode an adversary's power, influence, and will.
What makes IW different is the focus of its operations – a relevant population – and its strategic purpose – to gain or maintain control or influence over, and support of, that relevant population. In other words, the focus is on the legitimacy of a political authority to control or influence a relevant population.

Joint Staff, *Irregular Warfare Joint Operating Concept*, version 1.0
(Washington, DC: The Joint Staff, June 2007), pp. 5–6.

little initial bloodshed as possible. Coups tend to be instigated by small numbers within the system, to limit the secrecy of the plot and prevent its discovery. For these reasons, conducting a coup d'état requires nerve, timing, planning and luck, but little in the way of additional resources. Often the instigators of coups d'état come from the officer corps, as the

Table 5.2 Attributes of types of irregular warfare[15]

Type	Resources	Centre of gravity	Mechanism	Strategic orientation	Tactical orientation	Duration
Coup d'état	Few	Elites (organise)	Seizure of power	Offensive	Offensive	Immediate
Terrorism	Few	Elites (influence)	Coercion	Offensive	Offensive	Lengthy
Revolution	Vanguard, growing to many	Population (stimulate)	Popular support (uprising)	Defensive	Offensive	As quickly as possible
Insurgency	Varied, but often significant	Population (control)	Denial leading to victory over or withdrawal of opponent	Defensive, switching to offensive	Offensive, given local superiority	Lengthy
Civil war	Varies	Varies	Denial or negotiated settlement	Varies	Varies	Varies

military is the one government institution that can quickly crush such acts of rebellion. Those who conduct coups seek to gain power in order to change national policies or correct ethnic or religious exclusion – and gain wealth in the process.[16]

Terrorism

Terrorism also involves small numbers of individuals, operating in cells and groups, with relatively few resources needed in order to function. Groups or cells face resource constraints for a number of reasons, including effective security services which constrain group members' freedom of action, to causes which appeal to only a slim minority within a population. Terrorism deliberately targets the non-combatant civilian population and other symbols associated with the state (military and police forces, government buildings, monuments, etc.) or the ruling government's power base (e.g. the Shi'ite al-Aqsa Mosque in Samarra, Iraq) in order to spread fear disproportionate to the damage it causes. Groups choose terrorism as a means of using the severely limited resources at their disposal in unorthodox and dramatic attacks, which are often reported by media outlets, in order to compel or persuade one or more target audiences. Against adversaries, terrorism in its various forms can convince a target population and its leadership that the stakes of a conflict are not worth the current and potential future costs.[17] For domestic audiences, sympathisers and supporters, including states, acts of terrorism demonstrate a group's power, reach and competence, and can facilitate access to resources or even ownership of a particular cause between competing terrorist groups.[18]

Revolution

Revolution bears many similarities to a coup d'état, in that it requires an intellectual elite or 'vanguard' to succeed, but it also possesses a number of crucial differences. The primary goal of a revolution is to paralyse and collapse or overthrow an existing government, in order to redistribute power and resources. There are two critical components to a revolution: a cadre of political organisers who work within a population; and a population that is oppressed, exploited and frustrated enough that they might just turn to protest or violence if the right spark is provided. The cadre of organisers, under the direction of the vanguard, seeks to demonstrate the incompetence of the existing regime, conduct political agitation overtly and covertly, and elevate the consciousness of the oppressed population. At the appropriate time, or perhaps as the result of an action either by the revolutionaries or the regime in response, a critical mass of the population will rise up, overpower the control elements of the regime and allow the vanguard to assume power. Without the mass of the population behind it, revolutions are doomed to fail.

Insurgency

Insurgency has been the subject of recent scrutiny and revision largely as a result of the Global War on Terror and confusion surrounding the character of the violence in Iraq. Some authors suggest that our concept of this type of irregular warfare requires substantial revision and rethinking, given the change in context in which insurgencies now occur.[19] Insurgency shares a number of characteristics in common with other forms of irregular warfare. Successful revolutions place primary emphasis on organizing, educating and proselytising among the population to prepare them for the inevitable uprising against the system. Maoist and other agrarian-based insurgencies, for example, also stress the need to develop a 'shadow government', or parallel political structure, which controls the rural population and extracts resources without alienating its crucial support base. Some interpreters are prone to broaden the meaning of the term 'population', and by implication the support it provides to insurgents, to mean all the residents of a country. The level of support required for insurgencies to sink roots and operate successfully is context-specific, as in the case of clan- or tribal-based societies, in which these social units can be self-supporting. Insurgencies of this type may not require the support of the general population, but rather the spreading of enough instability, uncertainty and fear to prevent the population from assisting the insurgents' adversaries.

While theorists agree that the centre of gravity for an insurgency is popular support, a fundamental difference between revolutions and insurgencies is how resources gained from the population or from other sources are utilised. Insurgencies harness resources in order to conduct attacks using guerrilla tactics that are designed to inflict ever-increasing losses on government or occupying forces and tip the balance of forces in the insurgents' favour. Such tactics include hit-and-run raids, ambushes and, more recently, remote attacks using mortars, rocket launchers and improvised explosive devices. Guerrilla tactics are conducted on a scale and intensity by units organised along conventional military lines that are designed to achieve operational or strategic effects over time: the weakening of the resolve of their political adversaries and the withdrawal of competing, occupying and/or government forces. The insurgent political structure fills the subsequent vacuum and attempts to consolidate its hold over the population by a mixture of intimidation, coercion, co-option or terror. Insurgent groups also recruit among the population, levy taxes and convince the local residents that the government or other groups cannot protect them and that it is in their best individual and collective interest to support the insurgents actively or passively. Success for insurgent groups allows them to translate support into larger militias and battalions, regiments and divisions of guerrillas with which to conduct even more attacks. These attacks further put their adversaries on the tactical, operational and even strategic defensive. Should the circumstances permit, insurgent groups translate time and resources into conventional or other capabilities that assume the strategic offensive in an attempt to defeat their most powerful local and national adversaries and end the conflict once and for all.

Insurgency is also one of the most forgiving and flexible forms of irregular warfare in terms of defeat. Local and even regional defeat of guerrilla forces does not spell the end of most insurgencies. The insurgent shadow network structures embedded within the population, including a confederation of informers and supporters, mean that even if government or other forces return, the insurgent threat and presence remain. Time and space can allow insurgent groups to recover and recoup their losses. Given the time it takes to weaken their adversaries to the point of collapse, or to tip the balance of forces and translate resources into meaningful capabilities, insurgencies are almost always prolonged in nature. The character and popularity of the cause championed by insurgent leaders, as well as a willingness to compromise on their desired goals, is often critical in determining an insurgency's duration and likelihood of success. Where adversaries are unwilling or unable to compromise or negotiate, the insurgency is almost always likely to end only after one of them submits, is eradicated or collapses.

Civil war

Civil wars differ from other forms of irregular warfare in that they occupy a space between the boundary of conventional and irregular warfare.

Within civil wars the struggle is between competing and roughly matched factions within a territory for the control, recognition and legitimacy to govern a state. What makes these wars difficult to categorise is their wildly varying causes, scope and scale. Factions may espouse any one of a number of the causes that Bard O'Neill suggests (see table 5.1 above), e.g. within societies over differences in policies (the American Civil War, 1861–5) and the form of governance (the English Civil War, 1642–51), or over a desire for self-governance (Eritrea from Ethiopia, 1974–91), or disagreement over a negotiated settlement to a conflict (the Irish Civil War, 1922–3). The scope and scale of civil wars are also diverse: some last for short periods of time, while others can stretch over several decades, and casualties can range from tens of thousands into the millions. In some cases, former insurgents fight one another, whereas in the most devastating civil wars factions fielding large armies fight more or less conventionally to impose their will upon one another through the destruction of their adversary's fielded forces. Some reject civil wars as a form of irregular warfare for this reason; others object to its categorisation as such because the adversaries possess nearly the same capabilities. The key distinguishing aspect of civil wars is geographic in nature; such wars exist within identifiable territories between two or more factions that may or may not employ civilian militias, paramilitaries and unorthodox tactics.

In order to avoid potential confusion and bound the subsequent review of the subject, this chapter focuses largely on two forms of irregular warfare: insurgency and terrorism. One reason for this is historical in nature. Revolution, for example, has largely fallen out of favour as a preferred form of irregular warfare over the last half century, owing to changes in the international economic and political system. Stripped of their former political ideological impetus, the vast majority of revolutions over the past two decades have been peaceful in nature.[20] The globalisation of information and trade has only increased the economic divide between the post-industrial 'north' and the geographic 'south'. Although working conditions within the nations of the south can be appalling, manufacturing nevertheless creates economic opportunities for local entrepreneurs and workers alike. In addition, organising and maintaining a clandestine mass movement for several years is exceptionally difficult. The ideologies that fuelled the bulk of the revolutions over the past three centuries, egalitarianism and Marxism, have either been discredited or discarded owing partially to the collapse of their sponsors but also as a result of political and economic progress and reform. The only potential ideological heir to the throne of revolution is theological: for instance, a movement led by militant Salafi or other religious radicals who exploit conditions in a state that is sliding into the abyss of political collapse, as was the case in Iran in 1979. Revolution, in this case, occurs not as a result of careful planning and meticulous preparation. Instead, revolutions of this stripe are opportunistic in nature and rely heavily on chance and an ability to exploit the unfolding situation. The group that will prevail is the one that is sufficiently organised, and supported either by enough of the population or by force of arms, to seize and consolidate its power base.

The second reason to focus on insurgency and terrorism, as opposed to other forms of irregular warfare, is related to time and geographic scope. Coups d'état occur quickly if they are properly organised and luck favours the plotters. There is little that potential intervening powers can do to halt a coup that is taking place. If the plotters succeed, they become the de facto legitimate governing authority of the state and should be dealt with according to international rules and norms. If the plotters fail, they are likely to be executed by the state both as traitors and a potential future threat. Although morally repugnant to some, coups d'état are viewed by many outside political and business leaders pragmatically as a source of stability in troubled states when military leaders assume power. The coup that brought Pervez Musharref to power in Pakistan, for example, stabilised a weak political system characterised by a succession of corrupt or inept political leaders who were democratically elected. Civil wars, in contrast, are difficult to identify for reasons that will become evident. They vary so wildly in geographic and military scope, scale and cause as to be problematic as a definable category of irregular warfare, as the preceding section suggested. One method of exploring the complexities and identifying the continuities of irregular warfare, to make sense of the present and the future, is to look at its theory and practice throughout history.

The study of irregular warfare historically presents a number of unique challenges. Although the history of irregular warfare, in the form of bandit raids or other unconventional tactics, arguably existed long before more organised, conventional warfare by fielded armies, there are relatively few memoirs, much less theories of violence, by those conducting irregular warfare against militarily superior opponents prior to the nineteenth century. Classic texts on ancient warfare from across the globe, including Maurice's *Strategikon* (Byzantium), Sun Tzu's *The Art of War* (China) and Kautilya's *Arthasastra* (India), addressed such unconventional methods of fighting as raids, ambushes, stratagems and ruses as a method of gaining an advantage over an opponent prior to or during battle.[21] Other ancient texts, including epic poems, theological texts and historical narratives, suggest that irregular tactics were used to overcome formidable defences. The most famous example remains the Trojan Horse in Homer's *Iliad*, but far more accounts describe a common subterfuge: taking walled cities by using traitors inside them to open the gates to armies waiting outside.[22] In addition, some texts discuss the specific fighting qualities, or what scholars now call 'strategic culture' or 'ways of war', of irregular or barbarian opponents.[23] Indeed, some scholars have gone so far as to suggest that civilisations have distinct styles of fighting, either as a result of geography or as an explanation for their political and economic success.[24] Ancient and medieval texts, however, must be approached with caution. Among their problems are author bias, hearsay or fabricated evidence, lack of supporting evidence and, in many cases, few other surviving corroborating or contradictory accounts.[25] Scholars and practitioners are forced either to read between the lines of existing accounts and manuals on the art of war or make inferences from histories of powers that were confronted by and defeated irregular threats.[26] With the benefit of hindsight and contemporary knowledge, authors are also inclined to interpret portions of ancient texts as evidence of the historical practice and theoretical continuity of irregular warfare. For example, contemporary scholars suggest that the public and dramatic assassinations conducted by Jewish Zealots against leading Roman citizens and subjects, or by the Nizari Ismaili Assassin sect against medieval Christian and Muslim rulers, were not just acts of terrorism but the first recorded acts of suicide terrorism.[27] Not only was the context of such attacks completely different, but so too were the targets and intended effects. It is crucial not to cast modern connotations onto ancient texts without explaining key differences and providing sufficient background information.

Out of necessity, this section will survey some of the most important developments in irregular warfare theory or doctrine. Works by a number of other authors provide comprehensive surveys of irregular warfare campaigns and thinkers.[28] For the purposes of this chapter, irregular warfare as it is understood in the modern context begins with the end of limited war in the West in the eighteenth century. A number of social, economic, political and military changes spurred the development of irregular warfare from the eighteenth century until the end of the Second World War. The first change, associated with ideas perpetuated during the Enlightenment, was the desire to replace feudal monarchies with a more representative, equitable and just form of government. Western armies during the early and mid-eighteenth century were comprised of limited numbers of professional, uniformed soldiers, organised into battalions and regiments, whose drill, tactics and battlefield manoeuvres were highly stylised and scripted, and little had changed since the first manual-of-arms for pike, arquebus and musket was published in 1607.[29] Monarchs feared arming the citizenry, which was comprised largely of peasants. This fear was based on the thought that armed peasants would reject the status quo, organise and overwhelm the small standing forces of the monarchs. Such philosophers as John Locke questioned the moral and ethical basis of non-representative forms of government, including monarchies. Locke's libertarian ideas influenced thoughts on democracy among such revolutionaries as Alexander Hamilton and Thomas Jefferson, among others. Hand-in-hand with the development of the idea of representative government, such as a democracy, was the rise of one of the most potent forces to mobilise the population for war: nationalism. The rise of nationalism, and threats to nascent revolutionary governments in the American colonies and in France in the late eighteenth century from standing professional armies, led in turn to the development of conscription and the concept of 'the nation in arms'.

The American Revolutionary War (1775–83) is important in the modern history of irregular warfare. The details of the American Revolutionary War, including the role that the citizen-soldier militia of 'Minutemen' played in securing victory, are well known.[30] Most Americans are familiar with the basic details of the conflict but time, popular culture and national myth have shaped the public understanding of the war. The war had its fair share of brutality, including massacres committed by Continental and British forces alike.[31] Some firebrands at the time claimed that the British should have been more brutal in dealing with the upstart colonial population.[32] The war featured elements of irregular warfare familiar to the modern reader: unorthodox tactics used by colonial troops that had been shaped in fighting against native American tribes and in the North American theatre during the Seven Years' War against the French (1756–63);[33] and unconventional campaigns, including the pivotal insurgency conducted in South Carolina by such partisan leaders as Andrew Pickens and the most famous guerrilla leader during the campaign, Francis Marion.[34] These aspects of the American Revolutionary War are not what make it unique. Indeed, the Austrian Hapsburg empire fought campaigns against irregulars on its eastern borders. The English and French, as well as the Austrians, developed light infantry and other skirmishing forces almost a century prior to the American Revolutionary War, and Robert Rogers established 'Standing Orders' for his famed irregular Rangers in 1759.[35] What marks the American Revolutionary War as unique is the mark the fighting left on a Hessian officer, Johann Ewald.

Johann Ewald and partisan war

Johann Ewald served as an officer in an elite *Jäger* regiment recruited to fight on the side of the British crown against the rebels. *Jäger* were light-infantry skirmishers who operated in advance or independent of main-force combat units and were responsible for screening their movements, gathering information, and conducting probing attacks and raids against enemy camps and units. The fighting in British North America made a deep impression on many officers during the conflict, including the remarkably introspective Ewald.[36] Upon his return to Cassel in 1784, Ewald penned his

Box 5.2 What is doctrine?

Scholars agree on the purpose of doctrine, but not on its form. The purpose of doctrine is to transmit and share 'best practices' or 'lessons learned' about the conduct of warfare. But how are these practices and lessons codified, understood and transmitted? Andrew Birtle suggests that US Army counter-insurgency doctrine does not have to be published but can consist instead of 'custom, tradition, and accumulated experience that was transmitted from one generation of soldiers to the next through a combination of official and unofficial writings, curricular materials, conversations, and individual memories'. This chapter suggests that doctrine must be written down and published to be considered such.

See Andrew Birtle, *U.S. Army Counterinsurgency and Contingency Operations Doctrine, 1860–1941* (Washington, DC: US Army Center of Military History, 1998), p. 5.

Abhandlung über den kleinen Krieg, or *Treatise on Partisan War*, one of the first manuals, or what we would today call 'doctrine', on the unique character of and requirements for conducting and countering irregular warfare in the context of his day.[37] This work, as well as Ewald's other published works, including his diary, offer considerable insights into both the continuities of and changes in modern irregular warfare from the eighteenth century until today.[38]

As in works by other officers of his generation, Ewald offers a number of prescriptions on how to prepare and organise for and conduct partisan operations. However, he insists that a different mindset, skills and approach are necessary to succeed in partisan warfare. In a supreme historical irony, which turns the conclusions of recent scholarship on British success and American failure in irregular warfare in the twentieth century on its head, Ewald suggests that British troops 'were not really suitable for the small war, because they did not have sufficient patience for this difficult and laborious kind of warfare'.[39] Unlike the conventional units of his day, partisan leaders require independent thought and action in order to identify and seize opportunities, prevent ambush, retain mobility and make the best possible use of the terrain.[40] Although Ewald's advice was bound by the norms and codes of conduct of his day, many of his recommendations at the tactical level for light infantry or special operations forces' commanders either still rings true in modern doctrine or remains applicable today, including the commander's need to identify patterns in rebel attacks and quickly adapt and develop innovative counter-measures against them.[41]

Ewald differs from his contemporaries in his passing discussion on the nature of irregular warfare. The revolutionary ideals that inspired the American colonists had a significant impact on their operations. For example, Ewald was amazed when he observed the suffering that American forces were willing to endure, and the minimal supplies they required to fight effectively, for the cause of 'Liberty and Independence'.[42] As colonial powers were to discover after the end of the Second World War, and the United States and its coalition partners have discovered in Iraq, ideals such as nationalism and self-determination are potent motivating forces and extremely difficult to defeat unless one is willing either to apply relatively unrestricted force or provide an equally powerful, contrasting set of ideas. On the use of force and relations with the local population, Ewald's works highlight the dilemma that confronts all powers fighting irregular wars. To suggest that Ewald discusses winning 'the hearts and minds' of the population is to read too much into his observations and prescriptive advice. The dilemma confronting Ewald is how to gain potentially valuable support, including information about local irregular forces, from the population without alienating them. His works are filled with references and incidents where acts of kindness among the population, even towards known revolutionary leaders, yielded valuable information about the condition or location of American forces.[43] Trusting the population blindly, without verifying information gained through reconnaissance and other sources, was a formula for potential betrayal and disaster.[44] But Ewald also did not shirk from using force against the population – 'the place was ransacked and plundered because all the inhabitants were rebellious-minded' – either to punish known rebel sympathisers or when necessity dictated.[45] He understood, however, that force used out of necessity came at the cost of alienating support from segments of the population that either had supported or were willing to support his forces at the time.[46] The need to strike a balance between gaining the willing and demonstrated support of the population versus the requirement to control and coerce it is a consistent theme historically that separates those who have succeeded in irregular warfare and those who have failed.

The history of irregular warfare from the end of the eighteenth century until the First World War (1914–18) is filled with considerable political, social, economic and military change. The most violent episode in Western history during the nineteenth century, the Napoleonic Wars (1798–1815), saw the concept of 'the nation in arms' lead inexorably to much more destructive, total warfare and the harnessing of popular sentiment in raising armies against the occupying armies of Napoleon. The combination of weather, inadequate French supplies, vast geographic space and the incessant attacks by partisan forces in Russia under the command of such leaders as Denis Davidov led to the decimation and retreat of Napoleon's *Grande Armée*.[47] In Spain, French forces faced a more favorable climate and smaller geographic space that nonetheless contained much more rugged terrain and a population that had grown weary of and exceptionally hostile to French looting, reprisals and other depredations. The subsequent campaign waged by Spanish irregulars or '*guerrilleros*', operating in the countryside while

French field armies were occupied with garrison duties and contending with a small British expeditionary force, harassed and bled the army of Marshal Nicholas Soult white in a campaign noted for its duration and brutality.[48] It is from this conflict that the term 'guerrilla' was derived.

Other significant changes in the history of irregular warfare at this time include a number of revolutions and the development of theories of violence, followed by colonial conquest and writings reflecting on pacification campaigns and experience gained throughout Africa, Asia and America. The most noteworthy revolutions during this period were the French Revolutionary Napoleonic Wars (1789–98) and events during the so-called 'Year of Revolutions' which swept through Europe and parts of Latin America in 1848. The leaders of the French Revolution sought to change from a monarchy to a more equitable form of government, a republic. Republican ideals were ultimately corrupted by personal power and institutional paranoia, which both set the stage for Napoleon's rise to power and contributed to the lexicon of irregular warfare the term 'terrorism', which was first used to describe systemic and deliberate violence by the state to instil fear and preserve order among its citizenry.[49] The range of causes that spurred the Year of Revolutions relates to societal change stemming from the economic revolution in modes and means of production associated with the Industrial Revolution which figure prominently in the theories of Karl Marx and Louis Auguste Blanqui. Although the theories of both are largely footnotes to history today, the disagreements between them over the mechanism and methods for success of the revolution are worth exploring for one key reason: the intellectual points of departure between Blanqui and Marx have been echoed by such Latin American revolutionaries as Ernesto 'Che' Guevara and Carlos Marighella, and, most recently, between such militant Salafist terrorist authors as Ayman al-Zawahiri and Abu Musab al-Suri, as the subsequent sections will demonstrate.

Karl Marx, Louis Auguste Blanqui and socialist revolution

From the perspective of those seeking to overthrow the existing political system using irregular violence, the writings of Karl Marx and Louis Auguste Blanqui provided two contrasting yet related rationales for violence. Marx, who was decidedly the more intellectual of the two writers, contributed the theory of 'historical materialism' whose central tenets are well known but have also been misconstrued. Capitalism, according to Marx, contained internal contradictions that would lead to its own collapse. The pace of economic change outstrips the ability of the capitalist system controlling society to adjust to such change; the class inequalities inherent in the capitalist system and the social disruption caused by cycles of economic growth and collapse would impel those in control of the means of production, the workers, to revolt. In addition to this objective condition inherent in the system, Marx also wrote about the need to develop the subjective conditions for revolution. In particular, Marx saw the socialist workers' party as performing two vital tasks. The first task was to educate the masses of workers, or proletariat, about the inequities in the system through pamphlets, speeches and other means so that the party could exploit crises and foment revolution. The second task was to build the party infrastructure to organise the workers, increase the size of the organisation, and seize the initiative and power when the revolutionary moment presented itself. Revolution, in Marx's mind, was an historical inevitability that could be exploited by the revolutionary. The key to success in Marx's mind, however, was organisation and, above all else, patience that the internal contradictions would lead to revolution.[50]

Although Louis Blanqui largely agreed with Marx on the economic foundations of revolution, he differed in opinion on its social and organisational aspects. That the workers were exploited was unquestionable. However, Blanqui believed that the workers would rebel anyway, and as a result they could not be educated and should not be informed of the plans for revolution. Only the vanguard, or the intellectual elite that was freed from class bonds and formed into its own general staff, could truly understand the purpose and direct the course of the revolution. The best method for organisation, therefore, was the creation of secret societies that would be difficult for the state security apparatus to monitor and track. Proper organisation, thorough planning, a correct reading of the conditions, and boldness of action at the right place and time would create the subjective conditions for revolution.[51] In addition, Blanqui urged his co-conspirators to read about military tactics and organisation so that revolutionaries understood their purpose during the insurrection, organised the masses and fought in a more cohesive manner.[52] When the conditions were deemed ripe, the vanguard would lead the attacks against the key organs of the state. Revolutionary ideals were a necessary precondition but not sufficient to guarantee the success of the insurrection. The oppressed masses would not only follow the example set by the insurgents, but their revolutionary zeal could be harnessed in an effective military manner against any counter-attacks by the remaining forces of the state.[53] It was up to the leaders of the vanguard to organise the masses once they were committed to the struggle. Put simply, according to Blanqui's scheme the insurgent vanguard could create and manipulate the subjective conditions so that the revolution could succeed. Once the time had arrived for insurrection, the vanguard must not wait and continue to talk about revolution: it must seize the initiative and lead the revolution to victory.[54] Although Blanqui's technique for insurrection grew more sophisticated after each unsuccessful attempt, his appreciation and assessment of the social and economic factors of revolution remained virtually unchanged. In fact, one author has concluded that 'parts of Blanqui's thinking were frustratingly vague and immature', and his understanding of socialism was 'ideological chop suey'.[55] As Blanqui and those who followed him were to discover, perceiving that the conditions are right, assessing the chances for success objectively and accounting for differences in the context on irregular warfare are not easy tasks when revolutionary fervor colours one's perceptions.

Given the broad range and diverse perspectives that characterised socialist theories of revolution throughout the nineteenth and early twentieth centuries, it is surprising that there was relatively little by way of theory, doctrine or treatises written about how to counter the threat of irregular warfare. Indeed, while the leading military theorists of the nineteenth century, Carl von Clausewitz and Antoine Henri de Jomini, acknowledged the underlying power of, and the difficulties associated with facing a people in arms, they nevertheless paid scant attention to the subject in their works.[56] With the possible exception of Clausewitz, who grappled with a theoretical understanding of the nature of war and the place that battle played within it, the vast majority of military officers who put pen to paper were concerned less with irregular warfare than with fighting and winning conventional battles decisively in order to win wars quickly. At their worst, works on 'strategy' and 'the art of war' were tedious studies on lines of manoeuvre and battlefield formations.[57] Other works provided historical narratives of battles past, often those conducted with such skill by Napoleon, to illustrate principles of war and other maxims.[58]

In addition to divining the secret of decisive battle, military writers during this time were preoccupied with the changes to the art of war that technology was rendering. In 1815, the accurate range of a smoothbore musket was less than 100 yards, and cannons fired solid iron shot at targets in their line of sight. Lack of accuracy meant that commanders relied on mass to make up for the difference. Over the next century, the range of rifles increased almost ten-fold due to the development of rifling, cartridges, primers and the cylindro-conoidal bullet. The introduction of smokeless powder made the source of rifle fire difficult to pinpoint. Accurate fire and breech-loading meant that men could disperse, seek cover and still inflict numerous casualties. Advances in metallurgy and engineering led to the development of the first automatic weapons that could sustain rates of fire of several hundred rounds per minute, making the ground in front almost impassible, as well as long-range, breech-loading, indirect-fire artillery. Artillery could also fire hollow shells designed to burst upon impact, increasing their lethal radius. Breech-loading and powder cartridges allowed for high sustained rates of fire.[59] All of these advances created a 'storm of steel' on the battlefield, in which the number of casualties grew significantly, and against which frontal assaults were all but suicidal.[60]

Charles Callwell and imperial soldiering

In addition to significant advances in the range and lethality of military weapons, the nineteenth and early twentieth centuries were characterised by the race by European powers to secure overseas colonies at the expense of local populations throughout Asia and Africa. Although the sheer range of campaigns makes generalisations about them difficult, they all shared one thing in common. Nationalism, combined with feelings of divine purpose and a sense of racial or ethnic superiority, led military commanders from a number of nations to consider that they were fighting opponents who were mere 'savages' and therefore undeserving of courtesies and treatments due their civilised opponents. While some concepts and ideas from this era continue to be discussed in the current context of counter-insurgency, such as the oil-spot or ink-blot theory of French officer Joseph-Simon Galliéni (whereby the territorial control of adjacent garrisons combines and spreads like blots of ink on a sheet of paper), the brutality with which some of these campaigns were waged seemed reasonable to the participants at the time but appear cruel and inhuman today.[61] In South West Africa, for example, German General Lothar von Trotha waged a vicious campaign over three years (1904–7) that sought to annihilate the Heraro tribe.[62] Occasionally 'savages' inflicted significant defeats on imperial armies, as occurred during the disastrous First Afghan War (1839–42) fought by the British or at Little Big Horn in 1876, but defeats on this scale were a rarity.[63] A more common scenario involved small numbers, relative to the local population, of European or American forces conducting operations against the natives and relying on a combination of discipline, firepower, pluck and superior will to turn the tide of the campaign (see figure 5.2). More often than not, 'savage armies' obliged them by making mass charges against Western forces armed with rifles, artillery and, in some cases, machine guns. Perhaps the defining incident of this type of warfare was a battle near the town of Omdurman in Sudan on 2 September 1898. British forces and auxiliaries, numbering no more than 25,000, were confronted by an Ansar, or dervish, army of some 50,000. The Ansar army believed that their spiritual leader, Abdullah al-Taashi, was the Mahdi or imam prophesied to return and restore justice and greatness according to the Shi'ite interpretation of Islam. The results of the battle confirmed that religious zeal and courage, combined with primitive weapons and tactics, were no match for modern firepower in a set-piece battle. Almost half of the Ansar army was killed or wounded, while the British and their auxiliaries suffered just over 400 casualties.

Although military handbooks, or doctrine, largely reflected preoccupations with decisive battle in the face of destructive, modern technology, imperial and colonial campaigns in far-off lands were bound to make their presence felt within the literature. Irregular warfare, especially against tribes, was nevertheless largely considered as either an adjunct to major

Figure 5.2 Religion, zeal and numbers were no match for Western technology and military discipline at the close of the nineteenth century. In this popular depiction of imperial soldiering from 1900, greatly outnumbered US Marines fight against rebel Chinese 'Boxers' while attempting to relieve besieged legations in Peking.

war at best or an aberration fraught with danger but with little opportunity for honour or glory. As is often the case in the history of irregular warfare, events that cause national trauma and reflection provide the catalyst for an upsurge in interest and writing in the subject. In Ewald's time, it was the defeat inflicted upon the British forces and their Hessian allies despite the tactical prowess and success of the *Jäger*. The defining irregular war of the end of the nineteenth and the beginning of the twentieth centuries was that fought against Dutch farmers, or Boers, who were living in what is now called South Africa.

The Second Boer War (1899–1902), in common with other irregular wars, contained numerous different forms of war in different phases. The pretext for war was a failed coup d'état in 1895 backed by British immigrants and mine owners, including the prime minister of the Cape Colony, Cecil Rhodes. The goal of the failed coup was the overthrow of the Boer government in the Transvaal. After four years of uneasy truce, during which time Boer governments in the Transvaal and the Orange Free State made preparations for war, British demands and ambitions, and the rejection of Boer concessions, led to the issuing of ultimatums. The war officially began on 11 October 1899, with mixed results. The initial Boer offensive got bogged down with the sieges of Kimberley, Mafeking and Ladysmith, but nevertheless the Boers were able to inflict significant defeats on British forces, especially during 'Black Week' (10–15 December 1899) at the battles of Stormberg, Magersfontein and Colenso. The arrival of British reinforcements from throughout the Commonwealth resulted in the relief of the besieged towns. Faced with the defeat of their army, Boer leaders shifted to a mobile guerrilla warfare phase which the authors of the British official history of the war labelled 'the gadfly of regular armies, finding its natural prey in railways, convoys and isolated posts, and born exponents in the horsemen of the Free State'.[64] Operating in independent commandos, small numbers of Boer farmers used horses for mobility and relied on accurate fire using the latest magazine-fed Mauser rifles to conduct hit-and-run raids against isolated British detachments. The guerrilla phase lasted until the end of the war on 31 May 1902. Initially, British commanders, including Horatio Herbert Kitchener, had difficulty dealing with Boer tactics. The combination of British tactics intended to deny the Boers mobility and support, including forced resettlement of the Boer population into concentration camps, the destruction of Boer farmsteads, the construction of reinforcing blockhouses and the use of mobile columns to intercept Boer forces once detected, led to British victory, but not without domestic and international criticism. The Second Boer War was one of the first irregular wars that featured the prominent impact of timely media reporting and battlefield photography. The reporting of aspects of the war related to moral issues, augmented by photographs of dead British soldiers and emaciated Boer civilians, left the British public shocked and outraged at how the war had been handled.[65]

In addition to calls for reform of the British Army's outdated commissioning, officer development and training regimens, the Second Boer War stimulated public and professional interest in irregular wars. As a result, a number of handbooks and manuals were published on the subject. They ranged from Ernest Swinton's innovative and practical *Defence of Duffer's Drift*, designed as a primer for junior officers, to works that described functional dimensions of irregular warfare, illustrated by examples, such as Thomas Miller Maguire's *Guerrilla or Partisan Warfare* and William Heneker's *Bush Warfare*.[66] The most detailed and influential work, however, was written by Colonel Charles Callwell in 1896, with updated editions appearing in 1899 and 1906. What sets *Small Wars: Their Principles and Practice* apart from other contemporary works is Callwell's attempt to analyse comprehensively the realm of irregular warfare and present this assessment in a logically consistent manner, including classes of campaigns, types of adversary and the influence of different types of terrain upon operations, among other matters. Some of his advice is dated and can even be offensive to modern readers, especially on the subject of the pacification of local inhabitants. Callwell suggests that harsh punitive measures against villages, crops and livestock are required as a way of 'bringing such foes to reason . . . for they understand this mode of warfare and respect it'.[67] One must however appreciate that Callwell's work was a product of its time, and to dismiss it outright on these grounds would be remarkably short-sighted. He was one of the first authors to recognise the need for conventional forces to use their advantages against the key strengths of irregulars. For example, Callwell appreciated that irregular opponents did not have to fight decisively in order to win. Irregulars possessed the strategic advantages of time, manoeuvre, intelligence, limited supply requirements, and the initiative to accept battle at a time and place of their own choosing. In addition, Callwell also identified that irregular warfare was not limited to tribes who preferred such fighting culturally but was adopted by enemy commanders as a form of warfare either out of choice or necessity. In any event, he understood the stresses that guerrilla war imposed upon conventional forces, including the requirement to fight according to methods that ran contrary to well-established military principles and maxims such as mass and never dividing one's force. Although now taken as common sense, Callwell struck upon a key dimension of irregular warfare in 1896: 'The more irregular and the less organized the forces of the enemy are, the more independent do they become of strategical rules.'[68] In other words, irregular enemies organise and fight according to their own preferences and not according to yours. Conventional forces could defeat irregular adversaries but not by trying to fight them in a conventional manner. Such adversaries preferred to fight protracted campaigns, and Callwell also recognised that a number of 'preventable causes' might allow conventional forces to play into their adversary's hands, such as:

bad organization or they may follow from insufficient preparation . . . lack of zeal among subordinates, or they may be due to want of energy in high places. But one of the commonest causes of operations being unduly prolonged, is to be found in their having been allowed to drift into a desultory form of warfare, and this is a question of strategy and tactics.[69]

Fighting irregular enemies required flexibility on the part of the commander, constant vigilance and self-assessment, as well as an understanding of the enemy's preferences and the practical difficulties associated with irregular warfare – considerations that field commanders confronting irregular enemies today would do well to adopt.

The close of the nineteenth century until the start of the First World War saw a number of developments in the field of irregular warfare but little in the way of theory or doctrine development. Having quickly and decisively defeated Spanish forces in Cuba and the Philippines for the ostensible reason of freeing the local populations from Spanish oppression, the United States found itself engaged in struggles against local insurgents in the Philippines instead. Led by Emilio Aguinaldo, the Philippine insurgents fought a guerrilla campaign with the goal of prolonging the conflict long

Figure 5.3 Popular notions of the noble aspects of imperial soldiering, such as civilising 'savage' races, were challenged during the Second Boer War (1899–1902) and Philippine War (1899–1902). Newspaper reports of atrocities by British and American soldiers, and graphic photographs taken by reporters and soldiers that were subsequently published, drove home the brutal realities of irregular warfare to the public. According to the original caption, this photograph is of 'insurgent dead just as they fell in the trench near Santa Ana, February 5th, 1899'.

enough to influence the peace lobby in the United States. Instead of achieving this goal, guerrilla attacks led to the deployment of more troops and the adoption by the US forces of harsh tactics and policies very similar to those adopted by the British in South Africa (see figure 5.3).[70] The United States declared the war over with the capture of Philippine General Miguel Malvar in 1902. As in Great Britain, the harsh conduct of military forces against the civilian population, including charges of wartime atrocities, was reported in the press (see figure 5.3). Such reports led Congress to form the Lodge Committee in January 1902 to investigate the charges, although little came of the proceedings. Throughout Europe, the socialist revolutionary movement saw numerous debates, disagreements and schisms between rival claimants over when to take action, the form that action should take and who should be allowed to join each specific national social democrat political party. The more radical elements, dubbed anarchists, believed in 'propaganda by the deed' against the state and its supporting elements.[71] Although some of the tactics used by such groups in Britain, France and Russia were already well established, such as kidnapping and assassination, anarchists were among the first to conduct bombings using stable, high-yield explosives for their attacks. The successful assassination of Russian Tsar Alexander in 1881 by Russian anarchists prompted other groups to imitate their success, a pattern that would be repeated among various Marxist-Leninist terrorist groups throughout the 1960s and 1970s and among terrorist and insurgent groups today.

The First World War, Paul von Lettow-Vorbeck and T. E. Lawrence

Although it is an historical stretch to suggest that an act of terrorism started the First World War, there is little doubt that the assassination of Archduke Franz Ferdinand and his wife by members of a Serbian nationalist group provided the pretext for the event that would set the chain of mutual defence pacts and mobilisation orders in motion and lead to German troops violating Belgian neutrality. Once the front lines between armies stabilised in the West and East in 1915, there was little scope for irregular warfare on the Eurasian continent. Instead, British and German military and political leaders concocted a number of schemes designed to draw enemy attention and resources by conducting irregular warfare by proxy in each other's various colonial possessions or the territory of their enemy's allies. Some schemes seemed sound in theory but were executed ham-fistedly or were simply impractical. Among these were German attempts to foment *jihad* and other plots against Egypt. These attempts were designed to threaten British control of the Suez Canal, and without exception they failed for reasons of national chauvinism, inadequate resources, insufficient knowledge, and competing local and national interests.[72] Other independent rebellions took place. In the case of Ireland, the uprising in Dublin during Easter Week 1916 failed to achieve the objectives envisioned by the leaders of the Irish Republican Brotherhood but paved the way for the more successful urban insurgency planned and led with daring and skill by Michael Collins from 1918 to 1921.[73]

Other irregular campaigns during the First World War were driven by necessity or were accidental in nature. For example, the guerrilla campaign led by Paul von Lettow-Vorbeck in East Africa resulted from conventional victories that significantly depleted his force despite their success. For the next four years, Lettow-Vorbeck and his initial force of 3,000 Germans and 11,000 native *askaris* threatened the British East Africa Protectorate (Kenya) and largely gave battle at the time and place of their choosing while evading Commonwealth forces on a trek through Portuguese Mozambique, German East Africa (Tanzania) and British Rhodesia.[74] Three features of Lettow-Vorbeck's campaign stand out in particular. First, Lettow-Vorbeck and his officers conducted the campaign in mobile columns with a mixed force of Germans and Africans that retained a high level of unit cohesion until the end of the war, which is evident in the almost equal rates of casualties the force suffered.[75] Second, Lettow-Vorbeck's force largely subsisted off the land and captured supplies from 1916 onwards. Third, and perhaps most importantly, Lettow-Vorbeck and his force managed to frustrate a Commonwealth force that contained a number of South Africans who had fought the British during the Second Boer War, demonstrating that even those well-versed in irregular warfare face much greater challenges when trying to defeat an insurgency.[76] As impressive as Lettow-Vorbeck's achievements were, they were nonetheless eclipsed by the actions of a British officer fighting as part of the Arab Revolt in Transjordan.

Thomas Edward Lawrence, better known by his soubriquet 'Lawrence of Arabia', can be considered the progenitor of modern irregular warfare in the West. This conclusion is based on his ability to assess objectively the conditions that existed within his theatre of operations, intuit the strength of the Arab forces and the weaknesses of the Turks, and understand the local culture to the extent he did. Nowhere are these qualities exhibited better than in his account of the Arab Revolt published in the inaugural edition of the *Army Quarterly*. This account is stripped of both the prose and literary pretensions that fill his other accounts of the campaign, *Seven Pillars of Wisdom* and its abridged version, *Revolt in the Desert*. In 'The Evolution of a Revolt' Lawrence provides a brief background sketch of the Arab Revolt and the reasons for its early setbacks.[77] In particular, Lawrence suggests that British attempts to force the Arabs to fight according to modern European battlefield practices ran contrary to their cultural strengths and was doomed to fail. While recovering from an illness, Lawrence claims to have discovered a formula to assess the Arab Revolt strategically. This formula consisted of the following factors: the algebraic, or the area of the terrain and number of Turks required to control it; the biological, or the resources that the Turks needed to sustain their forces; and the psychological, or the morale of both the Turks and the Arabs.[78]

The weakest link in the Turkish garrison chain was the biological factor and, using superior Arab mobility in the desert where the Turks rarely ventured, Lawrence sought to stress it even further. Rather than battle Turkish forces in outposts or attempt the liberation of the holy city of Medina, he believed that the Arabs should strike against Turkish supplies: 'Our cards were speed and time, not hitting power, and these gave us strategical rather than tactical strength.'[79] Tactically his forces would fight 'tip and run, not pushes, but strokes'.[80] Lawrence also discriminated the strategic purpose for the violence, forcing the Turks to abandon Transjordan and freeing the Arabs from Turkish rule, from the tactical limitations and motivations of the tribes that were to conduct the operations. Individual tribes would fight their neighbours just as easily as the Turks. In order to solve this problem, Lawrence adopted two solutions. The first, and base, motivation was personal gain, and he secured sums of gold with which to maintain the loyalty of tribal chiefs, even though some of the funds were diverted and payment did not necessarily guarantee numbers for duty.[81] As much as Lawrence waxed eloquently about Arabs fighting for the idea of freedom, wealth and plunder sustained the Arab Revolt throughout the campaign. The second solution was to use a number of tribes individually so that they formed a 'ladder' on the way to Damascus.[82] To increase the range and destructiveness of the Arabs, and by extension the pressure that the tribes could put on Turkish supply lines, Lawrence secured modern rifles, machine guns, explosives and experts trained in their use, and tinned rations.[83]

Whether or not Lawrence deserves the laurels piled at his feet is a matter for debate. T. E. Lawrence remains an enigma to this day, filled with contradictions, not beyond pranks, and not always absolute with the truth.[84] Whether or not Lawrence could have succeeded in forcing the Turks to withdraw by guerrilla action alone is also a matter of conjecture. As it was, Lawrence's Arab forces secured the right flank of the three corps comprising the Egyptian Expeditionary Corps under the command of General Edmund Allenby and continued to harass Turkish supply lines, drawing off manpower to guard and repair them.[85] Yet Lawrence continues to be held in high esteem by modern irregular warfare specialists as one who is worthy of emulation. Indeed, one modern counter-insurgency specialist has gone so far as to imitate Lawrence's famous '27 Articles' as a method of transmitting important information to company commanders deploying to Iraq.[86] Lawrence was one of the first authors to outline how to conduct a successful unconventional campaign against a conventional opponent as well as to emphasise the psychological dimensions of irregular warfare over battle. Lawrence's written account of the objective and subjective conditions in Transjordan in 1916, regardless of whether it was real or fabricated after the fact, serves as one of the few examples of how such conditions can and should be accurately assessed.

Mao Tse-Tung and protracted people's war

One of the few socialist theorists who also read the subjective and objective conditions strategically after early failure was Mao Tse-Tung (Zedong). As with Lawrence, a number of Mao's claims about the revolution and his role in it are open to question.[87] A rival socialist predecessor of Mao, Vladimir Ilyich Ulyanov, or Lenin, had written extensively on revolution, including partisan warfare. But his impact on the revolution in Russia in 1917 had more to do with chance, support from the Imperial German government at a crucial juncture of his exile and the incompetence of the Tsarist regime than with reading and influencing the subjective conditions within the country.[88] As a young revolutionary dedicated to the socialist cause, Mao slavishly attempted to follow the now-accepted formula for Leninist proletariat revolution in his native China in 1921. Its failure, due primarily to the lack of meaningful numbers of oppressed urban workers fuelling the machine of capitalism, caused Mao to reflect upon the nature of revolution in China. Over the course of the next sixteen years, Mao succeeded in consolidating his hold on power of the Chinese Communist Party and expanding its base among the rural peasantry, despite aggressive attempts by the Chinese Nationalists to crush it. In 1937, however, the Japanese invaded China, and Nationalists and Communists were faced with an aggressive, competent adversary that initially swept away all attempts to stop it. The following year, Mao produced two complementary works on irregular warfare: the pamphlet entitled *Yu Chi Chan*, or 'On Guerrilla War', and a series of lectures at the Yenan Association for the Study of the War of Resistance against Japan entitled 'On Protracted War'. No work by an author on and practitioner of irregular warfare has before or since so accurately read most the subjective and objective conditions for success within its specific context, or provided a comprehensive roadmap that links battle to revolutionary victory, as Mao did in 'On Protracted War'.

As with most other significant military theorists, including Clausewitz, Mao's ideas are quoted, cited and too often utterly mischaracterised. For example, Mao's metaphor of the guerrilla fish swimming in the sea of the population is well known, and variations of it were cited in early speeches related to the Global War on Terrorism.[89] Glibly citing the metaphor, and understanding the difficulties and problems associated with isolating guerrillas from the population, are two completely different things, as most counter-insurgency practitioners understand. Mao's three-phase plan for revolutionary victory, for example, has been rigidly interpreted to provide the foil to advance arguments for why approaches to counter-insurgency plans for Iraq are in need of significant revision.[90] Part of the reason Mao has been misinterpreted is that his theory of warfare, like Clausewitz's, is descriptive rather than prescriptive. And like Clausewitz, Mao provides a framework for understanding the often contradictory relationships that exist between battles and campaigns in achieving the overall political aim of the war.

In 'On Protracted War', Mao sets out to prove that notions of quick victory are impossible and that maintaining a line of tactical defences against the Japanese will only result in the defeat of Chinese Communist forces. The Japanese are simply too well equipped and trained to be fought conventionally. Much like Lawrence, Mao understands that there are too few Japanese troops to conquer and occupy China.[91] China's strengths are its vast geographic space and the size of its population.[92] These strengths alone, however, are insufficient to defeat the Japanese. The Chinese peasants must be educated, trained, organized and equipped to fight, and this process will take time. In order to buy the required time, Mao suggests trading geographic space and conducting offensive action at the tactical level instead of slavishly trying to blunt every Japanese offensive and prevent the occupation of major Chinese cities.[93] Trading space, however, does not imply retreating before the Japanese. Tactical offensive action will take place in the spaces occupied by the Japanese in a 'war of jig-saw pattern' designed to threaten their supply lines.[94] In order to deal with such threats, the Japanese will be confronted with a dilemma: cede territory in their rear area to the guerrilla cadres, who would exploit the situation to recruit among the population, or divert units to garrison towns and secure supply lines, weakening the strategic offensive and making such units tactically vulnerable to attack and annihilation.[95] Mao states much of what is obvious and intuitive in irregular warfare at the tactical and strategic level: cause the enemy to disperse his forces, strike where the enemy is weak and inflict casualties, avoid pitched battles unless you have overwhelming force, time is a weapon that favours the guerrillas, etc.

Three related features distinguish 'On Protracted War' and its companion work for the Communist cadres, *On Guerrilla Warfare*, from other volumes on irregular warfare. The first feature is Mao's distinction between tactical action and its relationship to the overall strategic effort. Mao's discussion is aimed at those who rigidly advocate all-out offence or all-out defence. Both views, in Mao's estimation, are wrong, and what is required instead is a more nuanced appreciation of the relationship between offence and defence at the tactical and strategic levels of war. The second unique feature of Mao's theory is his framework for victory, which places tactical actions into an overall plan for victory. The three phases outlined by Mao – strategic defensive, stalemate and strategic offensive – outline an achievable vision of victory, provided the members of the Chinese Communist Party are patient and diligent enough.[96] Unlike other irregular warfare theorists before or since, Mao grasped that tactical guerrilla actions alone, however cleverly executed or destructive, are insufficient to drive an enemy from one's territory. Guerrilla action was designed not only to weaken the Japanese forces, improve the quality of Chinese forces in the 'university of war' and lead to the balance of forces tipping in favour of the Chinese Communists but also to allow the development of larger-scale military units to conduct mobile warfare in more conventional offensives.[97] The third and final distinctive feature of Mao's theory of irregular warfare, related to the last point, is the primacy of politics and the role that military action plays in support of it. Guerrilla action was designed not just to achieve military objectives. Such action first and foremost shielded the political activities of the Communist cadres, providing them with the breathing-space to organise and receive the support of the population. Mao devotes a portion of both works to the object of war, the role that politics plays and the need to mobilise the population for war.[98] In order to do this, the population must be educated as to why they are fighting and how victory will improve their lives. In addition, the Chinese Communists must demonstrate their moral superiority over the Japanese in deed and in action by following Mao's 'Three Rules and Eight Remarks'.[99] In this way the local peasants would see that the Chinese Communists were worthy of support. Military action alone could not achieve victory unless a critical mass of the Chinese population actively and willingly sustained and swelled the number of the guerrilla forces. The pivotal role that the population plays in irregular warfare, outlined so clearly by Mao, has figured prominently in almost all modern theory and doctrine, but the relationship between violence, ideology and politics continues to remain elusive, misunderstood and open to disagreement.

The Second World War

Although there were a number of other important irregular wars and incidents prior to 1939, including the Russian (1918–22), Irish (1922–3), and Spanish (1936–9) Civil Wars, US Marine interventions in the so-called 'Banana Wars' in Central and South America, the bombing of the financial district of Wall Street in New York (1920), and Arab and Jewish guerrilla and counter-guerrilla warfare in British-mandated Palestine, these events were overshadowed historically by a seemingly unstoppable string of German and Japanese victories at the start of the Second World War. Within Great Britain, the prospect of German invasion appeared all too real by the late summer of 1940. The British Army had lost most of its equipment earlier that year in battle or on the beaches of Dunkirk. To defend the island nation, Prime Minister Winston Churchill approved plans to create a cadre of civilian irregulars eventually labelled the 'Home Guard'. Among those selected to train the volunteers were Tom Wintringham and Bert Levy, who had fought together in the Spanish Civil War on the Loyalist side. Both Wintringham and Levy wrote short, mass-produced works designed as tactical training aids for civilian irregulars based on their experiences in Spain. Wintringham's *New Ways of War* and Levy's *Guerrilla Warfare* discussed guerrilla history, organisation, propaganda requirements, ambush techniques and methods to defeat German panzers.[100]

The German invasion of Great Britain was postponed and then cancelled, and so Wintringham and Levy's techniques were not put to the test there. The populations of other countries in Europe and Asia were not so fortunate. Harsh German and Japanese policies within the countries they had occupied, including brutal reprisals against villages suspected of supporting guerrillas or partisans, dealt with a tactical military problem but strategically proved ruinous. As the true nature of the German and Japanese occupations was revealed, a percentage of the local population in countries as diverse as Poland, Czechoslovakia, France, the Soviet Union, Malaya and French Indochina conducted active and passive resistance in response. Reprisals and indiscriminate sweeps, especially by German and other national auxiliaries behind their lines on the Eastern front, did not cow locals into submission but instead swelled partisan ranks.[101] For the Allied powers, resistance, and guerrilla and partisan movements in occupied Europe and Asia were a potential source of offensive support for plans to liberate countries. The actual contribution made by partisan and resistance movements, operating with the assistance of the British Special Operations Executive, the American Office of Strategic Services and the Soviet STAVKA, remains controversial, owing to lost or missing records, inflated claims by partisan and resistance groups, and the difficulties in assessing the impact of subversion, sabotage and ambush as a drain on the German and Japanese war effort.[102] What is certain, however, is that the ideals articulated by the Allies set the stage for the next chapter in modern irregular warfare.

American President Franklin Roosevelt and British Prime Minister Winston Churchill could not possibly have known how truly strong and problematic the future whirlwind would be when they issued the Atlantic Charter in August 1940. Although most of its points appeared innocuous, the third point – the right of all peoples to self-determination – would cause the greatest difficulties. In particular, the leaders of socialist or nationalist movements in colonial territories interpreted the Atlantic Charter as the basis for declarations of independence once the war was over. The most famous example occurred in French Indochina in September 1945, where Ho Chi Minh declared Vietnam independent using language borrowed from the US Declaration of Independence.[103] Within three years of the end of the Second World War, France, the Netherlands and Great Britain were fighting insurgent groups that used guerrilla and terrorist tactics in their colonies, including Malaya (Malaysia), Palestine, French Indochina (Vietnam, Laos and Cambodia) and the Dutch East Indies (Indonesia). In other cases, the struggle for post-war predominance between different groups raged in former monarchies, such as Yugoslavia, during the war. In the case of occupied Greece, the struggle for supremacy between a number of rival nationalist and socialist factions started as early as 1942 and developed into a civil war that concluded only in 1949.

To outside observers, the majority of the groups waging guerrilla or terrorist campaigns appeared to be Communist-inspired or -directed. This observation, combined with increasing tensions with and territorial gains by the Soviet Union, suggested that this wave of irregular warfare was part of a vast, socialist conspiracy to defeat the West. Nikita Khrushchev's speech in January 1961 that implied Soviet support for those fighting 'wars of national liberation' only cemented this perception and was arguably a key element in the American decision to intervene in Vietnam.

Insurgent strategies

Up until the American commitment of combat troops to Vietnam in 1965, irregular wars conducted against colonial powers, newly independent governments or other 'puppet' regimes followed four basic strategic approaches regardless of the group's political or religious ideology. In some cases, groups used these approaches independently, in parallel or in sequence, depending on their success (or lack thereof). The first attempted to imitate Mao's success in China by following his advice in 'On Protracted War'. The success of Mao's approach was based on the assumption of large geographic space and a sizeable rural peasant population. Vietnamese General Vo Nguyen Giap, the most famous student of Mao, applied the formula to great success against the French. Giap oversaw the growth of a large Viet Minh army that contained regular forces and guerrillas. The siege and defeat of the French base at Dien Bien Phu in 1954, although not precisely Mao's envisioned strategic offensive phase, was enough to convince political leaders in France that the war could not be won.[104] Since Vietnam, a number of insurgent groups have also attempted to apply Mao's ideas in their own country. Although Maoist-inspired insurgencies continue to be waged to this day in India and Nepal, the formula has had less success in such countries as Thailand, Sri Lanka, Peru and the Philippines as groups have emphasised the military aspects of the campaign, including acts of terrorism, at the expense of political considerations.[105]

The second approach that irregular groups used involved attempts to convince the colonial power that the costs of maintaining their hold over the country were unacceptable without fighting major battles. In most cases, geography dictated this choice; this is especially true where population density was high and massed guerrilla movement was impractical or unwise. Zionist groups in British-mandated Palestine, for example, conducted independent operations and some co-ordinated attacks, ranging from pipeline sabotage and assassination to car bombings. Two incidents in particular characterised the type of attack conducted by groups that included the Palmach, Lehi, the Stern Gang and Irgun: the bombing in July 1946 of the King David hotel, which housed numerous British-mandate offices, including that of the Secretariat and the Criminal Investigation Division; and the kidnapping and hanging of two British Army sergeants in reprisal for the death sentences carried out against three Irgun members in July 1947.[106] Factors that contributed to the British decision to turn the territory over to the United Nations included: 1) awkward questions in the British parliament about the cost of operations within the mandated territories; 2) media reporting of significant incidents; 3) the loss of credibility after security measures led to an increase in attacks in circumstances that echo more recently the spike in Iraqi insurgent violence in response to the 2007 force 'surge' led by General David Petraeus; and 4) the shocking nature of some attacks.

The third strategic approach was to seek a diplomatic resolution because the conflict had reached a stalemate. Insurgent groups prevailed upon outside parties and sought to gain the attention of the member states of the United Nations in the hope that their cause would be raised as an issue for resolution by the General Assembly. The leaders of the Algerian *Front de Libération Nationale* (FLN), for example, which was losing ground militarily against French forces, sponsored a general strike in 1957, as well as bomb-ings and other attacks, timed to maintain interest within the General Assembly on the subject of Algeria's future.[107] Indonesian leaders routinely prevailed on outside powers, including Britain, the United States and the United Nations, to resolve their on-again, off-again war to secure their inde-pendence from the Dutch (1945 to 1949).

The fourth and last strategic approach was something entirely different, which recalled the nineteenth-century anarchist motto 'propaganda by the deed'. Writers including Che Guevara, Régis Debray and Carlos Marighella made a fundamental break with established socialist revolu-tionary theory by suggesting that action take the place of organisation. Guevara and Debray, for example, suggested that the objective conditions within Latin America were ripe for revolution and that guerrilla action by a revolutionary vanguard could itself create the subjective conditions.[108] Guevara's experience in the Cuban Revolution (1956–8) only confirmed this.[109] The peasants and workers did not need to be educated or enlight-ened: the actions of a few would inspire, awaken and attract the masses to join the insurgency. Marighella, on the other hand, suggested that urban guerrilla action would reveal to the masses the true nature of the ruling regime. Urban guerrillas could find all the resources they needed within cities, including money, arms, media outlets and targets to attack. The regime would have difficulty locating the guerrillas. The vain attempts by the regime to do so would only demonstrate its incompetence as the guer-rillas continued to strike, and this led to reprisals and security measures that would impose hardships upon the population.[110] The rural popula-tion would eventually be involved in the struggle, but Marighella was vague on the details of this.[111] In their zeal, Guevara and Marighella con-vinced themselves of their own revolutionary prowess. Guevara, for example, failed to heed his own advice about when not to attempt guer-rilla warfare as he departed for Bolivia in 1966: 'Where a government has come into power through some form of popular vote, fraudulent or not, and maintains at least an appearance of constitutional legality, the guer-rilla outbreak cannot be promoted since the possibilities of peaceful strug-gle have not yet been exhausted.'[112] Considered the 'Guerrilla Enemy Number One' by the United States, perhaps even the Osama bin Laden of his generation, Guevara was tracked down by Bolivian Rangers and killed in October 1967. Although both Guevara and Marighella were killed by state security forces, their writings and example inspired a generation of Marxist-Leninist terrorists from 1967 until the collapse of the Soviet Union.

Developments in counter-insurgency

The current generation of irregular warfare experts derives much of its knowledge from the classic works written between 1960 and 1973 by Filipino, British, French and American authors with first-hand experience in locations such as the Philippines, Malaya, Kenya and Algeria.[113] Works by such authors as Robert Thompson, Frank Kitson, David Galula, Roger Trinquier, Napoleon Valeriano and Edward Lansdale continue to be read and held in high regard for the insights they provide.[114] After President John F. Kennedy officially made counter-insurgency a high national priority in 1962, most of these experts either shared their experiences in sponsored conferences and written works or they acted as advisors to the US government.[115] French Lieutenant-Colonel David Galula, for example, produced both of his written works, *Pacification in Algeria* and *Counterinsurgency Warfare*, while sponsored by the RAND Corporation and Harvard's Center for International Affairs in 1963 and 1964.[116] Robert Thompson, considered one of the foremost experts on pacification during the Malayan Emergency and the author of *Defeating Communist Insurgency*, served as head of the British Advisory Mission in South Vietnam from 1961 until 1965 and later as a personal advisor on counter-insurgency to President Richard Nixon.[117] Much of what these authors have to say is still useful for those preparing to deploy to Iraq and Afghanistan. Indeed, such is the market for these titles that the works of Galula, Trinquier and Valeriano have been reissued by their original publishers after remaining out of print for almost forty years (see figure 5.4). Given their range of experience and the quality of the works that these authors produced, it is not surprising that this era, which began with the Malayan Emergency in 1948 and ended with the US withdrawal of its combat forces from Vietnam in 1973, is considered the 'golden age of counter-insurgency'.

Doctrine

The 'golden age of counter-insurgency' was marked by two significant developments in modern irregular warfare: an explosion of doctrinal publications and the creation of specialised counter-guerrilla forces. As the preceding pages have outlined, authors as far back as the American Revolutionary War had attempted to distil lessons learned in fighting irregular adversaries for the benefit of officers faced with this threat in the future. Interest in partisan and small wars waxed during such conflicts but waned as military officers focused their efforts on the problems of

Figure 5.4 The French experience with irregular warfare in Indochina and Algeria led Roger Trinquier and David Galula to different conclusions about how to combat irregular foes. Here, French Foreign Legionnaires, backed by US-supplied tanks, conduct large-scale and ineffective sweeps against guerrilla Viet Minh forces in the Red River Valley in the year of the French defeat at Dien Bien Phu, 1954.

conventional warfare on land and sea and, later, in the air. Given the wealth of experience that a number of French and British officers had accumulated, it is surprising how few formal attempts were made to capture hard-won lessons in doctrine.[118] The mere existence of doctrine, however, does not guarantee success. Doctrine provides guidelines for commanders to review, digest, use and modify, provided it is read and understood. If used improperly and unimaginatively, doctrine can instead be misconstrued as a set of inviolate rules never to broken, becoming a set of intellectual handcuffs. The absence of doctrine, however, places an undue burden on the commander and his subordinates to improvise and make up techniques and procedures as they go along. As David Galula lamented, the lack of common doctrine to pacify regions in Algeria led to completely different practices being followed even in neighbouring regions, and these often changed as officers came and went.[119]

Published American doctrine on irregular war had existed as early as 1921 and was refined into a work that is still useful today: the Marine Corps' 1940 *Small Wars Manual*.[120] Among the lessons incorporated into this manual, which are having to be relearned painfully today, were: the need for liaison with US State Department officials; the role played by aviation in small wars; and guidelines for disarming the population, holding elections, establishing local security forces and withdrawing one's own forces.[121] A quarter of a century after the release of the *Small Wars Manual*, the Department of the Army and Headquarters, and the United States Marine Corps released a canon of field manuals and pamphlets from 1963 until 1973 which included: *FM 31-15, Operations against Irregular Forces*; *FM 31–16, Counterguerrilla Operations*; *DA-PAM 550-100, U.S. Army Handbook of Counterinsurgency Guidelines for Area Commanders: An Analysis of Criteria*; *DA-PAM 550–104, Human Factors Considerations of Undergrounds in Insurgencies*; *FMFMRP 12–40, Professional Knowledge Gained from Operational Experience in Vietnam 1965–1966*; and *FMFM 8–2, Counterinsurgency Operations*. As Colin Gray has noted, the American defence community has a short attention span and is largely ahistorical in its outlook.[122] A decade after the withdrawal of US forces from Vietnam, and with the refocusing of defence priorities back onto potential conflict with the Warsaw Pact in Europe, most of these doctrinal publications were shelved and forgotten.

Organisational adaptation

Doctrine, no matter how prolific, is only as useful as the soldiers who put it into practice. As Johann Ewald noted, soldiers who excelled at conventional warfare had difficulties in adapting to the less rigid, more individualistic style of fighting in irregular war. To help address this problem, authors including Johann Ewald, Charles Callwell and William Henecker had suggested that conventional forces should be augmented by forces skilled in partisan and guerrilla methods. Not surprisingly, this era saw the formation or development of a number of specialised military units skilled in guerrilla methods. The British in Malaya had developed the Ferret Force and the Malaya Scouts, as well as deploying 21 Special Air Service Regiment (SAS).[123] The French in Indochina in turn fielded the *Groupement de Commandos Mixtes Aéroportés* (GCMA), in which French commissioned and non-commissioned officers led groups of local tribesmen. The commanding officer of the GCMA during the battle of Dien Bien Phu was none other than Roger Trinquier.[124] Within the United States, President Kennedy elevated the status of the fledgling US Army Special Forces, or Green Berets, as the tip of America's spear in the fight against Communist insurgencies.

Other service commanders saw the way in which the political winds were blowing and approved the establishment of their own counter-guerrilla forces. Even Air Force General Curtis LeMay, who was not known for tact or subtlety, recognised the requirement, and he authorised the formation of a squadron, the 4400th Combat Crew Training Squadron, or 'Jungle Jim', to provide advice and training to foreign personnel in the use of air power against guerrillas.[125] As with doctrine, the uniquely qualified personnel of such special operations forces could not overcome military and political incompetence and misuse at the operational and strategic level.[126]

Principles of counter-insurgency

The legacy of the 'golden age of counter-insurgency' is both a blessing and a curse for those facing irregular threats today. There is little need to review doctrine or the works of Thompson, Kitson, Galula, Trinquier, Valeriano or Lansdale, as they agree on the fundamentals of counter-insurgency but emphasise different aspects. These works have led to a set of fairly well-understood principles for countering irregular warfare. Such principles incorporate aspects of, but are not limited to:[127]

- controlling the population and tracking their movements through the use of checkpoints, identification checks, forced relocation, and/or intimidation and coercion
- gaining the support of the population, often expressed in the phrase 'winning the hearts and minds', which can mean their active participation in local government and self-defence militias, and providing information to the authorities, usually by providing local security and stability; at the very least, the population should be prevented from supporting insurgents and terrorists (see figure 5.5)
- obtaining precise information on the organisation and location of insurgent and terrorist groups so they can be killed, captured or turned against their comrades
- creating, or improving the quality and quantity of, military, paramilitary and law enforcement forces so that they are competent enough to provide local security and stability, with limited outside assistance, as well as deny the insurgents and terrorists sanctuary; these forces must be able to accomplish these objectives in such a manner as not to be perceived by the population as tools of government oppression
- developing, or assisting in the development of, just and responsive governance and co-ordinated responses across all government agencies at the local, regional and national level to address the political, social and economic conditions that led to violence in the first place and inform ongoing and future actions against the insurgents and terrorists.

As with doctrine and forces trained in defeating terrorists and insurgents, knowledge of such principles alone is insufficient. The curse of this era can

Figure 5.5 The support of the population, which can include providing information on insurgents, terrorists and revolutionaries or taking direct action against them, is based in part on effective local governance. Such governance must be credible, responsive and honest, and based on intricately linking local needs with available resources. Understanding such often requires specific cultural information that can only be provided by direct contact with the population. Here, an American governor is photographed with locals in Zamboanga province, Mindanao, in the Philippines, 1900.

be summed up into two main problem areas: the 'big idea', and stressing performance over politics.

The first problem area, the 'big idea', begins while searching for solutions to deal with irregular threats. Practitioners rediscover or are introduced to campaign narratives and analysis, the details of a specific historical programme or works from the 'golden age of counter-insurgency'. Such analogues are appealing, as they appear to provide the answer to the current questions. For example, the iconic success story of this era, the British campaign in Malaya from 1948 to 1960, was mined for lessons of victory in counter-insurgency that are applicable today. Current practitioners have since drifted away from Malaya, given the unique attributes of that conflict, such as a racially distinct ethnic minority insurgent group and the existence of an integrated, functioning colonial civil administration, and have focused instead on the failed French campaign in Algeria (1954–62). Algeria is appealing in that the works of Trinquier and Galula are accessible and the conflict featured a tapestry of religious and cultural elements similar to those in Iraq today. In addition to Galula's 'rediscovered' works, Alastair Horne's narrative of the Algerian war, *A Savage War of Peace*, became a scarce commodity in the frenzy to read about the campaign. While there is a sizeable body of literature on the subject from this period that is being rediscovered, other conflicts for which there are few published details, or accounts that occurred after the 'golden age of counter-insurgency', are apt to overlooked. The various 'bush wars' of Africa and counter-insurgency and counter-terrorism campaigns in Central and South America during the 1970s and 1980s are rich with insights about insurgent and counter-insurgent adaptation, organisational learning, and the interactions between adversaries at the level of policy and strategy which influenced the character of those wars.[128]

As several scholars have pointed out, reasoning by analogy and looking to history for answers to today's problems contain a number of potential pitfalls.[129] One such pitfall is simplifying the past. In reviewing works produced during this time, those looking for answers are apt to take the principles, insights and conclusions they find at face value. What may be overlooked is the specific context of the conflict in which the works were written.[130] Some of this can be put down to time and resource constraints, ignorance or intellectual laziness. More often than not, other errors are based on sins of omission or commission by the original authors. Some authors, including Thompson and Kitson, compressed significant details and omitted nuances and the complexities of the campaigns to save space and ease readability. Contemporary accounts also suffered because participants often related the details of the conflict as they knew and understood them from their specific vantage point. Sins of commission include deliberately playing down negative aspects of or evidence contrary to the concepts and ideas put forth. Such accounts are often distilled down even further as they are read by those looking to find the wisdom contained within. Kitson and Thompson's works, in particular, depict a version of counter-insurgency that appears kinder and more humane than that painted by their French counterparts, Trinquier and Galula. Recent scholarship on the British campaign in Kenya (1952–60), in which Kitson played a major role, depicts the cruel and often expedient measures imposed upon the local population, challenging the traditional image of 'winning hearts and minds'.[131]

In simplifying the past, other details can be overlooked as well. For example, the most basic depiction of counter-insurgency identifies three primary actors: the insurgent group, the population and the government (i.e. counter-insurgent) forces. Both the insurgent group and the government seek to influence the population to gain their support. On a conceptual level, this is understandable. But for reasons that Clausewitz well understood, what separates war in theory from war in reality, regardless of the form it takes, are the details of and frictions between actors. Few campaigns during the 'golden age of counter-insurgency' involved monolithic insurgent groups, populations or governments. Petty jealousies, rivalries and struggles for predominance between competing factions, shifting allegiances, and indifference and incompetence between all three, as well as the practical difficulties of comprehending these, much less dealing directly with them, are the stuff of irregular warfare.[132] The irregular wars in Iraq and Afghanistan have been labelled 'complex' and 'difficult' for good reason: there are no clear-cut or easy solutions to them. Those directly dealing with Iraq and Afghanistan have been faced with a range of competing functional and political requirements, including minimising their own casualties, dealing with local tribal and militia leaders, and making decisions based on incomplete information in areas that have no clear moral dividing line. The labels 'complex' and 'difficult', however, can be applied to almost all irregular wars during this period, especially Vietnam and Algeria. The war in Vietnam was not a simple 'us-versus-them' conflict, with the population in between, that could have been resolved by invading the North and destroying its alleged centre of gravity, its army. As Harry Summers points out, this 'purely military' option was completely divorced from political reality, and therefore unwise and impractical.[133] The war in Vietnam was comprised of a number of nested and interrelated problems spiced with the vested interests of various groups. These groups included the US military, whose leaders acted according to their own individual and organisational imperatives, and competing social, political, economic and religious elements within South Vietnam, such as the montagnard hill tribes, an influential Buddhist minority and a social elite of Catholic Vietnamese. In Algeria, the French also did not face a single enemy. The conduct for which French forces are mostly remembered, involving torture and forced confessions, must be seen against the backdrop of a caustic sectarian war taking place within Algerian society. What is often overlooked in reviews of the campaign is bitter rivalry, torture, executions and purges conducted between various leaders and groups, as well as factions within the FLN, that claimed tens of thousands of lives.[134] If viewed at the time, the situation confronting French commanders and politicians bears little resemblance to the contemporary perception. Another aspect of oversimplification in the face of complex problems is jumping to snap judgements that the defeat of major powers in irregular wars is inevitable.[135]

The second and final problem associated with learning from the era can be summarised as the tendency to learn military lessons at the expense of political ones. All of the Coalition members engaged in Iraq and Afghanistan, but especially those with the preponderance of forces in theatre, continue to learn from and adapt to their adversaries. Current

Figure 5.6 Technology allows US and Coalition forces to obtain and manage vast amounts of information today in ways undreamt by practitioners from the 'golden age of counter-insurgency'. Military lessons continue to be learned and improvements made in operations, but the political wisdom of certain actions in Iraq, such as enlisting private militias, remains a subject of continuing debate. Here soldiers from the 10th Mountain Division process applicants for the 'Night's Guard', one of a number of private Iraqi security forces enlisted as part of the 'surge' of forces, 2007.

practitioners look back to the 'golden age of counter-insurgency' to identify potential techniques and tricks of the trade to improve their overall performance (see figure 5.6). Even the most traumatic event in recent American memory, the war in Vietnam, has been mined for potential relevant practices and potential guidance. Among the areas that have been investigated is the controversial interagency programme designed to eliminate the Viet Cong political and military infrastructure in South Vietnam code-named 'Project Phoenix'.[136] Reaching back to the past is laudable, especially if it saves lives and defeats the insurgency. The current trend, however, stresses improving the performance of the means used while divining little about the ends to be achieved. Countering irregular warfare has little to do with fighting more effectively against insurgents and terrorists oneself, as the principles outlined above suggest, but rather assisting local forces to create the conditions for security and stability from the bottom up while assisting the host nation government in its ability to govern credibly from the top down (see figure 5.6).[137] Studying Nixon's policy of 'Vietnamisation' for potential political insights applicable to Iraq, for example, is not to equate the latter with the former. The end result, the collapse of the Army of the Republic of Vietnam, was not due primarily to the removal of US air power from the equation. The assumptions behind the policy of Vietnamisation were sound, but its execution left something to be desired.[138] The bottom line was that the host nation, South Vietnam, did not possess military forces competent or trustworthy enough to protect the nation, nor did it have a political system worth defending. And yet, as Harry Summers related to a North Vietnamese colonel years after the fall of Saigon: 'You know, you never defeated us on the battlefield', to which the response was '[T]hat may be so . . . but it is also irrelevant.'[139]

Teasing out the details of irregular warfare, including the forms used and the reasons for success or failure, is not difficult after such conflicts end. Academics can state with certainty that the Irish Civil War began on 28 June 1922 and ended on 30 April 1923.[140] Usually the start and end of specific conflicts are tied to crucial events with the benefit of hindsight.[141] When faced with such wars now and in the future, however, even the most basic information is unclear and the subject of speculation. The cardinal error that a political leader or military commander could commit, according to Clausewitz, is misunderstanding the kind of war about to be undertaken and ensuring that the means applied is suited to the desired ends.[142] Problems for the political leader and military planner when they are confronted by insurgency or terrorism, or any other form of irregular warfare, occur for a number of related reasons: confusing differences in the most recent context of political violence for a change in the nature of warfare itself; conceiving the character of irregular warfare in absolute and static terms; mistaking the means and methods used by the adversary for the purpose of the violence; and uncertainty associated with the purpose of irregular violence.

The importance of context

At the risk of repetition, even the most cursory reading of military history and strategy conveys the clear message that all conflicts are unique to and shaped by their specific context. The Chechens, for example, have fought three irregular wars against Russia over the last 150 years. Although the geography has been the same in each case, the character of each conflict has been shaped by changes in society, technology, culture, information and a host of other factors. In order to understand the root causes and motivations behind irregular conflicts, some scholars suggest that cultural and language studies are crucial. Few would dispute this sound advice. Unfortunately, other authors have further interpreted this to mean that cultural and religious reasons alone explain violence, irregular or otherwise, as an end in and of itself. The implication of this conclusion is clear and disturbing: there is no room for negotiation or bargaining with those for whom violence forms an integral part of their religion and/or culture. Violence serves a purpose that suits the social context but nothing else. When cultural or religious warriors fight professional soldiers, the former are willing to adopt methods that the latter cannot or will not embrace. This advantage is crucial in explaining why militias, tribes and others using irregular tactics have frustrated and defeated more powerful adversaries with professional modern armies.

The kernel of truth behind such claims mistakes individual and group motivation, organisation and fighting style – in other words the technique of violence – for its purpose. Irregular warfare is no different from its regular counterpart in terms of the intended outcome. Those who adopt irregular means are looking to obtain power of one sort or another. That power is political in nature, and its possession allows the wielder to achieve control as well as conduct systemic change – from a redistribution of power and wealth within society all the way to recasting it according to a specific political or religious ideology. The purpose of violence, and the rationale for its use, has been remarkably similar from Auguste Blanqui to the current generation of militant Salafi *jihadists*. Che Guevara, for example, suggested that guerrillas were 'the *armed vanguard* of the great popular force that supports them' in which 'the guerrilla fighter is a social reformer . . . *[who] fights in order to change the social system* that keeps all his unarmed brothers in ignominy and social misery' in order to 'achieve an ideal, establish a new society . . . and to achieve, finally, the social justice for which they fight'.[143] Egyptian Sayyid Qutb, considered one of the most influential modern thinkers of the militant Salafi *jihadi* movement, used very similar language in 1966 to describe the catalyst for change: 'It is necessary that there should be a *vanguard* which sets out with this determination [creating a new system] and then keeps walking on the path.'[144] The ultimate purpose of this vanguard is almost identical to that spelled out by Guevara: 'Our foremost *objective is to change the practices of this society*. Our aim is to change the *Jahili* system at its very roots.'[145] Not much separates the ultimate purpose of today's insurgents and terrorists from those who struggled 50 and 150 years ago.

Although some militias and other groups limit the scope of their power to traditional ethnic and tribal lands, other groups have sought complete control within state borders. The reason for this is that power continues to be exercised most effectively at the state level in the international system. State leaders have a legitimacy that sub-state leaders and groups do not. Irregular warfare does differ from conventional warfare in terms of the form that violence takes and its functional purpose. As the preceding section suggests, heavy emphasis is placed on the organisation for and exploitation of the political aspects of conflict, regardless of the form of irregular warfare chosen. Violence serves the purpose of removing a threat to a group's control over a population, as well as permitting that group to expand sympathy for its cause and consolidate its support network and power base. Even militant Salafi *jihadists*, who have as their goal the remaking of all society according to the guidelines contained exclusively in the Qur'an, have understood that global revolution must occur one step at a time: 'When God restrained Muslims from Jihaad for a certain period, it was a question of strategy rather than of principle; this was a matter pertaining to the requirements of the movement and not to belief.'[146] For these very pragmatic reasons, bin Laden and Zawahiri have repeatedly stated that the first step in the realisation of this goal is the establishment of one such state (caliphate). The caliphate will serve as a beacon to the faithful by demonstrating that God's will is being realised through governance and social reforms according to radical Salafi norms, as Qutb so clearly indicated: 'The beauty of this new system cannot be appreciated unless it takes concrete form. Hence it is essential that a community arrange its affairs according to it and show it to the world. In order to bring this about, we need to initiate the movement of Islamic revival in some Muslim country.'[147]

Misunderstanding the character of violence

In addition to misunderstanding the purpose of irregular violence, political and military leaders are prone to misread the character of the violence. There is little likelihood of this occurring when groups are limited in size, purpose and issue, as was the case with such terrorist groups as the Palestine Liberation Organisation, the Popular Front for the Liberation of Palestine, the Red Army Front and the Japanese Red Army. Other cases of irregular violence, such as coups d'état, only succeed if the plot is clandestine until the moment that violent action is taken. Military and political leaders can misunderstand the character of irregular warfare in any one of a number of ways. In some cases, rather than viewing irregular warfare as a potential set of complex, embedded problems, the phenomenon is viewed instead in absolute terms or as a static phenomenon. In other words, instead of recognising that they might be faced with a series of intertwined irregular problems, or that its character is dynamic and may change or evolve over time, policy-makers and military planners may believe that they are confronting one phenomenon instead. Civil war, insurgency or terrorism each has 'prescribed' solutions. The thought that a civil war can occur within or at the same time as an insurgency, that the conflict in Iraq can remain uncoupled from the global phenomenon of militant Salafi *jihad* or that a humanitarian mission can morph into a robust manhunt, as was the case in Somalia, is potentially beyond comprehension.[148] Similar problems occur when the response to irregular warfare is conceived almost exclusively in military terms. At first glance, such misperceptions may appear trivial or academic until they are linked to policies, military operations and public perception in democracies.[149] The seemingly endless variety of labels used to encompass all of the irregular violence within Iraq – insurgency, terrorism, civil war and sectarian violence – without sufficiently explaining the changing character and complex nature of the conflict has led to military missteps, public confusion, and domestic and international opposition to the war. In addition, policy statements that grossly link the violence in Iraq to al-Qaeda only add mud to the already unclear water of public perception.

Mistaking means, methods and purpose

Irregular warfare can be difficult to understand owing to its character or the means and methods of violence used. There is a tendency to assume the type of irregular violence according to the methods and means used while overlooking the purpose it is designed to achieve. Put simply, there is a tendency to mistake the tactic, its strategic utility and the purpose of the violence (see figure 5.7). For example, there is a common misperception that insurgents only use guerrilla tactics. Acts of terrorism, such as bombings, assassinations, hijacking and kidnapping, are strictly the realm of terrorists. Noteworthy theorists, including Mao Tse-Tung and Che Guevara, would rail against such simplistic assessments of the use of violence within an insurgency (see figure 5.7). Both authors acknowledged the role that terrorism, as a tactic, could play in their overall campaign.[150] Other methods and techniques, such as sabotage, subversion and passive resistance, which have considerable tactical utility but are exceptionally difficult to identify and evaluate, have been confused as unique forms of irregular warfare with their own purpose.

Insurgents and terrorists are not limited to specific means or methods but instead make the best use of the available tools to suit the environment. During the portion of the French campaign in Algeria known as 'the battle of the Casbah', Algerian revolutionary Abane Ramdane believed that attacks by guerrilla units in the city were senseless and impractical, given the terrain and available resources. The complex urban terrain, range of potential targets and presence of international media outlets favoured the use of terrorist tactics for a variety of reasons. Tactically, such attacks were an efficient use of terrorist resources and were difficult for the French to prevent.[151] From a strategic perspective, the terrorist bombings were an effective means of achieving the wider goals of the insurgent cause: generating international recognition and sympathy for their cause or even driving the French out on their own.[152] Unlike insurgents, those who utilise terrorism exclusively do so not by choice but out of necessity. Insurgents have more options in the method and means of violence they use than does the terrorist, due largely to their ability to harness local discontent and grievances and turn available resources into a greater range of capabilities.

Figure 5.7 In an effort to grasp the nature of the war in which one is involved, there is a danger of oversimplifying complex aspects of irregular warfare, such as confusing the means used by insurgents, terrorists and revolutionaries for the ends they are trying to achieve. Those who conduct irregular warfare are first and foremost pragmatic opportunists when it comes to using the resources at hand. Viet Cong leaders, for example, paid little mind to the conceptual distinction between acts of terrorism and insurgency during the bombing campaign they conducted in Saigon. Bomb-damaged US officers' billet, Saigon, 1966.

Some writers draw linkages between the tactic of violence and the cultural arguments mentioned previously when they try to make sense out of suicide bombings conducted in London, Bali and elsewhere. Some of the Western curiosity surrounding so-called 'martyrdom operations' relates to the individual purpose and rationale for killing others and dying in the process. Only by understanding such motivations can states develop responses to address them. What is missing from such interpretations is a larger meaning or group purpose for the violence. According to Ayman al-Zawahiri, one of the co-founders of al-Qaeda and a frequent spokesman for it, the types of attack conducted in the name of al-Qaeda and its cause do more than just spread fear and test the faithful.[153] Terrorism is the only one of a number of means in a broader strategy of cumulative effects over time that will eventually achieve the goals of the militant Salafi *jihad*.[154] In the absence of a clear and concise 'game plan' along the lines of Mao's 'On

Protracted War', some writers, journalists and media pundits attribute a level of strategic genius to, and divine the specific intent, as well as purpose, of every successful terrorist attack or plot.

The reason policy-makers and others confuse means with ends is related to the nature of the organisations that conduct irregular warfare. Leaders of such groups rely on a variety of measures to prevent their detection and tracking by security forces and obtain the resources necessary to conduct their operations. One such measure is limiting the volume of or media by which information is disseminated. Group leaders also often change the scope and tone of their messages and tailor them to specific audiences.[155] In his early published statements and audio and video recordings, Osama bin Laden provided lengthy theological justification and historical evidence in support of his call for a global Islamic uprising.[156] The target of his audience was not Islamic scholars and imams, who would have questioned his interpretation of theology and history, but rather those with more limited knowledge who favoured action over debate. The earliest speeches in 1996 and 1998 spoke of resistance against American support for Israel and other 'apostate' governments, as well as the presence of American forces in the land of the two mosques (Saudi Arabia), among other goals.[157] In a taped statement in 2004, bin Laden suggested that the goal was economically weakening and bankrupting the United States.[158] In 1998 bin Laden had exhorted his followers that:

The ruling to kill the Americans and their allies – civilians and military – is an individual duty for every Muslim who can do it in any country in which it is possible to do it, in order to liberate the al-Aqsa Mosque and the holy mosque [Mecca] from their grip, and in order for their armies to move out of all the lands of Islam, defeated and unable to threaten any Muslim

whereas the 2006 much-publicised truce statement was directed at the American public.[159] In other words, al-Qaeda's goals and targets have changed, based on the speaker and the intended audience.

Other elements that complicate understanding of a group's goals result from internal changes and interactions between opponents at the strategic level over time. Given that terrorist and insurgent groups rely on a variety of clean or illicit means to support their activities, such as front companies, extortion, racketeering and smuggling, there is always a risk that the original goals of a group are subsumed by greed and a relish for local influence and power. The sums of money involved are not insubstantial. The loyalist Ulster Volunteer Force in Northern Ireland, for example, conducted such activities as fuel scams, video piracy, drug-dealing, counterfeiting, and running legitimate laundry and taxi services that netted the group's 350-odd members an annual income of over £3 million.[160] The group *Fuerzas Armadas Revolucionarias de Colombia*, or FARC, originally espoused a Marxist-Leninist platform of social reform and wealth redistribution when it was founded in 1962. Although the group's website, www.farcep.org/, continues to publish communiqués that continue the rhetoric, most analysts agree that the FARC now serves a much different purpose: providing protection to cartels and benefiting from the country's narcotics trade.[161]

Other internal or external events, such as struggles for power within organisations, the death or capture of influential leaders, or catalytic events can morph terrorist and insurgent objectives or goals, or even the form of irregular warfare, into something much more complicated. Consider for example the attack, carried out by al-Qaeda's Organisation of Holy War in Iraq, against the al-Askariya Mosque in Samarra in 2006. Prior to the attack, Coalition and Iraqi forces focused their efforts on a straightforward counter-insurgency campaign against roughly a dozen Sunni insurgent and terrorist groups.[162] The campaign was characterised by patrolling operations and large-scale sweeps of known or suspected insurgent sanctuaries.[163] Shi'ite groups and militias, including Muqtada al-Sadr's Madhi Army and the Supreme Islamic Iraqi Council's Badr Organisation, were either left largely untouched by Coalition forces or utilised in the fight against Sunni groups. The deliberate, systematic attack approved by Abu Musab al-Zarqawi, an al-Qaeda-affiliated leader, targeted one of the holiest shrines in Shi'a Islam.[164] Zarqawi allegedly intended the attack to spark a civil war between Shi'a and Sunnis. US and Coalition commanders prior to the attack were beginning to understand better the context and nature of the conflict and of the enemy in Iraq. Widespread sectarian violence, roving Shi'a death squads, continued car bombings and tit-for-tat executions challenged the commanders' understanding of and ability to respond to this evolution in irregular violence in the country. In addition, the Samarra attacks, subsequent sectarian violence and the death of Zarqawi have opened a rift between the uncompromising foreign fighters of al-Qaeda's Organisation for Holy War in Iraq and other indigenous Sunni insurgent groups that has led to US arming and support of the latter against the former.[165]

'Mirror-imaging'

Understanding irregular warfare is also difficult because policy-makers and military planners are prone to 'mirror-image' their irregular adversaries. Part of the reason for this is understandable. If the terrorist and insurgent violence is undertaken for a purpose, then surely the leaders of such movements must have a plan to translate tactical action into achieving stated ends. In addition, as the true scale of the insurgent and terrorist movement is understood through such tools as social network analysis, it is easy to be convinced of a 'master-plan' guiding it. In reality, there may be less of an initial plan for victory than the hope that action will somehow translate into purpose. Given enough time, however, most irregular warfare theorists from

Lawrence to Mao have developed a concept of operations that takes the current context of conflict into account. As the preceding review has demonstrated, revolutionary theorists have often disagreed on the appropriate method or mechanism for success in irregular warfare. Unfortunately for the current generation of practitioners dealing with the militant Salafi *jihad*, these debates continue to rage among their opponents. The debates encompass almost all aspects of strategy, including whether to fight the 'near' enemy (where the militant Salafi *jihadists* reside, most often states that are ostensibly Muslim but follow secular laws) or the 'far' enemy (the United States and other Western nations that represent the purported source of all things wrong and evil).[166] In addition, such writers and organisers as Abu Musab al-Suri (born Mustafa Setmariam Nasar), a former member of the Syrian Brotherhood with ties to Zarqawi's al-Qaeda's Organisation of Holy War in Iraq, have argued that the radical Salafi *jihad* conducts what was once labelled 'the propaganda by the deed' in an entirely decentralised and independent manner. Victory will eventually result from the cumulative effects of such activities.[167] Other writers argue that a more focused, sequential plan of action is necessary. Abu Bakr Naji outlines an approach that, in keeping with the principles of practice of irregular war, emphasises both the political and military dimensions of the struggle:

This plan requires: A military strategy working to disperse the efforts and forces of the enemy and to exhaust and drain its monetary and military capabilities; A media strategy targeting and focusing on two classes. [The first] class is the masses, in order to push a large number of them to join the jihad, offer positive support, and adopt a negative attitude toward those who do not join the ranks. The second class is the troops of the enemy who have lower salaries, in order to push them to join the ranks of the mujahids or at least flee from the service of the enemy.[168]

A core component of Naji's vision of success is a hierarchy of highly capable administrators who guide and manage the revolutionary masses, which harkens back to the earlier generation of socialist revolutionary theorists.[169] Insurgent and terrorist groups are not immune to the same internal bickering, squabbles, incompetence and problems that confront those who are trying to defeat them.

To sum up, irregular warfare is difficult to understand for a variety of reasons. One reason results from the belief that irregular violence takes unchanging, absolute forms. Those conducting irregular warfare ultimately have to be pragmatic about the violence they use, in order to survive, and leaders choose the violence that best suits the local conditions at the time. Different forms of violence can be used simultaneously, or in sequence, in an overall national or global campaign. The purpose of the violence can also change over time. Another reason irregular warfare is difficult to understand has to do with confusion over the method of violence employed for its purpose. This creates enough problems on its own, but intuiting the overarching purpose of groups conducting irregular warfare is not as simple as it may appear. Insurgent and terrorist leaders may not reveal their true goals at the time to their followers or in their public statements. In addition, published and available statements are often contradictory, and the message can change depending on the intended audience or over time. Finally, some mistake the complexity of irregular wars for changes in the nature of war. The very character of irregular wars can change as enemies adapt to one another, alliances are forged, rifts form between leaders and groups, or other actors join in the fight. In other words, irregular warfare is difficult to understand for precisely the reasons that Carl von Clausewitz suggested make all wars difficult: 'The consequences of the nature of War, how ends and means act in it, how in the modifications of reality it deviates sometimes more, sometimes less, from its strict original conception, fluctuating backwards and forwards.' To this Clausewitz added an important qualifier. No matter what form war takes or how puzzling it may appear to be to the participant and observer, war cannot escape its nature, 'always remaining under that strict conception [the nature of War] as under a supreme law'.[170] Despite its complexities and changes, this chapter has argued that many aspects of irregular warfare have remained and will remain remarkably consistent owing to the nature of all wars that Clausewitz so keenly deduced.

NOTES

1 Central Command's Operations Plan 1003–98 originally called for more than 400,000 troops. For a variety of reasons, Secretary of Defense Donald Rumsfeld insisted that those numbers be whittled down to as few as 4,000. The eventual compromise plan, known by many names including 'Cobra II', committed 145,000 to the initial invasion of Iraq. For a comprehensive narrative on the evolution of the plans to invade Iraq, see Michael R. Gordon and Bernard E. Trainor, *Cobra II: The Inside Story of the Invasion and Occupation of Iraq* (New York: Pantheon, 2006), pp. 26–54; 66–94; 115.

2 For a narrative on conventional force actions in Iraq from the start of operations to the fall of Baghdad, see Gordon and Trainor, *Cobra II*, pp. 182–433. The actions of US Army Special Forces during Operation Iraqi Freedom are outlined in the unclassified official history. See Charles H. Briscoe, Kenneth Finlayson and Robert W. Jones, Jr., eds., *All Roads Lead to Baghdad: Army Special Operations Forces in Iraq* (Fort Bragg, NC: ARSOC History Office, n.d.).

3 See for example Montgomery McFate, 'The Military Utility of Understanding Adversary Culture', *Joint Force Quarterly 38* (3rd Quarter, 2005): 42–8, and 'Honor among Them', *The Economist* 381, 8509 (23 December 2006): 36–40.

4 A conclusion reached by John Nagl in *Counterinsurgency Lessons from Malaya to Vietnam: Learning to Eat Soup with a Knife* (Westport, CT: Praeger, 2002). A paperback edition of the book was released with two new additions: a revised preface based on the author's experience as a battalion operations officer in Iraq and a new foreword written by the Army Chief of Staff, General Peter J. Schoomaker. The book has been issued to all Army general officers prior to deploying to Iraq.

5 See for example T. X. Hammes, *The Sling and the Stone: On War in the 21st Century* (St Paul, MN: Zenith, 2004). The concept of 4GW first appeared in William Lind, Keith Nightengale, John Schmitt, Joseph Sutton and Gary Wilson, 'The Changing Face of War: Into the Fourth Generation', *Marine Corps Gazette* 73:10 (October 1989): 22–6. The article is available online at www.d-n-i.net/fcs/4th gen war gazette.htm.

6 *FM 3-24 Counterinsurgency* (Washington, DC: Headquarters, Department of the Army, December 2006).

7 *AFDD 2.3-1, Foreign Internal Defense*, Coordination Draft (15 May 2007), supersedes AFDD 2-3.1 (10 May 2004).

8 Bruce Hoffman, *Inside Terrorism*, rev. and expanded edn (New York: Columbia University Press, 2006), pp. 3–20.

9 A key US policy goal is to build a global anti-terrorist environment or consensus in which terrorism is recognised as an international scourge. Analogies used to inform this policy are piracy and slavery; both still exist but are no longer seen as credible or legitimate. See for example the recent collection of essays in Joseph McMillan, ed., *'In the Same Light as Slavery': Building a Global Antiterrorist Consensus* (Washington, DC: National Defense University Press, 2006).

10 Bard E. O'Neill, *Insurgency and Terrorism: From Revolution to Apocalypse*, rev. edn (Washington, DC: Potomac Books, 2005), pp. 19–29.

11 Carl von Clausewitz, *On War*, ed. and trans. by Michael Howard and Peter Paret (Princeton, NJ: Princeton University Press, 1976), pp. 89; 119–21.

12 James Kiras, 'Irregular Warfare: Terrorism and Insurgency', in John Baylis, Eliot Cohen, James Wirz and Colin S. Gray, eds., *Strategy in the Contemporary World*, 2nd edn (Oxford: Oxford University Press, 2007), p. 179.

13 Osama bin Laden has repeated the desire to obtain legal sanction for and acquisition of nuclear weapons. See for example 'Jihad against Jews and Crusaders', first published in al-Quds al-Arabi in London on 28 February 1998 and translated and available at www.fas.org/irp/world/para/docs/980223-fatwa.htm, as well as the 2003 fatwa cited by bin Laden. See Nasir bin Hamd al-Fahd, 'A Treatise on the Legal Status of Using Weapons of Mass Destruction against Infidels' (May 2003). An example from popular

culture also illustrates the point. In the 1966 film *The Battle of Algiers*, captured Algerian guerrilla leader Larbi ben M'Hidi responds to a question about the ethics of concealing bombs in baskets by saying, 'Give us your bombers, and you can have our baskets.'

14 Daniel Byman does justice to this exceptionally difficult subject in *Deadly Connections: States that Sponsor Terrorism* (Cambridge: Cambridge University Press, 2005).

15 I freely acknowledge the intellectual debt I owe to Arial Merari for this chart. His comparison of forms of insurgency provided the inspiration for my own analysis that differentiates between forms of irregular warfare. See Merari, 'Terrorism as a Strategy of Insurgency', *Terrorism and Political Violence* 5:4 (Winter 1993): 220.

16 Edward Luttwak's short, concise handbook on the subject remains almost forty years after its publication the single best reference work on how and why coups are conducted: *Coup d'État: A Practical Handbook* (New York: Knopf, 1969).

17 Robert Pape, *Dying to Win: The Strategic Logic of Suicide Terrorism* (New York: Random House, 2005), pp. 20–3.

18 Mia Bloom, *Dying to Kill: The Allure of Suicide Terror* (New York: Columbia University Press, 2005), pp. 76–85.

19 See for example Steven Metz, *Rethinking Insurgency* (Carlisle Barracks, PA: Strategic Studies Institute, June 2007) and David Kilcullen, 'Counter-Insurgency *Redux*', *Survival* 48:4 (Winter 2006–7): 111–30.

20 Examples include Czechoslovakia's 'Velvet Revolution' (1989), Serbia's 'Bulldozer Revolution' (2000), Georgia's 'Rose Revolution' (2003), Ukraine's 'Orange Revolution' (2004–5), and Lebanon's 'Cedar Revolution' (2005).

21 See for example Maurikios, *Maurice's Strategikon: Handbook of Byzantine Military Strategy*, trans. George T. Dennis (Philadelphia, PA: University of Pennsylvania Press, 1984), pp. 52–7; 93–105; Harro von Senger, *The Book of Strategems: Tactics for Triumph and Survival*, trans. and ed. by Myron Gubitz (New York: Viking, 1991); and Ralph Sawyer, trans., *The Seven Military Classics of Ancient China* (Boulder, CO: Westview, 1993). The ancient Indian text by Kautilya, *Arthasastra*, provides little guidance on the tactics of fighting, as it is meant to be a manual on statecraft. Like Sun Tzu's *The Art of War*, Kautilya places some emphasis on spies, intelligence networks and using proxies in enemy states to foment unrest. See T. N. Ramaswamy, *Essentials of Indian Statecraft: Kautilya's* Arthasastra *for Contemporary Readers* (New York: Asia Publishing House, 1962), pp. 55–8; 60–1.

22 See for example acts of treachery during the Peloponnesian Wars that led to the fall of numerous cities, including Anactorium, Panactum and Oropus, in Robert Strassler, ed., *The Landmark Thucydides: A Comprehensive Guide to the Peloponnesian Wars* (New York: The Free Press, 1996), pp. 33; 250; 303; 515; Paul Bentley Kern, *Ancient Siege Warfare* (Bloomington, IN: Indiana University Press, 1999), pp. 21; 33–4; 59–60; 119.

23 Maurikios, *Maurice's Strategikon*, pp. 113–26.

24 Archer Jones wrote about Western persisting and Eastern raiding approaches to warfare in *The Art of War in the Western World* (New York: Barnes and Noble, 1987), pp. 54–7. Victor Davis Hanson suggests that Western civilisation, with its combination of democratic values, organisation and technology, has militarily, politically and economically prevailed over the despotic and unstable south and east in *Carnage and Culture: Landmark Battles in the Rise of Western Power* (New York: Doubleday, 2001).

25 In particular, Flavius Josephus's works, including his account of the Jewish uprising in AD 70, *The Jewish War*, have been the subject of considerable scholarly inquiry and criticism. See for example S. J. D. Cohen, *Josephus in Galilee and Rome: His Vita and Development as a Historian* (Leiden: E. J. Brill, 1979) and Tal Ilan and Jonathan Price, 'Seven Onomastic Problems in Josephus' "Bellum Judaicum,"' *The Jewish Quarterly Review* 84:2/3 (October 1993–January 1994): 189–208.

26 Robert Asprey, for example, begins his historical exploration of guerrilla warfare from the Persian empire under the rule of Darius in 531 BC; John Ellis, in contrast, goes back even further, to the actions of the Israelites against the Hittites as described in the Book of Joshua in the Bible. See Asprey, *War in the Shadows*, rev. edn (London: Little, Brown, 1994), pp. 3–4; Ellis, *From the Barrel of a Gun: A History of Guerrilla, Revolutionary and Counter-Insurgency Warfare, from the Romans to the Present*, rev. edn (London: Greenhill, 1995), p. 17.

27 Such works include Hoffman, *Inside Terrorism*, pp. 83–4, and Pape, *Dying to Win*, pp. 12–13. Critical scholarly treatments of the Zealots and Assassins are: Martin Hengel, *The Zealots: Investigations into the Jewish Freedom Movement in the Period from Herod I until 70 AD*, trans. David Smith (Edinburgh: T&T Clarke, 1989), and Farhad Daftary, *The Assassin Legends: Myths of the Isma'ilis* (London: I. B. Taurus, 1995).

28 See for example Asprey, *War in the Shadows*; Ellis, *From the Barrel of a Gun*; Walter Laqueur, *Guerrilla: A Historical and Critical Study* (Boston, MA: Little, Brown, 1976); and Anthony James Joes, *Guerrilla Conflict before the Cold War* (Westport, CT: Praeger, 1996).

29 Christer Jörgensen, *et al.*, *Fighting Techniques of the Early Modern World: Equipment, Combat Skills, and Tactics* (New York: St Martin's, 2006), p. 25.

30 Mark Kwasny, *Washington's Partisan War, 1775–1783* (Kent, OH: Kent State University Press, 1996).

31 See for examples the details of the Waxhaws massacre, conducted by the British Legion under the command of Banastre Tarleton, and the 'Pyles Massacre' perpetrated by Colonel Henry Lee's dragoons. See John Ferling, *Almost a Miracle: The American Victory in the War of Independence* (Oxford: Oxford University Press, 2007), pp. 436–7; 495–6.

32 *Ibid.*, 400–2.

33 Fred Anderson does a remarkable job in weaving together conventional and irregular military aspects of the war within their political context in *Crucible of War: The Seven Years' War and the Fate of Empire in British North America, 1754–1766* (New York: Knopf, 2000).

34 For details of Marion's exploits, see Daniel E. Fitz-Simons, 'Francis Marion the "Swamp Fox": An Anatomy of a Low Intensity Conflict', *Small Wars and Insurgencies* 6:1 (Spring 1995): 1–16. To put the 'Swamp Fox's' exploits in the context of the campaign in South Carolina, see Walter Edgar, *Partisans and Redcoats: The Southern Conflict That Turned the Tide of the American Revolution* (New York: Perennial, 2003).

35 Rogers' 'Standing Orders' consist of nineteen aphorisms and such common-sense advice as 'Don't forget nothing' and 'If we strike swamps, or soft ground, we spread out abreast, so it's hard to track us.' The Standing Orders continue to form part of the heritage of the American 75th Ranger Regiment, which draws its lineage from Rogers' Rangers, and are posted on the Regiment's website. See www.soc.mil/75thrr/75thrrorders.shtml.

36 Walter Laqueur, for example, summarises the 1789 work by Andreas Emmerich entitled *The Partisan in War or the Use of a Corps of Light Troops to an Army*. See Laqueur, 'The Origins of Guerrilla Doctrine', *Journal of Contemporary History* 10:3 (July 1975): 344–5.

37 This work will rely on the more tangible and defensible ground of published works. Other notable works on 'small wars' that preceded Ewald's were written by Armand François de la Croix in 1752 and Thomas Auguste 'Le Roy de Grandmaison in 1759. For details see Johann Ewald, *Treatise on Partisan Warfare*, trans. and annot. Robert Selig and David Curtis Skaggs (Westport, CT: Greenwood, 1991), n. 11, pp. 137–8.

38 Johann Ewald, *Diary of the American War: A Hessian Journal*, trans. and ed. Joseph Tustin (New Haven, CT: Yale University Press, 1979).

39 Laqueur, 'The Origins of Guerrilla Doctrine', Ewald quoted in 346.

40 Ewald, *Treatise on Partisan Warfare*, pp. 68; 80; 114; 183. J. F. C. Fuller provides a concise summary of, and considerable praise for, this work in his *British Light Infantry in the Nineteenth Century* (London: Hutchinson, 1925), pp. 137–51.

41 See for example the discussion of ambush measures and counter-measures contained in Ewald, *Diary of the American War*, pp. 57–8.

42 *Ibid.*, pp. 355; 341.

43 See for example Ewald, *Treatise on Partisan Warfare*, pp. 69; 70; 76; 78 and the anecdote about the Reverend Dr William Smith related in Ewald, *Diary of the American War*, pp. 92–3.

44 Ewald, *Treatise on Partisan Warfare*, p. 88.

45 Ewald, *Diary of the American War*, p. 57.

46 *Ibid.*, pp. 335–6.

47 Davidov captured some of his experiences leading partisan forces in his memoir. See Davidov, *In the Service of the Tsar against Napoleon*, trans. and ed. Gregory Troubetzkoy (London: Greenhill, 1999), pp. 83–161.

48 Ellis, *From the Barrel of a Gun*, pp. 73–6.

49 Hoffman, *Inside Terrorism*, pp. 3–4.

50 Marx's seminal works on the subject remains *Das Kapital* and the volume he penned with co-author Friedrich Engels, *The Communist Manifesto*. This section draws upon Robert Tucker's work, which separates the wheat from the Marxist intellectual chaff. See Tucker, *The Marxian Revolutionary Idea* (New York: Norton, 1969).

51 Samuel Bernstein, *Auguste Blanqui and the Art of Insurrection* (London: Lawrence and Wishart, 1971), p. 309.

52 Auguste Blanqui, 'Manual for an Armed Insurrection', trans. Andy Blunden (1866), available online at www.marxists.org/reference/archive/blanqui/1866/instructions1.htm.

53 Bernstein, *Auguste Blanqui and the Art of Insurrection*, pp. 309–10.

54 Blanqui, 'Manual for an Armed Insurrection'.

55 Bernstein, *Auguste Blanqui and the Art of Insurrection*, p. 299.

56 See for example Clausewitz, *On War*, pp. 479–83 and Antoine Henri de Jomini, *The Art of War*, trans. G. H. Mendell and W. P. Craighill, repr. edn (Westport, CT: Greenhill, 1971), pp. 31–6.

57 Illustrations of the type of diagrams that Clausewitz scorns are contained in Jomini, *The Art of War*, pp. 188–94 and J. B. Wheeler, *A Course of Instruction in the Elements of the Art and Science of War* (New York: Van Nostrand, 1879), pp. 16–18; 92, etc.

58 See for example the discussion of the three principles of war and nine maxims contained in the Sandhurst primer by P. L. MacDougall, *The Theory of War*, 3rd edn (London: Longman, Green, Longman and Roberts, 1862), pp. 51–2; 98–115.

59 For details see Trevor Dupuy, *The Evolution of Weapons and Warfare* (Fairfax, VA: HERO Books, 1984), pp. 190–202.

60 The phrase was developed by Ernst Jünger as the title of his First World War memoir. See Jünger, *Storm of Steel: From the Diary of a Storm-Trooper on the Western Front* (London: Chatto and Windus, 1930).

61 Douglas Porch's chapter on French practices in its colonies remains unsurpassed. See Porch, 'Bugeaud, Galliéni, Lyautey: The Development of French Colonial Warfare', in Peter Paret, ed., *Makers of Modern Strategy: From Machiavelli to the Nuclear Age* (Princeton, NJ: Princeton University Press, 1986), pp. 376–407.

62 A number of von Trotha's statements are reproduced in Gil Merom, *How Democracies Lose Small Wars* (Cambridge: Cambridge University Press, 2003), pp. 36–7.

63 The details of the First Afghan War, including the luckless retreat from Kabul, are contained in Patrick Macrory, *The Fierce Pawns* (New York: Lippencott, 1966), especially pp. 241–90.

64 Frederick Maurice and Maurice Grant, *History of the War in South Africa, 1899–1902*, vol. III (London: Hurst & Blackett, 1908), p. 93.

65 For details on media reporting of the war, see Denis Judd and Kevin Surridge, *The Boer War* (New York: Palgrave Macmillan, 2003), pp. 251–6.

66 Swinton's work remained in print until 1991, which is a testament to its quality and utility. See Swinton, *The Defence of Duffer's Drift* (London: Leo Cooper, 1991). See also T. Miller Maguire, *Guerrilla or Partisan Warfare* (London: Hugh Rees, 1904), and W. C. G. Heneker, *Bush Warfare* (London: Hugh Rees, 1907).

67 Charles Callwell, *Small Wars: Their Principles and Practice*, 3rd edn (London: GMSO, 1906), p. 41.

68 *Ibid.*, p. 52.

69 *Ibid.*, p. 99.

70 For details on the guerrilla war, including American policies and variations in their implementation on the islands of Panay, Luzon and Samar and in the predominantly Islamic area known as Moroland, see Brian Linn, *The Philippine War, 1899–1902* (Lawrence, KS: University Press of Kansas, 2000), pp. 185–321.

71 The phrase has been attributed to a number of anarchists, including Carlo Pisacane, Mikhail Bakunin and Paul Brousse. The latter used the phrase as the title for an article published in 1887. See Paul Avrich, *Anarchist Portraits* (Princeton, NJ: Princeton University Press, 1988), p. 244.

72 For German strategic objectives related to the *jihad* campaign and an assessment of sabotage and guerrilla warfare operations planned or conducted to support the 1915 Suez campaign, see Tilman Lüdke, *Jihad Made in Germany: Ottoman and German Propaganda and Intelligence Operations in the First World War* (Münster: Lit Verlag, 2005), pp. 33–8; 90–105. See also Hew Strachan, *The First World War, Volume I: To Arms* (Oxford: Oxford University Press, 2001), pp. 700–4.

73 On the rationale for violence and the conduct of the campaign, see Michael Collins, *The Path to Freedom* (Boulder, CO: Roberts Rinehart Publishers, 1996), pp. 63–74.

74 Paul von Lettow-Vorbeck, *My Reminiscences of East Africa*, 6th edn (Nashville, TN: Battery Press Reprints, 1990), p. 72.

75 When Lettow-Vorbeck's force surrendered on 25 November 1918, it numbered 155 Germans and 1,156 *askaris*. See Charles Miller, *Battle for the Bundu: The First World War in East Africa* (London: Purnell Book Services, 1974), pp. 325–6.

76 The most famous of the Second Boer War veterans fighting with the British in East Africa was future Field Marshal and South African Prime Minister Jan Christian Smuts. See Byron Farwell, *The Great War in Africa: 1914–1918* (New York: Norton, 1986), pp. 80–1.

77 Lawrence, 'Evolution of a Revolt', *Army Quarterly* 1 (October 1920): 55–6.

78 *Ibid.*, pp. 59–62.

79 *Ibid.*, p. 63.

80 *Ibid.*, p. 64.

81 A summary of monies paid early in the revolt is contained in 'Sherif Hussein's Administration' (*Arab Bulletin*, 26 November 1916), in Malcolm Brown, *Secret Dispatches from Arabia and Other Writings by T. E. Lawrence* (London: Bellew, 1991), pp. 61–4.

82 Lawrence, 'Evolution of a Revolt', p. 63.

83 *Ibid.*, pp. 63; 65–6.

84 See for example the assessments contained in Linda Tarver, 'In Wisdom's House: T. E. Lawrence and the Near East', *Journal of Contemporary History* 13 (1978): 585–608; Lawrence James, *The Golden Warrior: The Life and Legend of Lawrence of Arabia* (New York: Paragon House, 1993); and Suleiman Mousa, *T. E. Lawrence: An Arab View* (New York: Oxford University Press, 1966).

85 Matthew Hughes, *Allenby and British Strategy in the Middle East, 1917–1919* (London: Frank Cass, 1999), pp. 77–8.

86 David Kilcullen, 'Twenty-Eight Articles: Fundamentals of Company-Level Counterinsurgency' (March 2006), electronic document available online at www.d-n-i.net/fcs/pdf/kilcullen_28_articles.pdf.

87 Jung Cheng and Jon Halliday, *Mao: The Unknown Story* (New York: Knopf, 2005), pp. 233; 243.

88 V. I. Lenin, 'Partisan Warfare', in Franklin Mark Osanka, ed., *Modern Guerrilla Warfare* (New York: Free Press, 1962), pp. 65–79.

89 Mao Tse-Tung, *On Guerrilla Warfare*, trans. Samuel B. Griffith (New York: Praeger, 1961), p. 93. A variation of Mao's metaphor, 'draining the swamps,' was used by senior Department of Defense officials in speeches just after the 11 September 2001 (9/11) attacks.

90 Stephen Biddle, 'Seeing Baghdad, Thinking Saigon', *Foreign Affairs* 85:2 (March/April 2006): 2–14.

91 Mao Tse-Tung, 'On Protracted War', in *Selected Military Writings* (Peking: Foreign Languages Press, 1966), pp. 196–7. The full text is available online at www.marxists.org/reference/archive/mao/selected-works/volume-2/mswv2_09.htm.

92 Mao, 'On Protracted War', p. 201.

93 *Ibid.*, p. 255.

94 *Ibid.*, pp. 219–22.

95 *Ibid.*, pp. 248–50.

96 *Ibid.*, pp. 210–19.

97 Mao, *On Guerrilla Warfare*, p. 73.

98 Mao, 'On Protracted War', pp. 226–31 and 257–61, and Mao, *On Guerrilla Warfare*, pp. 88–93.

99 Contained in *ibid.*, p. 92.

100 Tom Wintringham, *New Ways of War* (Harmondsworth: Penguin, 1940), and 'Yank' Levy, *Guerrilla Warfare*, 2nd edn (Boulder, CO: Panther, 1964). The other work used by the Home Guard at this time was S. J. Cuthbert, *We Shall Fight in the Streets*, 2nd edn (Boulder, CO: Panther, 1965).

101 There is a wealth of literature recently published on this neglected subject that is rewriting the traditional interpretation of the German military in the Second World War, including Ben Shepherd, *War in the Wild East: The German Army and Soviet Partisans* (Cambridge, MA: Harvard University Press, 2004), Edward Westermann, *Hitler's Police Battalions: Enforcing Racial War in the East* (Lawrence, KS: University Press of Kansas, 2005) and Kenneth Slepyan, *Stalin's Guerrillas: Soviet Partisans in World War II* (Lawrence, KS: University Press of Kansas, 2006).

102 A point emphasised by one of the historians for the official history of the US Army in the Second World War on the value of the French resistance in the Normandy invasion. See Gordon Harrison, *Cross Channel Attack: The United States Army in World War II* (Washington, DC: US Army Center of Military History, 1989), p. 207.

103 The text of the speech is available online through a number of websites, including http://coombs.anu.edu.au/~vern/van_kien/declar.html and www.fordham.edu/halsall/mod/1945vietnam.html.

104 For details see Martin Windrow, *The Last Valley* (London: Weidenfeld & Nicolson, 2004), and Bernard Fall, *Hell in a Very Small Place: The Siege of Dien Bien Phu* (Philadelphia, PA: Lippencott, 1967), especially pp. 415–25.

105 A conclusion reached by Thomas Marks in *Maoist Insurgency since Vietnam* (London: Frank Cass, 1996), pp. 285–89.

106 Menachim Begin, *The Revolt: The Story of the Irgun*, trans. Samuel Katz, 7th edn (Jerusalem: Steinmatzky, 1977), pp. 212–37; 283–90.

107 Alistair Horne, *A Savage War of Peace: Algeria, 1954–1962* (New York: Penguin, 1985), pp. 245–7.

108 Brian Loveman and Thomas Davies, Jr., *Che Guevara: Guerrilla Warfare*, 3rd edn (Lanham, MD: SR Books, 2004), pp. 52–5.

109 Regis Debray, *Revolution in the Revolution? Armed Struggle and Political Struggle in Latin America* (London: Pelican, 1698), pp. 22–5.

110 Carlos Marighella, 'Minimanual of the Urban Guerrilla' (n.p., 1969). Available online at www.baader-meinhof.com/students/resources/print/minimanual/manualtext.html.

111 Carlos Marighella, *For the Liberation of Brazil*, trans. John Butt and Rosemary Sheed (Harmondsworth: Penguin, 1971), pp. 49–50.

112 Loveman and Davies, *Che Guevara*, p. 51.

113 The year 1960 marked the end of the Malayan Emergency. That same year, Frank Kitson published his account of the defeat of the Mau-Mau in Kenya: *Gangs and Counter-Gangs* (London: Barrie and Rockliff, 1960). French forces left Algeria in 1962, while 1973 marked the withdrawal of US forces from Vietnam.

114 Works not subsequently cited are Frank Kitson, *Low Intensity Operations: Subversion, Insurgency, Peace-Keeping* (London: Faber and Faber, 1971); Roger Trinquier, *Modern Warfare: A French View of Counterinsurgency* (New York: Praeger, 1964); Napoleon Valeriano and Charles Bohannan, *Counter-Guerrilla*

Operations: The Philippine Experience (New York: Praeger, 1962); and Edward Lansdale, *In the Midst of Wars: An American's Mission to Southeast Asia* (New York: Harper and Row, 1972).

115 See for example the list of participants at a symposium hosted by RAND in 1962. The report from the symposium has recently been reissued. See Stephen Hosmer and Sibylle Crane, *Counterinsurgency: A Symposium, April 16–20, 1962*, R412-1-ARPA (Santa Monica, CA: RAND, 2006), available online at www.rand.org/pubs/reports/2006/R412-1.pdf.

116 David Galula, *Counterinsurgency Warfare: Theory and Practice* (New York: Praeger, 1964). Galula's work for RAND was classified and remained forgotten until it was republished in 2006: *Pacification in Algeria, 1956–1958*, MG-478-1 (Santa Monica, CA: RAND, 2006).

117 Thompson's most noteworthy published works include *Defeating Communist Insurgency: Experiences in Malaya and Vietnam* (London: Chatto and Windus, 1966) and *Revolutionary Warfare in World Strategy, 1945–1969* (New York: Taplinger, 1970). The subtitle of Thompson's autobiography gives some idea of his sense of self-worth: *Make for the Hills: The Autobiography of the World's Leading Counterinsurgency Expert* (London: Leo Cooper, 1989).

118 The exceptions occurred in, but were specific to, the conflict in Malaya: *Despatch 5, Intelligence Summary: Lessons of the Malayan Emergency* and *The Conduct of Anti-Terrorist Operations, Malaya*, or ATOM. A summary of the development of these documents and their contents is contained in Tim Jones, *Postwar Counterinsurgency and the SAS, 1945–1952: A Special Kind of War* (London: Frank Cass, 2001), pp. 134–7.

119 Galula, *Pacification in Algeria*, pp. 64–8.

120 Headquarters, United States Marine Corps, *Small Wars Manual* (Washington, DC: Government Printing Office, 1940). Available online at www.smallwars.quantico.usmc.mil/sw_manual.asp. For details on the development of Marine Corps irregular warfare doctrine, see Keith Bickel, *Mars Learning: The Marine Corps' Development of Small Wars Doctrine, 1915–1940* (Boulder, CO: Westview Press, 2001).

121 HQ, USMC, *Small Wars Manual*, Ch. 9, 11–14.

122 Gray's assessment of the American way of war is both keenly insightful and disheartening at the same time. See Colin Gray, *Irregular Enemies and the Essence of Strategy: Can the American Way of War Adapt?* (Carlisle Barracks, PA: Strategic Studies Institute, 2006), pp. 30–49.

123 Ferret Force, the Malayan Scouts and 22 SAS Regiment are discussed in Alan Hoe and Eric Morris, *Re-enter the SAS: The Special Air Service and the Malayan Emergency* (London: Leo Cooper, 1994).

124 For details, see Howard Simpson, *Dien Bien Phu: The Epic Battle America Forgot* (Washington, DC: Brassey's, 1994), pp. 170–1, and Roger Trinquier, *Les Maquis d'Indochine: Les missions spéciales du service action* (Paris: Albatros, 1976).

125 An excellent assessment of the establishment of and problems with Jungle Jim is the essay by Edward Westermann which received an honorable

mention in the 2005–6 Cold War Essay Contest held at the Virginia Military Institute. See Westermann, 'Relegated to the Backseat: Farm Gate and the Failure of the Air Advisory Effort in South Vietnam, 1961–1963', in Donald Stoker, ed., *Military Advising and Assistance: From Mercenaries to Privatization, 1815–2007* (London: Routledge, 2007). For a longer view of Air Force preparations to conduct support to host nations, see Richard D. Newton, *Reinventing the Wheel: Structuring Air Forces for Foreign Internal Defense*, CADRE Report AU-ARI-CPSS-91-1 (Maxwell AFB, AL: Air University Press, August 1991).

126 A problem discussed in depth in James Kiras, *Special Operations and Strategy: From World War II to the War on Terrorism* (London: Routledge, 2006), pp. 58–82.

127 Anthony James Joes, for example, suggests a much more comprehensive list of principles and practices in a phased plan in *Resisting Rebellion: The History and Politics of Counterinsurgency* (Lexington, KY: University Press of Kentucky, 2004), pp. 232–55.

128 Such works include John Cann, *Counterinsurgency in Africa: The Portuguese Way of War, 1961–1974* (Westport, CT: Greenwood, 1997), Jose Bracamonte and David Spencer, *Strategy and Tactics of the Salvadoran FMLN Guerrillas: Last Battle of the Cold War, Blueprint for Future Conflicts* (Westport, CT: Greenwood, 1995) and David Spencer, *From Vietnam to El Salvador: The Saga of the FMLN Sappers and Other Guerrilla Special Forces in Latin America* (Westport, CT: Greenwood, 1996).

129 Peerless works on the subject remain Richard Neustadt and Ernest May, *Thinking in Time: The Uses of History for Decision Makers* (New York: The Free Press, 1988), and Yuen Foong Khong, *Analogies at War: Korea, Munich, Dien Bien Phu, and the Vietnam Decisions of 1965* (Princeton, NJ: Princeton University Press, 1992).

130 This obvious, but often overlooked, point is the basis of David Kilcullen's concern in 'Counter-Insurgency *Redux*', 111–30.

131 See for example David Anderson, *Histories of the Hanged: The Dirty War in Kenya and the End of Empire* (New York: Norton, 2005) and Caroline Elkins, *Imperial Reckoning: The Untold Story of Britain's Gulag in Kenya* (New York: Henry Holt, 2004).

132 Steven Metz's *Rethinking Insurgency* is a plea for the US military to look at counter-insurgency as a much more complicated phenomenon than current doctrine, planning and operations assume. See Metz, *Rethinking Insurgency*, pp. 12–42.

133 See Harry Summers, Jr.'s *On Strategy: The Vietnam War in Context*, 4th printing (Carlisle Barracks, PA: Strategic Studies Institute, 1983), p. 75.

134 A concise summary of the rivalries and religious dimension of the conflict is contained in Abder-Rahmane Derradji, *The Algerian Guerrilla Campaign: Strategy and Tactics* (Lampeter: The Edwin Mellen Press, 1997), pp. 213–17. For an inside account of these rivalries and the subsequent purges that took place, see Rémy Madoui, *J'ai été fellagha, officier et déserteur: Biographie du FLN à l'OAS* (Paris: Seuil, 1994), pp. 117–92.

135 Dale Walton does an exceptional job of outlining the strategic roads open to, but ultimately left unchosen by, US decision-makers during the Vietnam War in *The Myth of Inevitable U.S. Defeat in Vietnam* (London: Frank Cass, 2002), pp. 151–8.

136 Based on author's conversations with senior US defence policy-makers from 2004 to 2005. A recent published discussion of Phoenix is contained in Kurt M. Campbell and Richard Weitz, *Non-Military Strategies for Countering Islamist Terrorism: Lessons Learned from Past Counterinsurgencies*, Princeton Project on National Security Working Paper (Princeton, NJ: Woodrow Wilson Center, n.d.), pp. 19–20.

137 An assumption challenged by Metz in *Rethinking Insurgency*, pp. 42–9.

138 The basic details of how Vietnamisation was implemented are contained in James Collins, Jr., *The Development and Training of the South Vietnamese Army, 1950–1972*, Vietnam Studies (Washington, DC: Department of the Army, 1975), pp. 85–122. A comprehensive assessment of the rationale for the policy and its implementation can be found in James Willbanks, *Abandoning Vietnam: How America Left and South Vietnam Lost its War* (Lawrence, KS: University Press of Kansas, 2004).

139 Summers, *On Strategy*, p. 1.

140 Bill Kissane, *The Politics of the Irish Civil War* (Oxford: Oxford University Press, 2005), p. 1.

141 In the absence of a specific agreement to end hostilities, scholars choose significant events that they interpret as ending the conflict. There can be scholarly disagreement over such events and dates. Kissane chooses 30 April 1923, the ceasefire date between Republicans and supporters of the Irish Free State. Other scholars suggest that the Irish Civil War ended with Eamon de Valera's speech to Republican holdouts to lay down their arms on 24 May. See Kissane, *The Politics of the Irish Civil War*, p. 93; J. Bowyer Bell, *The Secret Army: The IRA, 1916–1979* (Cambridge, MA: MIT Press, 1980), p. 38.

142 Clausewitz, *On War*, p. 89.

143 Loveman and Davies, *Che Guevara*, pp. 52; 55.

144 Sayyid Qutb, *Milestones* (New Delhi: Islamic Book Service, 2002), p. 21.

145 *Ibid.*

146 *Ibid.*, p. 76.

147 *Ibid.*, p. 11.

148 The failure of senior US policy-makers to anticipate reactions by Somali warlords to the humanitarian relief mission is contained in Jonathon Stevenson, *Losing Mogadishu: Testing U.S. Policy in Somalia* (Annapolis, MD: Naval Institute Press, 1993).

149 Gil Merom argues that democracies lose small wars owing to a gap in credibility that grows over time between governments unable to win without resorting to brutality and the middle class which bears most of the costs of the war. It should be noted that Merom's three case studies focus on

democracies with conscripted armies. See Merom, *How Democracies Lose Small Wars*, pp. 33–60.

150   See for example Mao, *On Guerrilla Warfare*, pp. 21; 87, and Loveman and Davies, *Che Guevara*, pp. 60–1. It should be noted that Mao does not refer to terrorism specifically, but his statements on how to deal with traitors, collaborators and other counter-revolutionary elements, couched in euphemisms, suggest his intent.

151   Derradji, *The Algerian Guerrilla Campaign*, p. 161.

152   Derradji suggests that Rahmane first developed the idea for an urban terror campaign, a claim supported by Alistair Horne. Paul Aussaresses suggests that Larbi Ben M'Hidi, who received orders from Rahmane, saw the bombing campaign as a method of coercing the French to leave. *Ibid.*; Horne, *A Savage War of Peace*, p. 184; Aussaresses, *The Battle of the Casbah: Terrorism and Counter-Terrorism in Algeria, 1955–1957* (New York: Enigma, 2002), p. 65.

153   Lawrence Wright suggests that Zawahiri, far from being a subordinate to bin Laden, formed one-half of the whole which allowed the formation of al-Qaeda: 'Each man filled a need in the other. Zawahiri wanted money and contacts, which bin Laden had in abundance. Bin Laden, an idealist given to causes, sought direction; Zawahiri, a seasoned propagandist, supplied it.' See Lawrence Wright, *The Looming Tower: Al-Qaeda and the Road to 9/11* (New York: Knopf, 2006), p. 127.

154   See for example translations of excerpts from Ayman al-Zawahiri's *Knights under the Prophet's Banner* printed in *Al-Sharq al-Awsat*. 'Al-Sharq Al-Awsat Publishes Extracts from Al-Jihad Leader Al-Zawahiri's New Book', trans. and publ. the Foreign Broadcast Information Service, Version 2, GMP20020108000197 (2 December 2001): 72–5.

155   I owe an intellectual debt to Bard O'Neill, whose succinct analysis of the problems associated with insurgent goals remains unsurpassed. He identifies five problems: changing goals, conflicting goals, misleading rhetoric, ambiguous goals, and confusion of ultimate and intermediate goals. See O'Neill, *Insurgency and Terrorism*, pp. 29–31.

156   See for example the extensive and selective quotations from the Qur'an and radical interpretations of it in bin Laden's 1996 fatwa, published by the al-Islah newspaper in London on 2 September 1996, entitled 'Declaration of War against the Americans Occupying the Land of the Two Holy Places'. The translated text is available from numerous online sources, including www.pbs.org/newshour/terrorism/international/fatwa_1996.html.

157   See *ibid.* and 'Jihad against Jews and Crusaders' first published in *al-Quds al-Arabi* in London on 28 February 1998 and translated and available at www.fas.org/irp/world/para/docs/980223-fatwa.htm.

158   See 'Bin Laden: Goal is to Bankrupt the U.S.', CNN.com (1 November 2004), available online at www.cnn.com/2004/WORLD/meast/11/01/binladen.tape/.

159 See 'Jihad against Jews and Crusaders and Text: 'Bin Laden Tape, *BBC News* (19 January 2006), available online at news.bbc.co.uk/2/low/middle_east/ 4628932.stm.

160 Andrew Silke, 'Drink, Drugs, and Rock'n'Roll: Financing Loyalist Terrorism in Northern Ireland – Part Two', *Studies in Conflict and Terrorism* 23:2 (April 2000): 107–27.

161 Gabriel Marcella concludes that 'The tenacity with which the FARC fought to preserve its control over the coca production areas in Putumayo department in the fall of 2000 clearly demonstrates that the narcotics–guerrilla nexus is no longer a myth. Estimates run as high as $500 million per year for the amount of money that goes into insurgent coffers from the coca business through extortion and war taxes. This amount, enough to fund a formidable war machine, allowed FARC battalion[*sic*]-sized formations in 1997–98 to inflict serious defeats upon the Colombian army.' *Plan Columbia: The Strategic and Operational Imperatives* (Carlisle Barracks, PA: Strategic Studies Institute, April 2001), pp. 3–4.

162 For an open source listing of Sunni groups in Iraq prior to the bombing, see International Crisis Group, *In Their Own Words: Reading the Iraq Insurgency*, Middle East Report No. 50 (Brussels: International Crisis Group, February 2006), pp. 1–3.

163 The most notorious Sunni sanctuary was Fallujah, which was the object of two major operations in April and November 2004. The first operation, Vigilant Resolve, ended in the premature withdrawal of forces after a negotiated settlement. For details of the second operation, Phantom Fury, see John Ballard, *Fighting for Fallujah: A New Dawn for Iraq* (Westport, CT: Praeger, 2006).

164 The al-Askariya mosque is also known as the 'Tomb of the Two Imams' as it houses the remains of two of the twelve Shi'a Imams, Ali al-Hadi and Hasan al-Askari. According to one report, the perpetrators of the attack took six hours to place charges in selected points throughout the structure to inflict maximum damage. 'TRITON Quick Look Report: IED Attack on the Al Askariya Mosque in Samarra, 22 February 2006' (Faringdon: Hazard Management Solutions, 26 February 2006), p. 4.

165 John Ward Anderson, 'Sunni Insurgents Battle in Baghdad: Residents of Western Neighborhood Join Groups' Fight against Al-Qaeda in Iraq', *Washington Post* (1 June 2007): A11, and John Burns and Alissa Rubins, 'U.S. Arming Sunnis in Iraq to Battle Old Qaeda Allies', *New York Times* online edition (11 June 2007), accessed online at www.nytimes.com/2007/06/ 11/world/middleeast/11iraq.html?ex=1339214400&en=7c69df022224828 e&ei=5090&partner=rssuserland&emc=rss.

166 Marc Sageman, *Understanding Terror Networks* (Philadelphia, PA: University of Pennsylvania Press, 2004), pp. 25–48.

167 Al-Suri is perhaps best known for his 1,600-page manual, the title of which is roughly translated as 'The Call to Global Islamic Resistance'. See Murad

Batal al-Shishani, 'Abu Mus'ab al-Suri and the Third Generation of Salafi-Jihadists', *Terrorism Monitor* 3:16 (11 August 2005): 1–3.

168 Naji, *The Management of Savagery: The Most Critical Stage through which the Umma Will Pass*, trans. William Cants (West Point, NY: Combating Terrorism Center, 2006), p. 21. This document is available online at www.ctc.usma.edu/Management_of_Savagery.pdf.

169 *Ibid.*, pp. 23–36.

170 Carl von Clausewitz, *On War*, trans. J. J. Graham, vol. I (London: Routledge and Kegan Paul, 1956), p. 45.

FURTHER READING

Asprey, Robert, *War in the Shadows*, rev. edn (London: Little, Brown, 1994).
Offers a narrative history of guerrilla warfare and terrorism remarkable in its breadth from ancient times, starting with the Persian empire under the rule of Darius in 531 BC, until 1993.

Byman, Daniel, *Deadly Connections: States that Sponsor Terrorism* (Cambridge: Cambridge University Press, 2005).
A scholarly investigation of how and why states sponsor terrorist groups, and Byman offers a number of useful policy prescriptions to deal with such states.

Galula, David, *Pacification in Algeria, 1956–1958*, MG-478-1 (Santa Monica, CA: RAND, 2006).
Unlike Galula's more famous analysis of what succeeds and fails against insurgents, *Counterinsurgency Warfare*, this recently reprinted monograph provides a battalion-level view of the practical challenges associated with putting counter-insurgency theory into practice. In particular, it offers useful insights into the difficulties of not just controlling a local population, but eliciting their support as well.

Gray, Colin, *Irregular Enemies and the Essence of Strategy: Can the American Way of War Adapt?* (Carlisle Barracks, PA: Strategic Studies Institute, 2006), pp. 30–49.
Gray applies his exceptional powers of analysis in a comprehensive review of the elements that both identify the modern American way of war and contribute to its less-than-stellar strategic performance in more recent irregular wars.

O'Neill, Bard E., *Insurgency and Terrorism: From Revolution to Apocalypse*, rev. edn (Washington, DC: Potomac Books, 2005).
Remains one of the best single-volume analyses of the difference between forms of irregular violence and the factors that shape its character, conduct and response.

Joes, Anthony James, *Resisting Rebellion: The History and Politics of Counterinsurgency* (Lexington, KY: University Press of Kentucky, 2004).
Weaves together historical practice with an analysis of the principles of counter-insurgency over the past two centuries, which culminates in an analysis of how the Vietnam War could have been fought differently (and won).

Kilcullen, David, 'Counter-insurgency *Redux*', *Survival* 48:4 (Winter 2006–7): 111–30.
An article by perhaps the foremost practising intellect on the subject of irregular warfare, this suggests that the well-known principles of counter-insurgency developed after the Second World War need to be understood in the light of changes in the character of modern irregular war.

Kitson, Frank, *Low Intensity Operations: Subversion, Insurgency, Peace-Keeping* (London: Faber and Faber, 1971).
Contains the distilled experience and wisdom of a counter-insurgency warrior who fought in a number of Britain's post-colonial insurgencies, including Kenya. Although some parts of this work are dated, it remains one of the few works that demonstrates the crucial relationship between all levels of interaction in counter-insurgency, from the strategic down to the tactical.

Merari, Ariel, 'Terrorism as a Strategy of Insurgency', *Terrorism and Political Violence* 5:4 (Winter 1993): 213–51.
Extremely useful for the typology of violence that the author develops and for his assertion that terrorism is not merely a tactic of violence, but can form the basis for an approach to violence that has its own strategic direction.

Merom, Gil, *How Democracies Lose Small Wars* (Cambridge: Cambridge University Press, 2003).
Suggests that the character of violence in irregular warfare can contribute to a divergence in opinion between political elites in democracies and those with significant influence who bear the costs of the conflict.

Metz, Steven, *Rethinking Insurgency* (Carlisle Barracks, PA: Strategic Studies Institute, June 2007).
Strikes the same chord as David Kilcullen on the need to look at modern insurgencies in a different light but suggests that they are increasingly complicated for other reasons.

Nagl, John, *Counterinsurgency Lessons from Malaya and Vietnam: Learning to Eat Soup with a Knife* (Westport, CT: Praeger, 2002).
Suggests that organisational culture is the key to understanding how and why institutions such as the British and American Armies adapted differently to the challenges of irregular warfare in Malaya and Vietnam.

Sageman, Marc, *Understanding Terror Networks* (Philadelphia, PA: University of Pennsylvania Press, 2004).
Remains unprecedented for the clarity of analysis and expression of how modern-day Salafist terrorist cells and groups form on the basis of social networking.

Trinquier, Roger, *Modern Warfare: A French View of Counterinsurgency* (New York: Praeger, 1964).
Trinquier wrote this concise monograph following his experiences leading partisan forces in Indochina and combating insurgents and terrorists in Algeria. This work remains influential as the ultimate expression of the pragmatic, practitioner's expression that the means justifies the ends, regardless of the consequences.

CHAPTER 6

WEAPONS OF MASS DESTRUCTION

CONTENTS

KEY THEMES

- Weapons of mass destruction (WMDs) are treated as distinct from 'conventional' weapons, and their stockpiling and use are particularly controversial.
- WMDs are divided into four general types: radiological, biological, chemical and nuclear weapons.
- Although WMDs have rarely been used in combat in recent decades, their existence and proliferation play an important role in shaping the international security environment.
- The battlefield utility of some forms of WMDs, particularly nuclear weapons, is generally very high. However, the military usefulness of most WMDs – particularly radiological and current biological weapons – is questionable. Nonetheless, terrorists might find any form of WMD useful in inciting fear and causing economic and other damage.
- The period from 1945 to the end of the Cold War, the 'First Nuclear Age', was defined by the relations between the two superpowers. We are now in a 'Second Nuclear Age' in which an increasing number of actors possess nuclear weapons.
- Capability and credibility are vital factors in determining the success or failure of a deterrence threat.

While most of the chapters in this book focus chiefly on how warfare is conducted and only address weapons within that context, any discussion of 'weapons of mass destruction' (WMDs) must have a somewhat different focus. This is because these weapons have been placed in a special category, marking the weapons themselves as extraordinary and making their use uniquely controversial. Indeed, the term 'conventional weapons', which is generally applied to virtually all non-weapons of mass destruction, is telling, as it implies that such weapons are 'normal' and thus useable, unlike their WMD counterparts. This focus on the weapon itself is unusual and is in substantial contrast to the attitude towards conventional weapons, which are generally treated more like various tools in a tool chest, some of which are appropriate for particular jobs but not for others, but all of which are ethically acceptable in a general sense, even if many of them cannot ethically be used in every situation.

Any reasonable recounting of the overall WMD 'story', therefore, must address *why* these weapons have not been used in various situations where they would have promised military advantage. This is critically important because, in general, one should expect a weapon likely to yield military advantage to be used in warfare and its use not to be limited or prohibited by international agreement. Indeed, the very notion of prohibition seems slightly bizarre in regard to most conventional weapons. Few individuals would call for tanks, artillery, helicopters or any other 'conventional' weapons systems to be banned globally (although there have been efforts to ban or control the use of land mines, cluster munitions and certain other devices perceived as particularly dangerous to civilians). Instead, it is simply, and almost universally, assumed that for so long as these systems are militarily useful they will be fielded, and when and if they cease to be useful they will be consigned to museums, joining longbows, chariots, bronze cannon and thousands of other outmoded weapons.

There is, however, no question that at least some WMDs continue not only to be potentially useful on the battlefield but also, as the term 'WMD' itself implies, potentially devastating. This raises the interesting question of why limitations have arisen on the use of these weapons. Nor, it should be noted, have these limits simply been legal in character – the legality of the use of nuclear weapons, for instance, is still debated, but a good case could be made that, if used against military targets (particularly ones well removed from substantial civilian populations), their use could be legal, at minimum for those states recognised as 'legitimate' nuclear possessors by the Nuclear Non-Proliferation Treaty (NPT) 1968. However, despite the numerous wars fought by nuclear-armed states, none have used these weapons in combat since 1945. A major theme of this chapter is to explore why most powers armed with WMDs have shown considerable restraint in the use of such weapons – particularly nuclear arms, the most militarily useful 'class' of WMDs – and whether such restraint can be expected to endure.

Even the term 'weapons of mass destruction' is itself problematic, as it describes a wide variety of weapons, and there is no single, authoritative definition of what constitutes a WMD. However, the term generally is used to describe any and all nuclear, chemical, biological and radiological weapons, contrasting such devices with 'conventional' weapons – which, in essence, are all weapons that are *not* WMDs. Nonetheless, as we shall see, WMDs vary enormously in their characteristics and destructive capabilities.

The term 'WMD' can be deceptive, as the phrase 'mass destruction' evokes images of devastation over a broad area. Some WMDs, certainly, are capable of inflicting such cataclysmic damage – thermonuclear warheads, for example, can have a lethal radius measured in miles, with a large area around 'ground zero' (the point where the warhead is detonated) being utterly destroyed, buildings obliterated, and humans and animals instantaneously killed. However, a canister of mustard gas (a chemical weapon) is also considered a WMD, even though a modest quantity of that gas released on a busy city street would possibly kill no one – although a fair number of people would probably be hospitalised, some perhaps being very seriously injured – and there would be no structural damage to the buildings near the point of release. Similarly, in late 2001, WMDs were used in terrorist attacks in the United States: anthrax toxin (a biological weapon) was mailed to a number of targets, including various media outlets and the Capitol Hill offices of US Senator (and then Senate Majority Leader) Tom Daschle. Five individuals died and numerous others were hospitalised, but no other direct damage was inflicted, although a thorough (and very expensive) cleaning of certain locations through which the anthrax had passed was required. Needless to say, the damage inflicted on the United States by these WMD terrorist attacks was far smaller than that inflicted a short time before in the terrorist attacks of 11 September 2001 (9/11), which involved no WMDs (at least as the term is generally used).

We shall examine, in turn, the four major categories of WMDs, in approximate order of their general tactical utility in warfare between states, beginning with the militarily least useful form of WMD, radiological weapons. Nuclear weapons will receive the most attention, because these devices have profoundly shaped international politics since the end of the Second World War, and they remain the most powerful weapon yet devised by humankind.

Following a general description of the various types of WMDs and how they have been or may be utilised militarily by both state and non-state actors, the chapter will discuss how WMDs differ from conventional weapons, both in terms of perceptions about their use and in how they are employed politically. In regard to the latter, the concept of deterrence, particularly nuclear deterrence, will be explored with an eye to how these weapons have long been 'used without being used'. Following that, the chapter will examine the possible future exploitation of WMDs, particularly in light of what has often been called the Second Nuclear Age, the period since the end of the Cold War, which has seen continuing proliferation and an increasing possibility that nuclear weapons will again appear on the battlefield.

Radiological weapons

Until recently, radiological weapons were by far the least discussed WMD category – indeed, whether they even are a form of WMD is debatable, as many authors omit them altogether, restricting the WMD 'nameplate' to nuclear, biological and chemical weapons. However, they are included here because, particularly since the 9/11 terrorist attacks in the United States, public discussion of radiological weapons has increased greatly, and it has become increasingly common for defence professionals to treat radiological weapons as a form of WMD.

The first thing that one must understand in any discussion of radiological devices is that they are *not* nuclear weapons, even though they do contain radioactive materials. Unfortunately, many press accounts use the phrase 'dirty nukes' to describe radiological weapons – or, even worse, interchangeably to describe both radiological weapons and relatively crude nuclear devices. Actual nuclear weapons use fissile material, such as uranium^{235} or plutonium, to create a nuclear reaction and resulting explosion.

In a radiological weapon, no nuclear explosion occurs. A radiological device is simply a bomb that uses a conventional explosive to scatter radioactive material. This is not necessarily fissile material, which is expensive to produce and extremely difficult for terrorists and similar actors to acquire. More probably, the radioactive matter in question would be something such as cobalt^{60}, which is used for cancer radiotherapy and other legitimate purposes worldwide. Radioactive isotopes have a wide variety of uses in medicine, food irradiation (to kill bacteria) and other industries.

It should be noted that different radioactive substances have enormously varied levels of radioactivity. Even the slightest exposure to very 'hot' – that is, highly radioactive – material can result in fatal radiation poisoning. On the other hand, exposure to low levels of radiation might not adversely affect an individual's health. Indeed, human beings constantly receive small doses of 'background radiation' from their surroundings – sunlight, radioactive elements naturally present in soil and water, and so forth. Depending on the materials used and their quantity, exposure to the nuclear material scattered by a radiological bomb would present a variable health risk. Given that stealing (or otherwise surreptitiously obtaining) and handling extremely radioactive materials is very difficult, while less radioactive (though still quite dangerous) materials are used in medicine and industry throughout the world, often with few safeguards to prevent their theft, it seems most likely that a terrorist group's radiological weapon would present only a limited threat to the population of a targeted city. Exploding a conventional bomb is a far-from-optimal way to scatter radioactive material, and most probably only a small area would be very dangerously contaminated. Depending on the circumstances, the actual number of fatalities directly attributable to a radiological device could be quite small, even zero, although those close to the explosion would be likely to face long-term health risks, such as a greatly increased threat of developing cancer. However, tiny quantities of radioactive material would be spread over a much wider area, and that raises a potentially even more serious prospect: public panic and the probably long-term economic consequences related to cleaning up contaminated areas.

It is all too easy to imagine chaos in one of the world's major metropolitan areas if a radiological device were exploded in the heart of any of them. Most people, be they residents of London, New York, Moscow, Shanghai, São Paulo or any other great city, have little or no knowledge of radiation poisoning and would find it difficult calmly and accurately to assess the risk that they and their loved ones faced, especially in an environment in which

Figure 6.1 US Navy sailors during an exercise in which yellow smoke was used to simulate exposure to chemical, biological or radiological weapons.

they would be receiving very incomplete, and no doubt often inaccurate, information from panicky media reports. The number of fatal injuries occurring in the resulting mass exodus from the city would probably be enormously greater than the number of individuals directly killed by the bomb blast itself. Later, that community and the country to which it belonged would be faced with very difficult long-term economic and political questions. Some residents would never be willing to return, while others would demand a clean-up so comprehensive that its cost would be exorbitant, much of the city having to be abandoned for several years while it was on-going. The long-term local, and even national, economic repercussions might be severe, the direct and indirect costs mounting into the trillions, and it is even possible that a wide section of the victimised city would simply be abandoned, as prohibitive clean-up costs and public fear made reconstruction problems irresolvable.

This grim scenario illustrates a key characteristic of radiological weapons: they are militarily of very little use but, in the hands of terrorists, might present great dangers. During the Cold War, the United States and the Soviet Union showed little interest in radiological weapons; this was essentially because there was no military purpose that these weapons might serve that could not be better performed by nuclear weapons. Unlike in a nuclear attack, few enemy troops would be immediately killed or incapacitated by a radiological weapon, even if many of them would face long-term health risks. Moreover, if one's own troops were subsequently to operate in the polluted area, they also could face long-term health risks (see figure 6.1).

Today, no state is known to maintain a radiological arsenal. Thus, there has been little in the way of international efforts to create and implement treaties banning these weapons: there is little point in creating complex international agreements to prevent the stockpiling of weapons that states have no interest in possessing. However, terrorists might find such weapons very useful for furthering their goal of inflicting political and economic damage on a targeted society. Given their simple design and the very real possibility that a terrorist group would be able to acquire radioactive material suitable for use in such a device, it is entirely possible that at some point in the future terrorists will mount a radiological attack on an urban area somewhere in the world.

Biological weapons (BWs)

As noted above, biological warfare has been practised for thousands of years. However, the use of modern biological weapons (BWs) has been very limited. The most important attempt to practise biological warfare was Japan's in the Second World War, when it was chiefly aimed at the Chinese civilian population. The most notable efforts were those of the infamous Unit 731, based in Manchuria. Unit 731 conducted horrific experiments on human test subjects and devised a number of means to spread disease through the Chinese population, such as the release of fleas infected with bubonic plague.

In essence, BWs include a living pathogen of some type – a virus, for example – or a toxin produced by living organisms (toxins invented by humans are generally treated as chemical weapons). Weapons including a living pathogen tend to be more difficult to store and deliver than toxins are, because measures must be taken to ensure that the pathogen does not die before its intended target is exposed to it. In any event, the robustness of the agent is very important: a living virus that will die very quickly when exposed to sunlight, for example, is likely to have little utility as a BW.

Another important characteristic of a BW agent is infectivity. An actor using BWs would generally want a very tiny quantity of an agent in order to be capable of infecting individuals; the smaller the amount of agent required to infect an individual, the higher its infectivity. Closely related to this is pathogenicity, which relates to the percentage of individuals who will actually manifest the symptoms of a disease to which they have been exposed. A BW user would desire very high pathogenicity, so that the overwhelming majority of affected individuals would manifest disease symptoms after a BW attack. Similarly critical is virulence – in this context, essentially the severity of a particular disease. A BW designer would generally desire great virulence, although, in some cases, he or she might not want the agent actually to kill exposed individuals, preferring instead that they be disabled for a time. However, a BW that caused mild symptoms, such as those of the common cold, would be of little use, because even if the agent had high infectivity and pathogenicity, its virulence would be too low: individuals would be able to carry on with their military or other duties despite being ill.

The incubation period of a particular disease is another key characteristic of a BW. Generally speaking, in military operations a shorter incubation period is more desirable, as one would wish to disable or kill enemy troops as quickly as possible. A terrorist group, however, might find a longer incubation period desirable, as this might allow a communicable disease to spread far, infecting a great number of people, before public health authorities became aware of its existence.

Effective delivery of BWs presents many challenges. For instance, placing a BW agent on a ballistic missile may result in the destruction of most of the agent when the missile's warhead strikes its target. Moreover, a biological agent must generally be dispersed over a wide area if it is to be used effectively. Again, placement of a large quantity of an agent in a cruise or ballistic missile warhead may not be an effective way in which to spread the agent, as this will contaminate only a relatively small area, and much of the agent will be destroyed when the missile hits its target. Similar problems confront efforts to place a biological agent in an artillery shell. In general, the most effective way to deliver biological agents is in the form of an aerosol (for a liquid) or a dust cloud (for a solid). Under the conditions of a military operation, delivering a BW in this fashion would be difficult, as the targeted troops would of course attempt to destroy the slow-moving aircraft that was spraying the agent; also, the targeted troops might possess protective gear that would guard them against exposure to the agent. The civilian residents of a city at peace, on the other hand, might be much more vulnerable to this technique.

BWs can have targets other than humans. In fact, in nature many of the illnesses caused by BWs primarily afflict animals, not humans, and biological warfare aimed at an enemy's animals is possible. Notably, Germany attempted this in the First World War, seeking to infect Allied draft animals with anthrax and glanders. Today's modern armies obviously do not rely on draft animals for transport, but some experts have expressed concern about a possible terrorist attack intended to inflict economic damage by causing an epidemic among animals raised for food. Also, BWs can target plants, and a state could attempt to destroy its enemy's food supply by spreading such diseases as wheat blast or rice blast among crops. Indeed, when it maintained an active BW programme, the United States developed considerable expertise in this area and maintained a significant anti-crop biological arsenal (although it was never actually used).

As noted above, not all BWs have to be meant to kill: because such weapons cause illness, a user may match the agent used to the effects desired and, for one reason or another, may not desire that targeted individuals actually die as a result of the biological attack. One could develop a biological agent intended to cause temporary incapacitation, but not death. For example, Q fever, a highly infectious, but generally not fatal, illness can be used in BWs. However, *all* BWs intended for use against humans are banned by the Biological Weapons Convention (BWC), which was opened for signature in April 1972; non-lethality is irrelevant to legality under the convention. Similarly, the use of non-lethal chemical agents in warfare is banned under the Chemical Weapons Convention (CWC), which was opened for signature in January 1993. (This creates some interesting ethical questions: one may ask whether it is ethically reasonable that biological and chemical weapons that have temporary incapacitating, but not generally fatal, effects are banned. After all, the use of such agents in a military operation could decrease the number of deaths and debilitating wounds suffered by combatants, which would generally be considered to be ethically desirable.)

In any case, most offensive BW research over the years has been aimed at the development of lethal agents. Indeed, high lethality is generally considered a critical characteristic of BWs. It is, however, very easy to exaggerate the potential effectiveness of these weapons. This is because tiny quantities of most such substances are fatal. Thus, one often sees statistics indicating that a small quantity of a given BW could kill the entire population of the earth. While, in an absolute sense, such a statement might be true, it also assumes the effective delivery of that agent to every person on earth – a practical impossibility, of course.

Conversely, one should not forget that BWs are indiscriminate: when actually used in military operations, the user must be careful to ensure that his own troops are not placed in danger. Depending on the weapon, this may require injections of a protective vaccine, and such vaccines – the anthrax and smallpox vaccines, for example – often have a non-negligible rate of serious side-effects. Worse still, there may be no effective vaccine for a given disease, which would lead most potential BW users (except perhaps terrorists) to regard that disease as one unfit for use in biological warfare.

BWs and terrorism

Not all BWs facilitate the spread of communicable diseases – indeed, most do not. Biological agents such as the anthrax and botulinum toxins do not cause diseases that are typically spread by personal contact. Thus, an outbreak of disease is inherently limited. From a military standpoint, this may be highly desirable, as it ensures that no uncontrollable pandemic will occur that might affect the population of one's own state. However, there are biological agents that do spread communicable diseases, including Q fever, bubonic plague and smallpox.

Smallpox has received particular attention in the United States, where there has been great concern about the possibility that a terrorist group might obtain samples of the smallpox virus and undertake a bioterrorist

Figure 6.2 Italian firefighters participating in a WMD exercise. They are standing near a container suspected of carrying WMDs.

attack intended to create a mass epidemic. In the simplest scenarios, a terrorist group with access to a virus could simply infect a number of 'suicide bioterrorists' with the virus and use them to spread the disease. Because there is a considerable time (typically weeks) between the point at which a human becomes infectious and when he or she is immobilised by the disease, the terrorist volunteers would have ample time to travel on airliners, wander through busy shopping malls and undertake other activities that would bring them into close contact with others who might then be infected and, in the period before they in turn become symptomatic, unwittingly infect others. How well such a scheme – or a more sophisticated one – might work is much debated, but it could arguably cause a devastating multicountry smallpox outbreak: unless treated promptly, smallpox has a high rate of lethality.

Decades ago, Americans and great numbers of other people worldwide were routinely inoculated against smallpox, but as the disease was conquered the decision was made to cease routine inoculation, which does create serious (even lethal) side-effects in a small percentage of patients. In theory, two institutions – the US Center for Disease Control and Prevention and Russia's Vector State Research Centre of Virology and Biotechnology – hold the only known samples of the smallpox virus anywhere in the world, but there are suspicions that there may be other, 'outlaw' stocks of smallpox. Some observers have argued that the danger of terrorists obtaining access to the smallpox virus is sufficiently great that routine smallpox inoculation should be reintroduced, while others, emphasising the known negative effects of smallpox vaccine in some patients, argue that 'smallpox terror' is too unlikely to justify the human and financial costs of mass inoculation.

The debate in the United States over whether routine smallpox inoculation should be reintroduced is only one example of a larger problem related to BWs, particularly those that spread communicable diseases: how countries should prepare for the possibility of BW terrorism. A number of factors complicate such discussions. First, there has never been a truly large-scale BW terrorist attack using a readily communicable agent, so even experts rely on scenarios of uncertain accuracy. For example, depending on one's assumptions, the smallpox scenario cited above might result in a few dozen fatalities – or, at the opposite extreme, tens of millions of deaths might occur. A great number of variables would affect the seriousness of the outbreak: how competent the suicide bioterrorists were at spreading the disease; when and under what circumstances public health authorities became aware that a smallpox outbreak was occurring; how effective the procedures are for quarantining infected persons and vaccinating vulnerable populations; and so forth.

Obviously, no one knows with certainty where a future bioterrorist attack will occur or which agent will be used in the attack. Yet, despite the myriad unknowns, if they are to be prepared properly for biological terrorism, governments must decide long before an attack how much money and effort they will devote to preparing for a bioterrorist attack, and how they are going to spend those resources. Preparations concerning public health infrastructure, stockpiling of vaccines and which diseases will be routinely vaccinated against, and many others, are made in the hope that they will prove to be adequate in the event that a bioterrorist attack does occur.

The way in which BWs are produced makes it possible for terrorists or 'rogue' states to create fairly substantial quantities of BW agent secretly and at minimal cost. A BW laboratory is equipped similarly to a legitimate medical research facility and may do many of the same things – growing cultures in Petri dishes, for example. Moreover, access to knowledge relevant to the creation of BWs is not controllable: the basic principles of BW creation are derived from biology and medicine, and every country with a sizeable population contains a substantial number of individuals who possess the general intellectual tools necessary to create BWs. Given these facts, a knowledgeable terrorist could operate a small-scale BW laboratory literally in his or her apartment, while a state could run a much larger facility in a warehouse. Given the practical impossibility of controlling access to basic medical equipment, BW research by terrorists, much less by states, is not preventable, although one might succeed in controlling access to many of the most dangerous pathogens, the best example of this perhaps being the very tight control over access to the smallpox virus noted above.

While it is fairly simple to create crude BWs, however, such weapons might well be lacking in the characteristics necessary to make them highly effective. Ricin, for instance, is a highly lethal toxin readily derived from castor beans, which are quite easily obtained, and in 2003 British police uncovered an alleged plot by a number of Muslim men of North African origin to use ricin as a terror weapon (only one individual, however, was subsequently convicted of planning to spread ricin). Yet delivering ricin in a fashion that would kill large numbers of people is considerably more problematic, both because of the difficulty of effective dispersal and the fact that ricin is not very robust. Thus, even if a bioterrorist ricin attack had occurred, it is entirely possible that few Britons would have been killed.

In general, anthrax toxin is far superior to ricin as a BW, although effective delivery requires that it be inhaled into the lungs, as this will result in pulmonary anthrax, which is highly fatal. (Gastrointestinal or cutaneous anthrax result from the entry of the toxin into the digestive system or skin, respectively, and both, particularly the latter, tend to be far less fatal.) This is difficult, as it requires that the toxin be milled to a very specific size optimal for inhalation and lodging in the respiratory system. Moreover, inhalation of the anthrax is likely to occur only while the agent is actually floating in the air; once it is on the ground, it presents only a minimal danger to those around it. Thus, the most effective means to deliver the agent is to spray it over the targeted population using a very complex spraying system that disperses the toxin in a very precise fashion. Also, anti-clumping additives are required to prevent the finely milled anthrax from bunching together – and combining the latter with the anthrax requires considerable sophistication. In any case, even if the terrorists were capable of creating anthrax spores of a high quality, it would be extremely difficult for them (unless they obtained help from a state) to obtain the equipment necessary precisely to mill and spray the toxin, although they might be able to deliver anthrax using a relatively crude spraying system, such as that on a crop duster. Such methods would be of uncertain effectiveness (although any such large-scale BW attack would probably succeed in sowing terror among the targeted population).

When assessing the threat of a BW attack by terrorists, one should consider their level of sophistication and financial resources, the agents that might be used, how those agents might be dispersed, what the incubation time and level of pathogenicity and lethality are for the disease caused by the agent, and whether effective treatments exist for that disease. Potentially most important of all is whether the BW in question causes a communicable disease and what the characteristics of that disease are, as an uncontrolled outbreak of a very dangerous communicable disease could theoretically have worldwide effects and cause many millions of deaths.

BWs and states

This discussion of BWs has mainly focused on their possible use by terrorist groups. However, they do have potential military utility, and although no state today acknowledges possession of them, it is near-certain that a number of states do possess a biological arsenal – although precisely which states may have BWs remains a matter of contention.

Yet the aforementioned problems with effective dispersion of BWs, protection of one's own troops and other issues go far in explaining why BWs have not played a significant role on the modern battlefield. Thus, when President Richard Nixon decided in 1969 unilaterally to renounce US stockpiling and use of BWs, his declaration created relatively little controversy: many American observers of military affairs agreed that there were few, if any, roles in which BWs would be superior to other weapons, particularly nuclear ones, and that therefore there was little purpose in maintaining a large biological arsenal.

Under international pressure because of the US abandonment of BWs, the Soviet Union also announced that it would destroy its own biological stockpile, and both countries eventually acceded to the BWC. The convention has been joined by the great majority of the world's countries, although about two dozen states have not signed it. The BWC bars states from researching or stockpiling BWs for offensive purposes. However, it does not forbid research focused on improving defences against BWs, and thus states may create very small quantities of BWs for research purposes. Some critics have, however, argued that this provision allows states to skirt the BWC's ban on offensive research, as the line between offensive and defensive BW research can be hazy, given that even defensive research may yield knowledge useful to the development of BWs.

Various rogue states, including North Korea, Iran and Syria, for example, are considered to be likely possessors of a BW arsenal, and even such major powers as China and, as noted, Russia (see box 6.1) may possess these weapons. At present, given the difficulties involved and the international opprobrium that would accompany their use, it would seem unlikely that a major power is going to use BWs in warfare. However, the possibility that a rogue state or other relatively small actor might use such a weapon, either against an outside enemy or in an effort to commit genocide against some segment of its own population, should not be dismissed casually.

Although today's BWs may offer their users only limited military advantages, the possibility that they will again be used in combat should not be ignored. The section below on the use of chemical weapons in warfare also addresses many of the issues that a force defending against BWs must confront.

BWs in perspective

Today, interest in BWs appears to be minimal in most of the world's major states, although some of them may maintain secret research programmes.

Box 6.1 Cheating on arms control: the Soviet Union and the Biological Weapons Convention (BWC)

Although the Soviet Union was one of the original signatories to the BWC, Moscow proceeded to break that agreement in spectacular fashion, running an enormous biowarfare industry, costing the equivalent of billions of dollars a year, which produced enormous quantities of BWs. Nevertheless, for decades Moscow was fairly successful in keeping these efforts secret. Many outsiders believed that the Soviet Union was maintaining a BW arsenal, particularly after a strange incident in the town of Sverdlovsk, in which numerous residents died of anthrax poisoning. The Soviets claimed that 'the epidemic was caused by anthrax-contaminated bone meal in livestock feed and the consumption of meat from infected animals'. However, after the fall of the Soviet Union it was confirmed that the deaths were, in fact, the result of an accidental discharge of weaponised anthrax. It was not until Kenneth Alibek (Kanatjan Alibekov), a major figure in the Soviet BW programme, moved to the United States in 1992 and openly discussed Moscow's BW effort that substantial evidence of its size became available publicly. To this day, however, there are significant questions about the programme; particularly troubling is the fact that the Soviet BW programme was clearly very advanced – almost certainly the most sophisticated in the world – and although Moscow claims to have fully disclosed the details of its programme and to have ceased all research into offensive BWs, some critics doubt this and contend that Russian scientists may be continuing research into new and very deadly BWs.

Those states fielding BWs with an apparent willingness to use such weapons in warfare tend to be relatively weak, and merely by maintaining their arsenals they risk the censure of the international community – particularly since most such states have acceded to the BWC and are thus clearly obligated legally not to maintain a biological arsenal. In any case, BWs are obviously a poor substitute on the battlefield for nuclear or even, in most cases, chemical weapons. BWs do, however, appear far more threatening in the context of terrorism, for it is when used against a vulnerable civilian population that these devices are most likely to succeed in inflicting terrible casualties.

The number of fatalities that would occur as a result of a major bioterror attack would vary by several orders of magnitude depending on a variety of variables, including the biological agent used, how the terrorists attempted to spread the agent and how successful they were in doing so, the level of preparedness of public health officials, and so forth. In any case, however, bioterrorism clearly presents a very real threat in the twenty-first century, particularly if one or more states should prove willing to arm terrorists with sophisticated BWs and the means to deliver them effectively.

Box 6.2 'Super-BWs'?

Unfortunately, the world may be on the cusp of a technological revolution that would exponentially increase the military utility and lethality of BWs. The discussion has focused on 'known' BWs – those that have been or almost surely could be created using current technology. However, in recent years there has been an explosion of knowledge in the life sciences. Of particular importance to the current discussion is the rapidly advancing field of genetics (including the first complete mapping of the human genome) and the related rapid development of biotechnology. Increasing knowledge about the human body and how it counters disease promises great advances in medicine over the coming years, but, unfortunately, the on-going biotechnological revolution also creates a very real possibility that BWs far more dangerous than those fielded today may be created. For example, it may be possible to create weapons that cause new and extraordinarily lethal diseases against which there is no current medical defence; some authors have even speculated about the possible creation of 'ethnic bioweapons' tailored to attack only individuals having genetic markers associated with a particular group of humans. Although such grim possibilities are purely speculative at this point, they should be kept in mind when considering the possible future of BWs. In particular, if it clearly became feasible to develop 'super-BWs', powerful states may very well re-examine their decision to dismantle their biological arsenals. Also, of course, if such weapons should ever come into the possession of apocalyptically minded terrorists, either provided by a state sponsor or (much less likely) developed by the terrorists themselves, the results could be truly terrible.

Chemical weapons (CWs)

Chemical weapons, or CWs, are the only form of WMD to be used with some regularity in warfare during the twentieth century. Although the great majority of that century's wars saw no use of CWs, many tons of them were used in the First World War, and they also appeared in a small number of subsequent conflicts.

The Hague Convention of 1899 banned 'the use of projectiles the object of which is the diffusion of asphyxiating or deleterious gases'.[1] However, less than two decades later, in 1915, Germany – seeking a military 'edge' that would allow it to break the tactical deadlock on the Western front – began using chlorine gas; this was quickly followed by CW use by other belligerents. In total, probably fewer than 100,000 troops, the majority of them Russian (poison-gas fatalities on the Western front were actually relatively small), were killed by CWs during the war. However, a much greater number of troops – probably over 1 million – were wounded by them. Interestingly, the survivors of chemical attack included a young Austrian corporal, Adolf Hitler, who was blinded temporarily by mustard gas in 1918.

The horrible effects of the CWs used in the First World War – including death by asphyxiation and, for many survivors, terrible burns, long-term severe lung damage and other debilitating problems – resulted in renewed revulsion for CWs. However, this did not prevent CW use between the world wars. Notably, in the course of its conquest of Abyssinia (modern Ethiopia) in the mid-1930s, the Italian military used considerable quantities of CWs against its opponents, including by aerial bombardment.

Techniques for the delivery of CWs are generally similar to those used for BWs. During the First World War, these included artillery shells and CW projectors (essentially mortars that fired a canister of CWs), and CW artillery shells continue to be stockpiled by some countries. CW-tipped warheads can also be placed on cruise and ballistic missiles. Effective dissemination of a chemical agent using such techniques does, however, present major challenges. When explosives are used to aerosolise and disperse a liquid chemical agent, they tend to destroy much of the agent; moreover, some agents are flammable and will often catch fire (thus destroying the agent) when explosives are used. Aircraft can also be used for the delivery of chemical weapons. For safety and other reasons, many devices for the delivery of CWs are binary. Rather than the agent itself, a binary device – such as an artillery shell or bomb – will contain two or more chemical precursors, which are separated from each other while the weapon is in storage. After the munition is fired, the precursors mix together, creating the deadly chemical agent.

Difficulties in effective dispersion are one of the key disadvantages of both BWs and CWs. As with biological agents, regardless of how CWs are delivered, climatic factors, particularly wind direction and speed, are critical to their effective diffusion. Indeed, on many occasions during the First World War, troops were exposed to chemical agents dispersed by their own side when the wind direction changed, blowing the CW back to their own lines.

During the Second World War, both Axis and Allied forces maintained CW stockpiles and declared their willingness to retaliate in kind against enemy use of such weapons. Yet in the European theatre, both sides refrained from first-use of CW, although Germany did seriously consider CW use against Allied troops. (There was, however, some use of CWs by Japan in China – see p. 299.) Precisely why neither side used CWs in the European theatre is complex and, to some degree, open to debate, but it appears that concerns about the political impact of first-use of CWs and fear of chemical retaliation against one's own troops (and, for Germany in the latter part of the war, fear that such use would result in Allied bombers dropping massive amounts of CWs on German cities) encouraged restraint on both sides. While the Third Reich did not use CWs against Allied soldiers, it did practise another, far more repellent, form of chemical warfare: the use, in such death camps as Auschwitz, of poisonous gas to murder victims of the Holocaust (see p. 309).

Saddam Hussein's Iraq repeatedly used CWs to terrorise civilian populations. In the Iran–Iraq War of 1980–8, Iraq launched missiles armed with CWs against Iranian cities, killing thousands and causing public panic; Iran is alleged to have retaliated with its own chemical attacks on Iraqi forces. In the latter part of that conflict, Saddam's government also used CWs against Iraqi Kurdish civilians, apparently as part of a genocidal campaign against them; thousands of Kurds died as a result.

During the Cold War, the United States and the Soviet Union amassed large CW stockpiles, and both superpowers were prepared to use them in the course of a Third World War, but CWs were decidedly less important in military planning than were nuclear weapons. As with BWs, there were serious questions concerning how great the military utility of these weapons would actually be, especially given the unpredictability of their dispersion and the related possibility that winds would drive them back on one's own troops, and, again like BWs, there were few military missions that CWs could accomplish that might not be better performed by nuclear weapons. In general, however, CWs may be judged as having real potential military utility. Although they also have considerable weaknesses, against a poorly prepared opponent modern CWs may be devastating, combining very high lethality with rapidity of action. This means that CWs are likely to be far more useful on a battlefield than BWs. There are four major classes of CW: choking (or pulmonary), blood, blister and nerve agents.

The first modern CW used in combat, chlorine, was a choking agent, while phosgene – a particularly dangerous choking agent – caused far more fatalities in the First World War than did any other CW. Choking agents cause damage to the lungs, and exposure to phosgene can result in pulmonary oedema – a build-up of fluid in the lungs that can kill an individual. In general, choking agents are regarded as 'outmoded' CWs, but some are perhaps still in the arsenals of a small number of states.

Blood agents prevent the body from utilising oxygen properly, causing suffocation. (The term 'blood agent' is somewhat deceptive, as the agent does not actually poison the blood; rather, the agent is distributed throughout the body by the blood.) Hydrogen cyanide and cyanogen chloride (generally referred to as CK) were first used on the battlefield in the First World War. Moreover, hydrogen cyanide, commonly known by the German trade-name Zyklon B, was used in the Holocaust. Most notably, the agent was used at the enormous Auschwitz camp complex, located near Kraków, Poland. Like the choking agents, blood agents are generally considered obsolescent. However, there are reports indicating that hydrogen cyanide was used by Iraq in the Iran–Iraq War against both Iran and Iraqi Kurds, and by the Syrian government as part of its brutal campaign to put down an uprising by the Muslim Brotherhood, an Islamist group, in the city of Hama.

Blister agents, as the name implies, have terrible effects on human skin, with exposure causing blistering and burns; if inhaled, they damage the human respiratory system. Of the blister agents, mustard is by far the best-known, and, although it caused relatively few fatalities in the First World War, it was perhaps the most feared of the CWs used in that conflict because of the excruciatingly painful wounds that it inflicted on victims. Several countries probably have CW arsenals that include blister agents.

Nerve agents are, generally speaking, the most advanced of today's CWs. These weapons attack the human nervous system, causing rapid death unless the victim receives an antidote, such as atropine. The best-known classes of nerve agent are the G- and V-series. The first of the G-series agents, GA (more commonly referred to as tabun), was developed by German scientists in 1936, and the last of them, GF (cyclosarin), was first synthesised in 1949. However, G-series agents continue to be regarded as highly lethal modern CWs. The even more advanced V-series agents were invented somewhat later, the first and best-known of them, VX, being developed by the United Kingdom in 1952.

Later still, the Soviet Union secretly developed the Novichok nerve agents in the 1980s and early 1990s; the existence of these weapons was not publicly known until 1992, when the programme was exposed in the Russian media. Interestingly, Russia had not previously informed the United States of the existence of the Novichok agents, despite the existence of a 1989 agreement between the two countries, known as the Wyoming Memorandum of Understanding (MOU), to share information of their respective CW programmes. Moreover, a Russian scientist who 'blew the whistle' on the program, Vil Mirzayanov, was subsequently prosecuted for releasing state secrets, although charges against him were eventually dropped.

It should be noted that, as with BWs, not all chemical agents are lethal – some are non-lethal incapacitating agents. Indeed, the most familiar types of CW are riot control agents such as CS, CN and OC, which are commonly known as tear gas, mace and pepper spray respectively. The CWC effectively bans military use of non-lethal CWs, but does not prohibit the use of such agents in domestic policing. These substances are often used to disperse rioters and protesters, as well as to subdue suspects without the use of lethal force. In some countries, riot control agents are also available to individual citizens, who may carry them for self-defence purposes. In addition, non-lethal chemical agents have been created specifically for military use. Of these, the most notable is known by its NATO codename, BZ. This agent was first developed by the United States in the 1960s. BZ has very severe psychological effects which, if untreated, last for several days. These include hallucinations and other mental disturbances broadly similar to those caused by such psychotropic narcotics as LSD.

Military use of CWs

In general, current CWs have greater potential utility on the battlefield than do their biological counterparts. While they present some of the

Box 6.3 Terrorist use of BWs

The agent GB (commonly called sarin) is a particularly well-known nerve agent. In the most noted use of CWs in a terrorist incident to date, the religious group Aum Shinrikyo used sarin in a 1995 attack on the Tokyo subway, killing a dozen people and injuring hundreds more. Five terrorist teams attempted to contaminate a number of subway lines. Each team consisted of two individuals, one of whom sur-reptitiously carried plastic bags of sarin onto a subway train and proceeded to punc-ture the bags with an umbrella tip and exit the train at a prearranged station; the other team member acted as a getaway driver. Sarin is an extremely dangerous agent, and the attack on the Tokyo subway system could have been truly devastat-ing, with hundreds, or even thousands, of deaths. Fortunately, however, the sarin used was of low quality and the means by which it was disseminated very ineffi-cient; the number of serious injuries and fatalities was thus minimised.

The Tokyo subway attack was not, however, the only use of a CW by terrorists. In 2007, for example, Iraqi insurgents began to use chlorine gas in terrorist actions, including suicide attacks. Since chlorine has many legitimate uses (such as in sewage treatment), it is a readily available chemical. For the reasons noted above, chlorine gas is not generally considered a particularly useful weapon against today's modern militaries, but it has inflicted considerable numbers of fatalities and other casualties on Iraqi civilians.

same difficulties, such as ensuring that the agent is dispersed properly and preventing one's own troops from being exposed to the agent, most CWs very quickly affect the health, and thus military effectiveness, of exposed individuals. While such an agent as sarin can kill within minutes of exposure, the long time between exposure and death usual for BWs allows the exposed individual to continue performing his or her duties without hindrance for days or even weeks. Moreover, given that advanced military forces carefully monitor their troops for exposure to BWs, it is likely that endangered personnel would quickly receive appropriate treat-ment that, depending on the agent, might well prevent the great major-ity of them from even falling ill, much less dying. In addition, as noted above, for numerous biological agents, such as smallpox and yellow fever, vaccines are available that allow individuals to be inoculated before expo-sure.

Protecting troops against CWs may require that they wear bulky and uncomfortable protective gear. Particularly in warm climates and/or when a mask is worn, such equipment impedes the conduct of military opera-tions, making it more difficult for soldiers to perform tasks ranging from fighting to driving to equipment maintenance. The same is true of operat-ing in areas where BWs may be, or have been, used (an environment heavily contaminated with the radioactive by-products of nuclear weapons use presents even greater challenges). However, when protective gear is used properly, it is highly effective in shielding troops from exposure to dangerous agents. As the problem with protective gear illustrates, one of the most important effects of both chemical and biological weapons (CBWs) is the inconvenience caused by them. Such weapons create a hostile physical environment that presents special operational problems and thus slows down military operations. Thus, even if CBWs have little direct effect in terms of casualties, a relatively weak state facing a much stronger opponent may be tempted to use these weapons. Indeed, even merely possessing (or being presumed to possess) them may present very substantial difficulties for the enemy. In both the 1991 Gulf War and the 2003 invasion of Iraq, the United States and its allies took careful measures to protect troops from possible CBWs exposure. It is notable that one of the great difficulties for commanders confronting the possible use of CBWs is determining how much emphasis should be placed on defensive preparations, for the simple reason that time and energy devoted to possible chemical or biological attack could be spent on other important tasks.

Advanced militaries spend an enormous amount of capital on chemical (and biological) defence and devote valuable training time to mastering appropriate defence techniques, and much can be done to hamper the lethality of chemical warfare. For example, detection and early warning devices, as well as masks, suits and other protective gear, can be made available to units, along with training time devoted to the proper use of such equipment; vehicles can be fitted out with air filtration systems that can protect occupants from contaminated air; a naval vessel can be constructed so that there is a capacity to 'pre-wet' the ship so as to prevent agents from settling and make the ship's core a 'citadel' with filtered air (see figure 6.3). Additionally, it should be noted that the sort of defences that protect military forces from chemical and biological attack are also useful in guarding against nuclear contamination. Indeed, one of the few things that the various WMDs do share in common is that they all present unusual and difficult contamination problems that require substantial forethought and planning if they are to be addressed successfully.

As the above indicates, even though CWs do have considerable potential military utility, battlefield defence against such weapons is quite feasible. Like BWs, CWs are potentially most effective not against well-equipped, advanced military forces but as a terror weapon aimed at civilian populations. However, the fact that CWs do not spread a communicable disease strictly limits their ability to inflict casualties. While, at least in theory, an epidemic resulting from BW use could cause hundreds of millions of deaths, only individuals directly exposed to CWs suffer harm. With that said, however, if a large amount were dispersed in a suitable fashion, it is entirely conceivable that a highly lethal agent could inflict tens of thousands of fatalities in a compact and highly populated urban area.

Figure 6.3 The guided-missile destroyer USS *Boxer* performs a test of the ship's counter-measure water wash-down system, which coats the ship with water so as to prevent chemical, biological or radioactive materials from settling.

Nuclear weapons

The first nuclear devices ever developed were the type known as fission weapons, but they were of two different designs. In a simple 'gun-type' design, a conventional explosive is used to drive two separate sub-critical masses together, forming a critical mass and setting off a nuclear chain reaction. The first nuclear weapon used in warfare, 'Little Boy', which was dropped on Hiroshima, Japan, on 6 August 1945, was a gun-type device. The somewhat more complex 'implosion' warhead uses a conventional explosive to implode a sub-critical mass, which looks like a round ball with a hollow core. This design uses fissile material more efficiently than the gun-type device and is therefore 'cleaner': a greater percentage of the fissile material is consumed in the nuclear explosion, leaving less of this highly radioactive matter behind as fallout. The first nuclear weapon ever tested, in the 'Trinity' test on 16 July 1945 at Los Alamos, New Mexico, was an implosion device, as was 'Fat Man' – the second, and heretofore last, nuclear weapon to be used in warfare. The latter weapon was dropped on Nagasaki, Japan, on 9 August 1945.

The period of American 'nuclear monopoly' was brief. Even before the first nuclear test, Soviet intelligence had already infiltrated the highly secret US nuclear development programme, known as the Manhattan Project, and was receiving stolen technical data, which was used to advance the Soviets' own secret nuclear programme. In August 1949, the Soviets exploded their own atomic device.

A few years later, the next major development in nuclear weapons technology occurred when the United States conducted the first test of a thermonuclear weapon, in October 1952. Thermonuclear weapons use an initial fission explosion to create the conditions for nuclear fusion. Thus, thermonuclear weapons are sometimes called fusion or, more accurately, fission-fusion, devices; also, these weapons are often referred to as 'hydrogen bombs' or 'H-bombs'. Theoretically, there is no limit to the potential yield – that is, explosive force – of a thermonuclear warhead.

Nuclear weapons yield is measured in kilotons and megatons. A kiloton is equal to the explosive force of 1,000 tons of TNT (dynamite); a megaton is the equivalent of 1 million tons of TNT. Nuclear weapons have been created with an enormous range of yields. The largest nuclear device ever tested (nicknamed the 'Tsar Bomba' in the West) was a Soviet warhead with a yield of about 50 megatons. By contrast, some tactical nuclear weapons have a yield measured as a fraction of a kiloton. It is important to understand that nuclear weapons can vary enormously not only in yield but in many other essential characteristics. Weapons designers are tasked with creating warheads that can accomplish particular military objectives, and those objectives, in turn, are shaped by the political goals of a state and its military doctrine.

Many authors erroneously refer to nuclear weapons with very high yields, particularly those in the megaton-range, as 'city-busters', assuming that they are designed to be used primarily against civilian targets. In fact, such high-yield weapons are more likely to be used against very 'hard' targets, such as concrete missile silos, command bunkers and similar installations. Urban-industrial targets, by contrast, are 'soft': it requires relatively little explosive pressure to destroy office buildings and similar structures. Such considerations are significant for war planners for numerous reasons, including the fact that the size of a nuclear device is related to its yield (the higher the yield, the more fissile material is required); how many nuclear warheads a missile may carry is related to the weight of those warheads. In general, nuclear warheads have become progressively smaller in yield over the decades as accuracy has improved. This, of course, is because when a warhead lands on, or very close to, a target, that target is exposed to much more explosive force than when the warhead misses by a considerable distance.

Nuclear weapons are often divided into two major categories: tactical nuclear weapons (TNWs) and strategic nuclear weapons. The distinction between the two can be fuzzy, but, in general, it would be accurate to say that TNWs are delivered at shorter ranges and are intended for battlefield use. Possible means of delivery for TNWs include tactical aircraft (such as fighter aeroplanes), artillery shells, short-range missiles, cruise missiles and so forth. The United States and the Soviet Union even developed nuclear-tipped torpedoes and nuclear depth charges for use in naval warfare. The Cold War superpowers each built enormous tactical nuclear arsenals, with thousands of these devices kept in Europe for possible use in a Third World War. Today, the great majority of the American TNWs have been removed from Europe, although a modest number of weapons that could be delivered by tactical aircraft remain. Russia has not revealed in detail the current status of its tactical nuclear arsenal, although it is quite possible that several thousand TNWs remain in European Russia. The overall number of TNWs maintained by Russia and the United States is not limited by arms control treaties between those two countries; rather, existing treaties focus on strategic nuclear weapons.

Strategic nuclear warheads generally have a larger yield and are delivered at long range, using intercontinental ballistic missiles (ICBMs), submarine-launched ballistic missiles (SLBMs) or heavy bombers. These three means of delivery together constitute the classic Cold War triad. The basic logic underlying the triad is that it is desirable for a nuclear state to possess multiple methods of delivering its strategic nuclear warheads, as this helps to ensure that it may do so reliably, particularly if it is the victim of a devastating first strike inflicted by a nuclear-armed enemy. Each of the three 'legs' of the Cold War triad was developed because it possessed specific advantages.

Bombers were the first means used for nuclear delivery. Originally, bombers carried simple, unguided (and thus relatively inaccurate) gravity bombs, such as those dropped on Hiroshima and Nagasaki, but nuclear-armed bombers can now carry advanced weapons systems, such as nuclear-tipped cruise missiles, which contain highly accurate modern guidance systems. Importantly, bombers may be recalled before their mission is completed. Thus, for example, if a state believes that a nuclear attack may be imminent and sends bombers out with the intent of delivering a retaliatory strike, its leaders may cancel the bombing mission if they soon thereafter discover that an attack will not, in fact, occur. Using a ballistic missile, by contrast, is more like firing a pistol: once the trigger is pulled, the bullet cannot be recalled. Moreover, bomber pilots may be tasked with the job of locating and destroying targets whose precise position is not known. Again, this is a mission that cannot be performed by ballistic missiles, which must be targeted to hit a specific point before they are fired.

The great advantage of SLBMs is the difficulty that an enemy is likely to encounter in locating and sinking the ballistic missile submarines (colloquially known in the US Navy as 'boomers') on which they are placed. A single ballistic missile submarine may contain many nuclear warheads. For instance, Ohio class ballistic missile submarines, which are at present the only American submarines tasked with carrying strategic nuclear weapons, carry twenty-four Trident II SLBMs, each of which is designed to carry up to eight warheads. For most of the Cold War, ICBMs enjoyed a great advantage over SLBMs in their accuracy, as measured by circular error probability (CEP), which, in essence, is the size of the circle surrounding a target in which half of the weapons fired at that target may be expected to land. For example, if 50 per cent of the warheads fired at a target fell within 1 mile of it, but 50 per cent landed more than 1 mile from it, then the CEP would be 1 mile. However, the development in recent decades of highly accurate SLBM warheads has greatly eroded this specific advantage. Unlike bombers, which are vulnerable to air defences (such as fighter aircraft), ballistic missiles (either land- or sea-based) and the warheads that they carry are very difficult to destroy, although some countries, particularly the United States, are now developing ballistic missile defences (BMD). Moreover, ballistic missiles can deliver their weapons payload with enormous speed, a particularly important factor in a first strike, as it would leave the enemy with only a matter of minutes to make critical strategic decisions before the warheads struck (see figure 6.4).

During the Cold War, the United States and the Soviet Union developed enormous nuclear arsenals: by the late 1970s, they possessed tens of thousands of tactical and strategic warheads. The sheer destructive power of these arsenals, and the fear that they would actually be used in warfare, resulted in a very strong emphasis throughout the Cold War on deterrence theory.

The nightmare of nuclear terrorism

Particularly since the 9/11 attacks, there has been enormous concern about the possibility that terrorists might acquire nuclear weapons. Certainly, terrorist acquisition of a nuclear device would present a 'nightmare scenario'. As noted above, certain chemical or biological agents could be used

Figure 6.4 A Standard Missile Three (SM-3) is launched from the US Navy Aegis cruiser USS *Lake Erie* in a ballistic missile defence test.

by terrorists to inflict an enormous number of casualties, although there is considerable reason to doubt whether a terrorist group would be able to deliver an agent in a fashion efficient enough to cause truly large numbers of casualties. However, if a nuclear weapon were smuggled into the centre of a major urban area and detonated, it would surely cause a horrifying number of casualties.

Actually acquiring nuclear weapons has, however, thus far proved difficult for terrorists, and it is improbable that even a wealthy and sophisticated terrorist group would actually be able to build a nuclear device, even if it somehow acquired the necessary fissile material (which itself would be no small feat). While the basic principles underlying the construction of a nuclear weapon are well known, actually building such a device would require very advanced engineering that would probably be beyond a terrorist organisation's capabilities. Thus, the more likely route for terrorist nuclear acquisition would be obtaining an already existing nuclear weapon, either by theft or gift.

Ever since the fall of the Soviet Union there have been periodic rumours that Soviet nuclear weapons have 'disappeared', presumably having been stolen by greedy military officers seeking to resell the devices, but these claims have never been confirmed and are probably unfounded. However, it is not impossible that a nuclear weapon might one day be acquired by terrorists. For instance, a particularly worrisome scenario is presented by Pakistan, a state that contains a very substantial number of individuals (including powerful ones) who are sympathetic to al-Qaeda and similar groups. The current Pakistani government is fairly cautious and prudent, but also fragile – and most observers believe that an internal coup or civil war in that country is entirely possible. In that event, the entire Pakistani nuclear arsenal could fall into the hands of Islamist radicals, and the latter might well be inclined to hand over one or more weapons to a terrorist group intent on mass destruction.

It is very difficult to estimate with precision the number of casualties that might be inflicted by a nuclear terrorist attack, as these would vary greatly depending on the explosive yield of the weapon, the layout and population density of the urban area in which it was detonated, wind speed and direction (which is important in calculating the effects of fallout), and many other factors. Certainly, any such attack would be a monstrous event with substantial international political repercussions.

Unacceptable weapons?

Even though WMDs differ radically in their destructive power, they are similar insofar as there is a general sense that the acquisition and use of WMDs is considered particularly controversial. Indeed, the possession, much less the use, of two classes of WMDs, chemical and biological weapons, is banned outright in treaties to which the overwhelming majority of countries are signatories. However, as noted above, not all signatories actually obey their obligations under the Chemical and Biological Weapons Conventions – and this may include such major states as China and Russia.

Similarly, the NPT restricts legal possession of nuclear weapons to just five states: China, Great Britain, France, Russia and the United States. All other signatories to the NPT legally renounce the right to build or possess nuclear weapons. However, some of these signatories, such as Iran, may be attempting to break the treaty's restrictions. Moreover, three countries that have never signed the NPT are known to possess nuclear weapons (India, Pakistan and Israel), while North Korea – which apparently conducted a nuclear test in 2006 and can be presumed to have a nuclear arsenal – is a former party to the treaty but withdrew from it in 2003. Indeed, even though the number of states that actually possess nuclear weapons is small, it should be noted that that group includes roughly half of humanity, including the three most populous states in the world – so, at least by some measures, nuclear possession is hardly unusual.

Why, one might ask, are WMDs regarded as different and their use, presumably, somehow less ethical than the use of conventional weapons – even though, in total, the weapons lumped in the latter category have killed an enormously greater number of human beings than have WMDs? Part of the answer to this question surely lies in the fact that WMDs touch emotional 'triggers' in many observers. For instance, while BWs as we know them today are a comparatively recent innovation, disease and poison have been used in warfare for millennia. For example, poisoning wells by throwing animal or human corpses into them is a very old practice. Yet in many cultures, such practices carry a taint, being seen as cowardly or wicked. There are many reasons this might be so – the indiscriminate fashion in which communicable disease strikes both warriors and non-combatants, the fear engendered by 'invisible killers', and so forth – but, in any case, 'war by disease' has unquestionably had a poor reputation in many times and places, and this very much influences perceptions of BWs.

Chemical, radiological and nuclear weapons are also viewed negatively, but the last of these, unlike its 'cousins', have a decidedly more mixed standing. Although many denounce the very possession of nuclear weapons as immoral, it is also clear that great numbers of people worldwide – both leaders and ordinary citizens – associate these devices with international standing and great power status. Indeed, despite their diplomatic and economic repercussions, the 1998 nuclear tests by India and Pakistan appear to have been popular domestically. Many millions of Indians and Pakistanis saw their country's successful nuclear tests as proof of its technological prowess and status on the world stage – in short, as a source of pride. Similarly, the government of Iran today appears to be moving ever closer to obtaining a nuclear arsenal, and despite threats by the international community of sanctions and other punishment, many Iranians support their government in its quest to become a nuclear weapons state. Clearly, great numbers of people worldwide regard nuclear weapons differently from the way they do chemical, biological or radiological weapons. While there is a general view that nuclear devices are morally problematic in character – and it is obvious that the effects of their use can be horrifying – they are far from universally despised. Rather, this 'absolute weapon',[2] as Bernard Brodie famously dubbed the atomic bomb, is feared and hated for its killing power but, at the same time, is seen as granting a special status in the international community. (If nuclear weapons did not, and simply brought disrepute upon a state, it is difficult to see why Britain and France, neither of which is likely in the foreseeable future to face critical security threats of the sort that can be addressed by nuclear possession, and both of which, in any case, are members of NATO and therefore protected by the American 'nuclear umbrella', do not surrender their small, and very expensive, national arsenals.) The nuclear club is a very exclusive one, even if it is growing.

Despite the disapproving attitude towards CBWs, however, numerous countries clearly see them as offering advantages significant enough to make it worthwhile spending significant sums obtaining and maintaining CBW stockpiles. A particularly notable example is provided by Iraq. As part of the armistice agreement ending the 1991 Gulf War, Iraq agreed to surrender its CBW arsenal (as well as end its effort to obtain nuclear weapons) and submit to UN inspections that would ensure that its WMD stockpile was destroyed and its capability to make further weapons dismantled. For more than a decade thereafter, an elaborate game ensued in which Iraq would sometimes appear to co-operate partially with inspectors but would also endeavour to thwart their efforts and stymie their investigations. Many governments and intelligence agencies worldwide believed that Iraq was secretly maintaining a CBW arsenal, and seizing Saddam Hussein's supposed WMD arsenal was a major motive for the 2003 American-led invasion of Iraq. However, it now appears that Iraq actually did dispose of its CBW arsenal in the months following the end of the 1991 conflict.

Why would Saddam undertake an elaborate hoax to convince outsiders that his country was defying an international agreement – a ruse that encouraged the UN Security Council (UNSC) to maintain economically ruinous sanctions on Iraq and inclined American political leaders to believe that Iraq's dictator was incorrigible and must be overthrown? It now appears that one of his chief motives was his fear of Iran and belief that a CBW arsenal was important to discourage Iranian aggression, as well as possible uprisings by internal enemies. The Iraqi leader apparently hoped to 'bluff' potential internal and external enemies into believing in a non-existent CBW arsenal while not so flagrantly violating the 1991 ceasefire that the UNSC, or a US-organised coalition acting without UNSC authorisation, would invade Iraq. Eventually, of course, Saddam lost his dangerous wager, but the fact that he made it is indicative of how important a leader might believe a CBW arsenal to be.

The Iraqi example highlights a characteristic notable in regard to all forms of WMDs (and, for that matter, conventional weapons): the psychological impact on leaders and populations. The curious mixture of revulsion and pride often felt in regard to nuclear weapons was discussed above, but this is only one aspect of what one might call the psychology of WMD acquisition. States desire particular weapons for their direct military potential (what they would do on the battlefield) but also for what they indirectly promise (which can include factors as varied as their possible deterrence value and the possible positive economic consequences for particular corporations and communities that would accompany acquisition of a given system), as well as for relatively intangible factors, such as prestige or their value as a 'statement' of national greatness. These assorted factors may be of greatly varying importance depending on the weapon under consideration, and every government will weigh them according to its own unique calculus. This highlights the importance of strategic culture.

States have distinct strategic cultures that profoundly shape how they 'do strategy' – culture influences human behaviour generally, including strategic decision-making. Leaders' values and preferred methods for obtaining goals, the preferred national 'style' of warmaking and many other areas are all influenced by culture. Like any other individuals, leaders are shaped by their life experiences, and culture plays an enormous influence in shaping those experiences; humans can strive to be aware of how culture has shaped their views and behaviour, but actually escaping the bonds of culture is impossible.

Strategic culture certainly reflects the general culture of a state's population, including the general interpretation of historical experiences and other shared beliefs that shape public attitudes towards strategy and war, but it is also influenced by the specific life experiences of the individuals who make strategy (and strategic culture can certainly change over time, although how rapidly and profoundly it may do so is debated). Therefore, it is not possible to assess strategic culture simply by looking at the general culture of a country. It is also necessary to study: which classes and regions a state's political and military leaders come from, and their educations; their religious and ideological beliefs, as well as other attitudes (and how they may differ from those of the general population); and many other factors that shape decision-making. Understanding the influence of strategic culture, in turn, can provide valuable insights into why a state might acquire WMDs – and under what circumstances it might use such weapons aggressively.

Clearly, a simple distinction between 'good' and 'bad' weapons is insufficiently nuanced to explain fully why countries acquire, or do not acquire,

WMDs. Given the broad assortment of pressures and threats present in the international security environment, as well as the variety of strategic cultures worldwide, it is hardly surprising that diverse states demonstrate a broad range of attitudes towards WMD acquisition and use.

Deterrence

Deterrence is not a concept unique to the nuclear era; indeed, deterrence has been practised throughout human history. At its core, the concept is a simple one: using threats, explicit or implicit, to prevent a potential foe from doing something undesirable, such as, for example, starting a war over a disputed piece of territory. In order to prevent the 'deterree' from starting a war, the 'deterrer' must convince the deterree that doing so is likely to be unprofitable.

There are two main ways in which the deterring side may do this. First, it may try to impress upon its counterpart that any war that the latter launched to gain the territory would be unsuccessful. This is deterrence by denial: if the deterrence attempt is successful, the deterree believes that its goals would not be achieved, and thus it will not launch a war. Alternatively, the deterrer may attempt to convince the deterree that even if the latter did achieve its goals, it would pay a prohibitive price to do so: it may win the territory, but it would be a victory costing more than it is worth. This is deterrence by punishment. These two forms of deterrence are not mutually exclusive, and, indeed, the most potent deterrence threats generally combine aspects of each. For instance, the deterrer may try to convince its opponent that it would both fail to gain the disputed territory *and* pay a high price – in military, financial and/or other losses – for its failed effort.

The flip side of deterrence is compellence, convincing an opponent to perform an action that he or she believes is not in his or her best interests and, thus, would not agree to except under duress. For example, in the period immediately after 9/11 the United States attempted to convince the Taliban government of Afghanistan to hand over Osama bin Laden, leader of the al-Qaeda terrorist network. Bin Laden had been living in Afghanistan for several years under the protection of that country's Taliban government. Washington warned Taliban leaders that if they did not turn bin Laden over, it would invade Afghanistan and overthrow their regime. In this case, compellance was not successful – the Taliban did not surrender bin Laden. In response, the United States carried out its threat, invading Afghanistan and destroying the Taliban government.

Both deterrence and compellence are forms of coercion. If deterrence or compellence is successful, the deterred or 'compelled' party will shape its behaviour so that it is in accordance with the demands placed upon it. In either case, the state whose behaviour is to be shaped may refuse to co-operate – and in such a case deterrence or compellence has failed. At that point, the would-be coercing power must either carry out its threat – which, in any scenario involving WMDs, carries many dangers, including the possibility (or, depending on what the deterrence or compellance threat was, even the certainty) of catastrophic violence – or 'back down', accepting that it has failed to deter or compel its opponent.

While deterrence has always been a key aspect of international politics and diplomacy, during the Cold War the concept was absolutely critical: particularly in the West, scholars and policy-makers obsessed over how to ensure that neither superpower would make a misstep that would result in a Third World War (see box 6.4). As a result, a sophisticated body of deterrence theory soon developed.

Because nuclear weapons are capable of inflicting overwhelming damage and can be delivered very rapidly, they presented deterrence theorists and policy-makers with new problems. While states had always had to worry about surprise attacks, technology limitations placed constraints on the ability of aggressors to launch speedy and devastating attacks. Moreover, geography provided many states with a substantial degree of protection. However, the ability of nuclear weapons to be delivered by aircraft – and, particularly, ballistic missiles – could make geographic factors almost irrelevant. A nuclear war could be fought, and a state or states utterly destroyed, in an afternoon.

How easy, or difficult, it would be to deter a given country is a matter of conjecture, not an exact science. As noted above, in order for deterrence to work, the deterred party must 'consent' to deterrence – that is to say, it has the option of accepting the possible consequences of its action and of *not* being deterred. Thus, the success of deterrence can never be guaranteed. However, various factors – credibility and capability – are likely to have a great impact on the success of a specific deterrence threat. Credibility greatly affects the likely success of deterrence threats, and it, in turn, is determined largely by the past actions of the would-be deterrer and the perceived appropriateness of the threat to the situation at hand. Thus, a state with a long record of blustering and making idle threats that are never carried through is likely to have much less credibility than one with a reputation for always carrying out threats if the demands that it puts forth are not met.

This highlights one of the severe limitations faced by nuclear powers: the political and military consequences of using nuclear weapons would be so serious that possession of these weapons is relevant only in a very limited set of circumstances. For instance, in 1982 Argentina invaded the Falkland Islands, a British possession claimed by both countries. Britain was a nuclear power, and Argentina had good reason to worry that Britain would defend the islands militarily, although Argentina appears to have greatly underestimated the likelihood that Britain's Thatcher government would do so. But Britain's nuclear status does not appear to have been factored very seriously into either Argentine or British decision-making. Simply put, Argentina,

Box 6.4 The first-strike quandary and the Cuban missile crisis

One of the great difficulties of nuclear strategy is coping with the challenges presented by the possibility of a first strike. Because of the speed with which nuclear war could be fought, there might be no time to mobilise reserve forces, much less build new weapons – states would rely on those which they had available. Thus, there is a natural, and very dangerous, tendency for states in a crisis to wish to 'land the first punch', inflicting devastating damage on the enemy polity and, hopefully, damaging it so severely that it is unable to retaliate effectively. This encourages crisis instability – even if neither side wants war and would prefer that the crisis be resolved peacefully, the threat of a first strike may inspire such fear in one side that it chooses to launch its own first strike, even if it does not wish to be aggressive.

During the Cuban missile crisis of October 1962, many observers feared precisely this outcome. The crisis resulted from the decision of Soviet leader Nikita Khrushchev secretly to deploy nuclear-armed missiles in Cuba, a state ruled by Soviet ally Fidel Castro and located only a short distance from Florida. At the time, the United States enjoyed a very considerable advantage over the Soviet Union both in its number of nuclear weapons and in its ability to deliver them to the soil of the enemy superpower. The Soviets hoped to decrease the US advantage by placing medium-range ballistic missiles in Cuba. Not only would this put missiles within range of key targets on the US East Coast, but, because of the modest distances involved, their warheads would be able to strike Washington DC within a matter of minutes after firing, providing only minimal warning time from launch to impact. Moreover, Khrushchev hoped that once the deployment was publicly announced it would discourage the United States from possibly invading Cuba in the future and overthrowing its Communist government (in the previous year, the United States had sponsored the disastrous Bay of Pigs invasion undertaken by anti-Castro Cuban exiles).

Once it had discovered that the deployment was underway – thanks to intelligence flights over Cuba by US reconnaissance aircraft – the United States considered a number of options, including an invasion of Cuba, but President John F. Kennedy soon decided on the relatively cautious course of confronting the Soviets publicly while blockading Cuba. The crisis continued for about two weeks, Washington and Moscow eventually agreeing to a private compromise arrangement in which the Soviets removed nuclear weapons from Cuba, while Kennedy agreed not to invade Cuba in the future and to remove US nuclear-armed missiles deployed in Turkey.

rightly, assumed that Britain did not consider the Falklands to be worth the enormous diplomatic and other costs that would accompany a nuclear threat, much less the actual use of nuclear weapons. As the Falklands example illustrates, possession of nuclear weapons is not even a reasonably reliable guarantee against military attack in many circumstances.

Capability is a relatively simple concept: a state either has or does not have the ability to carry out a threatened action. In some cases, capability is not at issue, and the would-be deterrer clearly has the ability to inflict a particular punishment, the only question being whether it has the will to do so. Sometimes, however, capability may be questionable. This is particularly notable in regard to second-strike deterrence threats. The purpose of such threats – which played a very large role in Cold War deterrence – is to deter a foe from attempting a nuclear first strike. Essentially, the state threatening a second strike is trying to convince its potential foe that even a very well-organised nuclear first strike would not eliminate its ability to retaliate. Thus, a first strike would be a 'murder-suicide', with the attacked state, even as it was in its death throes, lashing out at its aggressor.

Clearly, such a threat can have a high credibility: a state that had suffered a nuclear strike would wish to take revenge on its enemy. However, whether it could actually do so would depend on many factors. A successful first strike would enormously damage the nuclear arsenal, communications network and other relevant assets of the victim state. Thus, in order to preserve second-strike capability, each of the superpowers spent many billions of dollars during the Cold War building large and diverse arsenals, and highly robust command, control and communications networks, and otherwise seeking to ensure that its peer believed that even the most successful first strike would not preclude devastating retaliation.

Credibility and capability are central to deterrence because of their influence over severity and surety of punishment. Deterrence is, ultimately, based on threatened punishment, and in order to succeed the would-be deterrer must issue a threat that is properly 'balanced'. The punishment threatened must be severe enough to dissuade the other party from an action but not be so severe as to be implausible. Thus, the more centrally a deterring state's interests are threatened – particularly if its population, form of government, territory and other most vital assets are placed in danger – the more severe a punishment may be while still remaining credible. The greater the severity and surety of punishment, the greater the likelihood of deterrence success; if one of these critical factors is missing – the threatened punishment is too minor or it seems unlikely that the threat can be carried out – deterrence can be expected to fail.

As noted above, however, it is the would-be deterree who ultimately casts the deciding vote in whether a deterrence threat will succeed. If a leader is risk-averse and places a high value on the avoidance of punishment, deterrence threats are likely to succeed. If, however, a leader is reckless and places a much higher value on potential gains than on potential losses, successful deterrence is much less likely. Moreover, if a leader simply believes that there is some overriding imperative – religious, political or otherwise – that makes it utterly and totally unacceptable to do as the would-be deterrer wishes, deterrence failure is certain.

In this regard, such rogue states as Iran and North Korea are of particular interest. It is generally assumed, probably rightly, that such powers as the five states acknowledged as 'legitimate' nuclear-armed powers by the NPT – Britain, China, France, Russia and the United States – are relatively cautious and sensitive to deterrence threats and, therefore, are unlikely to take reckless actions that would lead to nuclear conflict. Many observers, however, are not confident that 'Cold War deterrence' would work against all nuclear-armed rogues.

Nuclear conflict in a Cold War context

The phrase 'nuclear war' is often used offhandedly to mean an essentially unlimited conflict: a simple exchange of warheads, with combatants showing no regard for civilian life and property, whose ultimate outcome is, inevitably, the destruction of the human species, or at least a very great portion of it. This, indeed, is one possible type of nuclear conflict, and during the Cold War the possibility of such a conflict – not unreasonably – aroused fear worldwide. A full-scale nuclear exchange between the superpowers could have involved tens of thousands of warheads, the targeting of major cities in Asia, Europe, North America and possibly elsewhere, and uncertain – but possibly globally devastating – environmental damage. However, this sort of 'maximum' conflict is only one of the possible types of nuclear war.

At the other extreme, nuclear weapons could – at least in theory – be used in a fashion that would cause no civilian casualties and only minimal, mostly local, environmental consequences. For example, use of a relatively low-yield tactical nuclear weapon against a ship or a command bunker located in a very rural area might fit into this category. Of course, given the international outrage that would surely follow from even the most discriminating use imaginable of a nuclear weapon (and the less discriminate nuclear retaliation that might follow if a nuclear-armed state were attacked), there are relatively few plausible scenarios in which such limited nuclear use might occur.

In discussing nuclear conflict, it is common to make a distinction between counterforce and countervalue targets. The first category includes targets of military/strategic value to a government, such as military forces (including, even especially, nuclear forces), certain government facilities, communications networks, the leadership itself and similar targets. The second is composed of things that a government would value for their own sake, aside from their military value, such as the population, industrial and transportation infrastructure, and so forth. It should be noted that the two categories are not mutually exclusive: many things – such as the leadership or the communications network, for example – may be considered both counterforce and countervalue targets. However, speaking generally, it would be reasonable to say that counterforce targets are of a military/strategic character, while countervalue targets are not. A carefully constrained nuclear attack would therefore probably be focused on counterforce targets, avoiding collateral damage as far as possible.

Between the most extreme and limited types of nuclear war falls a broad variety of possible conflicts. It is certainly possible to imagine conflicts involving only the limited use of nuclear weapons, perhaps even to send a 'signal' to the opponent. During the Cold War, the United States and Soviet Union contemplated many possible warfighting scenarios involving a limited use of nuclear weapons. Examining the United States' attitude towards nuclear weapons is particularly interesting for the purposes at hand, because its nuclear strategy was essentially built on the belief that the Warsaw Pact possessed overall military superiority in Northern Europe, which was thought to be the likely main theatre in a future war. A major fear was that the Soviet Union and its allies might launch an invasion, centered on the then West Germany, which would punch rapidly through NATO's front-line troops, throwing the defenders into disarray and allowing a rapid Soviet advance to the English Channel. A possible solution to this threat was seen in the use of nuclear weapons.

The notion of extended deterrence is critical to understanding the NATO nuclear deterrence problem of the Cold War, as well as many possible crises involving rogue states or other actors. The chief immediate deterrence goal of the United States during the Cold War was not to protect its own homeland against Soviet attack. Rather, Washington was trying to protect its NATO allies from invasion, and a potential foe is always likely to question a state's willingness to suffer massive damage on behalf of its allies. Thus, maintaining a high level of credibility was critical, because it was feared that if the Soviet leaders became convinced that the United States would not accept enormous damage on behalf of its allies, they would proceed to invade Western Europe. NATO's European members worried that the United States would actually desert them in their time of need, accepting a Soviet conquest of Western Europe in exchange (at least temporarily) for not suffering the horrors of nuclear attack on its own homeland.

If, however, the United States did not quickly abandon its European allies, it would then have confronted all the problems described previously in regard to managing escalation, including the very real possibilities either of accidentally allowing the escalation process to slip out of control, the result being a massive nuclear exchange, or of failing to escalate quickly and boldly enough to convince Soviet leaders (assuming, of course, that they could be convinced) to abandon their invasion and evacuate NATO territory.

Fortunately, we do not know with certainty how well NATO armies would have been able to cope with a nuclear environment. However, it is easy to imagine the struggles that warfighters might have encountered after even a limited nuclear exchange. First, operating in a radioactive environment, which would require the use of stifling protective suits, would be exceedingly difficult; goods (including food and water) might be contaminated with radioactive materials; both mass media and military communications networks would be damaged and perhaps fatally undermined; enormous numbers of civilian and military casualties would overwhelm medical facilities of all kinds; panicked civilians, desperate to escape dangerous areas, would clog the transportation infrastructure, delaying troop movements and degrading, if not collapsing, the military logistic network; and there would probably be severe damage to the public utility infrastructure, with electricity, safe drinking water and other necessities suddenly unavailable to soldiers and civilians alike. Many soldiers, confronted with unbelievable stress, would be strongly tempted to throw off their own uniforms and assist their loved ones in fleeing. Moreover, this might have occurred in a very compressed timeframe, with highly civilised societies reduced to Hobbesian chaos – and all of this occurring in a situation where an even more terrifying large-scale nuclear exchange loomed as a distinct possibility.

The vision of precisely how nuclear weapons would be used in the defence of Europe, however, changed over time, and it should be emphasised that there was never an entirely concrete, unalterable vision of what form a nuclear defence would take. In general, however, it would be accurate to say that the early US vision of how to defend NATO-Europe relied on the capability of the bombers in the US Air Force's Strategic Air Command (SAC) to 'leap-frog' past Soviet forces in the field and strike directly at the Soviet homeland, destroying the government, communications, and military infrastructure of the Soviet Union. In short, in these early years many American officials envisioned a quite brief (and, critically, very one-sided) nuclear war.

The thinking of this era is generally associated with the concept of massive retaliation, although that term was not coined until 1954, when it was used in a speech by Secretary of State John Foster Dulles. Massive retaliation is commonly misrepresented as a very simplistic doctrine in which any provocation by the Soviet Union would be met by a nuclear response, but the actual concept was rather more nuanced. Dulles actually referred to a US ability to respond to threats 'at places and with means of our own choosing'.[3] This ambiguous formulation clearly did not rule out the possibility of an all-out nuclear attack, but it also did not clarify under precisely what circumstances the United States would use nuclear weapons. Indeed, the critics of massive retaliation largely focused on its perceived lack of credibility in all but the most extreme situations; certainly, the Soviet

Union had good reason to fear that the United States actually would resort to nuclear force to defend Western Europe, but it also had reason to doubt that the Americans would do the same in response to a provocative act in more marginal strategic regions.

A threat that is excessively severe may be perceived as being incredible. Moscow did many things of which the United States disapproved – for example, attempting to increase its influence in Southeast Asia, Africa and elsewhere – but even during the years in which massive retaliation was espoused, Washington did not really attempt to use its nuclear arsenal to dissuade the Soviets from such actions. This cautious stance was prudent, since casual use of nuclear threats would have been extremely dangerous, surely leading to many crises, any one of which might have resulted in nuclear war. Even aside from the possibility that the Soviet Union would have been goaded into a nuclear first strike, however, there was the probability that, sooner or later, Soviet leaders would have refused to believe American threats, especially regarding relatively petty issues. Thus, they would have been tempted to 'call the bluff', forcing Washington either to carry through its threat, the result being nuclear war, or risk humiliation and the loss of credibility.

Criticisms of massive retaliation, as well as the growing availability of relatively small TNWs – and the growing size of the Soviet nuclear arsenal, which increasingly undermined massive retaliation's credibility – encouraged a shift in focus over time, with an increasing interest in limited nuclear alternatives. Under the right conditions, nuclear weapons could allow numerically inferior NATO forces to defeat enemy forces of greater size, and, beginning in the 1950s, TNWs began to be dispersed throughout the US military. Academics, military officers, government officials and others debated intensely whether a nuclear war could be very limited in scope.

Perhaps, some argued, nuclear weapons could be used to signal seriousness to an opponent, making clear the willingness to escalate to nuclear use and encouraging the opponent to back down. If a state can control its opponent's behaviour by 'ratcheting up' the level of potential risk and violence in a conflict, it is said to enjoy escalation dominance; this puts it in a position to coerce its opponent into surrendering. Of course, dominance is dependent on the opponent actually being willing to accept defeat. To use a metaphor made famous by the nuclear strategist Herman Kahn, one can envision a military conflict as a ladder with many rungs – an escalation ladder. If NATO had been the first to employ nuclear weapons in a conflict with the Warsaw Pact (in the West, it was a common, although very questionable, assumption that this would be the case), it could have limited their use in various ways – only using nuclear weapons against military targets, for example, or even refusing to use such weapons except against invading enemy troops operating on NATO soil. The hope was that such a constrained exercise of military force would convince the Soviet Union that further aggression would be unprofitable. However, the actual Soviet response could have been very different. Indeed, if it had wished to do so, Moscow could have responded with its own escalation, leaping further up the ladder – which, in turn, would have left NATO with the decision of whether itself to back down or continue the process of escalation.

For a time, nuclear weapons were seemingly being integrated into the mainstream of US forces: in the late 1950s, the US Army even reorganised into 'pentomic' divisions, a force structure constructed with fighting and surviving on the nuclear battlefield in mind. However, TNWs never did become a fully and uncritically accepted part of the US arsenal (indeed, the pentomic division structure itself was soon abandoned), and NATO leaders did not achieve a common understanding of when defensive nuclear use should occur. NATO policy remained vague: a 'no-first-use' policy regarding nuclear weapons was never announced, but NATO also never stated explicitly when nuclear weapons would be used. As time passed, and the Soviet arsenal grew ever larger, there was considerable worry in NATO-Europe that the Soviet Union might be able to sever the 'transatlantic link' with the United States.

During the early period of the Kennedy Administration, the United States attempted to maximise its freedom of action through the doctrine of flexible response, which was shaped largely by criticisms of massive retaliation. Flexible response was intended to provide a president with a long menu of conventional, tactical nuclear and strategic nuclear options that could be implemented as appropriate. Thus, the thinking went, the United States would be better prepared to cope with situations, such as Soviet adventurism in the Third World, in which the use of nuclear weapons would be inappropriate.

Over time, however, the United States moved away intellectually from flexible response and towards mutually assured destruction (MAD), which was essentially based on a belief that a nuclear war could not, in any meaningful sense, be 'won': that Soviet forces would be able to inflict such massive damage on the United States even in a second strike that both societies would simply be destroyed. This of course made a first strike, at least against the Soviet homeland, unacceptable.

As a strategic planning concept, MAD grew out of a budgeting exercise conducted by Secretary of Defense Robert S. McNamara (he actually referred to 'assured destruction'; the catchier term 'MAD' was coined by Donald Brennan, a critic of the exercise). If there was no plausible first-strike role for US forces, then their core purpose would be to avert a Soviet strike against the United States. McNamara believed that a Soviet first strike could be averted if the United States possessed a nuclear arsenal sufficiently large and secure to inflict devastating countervalue damage on the USSR. His stated requirements were that the surviving US nuclear arsenal should be

Figure 6.5 The YB-52, a prototype version of the B-52 bomber, lands on a dry lake at Edwards Air Base, 1953. The B-52 is still used today by the US Air Force to carry nuclear weapons.

able to destroy 30 per cent of the Soviet Union's population, 50 per cent of its industrial capacity and devastate its 150 most important cities. However, the United States never really implemented 'MAD assumptions' into its nuclear war planning, always maintaining a far larger and more diverse nuclear arsenal – as well as a more complex targeting scheme – than the very simple requirements of MAD-based planning would have dictated.

One can understand, given the increasing size of the Soviet nuclear arsenal, why US leaders began to think in terms of mutual, rather than one-sided, nuclear devastation. However, this MAD-centered vision also had some curious side-effects, encouraging, for example, many to argue against ballistic missile defences because they feared that such defences might undermine the mutual character of assured destruction and thus upset the 'nuclear balance'. Those who made this argument had, in essence, accepted the notion that mutual vulnerability was the best possible condition in a world with two nuclear-armed superpowers.

MAD, however, never offered a satisfactory answer to many of the critical military questions facing the United States and NATO (most importantly, perhaps, it did not offer a clear role for nuclear weapons if the effort to deter a Soviet conventional invasion of Western Europe failed). Over time, American leaders tried to move away from MAD, the Nixon Administration moving slightly away from MAD and the Carter Administration putting forward the concept of countervailing strategy, a carefully stated doctrine that did not outrightly reject MAD but was clearly not based on its core premises. The Reagan Administration moved still further away from MAD in its nuclear doctrine. Moreover, in 1983 Reagan proposed the Strategic Defense Initiative (SDI), more commonly known as 'Star Wars', a ballistic missile defence system that would, it was hoped, allow a sufficiently robust defence against nuclear missiles as to make it very difficult for an aggressor to be confident of his ability to carry out a successful first strike. SDI challenged the essential premise of MAD, which was that stability supposedly resulted from the *mutual* character of assured destruction.

The twists and turns in US thinking about nuclear weapons illustrate the difficulties inherent in attempting to build a coherent strategy that accounts for both deterrence and possible warfighting – and the risks that accompany any nuclear strategy. Each possible nuclear doctrine involves trade-offs, some risks being lessened and others increased, and nuclear weapons do not offer a simple solution to all of a state's security needs. Moreover, it should be noted that the great swings in American thinking about nuclear war occurred in the relatively stable security environment of the Cold War, and decisions were made primarily in reference to a single potential foe, the Soviet Union. In the relatively freewheeling security environment of the twenty-first century, with its great variety of actors, including potentially unpredictable rogue states and terrorist groups, the creation of a satisfactory nuclear doctrine may prove to be even more challenging.

The Second Nuclear Age

Some academics and other observers argue that the world is in the early phase of a 'Second Nuclear Age', as distinct from the 'First Nuclear Age' (which lasted, approximately, from 1945 to the fall of the Soviet Union in 1991), in a number of key respects. One of the most important of these characteristics is the likelihood of an increasing unreliability of deterrence.

There are two forms of nuclear proliferation: when weapons proliferate horizontally, the number of states possessing nuclear weapons increases, but when vertical proliferation occurs, the total number of nuclear weapons in existence increases. In general, the Cold War era was one of relatively modest horizontal proliferation, the number of states possessing these weapons growing only slowly over the decades. However, the total number of nuclear weapons increased dramatically over the early decades of the Cold War, the great majority of those weapons belonging either to Washington or Moscow. In recent years, however, the actual number of nuclear weapons on earth has decreased: we are experiencing 'vertical deproliferation' as Russia and the United States allow their nuclear arsenals to constrict in size. However, horizontal proliferation is proceeding, India and Pakistan testing nuclear weapons in 1998 (although both possessed nuclear weapons capabilities well before that year, and India even conducted a 'peaceful' nuclear test in 1974), North Korea apparently testing a nuclear weapon in October 2006, and Iran appearing to be well along in its own nuclear programme. It is impossible to say how many, if any, new possessors of nuclear weapons will appear over the next few decades, but there are some reasons to believe that it will be a substantial number.

First, it should be kept in mind that nuclear weapons have now existed for over sixty years. Basic nuclear weapons technology is not, in any reasonable use of the term, 'cutting-edge'. There are many thousands of individuals on earth who possess at least some of the knowledge and skills required to build a nuclear device, and many of them are citizens of – or are simply willing to work for – states that may desire nuclear weapons. The career of a single individual, Pakistani scientist and engineer A. Q. Khan, illustrates this fact well. Khan worked in Europe during the 1970s and stole technical information related to uranium enrichment. He became central to Pakistan's nuclear weapons development effort and eventually built up an international network that provided nuclear weapons-related parts and technology to various would-be proliferators, apparently including Iran and North Korea. The government of Pakistan contends that it was unaware of Khan's nuclear sales to foreign governments, although the huge scope of Khan's activities – and his frequent visits to countries, such as North Korea, that are not known chiefly for their tourist attractions – casts some doubt on this claim. In any event, however, Khan's career demonstrates how an individual with the right knowledge and resources can contribute greatly to horizontal proliferation.

Second, if one or more particular states obtain, or appear to be close to obtaining, nuclear weapons, this may convince certain other states that they should build nuclear weapons. We have seen this phenomenon to a limited degree in the past – for example, India's determination to have a nuclear capability was clearly a major driver of Pakistan's nuclear programme, while India's own nuclear efforts were largely driven by its concern about China's nuclear arsenal – and we may see more extreme cases of it in the future. For instance, there has been speculation that Iranian acquisition of nuclear weapons might drive several other Middle Eastern states, possibly including Saudi Arabia, Turkey and/or Egypt, to seek nuclear weapons. A country such as Iran obtaining nuclear weapons might indirectly result in proliferation by numerous other states – and that could make other states feel threatened in turn, thus encouraging further proliferation.

Third, and most importantly, nuclear weapons continue to have great utility both on and off the battlefield. Diplomatically, nuclear weapons bring (potentially considerable) benefits in terms of prestige, ability to practise nuclear deterrence and coercion, and other areas. Indeed, a nuclear-armed state may be able to dissuade a more powerful opponent even from taking military action against it. Many observers, for example, have speculated that if Iraq had possessed nuclear weapons when it invaded Kuwait in 1990, the US-led force that eventually liberated Kuwait would never have been assembled. Indeed, it is quite possible that today Saddam Hussein could still be alive, in office, and more affluent and powerful than ever. This, in turn, ultimately flows from the fact that nuclear weapons remain the most powerful weapons yet devised by humankind.

Warfare as practised by the United States and other militarily advanced states, the kind of combat that often is discussed in relation to the arguably on-going Revolution in Military Affairs, or RMA (see chapter 2), places states with less technologically advanced equipment and less well-trained personnel in an unenviable position. As numerous conflicts, particularly the 1991 Gulf War, have demonstrated, a relatively mediocre conventional force using conventional tactics is no match for a first-rate military, even if the latter is smaller. Under current conditions, and regardless of whether one is fighting at land, on sea or in the air, quality of personnel and equipment generally trumps quantity. If, however, nuclear weapons are brought into the equation, the situation can be radically altered, and even an otherwise weak force may be able, at least temporarily, to enjoy a critical advantage over a far more powerful enemy.

Nuclear conflict: future possibilities

Unfortunately, while concerns over a US–Soviet confrontation in Europe are safely relegated to the past, the occurrence of a limited nuclear conflict somewhere in the world remains entirely possible. Some of the many possibilities include:

- an Indian–Pakistani nuclear exchange
- an Israeli–Iranian nuclear war (assuming, of course, that Tehran obtains nuclear weapons)
- North Korean nuclear use against South Korea and/or Japan, which would probably result in an American nuclear response against North Korea.

Any of these events would result in an enormous humanitarian disaster, although, again, the exact circumstances of a conflict would play a key role in determining the extent of the damage.

Most importantly, there would be the issue of what is targeted. It is possible, as previously noted, that nuclear weapons might be used – probably out of desperation – in a strictly battlefield role, and perhaps it would be possible to limit a conflict to tactical nuclear use. Alternatively, however, it is possible that a state may use its nuclear arsenal in a much different manner, perhaps even undertaking a first strike intended to maximise civilian casualties. Such an action would not fit the vision of the escalation ladder, which presumes that intentional attacks on civilian populations would be near the ladder's top – and even strikes on military and other government facilities that happened to be located in or near cities would be very high on the escalation ladder, and thus most probably avoided. However, the ladder – and similar Cold War deterrence and warfighting concepts – is built on the assumption of foes who are reasonably similar in what they value and fear. However, as an increasingly diverse group of states acquires nuclear weapons, there is no guarantee that this will continue to be the case (see box 6.5).

Fortunately, at least for now, the danger of a civilisationally devastating nuclear war appears to have receded greatly. However, the possibility in a given year of a nuclear war occurring somewhere in the world is much higher than it was during most of the Cold War. Some of the reasons for this are obvious, such as the fact that more states possess nuclear weapons and that, presumably, the more nuclear-armed actors there are, the greater the likelihood that one of them will actually decide to use its weapons. However, there also are more subtle reasons: the actors involved may be different in critical ways.

Ultimately, what we know about the avoidance of nuclear conflict is based on the behaviour of a small sample of actors over, historically speaking, a rather brief time. We do not have a sufficiently large body of historical evidence to make highly trustworthy predictions about the future use, or non-use, of nuclear weapons. With that in mind, however, it does appear that horizontal proliferation is a continuing trend. While there was considerable optimism immediately after the Cold War that a 'nuclear-free' world was possible, most observers now treat this as, at best, a distant hope. There is substantial reason to believe that the number of nuclear-armed states will continue to increase over time, although the actual rate of that increase is highly debatable.

Given this uncertain, and possibly quite hazardous, international security environment, missile defences are likely to become increasingly important in the future. When SDI was announced, its would-be architects were faced with the daunting task of discovering how to build a highly reliable defensive shield that would destroy the great majority of many thousands of nuclear warheads. Even with today's far more advanced computer processing power and other technological advances, this would be an extremely difficult and expensive task. However, against the small arsenals of most of the current and likely future nuclear states, missile defence might prove quite feasible, and missile defences can enormously

Box 6.5 Different leaders, different goals

Leaders may vary enormously in what they most value, what risks they are willing to take and other attitudes relevant to WMD use. Even leaders within the same broad political tradition have diverse priorities and beliefs – Bill Clinton and George W. Bush are both recent US presidents, but they are quite distinct personalities. The differences between two leaders from very dissimilar political and strategic cultures – for example, a US president and a North Korean ruler or Iranian president – may be so great that it is difficult for either to comprehend accurately what motivates the other. The possibility for misunderstanding, missed signals and other communication breakdowns is high when two such leaders are interacting. This is especially the case when leaders engage in 'mirror-imaging'. That term, which came into common use during the Cold War, relates to the tendency to assume that another individual shares one's own general value hierarchy, reasons in a similar fashion and is otherwise quite similar to oneself. Western diplomats and other leaders often, and arguably quite justifiably, were criticised for tending to mirror-image Soviet leaders, paying insufficient attention to the specifics of Marxist-Leninist ideology and the Russian-Soviet historical experience and culture. Of course, there was no US–Soviet nuclear conflict, so, presumably, deterrence 'worked' sufficiently well overall. However, there is no guarantee that it will continue to work in the future.

Leaders – like any other human beings – ultimately decide what they value, and those choices will not always appear reasonable and responsible to outside observers. One can think of many historical examples of states, even great powers, which had unsavoury or bizarre goals – Hitler's Germany is an obvious twentieth-century example, but Stalin's Soviet Union and Mao's China also both acted murderously towards perceived internal enemies and pursued various goals that were in line with state ideology but that an outside observer might have judged imprudent or abnormal. If great powers can act unpredictably, one can certainly imagine that a state like North Korea, which is isolated from the global media, ruled by an eccentric autocrat and promotes a strange, hyper-nationalistic variant of Communism, might act in a surprising fashion.

complicate nuclear warplanning. When a state launches a nuclear attack on a country with a missile defence, the attacker cannot know which of its warheads will break though the defence and land on target; when the attacking country has only a small number of nuclear weapons, they might all be intercepted by the missile defence. Given these potential defensive advantages, it is entirely plausible that numerous states, some of which have nuclear arsenals and some of which do not, will build missile defences in coming years.

Of course, the possibility of nuclear conflict does not preclude the possible use of CBWs. It is likely that we will again see the use of CBWs by states that are not nuclear-armed. Indeed, it is even possible that the use of CBWs may be the catalyst for the next use of nuclear weapons, as a nuclear-armed state could decide to retaliate for CBW use with nuclear weapons. It is the policy of several nuclear-armed states to maintain the option to retaliate in this fashion.

Overall, given continuing horizontal proliferation, the military usefulness of nuclear weapons and similar factors, it is reasonable to suppose it is probable that at some point in the Second Nuclear Age the alleged taboo against nuclear use will be broken. Although some authors believe that there genuinely is a strong taboo that will probably prevent nuclear weapons from being used again in warfare, it is notable that since the invention of these devices no nuclear power has been confronted with a situation in which *not* using nuclear weapons would have immediate and catastrophic consequences. For instance, no nuclear-armed state has chosen to allow its military to be utterly destroyed in conventional battle or permitted itself to be conquered outright by an invader rather than resort to the use of nuclear weapons. Such extreme situations would provide real tests of whether the norm against nuclear use truly is strong enough to be described as a taboo. Moreover, as discussed above, there is no guarantee – especially given the continuing horizontal proliferation of nuclear weapons – that all future leaders of nuclear-armed powers will have a very high threshold for nuclear use.

The occurrence of one nuclear conflict would of course not ensure that there would be many such wars. However, the possibility of a progressive 'normalisation' of nuclear (not to mention CB) weapons should not be dismissed casually. Perceptions concerning the military usability of WMDs are shaped continuously by the behaviour of the actors possessing such weapons; if a number of state and non-state entities prove willing to use WMDs, it may be that the high 'wall' separating conventional weapons from WMDs will slowly break down, leading to an increasing willingness to use the latter in combat.

At present, WMDs are largely 'dormant' in regard to actual warfighting, having been – at least till now – rejected as useable military instruments by the great powers. They do, however, play an important role in shaping the international security environment, and their existence, and particularly the possibility of WMD proliferation, drives many political events. Certainly, the (albeit mistaken) belief that Iraq was rebuilding its CB arsenal was one of the key reasons for the 2003 invasion of that country. Moreover, the apparent efforts by North Korea and Iran to obtain nuclear weapons have created two of the most significant on-going diplomatic predicaments facing the UNSC, among other international bodies.

With regard to WMDs, and particularly nuclear weapons, the period from the end of the Cold War to the present might reasonably be described as a transitional stage – the early period of the Second Nuclear Age, whose characteristics are becoming increasingly clear over time. While there were numerous states that possessed WMDs, the First Nuclear Age was essentially defined by two superstates with gargantuan nuclear arsenals facing off, humanity's fate resting on the decisions made by the two powers. The Second Nuclear Age that we have entered, by contrast, will surely not have such a simple, straightforward narrative. Rather, an assortment of relationships among various states that possess WMDs – the number of which is, of course, growing over time – will be significant. Most probably, various scenarios will unfold in different parts of the world. In some cases, countries will use WMDs to bully their less well-armed neighbours, but there will be other states that obtain WMDs and use these devices in a responsible, defensively orientated manner. Sometimes, one or more great powers – whether or not acting under the aegis of the UN – will perhaps choose to use force to prevent a specific instance of proliferation; on other occasions, proliferation will proceed without meaningful interference by outside powers. Some of the states that today are at odds with each other may find that mutual possession of devastating weapons 'cools the passions', and their leaders will find it prudent to seek compromise and the diminishment of tensions rather than military victory. Other states will probably not be so accommodating and will continue down a course that leads to a war fought with WMDs.

NOTES

1   1899 Hague Convention, Declaration II: *Declaration on the Use of Projectiles the Object of Which is the Diffusion of Asphyxiating or Deleterious Gases*, 29 July 1899; accessed from the Avalon Project at Yale Law School, www.yale.edu/lawweb/avalon/lawofwar/dec99-02.htm.
2   Bernard Brodie, *The Absolute Weapon: Atomic Power and World Order* (New York: Harcourt, Brace, 1946).
3   Quoted in David M. Kunsman and Douglas B. Lawson, *A Primer on U.S. Strategic Nuclear Policy*, Sandia Report SAND2001-0053 (Albuquerque, NM: Sandia National Laboratories, 2001), p. 99. Accessed at www.nti.org/e_research/official_docs/labs/prim_us_nuc_pol.pdf.

FURTHER READING

Alibek, Ken and Handelman, Stephen, *Biohazard: The Chilling True Story of the Largest Covert Biological Weapons Program in the World – Told from Inside by the Man Who Ran It* (New York: Random House, 1999).

Contains a great deal of detail about the size and character of the Soviet biological warfare programme.

Barnaby, Frank, *How to Build a Nuclear Bomb: And Other Weapons of Mass Destruction* (New York: Nation Books, 2004).
Explains in accessible language the steps that a state or terrorist group must take if it is to build WMDs.

Cirincione, Joseph, Wolfsthal, Jon. B., and Rajkumar, Mirium, *Deadly Arsenals: Nuclear, Biological, and Chemical Threats*, 2nd rev. and expanded edn (Washington, DC: Carnegie Endowment for International Peace, 2007).
Addresses many proliferation-related issues and includes detailed discussion of numerous states and their arsenals.

Croddy, Eric A. with Perez-Armendariz, Clarisa and Hart, John, *Chemical and Biological Warfare: A Comprehensive Survey for the Concerned Citizen* (New York: Copernicus Books, 2002).
Provides much useful information on both chemical and biological weapons.

   and Wirtz, James J., eds., *Weapons of Mass Destruction: An Encyclopedia of Worldwide Policy, Technology, and History* (Santa Barbara, CA: ABC-CLIO, 2004).
Contains information on an enormous variety of topics and issues related to WMDs.

Freedman, Lawrence, *The Evolution of Nuclear Strategy*, 3rd edn (New York: Palgrave MacMillan, 2003).
Offers an excellent, detailed discussion of how the nuclear strategy of various states has developed over time.

Langewiesche, William, *The Atomic Bazaar: The Rise of the Nuclear Poor* (New York: Farrar, Straus and Giroux, 2007).
Discusses many of the key issues related to nuclear proliferation, particularly the possibility that terrorist groups will obtain nuclear weapons.

Harris, Robert and Paxman, Jeremy, *A Higher Form of Killing: The Secret History of Chemical and Biological Warfare*, rev. and updated edn (New York: Random House, 2002).
Co-written by a popular novelist and a well-known journalist, this work is an accessible history of the development of CB warfare.

Gray, Colin S., *The Second Nuclear Age* (Boulder, CO: Lynne Rienner, 1999).
This insightful book addresses the character of the Second Nuclear Age, including the possibility that WMDs will be used in warfare.

Sagan, Scott D. and Waltz, Kenneth N., *The Spread of Nuclear Weapons: A Debate Renewed*, 2nd edn (New York: W. W. Norton, 2002).
Two scholars of international relations debate what the likely impact of the spread of nuclear weapons will be on the global security environment.

Tucker, Jonathan, *War of Nerves: Chemical Warfare from World War I to Al-Qaeda* (New York: Pantheon, 2006).
Provides a very detailed history of the development and use of chemical weapons.

Walton, C. Dale, 'Navigating the Second Nuclear Age: Proliferation and Deterrence in this Century', *Global Dialogue* 8:1 (Winter/Spring 2006): 22–31.
Briefly discusses horizontal proliferation in this century and how Western states can best address the dangers presented by this phenomenon.

GLOSSARY

Air superiority
The ability to use air power at a given time and in a given place without prohibitive interference from the enemy.

Air supremacy
Air superiority in which the enemy is incapable of effective interference.

Aircraft carrier
A warship designed to carry and operate numerous fixed-wing aircraft at sea.

Amphibious operation
The landing of military forces from the sea on a hostile or potentially hostile shore.

Attrition
The reduction of the effectiveness of a military formation caused by the loss of equipment and/or personnel.

Battalion
A military unit usually consisting of 500–1,200 troops divided into 4 to 6 *companies*. Two or more battalions may be grouped into a *brigade*, or one or more may constitute a *regiment*.

Battlefleet
A fleet, usually composed of the most powerful warships, designed to contest *command of the sea* in combat with the enemy.

Battlegroup
A flexible *combined-arms* force usually created around the nucleus of a *battalion/regiment*-sized infantry or armoured unit and augmented with other arms.

Battleship
A large, heavily armoured warship armed primarily with large-calibre guns. Until the mid-twentieth century these were the largest and most powerful warships.

Battlespace dominance
A US concept that encompasses the ability to dominate the three-dimensional battlespace by establishing zones of superiority around deployed forces.

Blockade
An attempt to deny access to a particular area. Often associated with attempts to cut off maritime trade to enemy ports.

Blue water
A colloquial term used to refer to the *high seas*.

Brigade	A military unit consisting of two to five *battalions* or *regiments*. Two or more brigades may be grouped into a *division*.
Brown water	A colloquial term used to refer to inshore sea areas, estuaries and deltas.
C2	An abbreviation to represent the military functions of *command* and *control*. The process by which a commander exercises *command* and *control* of their forces in order to direct, organise and co-ordinate their activities to maximum effect.
C3I	An abbreviation to represent the following military functions: *command, control,* communications and intelligence.
C4ISR	An abbreviation to represent the following military functions: *command, control,* communications, intelligence, surveillance and reconnaissance.
C4ISTAR	An abbreviation to represent the following military functions: *command, control,* communications, intelligence, surveillance, target acquisition and reconnaissance.
Campaigns	A connected series of *tactical* engagements designed to achieve a *strategic* objective.
Capital ship	The most powerful and influential type of warship, often valued for its symbolic as much as for its military value.
Centre of gravity	Characteristics, capabilities or locations that are key to the ability of an organisation to function effectively.
Close air support	Air attacks launched against enemy targets in close proximity to friendly forces.
Close operations	Operations on or near the enemy front line, as opposed to *deep operations,* conducted far into the enemy's rear areas.
Combined arms	The integration of different arms into a single system to achieve a complementary effect. *Battle-groups,* for example, are designed to exploit the benefits of combined arms.
Combined operations	Traditionally, a term used to describe what would now be called *joint operations*. In modern nomenclature, the term is used to describe multinational operations.
Command	The authority to *control* the activity and organisation of armed forces.

Command of the sea	The ability to use the sea and to deny that use to the enemy.
Company	A military unit consisting of 100–200 troops, divided into 2 to 5 platoons.
Control	The process by which a commander directs, organises and co-ordinates the activities of the forces under his *command*.
Corps	A military unit consisting of two or more *divisions*. Derived from the French term *corps d'armée* ('body of the army'), traditionally a corps was a *combined-arms* force capable of fighting independently for a limited period of time.
Corvette	A small warship, usually lightly armed.
Cruiser	A powerful warship, less heavily armed and armoured than a *battleship*, often designed to conduct *scouting* and *screening* operations in support of the *battlefleet* or to protect/attack trade or to project power overseas.
Damage control	Controlling the damage caused to ships by enemy action in naval warfare.
Deep operations	Large-scale, simultaneous attacks against enemy reserve and rear areas as well as the front line. Deep operations can be performed by remote firepower (air, artillery and missile attack) and by the rapid exploitation of breakthroughs by mobile forces.
Destroyer	A capable *flotilla* vessel designed to fulfil a range of missions that include anti-submarine operations, air defence and various escort duties, but that is capable of operating in support of the *battlefleet*.
Division	A large, usually *combined-arms*, military unit consisting of two or more *brigades*. Two or more divisions may be grouped together into a *corps*.
Doctrine	The principles that are intended to guide the actions of military forces.
Double envelopment	Simultaneous movement around the flanks of the enemy designed to achieve, or to threaten to achieve, the encirclement of the enemy.
Dreadnought	British *battleship* launched in 1906 that, by its exclusive armament of heavy-calibre guns and new steam turbine engines, revolutionised battleship construction, lending its name to subsequent vessels of this type.

Echelon	As a formation, describes the use of multiple reserve formations to create successive waves of attack. Generically, the term 'second echelon' is sometimes used to describe all of the forces that follow on from the initial attacking forces.
Effects-based operations	Rather than prioritising the destruction of enemy forces through the application of military power, this is an approach that focuses first on establishing the broad end states that need to be delivered (the 'effect') and then choosing the most appropriate range of instruments to achieve it (of which military power may be only one). It is a process designed to produce better *strategic performance*.
Envelopment	Movement around or over the enemy.
Expeditionary operations	Operations where military force is projected and sustained at some distance from the home bases, usually across the seas.
Fire control	The control and direction of artillery fire, particularly from warships.
Fleet in being	The maintenance of one's own fleet intact in the hope that its continued existence will deny options to the enemy.
Flotilla	A formation of smaller warships, sometimes included as part of a larger fleet.
Fourth-Generation Warfare/4GW	Warfare dominated by the use of insurgency by non-state actors deliberately to target the political and social vulnerabilities of adversary states.
Frigate	A *flotilla* vessel, usually optimised to focus on either anti-submarine warfare or air defence.
Friction	Those factors that make the practice of warfare more difficult than its theory, including fear, chance, uncertainty and physical exertion.
Grand strategy	The application of national resources to achieve national/alliance policy objectives.
Green water	A colloquial term used to refer to coastal waters, archipelagos and sea areas above the continental shelf.
Guerre de course	An attack on enemy merchant shipping at sea.
Gunboat diplomacy	The use of naval forces in support of diplomatic activity. It is often associated with the coercive use of naval forces in situations short of armed conflict.
High seas	The area of the sea beyond *territorial seas*. Navies are free to navigate through the high seas without restriction.

Innocent passage	The right provided for under *UNCLOS* for ships to transit the territorial seas of other states provided they do not engage in military activity.
Insurgency	An organised movement aimed at the overthrow of a constituted government through the use of subversion and armed conflict. Like *terrorism*, however, insurgency is a contested concept. Its essence is the combination of irregular warfare techniques and political ideology.
Integration	The development of closer, complementary interaction between elements within a military system. Generically, integration is required for effective performance in all aspects of warfare whether *command* and *control*, *logistics*, *combined arms* or *joint* operations. The term has acquired specific importance in relation to contemporary debates regarding the creation of a *system of systems*.
Interdiction	Actions to divert, disrupt or destroy the enemy before they reach the area of battle.
Jihad	An Islamic term meaning 'holy war', but also the personal struggle for piety in accordance with the will of Allah. As regards holy war, traditional Sunni scholars developed numerous qualifying conditions under which violence could be used. Supporters of Osama bin Laden reject these in favour of principles practised by the prophet Mohammed. In their eyes, people who will not subscribe to those principles can and should be killed.
Joint operations	Operations involving the integration of land, air and/or naval forces.
Linear tactics	A tactical system based upon the use of troops deployed in line, designed to maximise firepower and minimise problems of command and control. Characteristic of warfare in the nineteenth and early twentieth centuries.
Littoral	The coastal region. Sometimes identified as coastal sea areas and the area of land susceptible to influence and support from the sea.
Logistics	The art of moving armed forces and keeping them supplied.
Manoeuvre	The movement of forces to occupy advantageous positions.

Manoeuvre warfare	The application of the *manoeuvrist approach* to warfighting.
Manoeuvrist approach	A philosophy of war based upon the principle of defeating the enemy by attacking such intangibles as cohesion and will to fight rather than focusing on destroying the enemy's materiel. Despite its label, manoeuvre is not necessarily a prerequisite for a manoeuvrist approach to war.
Mechanised forces	Mobile forces where the transport is usually composed of armoured, armed, and (often) tracked vehicles. The transport is designed to contribute to combat operations by providing protection and fire support.
Military transformation	Generically, 'major change' in the way warfare is conducted. More specifically, it refers to the contemporary idea of US military reform focusing on such ideas as network-centric warfare, modularisation and an expeditionary focus.
Mission command	A command philosophy based on the principles of decentralisation of responsibility and the use of initiative. Classically, subordinates are informed of what they must achieve (the mission) but are allowed to use their own judgement on how this should be best achieved given local conditions.
Motorised forces	Mobile forces where the transport is usually composed of wheeled and unarmoured vehicles. The transport is not usually designed to take part in combat.
Naval diplomacy	The use of naval forces in support of diplomatic activity.
Operational art	The execution of the *operational level* of command.
Operational level	The level at which campaigns and major operations are planned, sequenced and directed.
Outflank	Movement around the enemy flanks. Although often used synonymously with the term *envelopment*, envelopment often implies a much deeper outflanking movement designed to pin and encircle the enemy.
Policy	In relation to strategic theory, policy is simply politics. Policy differs from *strategy* in that policy sets the ends to which strategy is directed.
Power projection	The ability to project military power overseas.
Radar	An acronym for Radio Detection and Ranging. The use of electromagnetic waves to detect the

	range, altitude, bearing and speed of moving objects such as aircraft, ships and vehicles and also the position of fixed installations.
Regiment	A tactical or administrative grouping of one or more *battalions*.
Revolution in Military Affairs (RMA)	The notion that combinations of new technology (particularly in information technology and precision-guided missiles) and new operational concepts have resulted in a paradigm shift in the conduct of warface.
Scouting	Activity designed to locate the enemy.
Screening	Activity designed to protect your forces from enemy observation and enemy action.
Sea Basing	The basing of military capabilities, such as troops, fire support, *logistics* and *command* and *control,* on ships offshore.
Sea control	The ability to use an area of the sea for one's own purposes and to deny that use to the enemy for a given period of time.
Sea denial	The attempt to prevent an opponent from gaining use of the sea.
Sealift	The ability to transport goods and personnel by sea.
Sea lines of communication	Commercial shipping routes and sea routes connecting military forces to their sources of supply and reinforcement.
Shock	A psychological state marked by fear and disorientation. Shock is a desirable state to induce in an enemy because it may result in slowed, uncoordinated, and irrelevant activity. Translated through to military organisations, 'systemic shock' undermines the capacity of a military force to operate effectively and may result in heavy defeat without the infliction of large amounts of physical destruction.
Sonar	An acronym for Sound, Navigation and Ranging. The use of sound waves to detect objects under water.
Space Force Application	The use of space for military purposes, employing weapons systems as opposed to reconnaissance and communications platforms. Defined by US Strategic Command as encompassing 'combat operations in, through and from space to influence the course and outcome of conflict'.

Squadron	A small formation of aircraft, ships or mobile ground forces such as cavalry or tanks.
Strategy	Multiple definitions exist. Fundamentally, strategy is the bridge between the means available and the ends set by *policy*. It can be considered the planning and application of military resources to help achieve *grand strategy*.
Strategic effect	In air power doctrine, the use of air power against designated *centres of gravity* to produce higher-order political effects. In *strategy*, any action that has an impact on the relationship between means and ends.
Strategic performance	The degree to which an action moves one measurably towards the achievement of the desired political goals.
Suppression	The neutralisation, rather than destruction, of forces through the psychological effect of firepower. Typically, 'suppressive fire' forces an enemy to remain in cover, pins them and prevents them from firing themselves by rendering them unable (through *shock* or disorientation) or unwilling (through fear) to expose themselves.
System	A set of interrelated parts that together constitute a whole. Military organisations are made up of a multitude of systems, such as administrative systems, logistic systems and training systems.
System of systems	A concept in which very high degrees of *integration* between different military systems, facilitated by improvements in data transfer and *C4ISR*, produce something more resembling a single *system*. In theory, this should dramatically improve the co-operation, co-ordination, speed and flexibility of a military organisation.
Tactics	The conduct of battles and engagements.
Territorial seas	Under *UNCLOS* these are defined as areas up to 12 miles off the adjacent coast. States enjoy sovereignty within this region, and the activities of outside naval forces are circumscribed, notwithstanding a right to *innocent passage*.
Terrorism	A basic definition might be: 'The of use of violence, or the threat of violence, to create fear.' Terrorism is a strategy in which violence is important for the psychological effect that it

	produces. However, terrorism is a contested concept, not least because it has associated moral, political and pejorative connotations. A multitude of different definitions exist.
UNCLOS	The Third UN Convention on the Law of the Sea that was signed in 1982 and came into effect in 1997.
Vertical envelopment	Moving over the enemy in order to threaten their flanks or rear. This may be executed through air-mobile (helicopterborne) or airborne (parachute or glider) forces.
WMDs	Weapons of mass destruction. A collective term for nuclear, radiological, biological and chemical weapons focusing on their capacity for large-scale indiscriminate damage. Often also referred to as 'Weapons of Mass Effect' because of the potential political, coercive and moral impacts associated with their use or threat of use.

INDEX

Note: Page numbers in bold refer to Tables and Boxes; those in italics refer to Figures